SEXUAL VIOLENCE
AT CANADIAN
UNIVERSITIES

SEXUAL VIOLENCE
AT CANADIAN
UNIVERSITIES

Activism, Institutional Responses, and Strategies for Change

Elizabeth Quinlan, Andrea Quinlan,
Curtis Fogel, Gail Taylor, editors

WILFRID LAURIER
UNIVERSITY PRESS

Wilfrid Laurier University Press acknowledges the support of the Canada Council for the Arts for our publishing program. We acknowledge the financial support of the Government of Canada through the Canada Book Fund for our publishing activities. This work was supported by the Research Support Fund.

Library and Archives Canada Cataloguing in Publication

Sexual violence at Canadian universities : activism, institutional responses, and strategies for change / Elizabeth Quinlan, Andrea Quinlan, Curtis Fogel, and Gail Taylor, editors.

Includes bibliographical references and index.
Issued in print and electronic formats.
ISBN 978-1-77112-283-2 (softcover).—ISBN 978-1-77112-284-9 (PDF).—ISBN 978-1-77112-285-6 (EPUB)

1. Rape in universities and colleges—Canada. I. Quinlan, Elizabeth, [date], editor II. Quinlan, Andrea, [date], editor III. Fogel, Curtis, 1983–, editor IV. Taylor, Gail, editor

LB2345.3.R37S49 2017   371.7'820971   C2017-901724-1
                                                     C2017-901725-X

Cover design by hwtstudio.com. Interior design by Angela Booth Malleau.

This book is printed on FSC® certified paper and is certified Ecologo. It contains post-consumer fibre, is processed chlorine free, and is manufactured using biogas energy.

Printed in Canada

Every reasonable effort has been made to acquire permission for copyright material used in this text, and to acknowledge all such indebtedness accurately. Any errors and omissions called to the publisher's attention will be corrected in future printings.

CONTENTS

SEXUAL VIOLENCE IN THE IVORY TOWER

Elizabeth Quinlan

Several recent incidents of sexual violence on Canadian campuses have gar-nered considerable media coverage. The stories draw particular attention to the perniciousness of a rape culture on campus and the inadequacy of Cana-dian universities' prevention and response to sexual violence.

During orientation week at Saint Mary's University (SMU) in the fall of 2013, senior students led several hundred first-year students in a chant that glorified nonconsensual sex with underage girls. A videotape of the cheer appearing on social media sparked outrage across the country. The president of the student union resigned the following day, declaring that the chant was the biggest mistake of his life while admitting that he, along with many others, had recited the chant every year since coming to the university. Shortly thereafter, the university announced the formation of a ten-member President's Council, chaired by a Dalhousie professor in law and ethics, to make recommendations that would attempt to foster "cultural change that prevents sexual violence, and inspires respectful behaviour and a safe learning environment" (President's Council, 2013, p. 16).

Within days of the uncovering of the Saint Mary's chant, a similar cheer surfaced at the University of British Columbia (UBC), followed by a quick succession of reported sexual assaults on the UBC campus the next month. Students reported the chant had been used for 20 years. The story found ample purchase in the traditional media. In response, the university president struck the Task Force on Intersectional Gender-Based Violence and Aboriginal Ste-reotypes to develop "actionable recommendations" addressing the violence rendered visible by the revelations of the chant (University of British Colum-bia, 2014).

Later that fall, a Lakehead University student who had been sexually assaulted by a fellow student a year earlier went to the media with her story. After several unsuccessful attempts to lodge a formal complaint and arrange her classes to avoid the perpetrator, she was instructed to obtain written documentation of her "learning disability" from a campus doctor as the best way to avoid having to write her exams in the same room as the perpetrator. She told the media that she didn't blame the university for the actions of her fellow student, but did hold it responsible for its injurious response to her requests for help. Soon after, the president formed a task force with a mandate to reduce or eliminate incidents of sexual assault and to ensure that when reporting, survivors would have access to counselling, assistance with medical care and academic concerns, and support in choices regarding reporting of the crime to law authorities. In particular, the task force was mandated to make recommendations regarding changes to the Code of Student Behaviour and Disciplinary Procedures, and the Employee Code of Conduct.

While the task forces at SMU, UBC, and Lakehead were developing recommendations to address sexual violence on their campuses, in early December 2014 a female dental student alerted the administration at Dalhousie University to the posts from a Facebook group of 13 male dental students, which promoted the use of sexual violence against their fellow female students. One particularly offensive post appeared on the 25th anniversary of the Montreal Massacre. Like the 14 engineering students killed at l'École Polytechnique de Montréal, the female dental students were pursuing careers in a traditionally male preserve. The female dental student at Dalhousie who alerted the administration wanted to lodge a formal complaint, but was dissuaded from doing so in a meeting with the administrators. A week later, the media obtained screenshots of the offending posts from an unknown source. Public outrage ensued. An online petition pressing the university to expel the students garnered 1000 signatures in a single afternoon. By mid-January, the number of signatures shot up to 50,000. While the provincial government was announcing it would monitor the situation, alumni across the country were removing their diplomas from their office walls and professional dental associations in various provinces were requesting the names of the Facebook group members, a request that the university refused, arguing it would violate the students' privacy. In early January, the 13 group members were suspended, only later to be offered alternative delivery formats for their courses so they could graduate on schedule. A number of fourth-year female students wrote an open letter to the president to convey their discomfort with the restorative justice process they felt pressured to accept in place of a formal complaint. The president of the university launched a task force in early January 2015.

As events at Dalhousie were continuing to solicit considerable media attention, in February 2014 a sexual assault was reported in Thunder Bay. The alleged perpetrators were two University of Ottawa (UofO) hockey team members. A criminal investigation was initiated. A month later, the female president of the university's student union went public with an online discussion in which five male students directed violently misogynist comments toward her. The next day, the hockey team was suspended, and several months later the hockey coach was fired and the university president established a 15-member task force to provide recommendations on how to foster a culture that prevents sexual violence.

In the fall of 2015, UBC was in the news again, with several women alerting the media about the university's delayed reaction to numerous complaints of sexual violence by a male doctoral student. UBC officials urged the complainants to pursue mediation and to keep quiet (Mayor, 2015). Later that year, coverage of the story by the CBC's *Fifth Estate* brought an announcement from the university that the doctoral student had been expelled ("School of Secrets," 2015).

The spring of 2016 brought a fresh round of campus sexual violence stories on the front pages of the national news outlets (Crabb, 2016). A student group at Brandon University revealed that the administration had required a student to sign a contract agreeing to not speak publicly about an assault, after she disclosed the incident to the university in September 2015. Failing to comply with the terms of the contract was to risk a range of disciplinary actions, including expulsion. Shortly after the initial media reports, eight more alleged survivors came forward, including the former student president, who was told by the senior administrator to whom she had reported sexual harassment by a faculty member that filing a formal complaint "isn't going to be in your best interest … you're in a position of leadership, you're a woman, this is something that happens to you and you just need to learn how to deal with it" (Macyshon, 2016). The university reply to the flood of media coverage included an announcement that, following the September 2015 incident, a task force had been established to examine services and supports (Crabb, 2016).

On the heels of the Brandon story, a Brock University student who was sexually harassed by a professor in the fall of 2015 went to the media to describe the university's response to her complaint. During and following the university's internal investigation of her complaint, the student was warned to keep quiet about the incident (Sawa, 2016). Within a month of the media story, another student came forward to the local newspaper with similar allegations of sexual harassment the previous year and the university's mishandling of her complaint (Firth, 2016). The university president was quick to announce the establishment of the Human Rights Task Force, mandated to review all the campus policies and procedures related to sexual violence.

This collection addresses sexual violence on college and university campuses in Canada. The contributing chapters, based on empirical studies, commentaries, and activist narratives, were written amid controversy, turbulence, and widespread public debate about sexual violence on Canadian campuses, reflected in part by the high-profile cases described above. As one of the most frequent violent crimes against women in Canada, sexual violence is at the forefront of our most pressing social problems. Coincident with the accelerating numbers of women working and learning on university and college campuses, rates of sexual assaults on campuses have risen. Sexual violence traumatizes survivors and degrades their quality of life in the aftermath, sometimes for many years. It also has debilitating consequences for the institutions, compromising the academic success of survivors, witnesses, and those to whom survivors disclose, as well as the work capacity of institutions' staff and faculty. Not surprisingly, then, the causes and consequences of, and solutions to, sexual violence are of increasing importance to members of university communities and the public alike: the rise of university task forces on the topic is but one indication of this growing concern.

The thematic structure of the collection takes up the problem of sexual violence as both an individual experience and a confluence of structural forces. The book links theory and praxis in relation to sexual assault on campuses across subject areas of violent campus spaces in university sports and cyberspace, institutional responses to sexual assault, anti-violence activism on and off the campus, and strategies for change. To set the stage for what is to follow in the collection, this introductory chapter discusses the prevalence of campus sexual violence, dimensions of rape culture, and the rising tide of activism and its effects on institutional responses to campus sexual violence as reflected by legislation and reports from the task forces mentioned above.

PREVALENCE

Sexual violence, according to the World Health Organization (2002), is "any sexual act, attempt to obtain a sexual act, any unwanted sexual comments or advances, or acts to traffic, or otherwise directed, against a person's sexuality using coercion, by any person regardless of their relationship to the victim in any setting, including but not limited to home and work" (p. 149). The incidents of sexual violence discussed above received considerable public attention, but they are not isolated occurrences. Sexual victimization affects as many as 33% of Canadian female university students (DeKeseredy, Schwartz, & Tait, 1993; Newton-Taylor, DeWit, & Gliksman, 1998). More recently, Senn et al. (2014) found no improvement in prevalence rates, with 35% of first-year university women experiencing at least one completed or attempted rape since age 14. In the United States, where data collection is legislatively required and more standardized, one in five women is sexually assaulted during her years of post-secondary education. Prevalence of sexual violence is found to be higher in earlier years of college (Smith, White, & Holland, 2003). While sexual violence also affects university staff and faculty, students are the more frequent targets (Statistics Canada, 2010). The overwhelming majority of campus sexual assaults (60%) are committed by serial perpetrators, each averaging between five and six assaults (Lisak & Miller, 2002), a startling statistic that affirms our institutions' lack of capacity to effectively intervene.

Men are also sexually assaulted. Krebs, Linkquist, Warner, Fisher, and Martin (2007) estimate that approximately 6% of college males are survivors of sexual assault. However, the prevalence of female-identified survivors remains significantly higher and is therefore the focus of many of the authors in this collection.

Prevalence rates are associated with alcohol and drug consumption (Krug, Dahlberg, Mercy, Zwi, & Lozano, 2002). Research on the link between alcohol consumption and sexual victimization confirms that sexual aggressors take advantage of the permissive environment of bars and other public drinking establishments to initiate predatory sexual overtures (Graham, Bernards, Abbey, Dumas, & Wells, 2010). Notably, in their study of individuals who presented to a hospital-based referral sexual assault service in Vancouver, McGregor et al. (2004) found that the incidence of drug-facilitated sexual assault in Vancouver has shown a sustained increase among younger women in the last 15 years.

The level of risk of being sexual assaulted has been found to be no different for students attending universities and colleges with heightened security measures, such as fenced boundaries, security checks at campus entrances, high ratios of security/patrol officers to students, self-defence courses, and off-campus safe-walk programs (Cass, 2007). This finding debunks the common rape myth that assaults are perpetrated by strangers and occur at night in unlit alleyways. The notion that targets can protect themselves from sexual assault by avoiding dark alleys and being alone at night is an associated myth. In fact, most assaults are perpetrated by individuals known to the survivor. A University of Alberta study found that only 8% of the reported cases of unwanted sexual experiences were perpetrated by strangers (University of Alberta Sexual Assault Centre, 2001).

When asked if sexual assault is a problem on campuses, fully one-third of presidents of American colleges and universities agreed or strongly agreed that sexual assault was prevalent in post-secondary institutions. Yet, very few (6%) believed that sexual assault commonly occurred at their own institution (Jaskchik & Lederman, 2015). While there has been no known comparable study in Canada, it could be assumed that the results would be similar. But, how such results might be affected by the recent wave of highly publicized sexual violence on Canadian campuses remains an open question.

RAPE CULTURE ON CAMPUS

Attitudes and behaviours that condone sexual violence in all its forms resonate throughout North American society. The complex social processes by which sexual violence is treated as normal, natural, and insignificant are captured in the very term "rape culture," a term that made its way into mainstream social psychology in the 1980s (Gavey, 2005) and has since re-emerged in public discourse of recent mainstream media coverage of campus sexual violence (e.g., "Dalhousie Won't Release Names," 2015; Hampson, 2015; Ormiston, 2014). Sexual violence is normalized through the words and images of popular culture (e.g., jokes, TV, music, advertising, and the Internet). It is arguably no accident that the phrase "hate fuck," used in the Dalhousie Facebook posts, was associated with the story about Jian Ghomeshi, the CBC host who was charged with sexual violence a few months prior to the posts. Other content of the Dalhousie Facebook group posts appeared in the popular TV show *Family Guy* and the Hollywood movie *Hall Pass*. While mainstream popular culture eroticizes sexual violence, feminists have long argued that there is nothing sexual about the act of rape; rather, it is an act of hatred that uses sex to erase the identity and agency of the survivors while keeping all women in a constant state of fear (Brownmiller, 1975). Gavey (2005) more recently has argued that sexual violence is encoded in the normative patterns of heterosexuality. The naturalness of female sexual passivity and of male sexual force is cemented together in the heterosexuality model in such a way that a woman's consent can always be questioned. The model provides a perfect cover for sexual violence: it was "just sex" (Gavey, 2005). These deep-seated understandings are integral to a culture of rape.

The norms of a rape culture are particularly pernicious in male-dominated spheres of the military, law enforcement, and other hyper-masculine institutions. On campuses these norms prevail in university sports, fraternities, and disciplines that have historically been occupied by men, such as engineering, natural sciences, and some of the medical professions. These spaces of violence are explored in the chapters in Part III of this collection: Judy Haiven explores the context of male-dominated engineering and business schools, Curtis Fogel's chapter examines Canadian university sports, and Andrea Quinlan takes up the more recently identified violent space of social media.

THE RISING TIDE OF ACTIVISM

Anti-violence activists of the early 1970s in Canada can take credit for establishing the early rape crisis centres, supported by their consciousness-raising groups and political action aimed at legislative changes (Quinlan, 2017). A new generation of activists is now pressing for change, asking important questions about institutional wrongdoing, and demanding that their universities are made safe for work and study. Such activism is responsible, at least in part, for the public protest sparked by the publicized incidents of sexual violence described above. Similar to the effect of the consciousness raising of the 1960s, as more incidents of sexual violence come out of the shadows, activists demand greater public scrutiny of our universities.

They are drawing attention to the fact that post-secondary institutions have largely been reactive, rather than preventative, in addressing sexual violence (Hertzog & Yeilding, 2009), and they have not let their institutions go unaccountable. While many have a vested interest in solving the problem of campus sexual violence — faculty, parents, alumni, campus security forces, and campus counsellors, to name a few — it is the students who have led the recent charge. They are asking why they find danger in a place where they expected to find safety. The sexual harassment offices and policies, affirmative action programs, and status of women advisory committees—established in the late 1980s and early 1990s as the hard-won results of second-wave feminists storming the ivory tower—have not lived up to the promise of making campuses safe for women.

In the United States, the mattress carried around Columbia University campus by Emma Sulkowicz, a survivor whose rapist remained at large on campus, is iconic of the growing movement (Svokos, 2014). After carrying her mattress around campus throughout the 2014–2015 academic year to symbolize the weight of her rape on her life, Ms. Sulkowicz lugged it across the stage at her graduation ceremony. The university president refused to shake her hand—a breach of the custom of the processional (Taylor, 2015). The perpetrator, who was later cleared of the crime in what Ms. Sulkowicz said was a flawed university disciplinary proceeding, also walked across the stage at the same ceremony.

The nationwide Know Your IX campaign in the United States, started in 2013 by two survivors, educates students of their right to an education free from gender-based violence. The rights enshrined under Title IX of the 1972

Education Act prohibit sex discrimination in educational institutions that receive federal government funding and spell out procedures that must be in place to protect survivors of sexual violence. The grassroots campaign was launched by the survivors who posted two sentences on social media: "We think rape is bad. We will help you" (Baker, 2013). Both campaign founders had been stonewalled by their respective institutions when they brought forward their complaints of sexual assault. One was refused any information about pursuing disciplinary action from her class dean and instead urged to "get a job at Starbucks or Barnes and Noble, and come back after he's graduated" (Bolger, 2013). Yet, the campaign can now boast a large presence on social media with extensive information for other activists mounting campaigns in their own locales at both post-secondary and secondary education institutions.

In Canada, activists have steadfastly pursued their own campaigns. The largest student organization, the Canadian Federation of Students, founded in 1981, has been an outspoken critic of universities' response to sexual violence, beginning with the No Means No campaign, initiated over 20 years ago. The federation, which represents over 500,000 students from 80 member locals across the country, regularly hosts national and provincial Consent Culture forums and lobbies both provincial and federal governments on campus sexual violence issues, most recently to ensure that sexual violence–specific policies are mandated at all post-secondary institutions across the country. In response to universities' mishandling of recent incidents of sexual violence, activist groups have formed on Canadian university campuses. For example, in the spring of 2016, students at Brandon University formed a student advocacy group, We Believe Survivors, to expose the university's practice of forcing disclosing victims to sign a behavioural contract (a.k.a. gag order), mentioned above. The group's name mirrored that of a public campaign that had galvanized national outrage about the not-guilty verdict in Jian Ghomeshi's sexual assault trial issued a few weeks prior.

Anti-violence activist campaigns in Canada and the United States recently received the endorsement of Lady Gaga in her video "Til It Happens to You," released in September 2015 (Donnelly, 2015). The award-winning documentary *The Hunting Ground* has also escalated public interest in campus sexual violence, which in turn has emboldened more survivors to come forward and challenge their institutions.

In the past several years, there has been an increase in the number of survivors who have launched legal suits charging their universities with failing to protect members of the student population. Notable Canadian cases include the suit against York University by a 17-year-old woman who was raped in her residence room in 2007 and the case against Carleton University brought by a woman who was sexually assaulted in the university's chemistry lab. More recently, in early 2015, a woman who was sexually assaulted by a fellow graduate student at York University launched a human rights complaint against her university (Gray, 2015). Another human rights complaint has been initiated by survivors at the University of British Columbia to protest the fact that Dmitry Mordvinov, a fellow graduate student, was allowed to remain on campus after the university administrators were aware of complaints independently brought forward by at least six women over the previous year and half (Canadian Press, 2016). These types of legal suits against universities challenge the institutions to acknowledge their duty to care for members of their campus community.

Risking stigma, humiliation, and possible retribution from the perpetrators and their institutions of learning, survivors and their allies such as the legal complainants, We Believe Survivors at Brandon University, and Ms. Sulkowicz and Know Your IX leaders south of the border are breaking the silence about campus sexual violence. Other long-standing activist undertakings at two prominent Canadian universities are explored in depth in the chapters in Part IV of this collection: "The Coalition Against Sexual Assault: Activism Then and Now at the University of Saskatchewan," written by Elizabeth Quinlan and Gail Lasiuk, and "Collective Conversations, Collective Action: York University's Sexual Assault Survivors' Support Line and Students Organizing for Campus Safety," authored by Jenna MacKay, Ursula Wolfe, and Alex Rutherford.

The recent wave of activism has opened the aperture for the expression of public outrage. However, with so many demands on the collective commitment to social justice, the tide of indifference might just as easily sweep back in. To be fully effective, the demands of activists will require continued widespread public pressure, policy change, and litigation. As James Hodgson (2010) reported in his expert testimony in Jane Doe's legal trial, the precedent-setting case regarding the Metropolitan Toronto Police's mishandling of rape, "traditionally, status apparatus has not treated gender issues and gender crimes with an equitable and appropriate level of importance until such time as public or political pressure or litigation induce policy and procedure change" (p. 173). Indeed, the rising tide of activism has penetrated government policy circles and university administrations.

Reverberations from governments

The provinces of Ontario and British Columbia recently introduced legislation requiring colleges and universities to create sexual assault policies, complaints procedures, response protocols, effective training and prevention programs, and support services for survivors of sexual assault, as well as publicly report all incidents of sexual violence on their campuses (Bill 23, 2016; Ontario

Government, 2016). Similar legislation is promised in Manitoba and Nova Scotia (Bill 15, 2016; Bill 114, 2015). Other provinces are signalling moves in the same direction. For instance, the Saskatchewan government has "encouraged" the province's post-secondary institutions to develop sexual assault policies and submit them to the Minister of Advanced Education for review (Brigden, 2016). Prior to the introduction of provincial legislation, slightly less than 10% of English-speaking universities and colleges had specific sexual assault policies (Mathieu, 2014). Since the legislative initiatives, most universities have created some form of policy, although they differ sharply on their comprehensiveness and the degree to which they are stand-alone policies. (See the chapter "Institutional Betrayal and Sexual Violence in the Corporate University" for results of an environmental scan of campus sexual assault policies.)

South of the border, the U.S. government is currently undertaking close to 300 investigations of post-secondary institutions' violation of Title IX (Axon, 2016). Early 2014 brought a White House task force on campus sexual assault and the introduction of the Campus Accountability and Safety Act in the United States, which imposes new reporting requirements for universities receiving federal funds, extends the focus to non-stranger assault, and modifies the all-or-nothing withdrawal of funding for Title IX violations. Recently introduced state legislation in California and New York puts the onus on the perpetrator to prove consent, and universities in Virginia are now legally required to mark perpetrators' transcripts, preventing them from moving from one university to another without notice. In their chapter "Responding to Sexual Assault on Campus: What Can Canadian Universities Learn from U.S. Law and Policy?" Elizabeth Sheehy and Daphne Gilbert explore the U.S. legal framework governing campus sexual violence for its applicability to Canadian universities.

Reverberations within university administrations: Results of task forces

Within a short time of the public outcry following most of the incidents of campus sexual violence described at this chapter's opening, university administrations in Canada announced the establishment of task forces.[1] The sizes of the task forces range from 3 members (Dalhousie) to 24 members (Lakehead). Composition varies from those with direct association to the particular university (UBC), to a mixture of university personnel and community-based activists (UofO), to experts external to the university (Dalhousie). These working groups came together for a short period of intense effort, and once they produced a report, dispersed. Their reports are now public-domain documents.

The reports tend to focus on particular dimensions of the incident of sexual violence that led to their formation. The prevention training recommended by the UofO task force targets the men's hockey team (University of Ottawa,

2015). Dalhousie's task force advocates attention to social media in the university's existing policies, more public disclosure of institutional processes, and structural changes in the Faculty of Dentistry to address the historical gender segregation in the training and practice of dentistry—in other words, to integrate Dental Hygiene within the Faculty of Dentistry (Dalhousie University, 2015). Both the SMU President's Council and UBC's task force include increased oversight by the university of orientation activities (President's Council, 2013; University of British Columbia, 2014). UBC goes further to recommend a mandatory pre-arrival online orientation module for all new students highlighting the values of a respectful, inclusive, safe environment for all students.

All reports highlight the importance of awareness education and training as a pivotal mechanism to lasting change. The UBC report calls for professional development modules on gender-based and anti-Indigenous violence for faculty, teaching assistants, and staff, as well as curriculum development in new and existing courses to acknowledge diversity. Lakehead's task force recommends educational sessions for new students and peer-support training of staff by community-based sexual assault organizations (Lakehead University, 2013). Both SMU's council and UofO's task force endorse Bringing in the Bystander training, which is discussed further in this collection's chapter by Anne Forrest and Charlene Senn. The UofO task force goes further by suggesting that all members of the senior administration participate in awareness training by fall 2015 to demonstrate the university leadership's commitment to preventing sexual violence. Less specifically, but perhaps informed by a similar sentiment, Dalhousie's task force adds the caveat to their proposal for improved education programs that they "should not be seen as a substitute for leadership and institutional commitment to confronting inequality" (p. 85).

These task force reports reveal deficiencies in campus sexual assault policies, including commitment to safeguarding the confidentiality of whistleblowers and processes to investigate, adjudicate, and sanction sexual violence. Lakehead's task force produced a sexual misconduct policy and protocol that was held up as a shining example by the media and many outside observers, perhaps because it was one of the first to emanate from the recent storm of controversies. SMU's council calls for a revision of the sexual assault policy written in 2008 to strengthen the formal investigation and adjudication procedures because the existing policy leaves all investigations to the criminal domain. Brandon's task force advocates for a stand-alone sexual assault policy. Both UBC's and Lakehead's task forces recommend a review of existing policies. Dalhousie's task force recommendation on policy is the least ambitious. With the exception of the inadequate protection from retaliation against whistleblowers and others who lodge complaints, this force found "on the whole, the University's policies and procedures for dealing with equity issues are as good as or better than other Canadian universities. We do not see a need to redraft them" (p. 3).

Both the UofO and Dalhousie task force reports refer to a climate of distrust and suspicion about the extent of the university's commitment to addressing sexual violence. From their consultations with more than 200 individuals, Dalhousie's task force found there was considerable perception of a "cover up," with the Facebook posts being "swept under the rug" (p. 63) in order to preserve the university's reputation. Transparency is a key requirement for revitalized confidence in the universities among students, faculty, and staff. As the authors of the Dalhousie report note, "An institution's response to allegations of sexual violence must not only be fair, it must be seen to be fair. Even when the 'right' outcome is reached, people will feel that justice was not served if the process was not fair" (Dalhousie University, 2015, p. 48). The Faculty of Dentistry has no formal complaint process, and as the authors note, "people seem afraid to complain informally for fear of retaliation ... and, they had little confidence that anything would be done anyway" (p. 3). Similarly, UofO Task Force consultees communicated their limited confidence in the university, in part because of the many still-to-be-implemented recommendations from the Harassment Working Group of a decade ago. Task forces may go a step towards repairing the loss of trust if they are seen as honest efforts of self-examination on the part of the institution, with the capacity to respond to suggestions for improvement. However, the real test of institutional commitment comes with the implementation of the recommendations.

The burning question is, are the task forces simply reactive crisis-management tools designed to assuage the public's concerns about a recent widely publicized incident of sexual violence? Can they produce the desired result of restoring public confidence in the universities to address the problem of campus sexual assault? While we might never know universities' actual intention, public confidence in Brandon University was certainly undermined by the allegations of plagiarism following revelations of a surprising resemblance between that task force's recommendations and those previously published at Queen's University (Johnston, 2016).

To their credit, each of the reports includes accountability mechanisms and structural changes to implement the recommendations, with regular reporting to the public for the first few years of their implementation. Results from the more recently established task forces (Brandon and Brock) are not yet available in their entirety. Public reports on progress of implementation at UofO and SMU have been made public; however, too few details are provided to make an adequate assessment of progress.

Furthermore, many recommendations are too vague to know if they have been implemented to the extent intended. For instance, the UBC report promised "appropriate resources, authority, and responsibility to oversee, coordinate, and support academic and non-academic units in enhancing the culture of equality and accountability" (University of British Columbia, 2014). But the follow-up report, *UBC's Response to the Task Force Recommendations* (May 13, 2014), identifies individuals and institutional positions responsible for the implementation of each recommendation but without associated timelines or consequences of lack of action.

Recommendations for new positions (e.g., SMU's new senior position in Student Services with a mandate of student safety, Dalhousie's Ombudsperson's Office, UofO's recently created Human Rights Office) do not include such crucial details as specification of duties, implications for existing procedures and policies, and reporting lines. Where reporting lines are specified and involve senior administration, potential conflicts of interest are not addressed in the reports.

The individuals consulted on the draft recommendations from UBC's task force expressed concern over the institution's lack of commitment to dedicated funding for all faculties and departments to integrate equity goals into their core processes. As a result of the consultation, the report's wording was adjusted to "necessary resources and supports should be made available to faculties and departments to build equity goals into core processes" (University of British Columbia, 2014, p. 26). However, this addition does little to clarify or answer the question of who determines the level of resourcing necessary to attain the goals.

The public's recent attentiveness to the problem of sexual violence has undoubtedly caused discomfort among some decision makers in the universities. As the authors of the Dalhousie task force report sympathetically note regarding the ill effects of the public scrutiny of the offending Facebook posts, "Every action was subject to intense scrutiny and a barrage of passionate commentary from every point of view" (Dalhousie University, 2015, p. 48). Yet is this not what every leader in our publicly funded educational institutions should expect? Is a widespread discourse on events within and about our public institutions not a sign of a healthy democracy?

The task forces and their reports signify an important juncture for Canadian universities. They reflect a growing strident activism directed to sexual violence taking hold across the country. At the same time, the task forces and resulting reports are indications of the flagrant inadequacies of our institutions to address the social problem. A resolution to the turmoil and controversies remains to be seen.

THE COLLECTION

The topic of sexual violence in general and sexual violence on campus in particular is an incendiary, polarizing one, with many diverse interests directing the public discourse. Taken together, the authors of the chapters in this collection represent a variety of social and institutional locations, as indicated by their biographies at the end of the collection. They, therefore, approach this urgent and complex topic with diverse viewpoints. While some chapters are written from the perspectives of emerging and established academics, others are written from the perspective of activists—Julie Lalonde (Chapter 13) and Andrea Gunraj (Chapter 8). Although Judy Haiven (Chapter 5) is a university professor, her chapter is reflectively written from the vantage of a long-standing activist.

The volume reflects an important historical moment in the life of Canadian universities—a moment when the high-profile stories of sexual violence on Canadian campuses described at the beginning of this chapter were at the forefront of an expansive public controversy about campus sexual violence. Thus, the stories appear in a number of chapters, although the authors refer to them for different purposes and from their distinct theoretical perspectives.

As editors, we have let the chapter authors choose their own terminology to identify individuals who have experienced sexual violence, acknowledging the considerable debate within the scholarship in this regard. The chapters by Andrea Gunraj (Chapter 8); Madison Trusolino (Chapter 4); and Jenna MacKay, Ursula Wolfe, and Alex Rutherford (Chapter 12) all address events at the same institution, York University, but from different vantages. The chapters by Julie Lalonde and by Elizabeth Sheehy and Daphne Gilbert were originally located in other sources and are reprinted here with permission; we have included them because they explore aspects of the subject not found elsewhere in the collection.

The collection is set apart from other sources, which are either not specific to on-campus sexual violence, although Canadian (e.g., Johnson & Dawson, 2011; Sheehy, 2012), or specific to on-campus, but not to the Canadian context (e.g., Bohmer & Parrot, 1993; Fisher, Daigle, & Cullen, 2009).

This book is divided into five sections. The first section, "Campus Sexual Violence: Impacts, Voids, and Institutional Betrayals," introduces the reader to the dimensions of campus sexual violence. Although experienced in a plethora of ways, sexual violence unilaterally violates individuals' rights, dignity, and integrity. Students in particular experience a range of psychological, cognitive, and social difficulties that interfere significantly with continuing their studies, which is the focus of Lana Stermac, Sarah Horowitz, and Sheena Bance's chapter, "Sexual Coercion on Campus: The Impact of Victimization and Disclosure on the Educational Experiences of Canadian Women." In their examination of educational impacts of sexual victimization, their chapter brings attention to the cultural diversity of the student population on many Canadian campuses and thereby makes a persuasive case for Canada-specific research compared to countries like the United States. In the following chapter, "Campus Violence, Indigenous Women, and the Policy Void," Carrie Bourassa and co-authors take up the void of data, policies, and programs relevant to Indigenous women on campuses. They attribute the effects of colonization to the indifference of contemporary post-secondary institutions to the cultural values, knowledge practices, and histories of First Nations. In so doing, they emphasize the intersections of colonization, racism, and sexism in the discussion of sexual violence, which traditionally has focused exclusively on gender as an axis of social inequality. While we know that a disproportionately higher number of Indigenous women are subjected to sexual violence in the general population, Bourassa et al. set out to find corresponding data on campus-specific violence. Their chapter reports on their environmental scan of English-speaking Canadian universities for their collection of demographic information on Indigenous survivors of violence on campus. In the section's final chapter, "Institutional Betrayal and Sexual Violence in the Corporate University," Elizabeth Quinlan takes up the effect of the accelerating corporatization of our post-secondary institutions. One such effect is a sense of being betrayed by the institutions to which survivors of sexual violence turn. The notion of betrayal is then extended to student populations, who seek post-secondary education while assuming their universities will attend to the problem of sexual violence. The chapter closes with an analysis of two forms of empirical data related to existing campus sexual violence resources and supports: an environmental scan and a survey of students' perceptions.

The second section, "Violent Spaces on Canadian University Campuses," explores a number of campus spaces that are particularly prone to sexual violence. The opening chapter, "'It's Not about One Bad Apple': The 2007 York University Vanier Residence Rapes," by Madison Trusolino, focuses on residences as a site of sexual violence and the link between the geopolitical location of the York campus and the element of race, ethnicity, and "otherness" so often implicitly embedded in the rape myth of the stranger lurking in the shadows. The next chapter, "Rape Chant at Saint Mary's University: A Convergence of Business School Ethics, Alcohol Consumption, and Varsity Sport," by Judy Haiven, situates the rape chant at Saint Mary's University, described above, within the triad of business school ethics, university sports, and the glorification of alcohol consumption. Haiven introduces the historical dimensions of misogyny on campus as a backdrop to the button campaign she initiated to raise awareness. From her many years as a social activist, Haiven knew the value of button campaigns as a strategy of changing public consciousness and galvanizing others into action, as buttons visually and readily proclaim the importance of an issue. Her chapter details the events that led to her button campaign and the outcome she found disappointing.

Andrea Quinlan's chapter, "Violent Bodies in Campus Cyberspaces," explores campus sexual violence that occurs in online spaces. Examining two recent cases of online sexual violence at Dalhousie University and the University of Ottawa, Quinlan argues that cyberspace can be a site where sexual violence and rape culture on campus are not merely reflected, but also reproduced and thereby perpetuated. Equally, it is a space of resistance to sexual violence. She draws on feminist literatures of technology and sexual violence, and proposes that by understanding the relations between violent bodies and technologies, some of the material consequences of online sexual violence on campus come into view. The section closes with Curtis Fogel's chapter, "Precarious Masculinity and Rape Culture in Canadian University Sport." Using a case study approach, Fogel examines how and why university athletes engage in sexual violence against their teammates and against female students, often in the form of gang rapes. Drawing on feminist theories of masculinity and sex-role socialization, Fogel develops a concept of "precarious masculinity" to shed light on athletes' use of sexual violence. He argues that in the context of sport, where fierce hierarchies of masculinity prevail and masculine status can be lost in an instant due to injury or poor athletic performance, athletes use sexual violence in an attempt to stabilize their otherwise unstable gender identities.

The third section, "Institutional Prevention and Responses to Sexual Violence," presents two very different sexual assault prevention programs for post-secondary application, followed by a critical review of an institutional response to sexual violence on campuses in Nova Scotia.

The first chapter, "Women as Experts: Origins and Developments of METRAC's Campus Safety Audit," by Andrea Gunraj, traces the evolution of the Campus Safety Audit Process over a period of 20 years with reference to its signature tools of critical reflection and multi-stakeholder involvement that includes students, faculty, administration, and community members. The campus audit grew out of the Women's Safety Audit Process conceived in 1989 and used across Canada and around the world. Based on anti-oppressive, intersectional feminist perspective and principles of social justice and women-as-experts, METRAC's participatory audit process trains community members and stakeholders to identify and prioritize locally relevant concerns. Changes to the audit process have been made since the beginnings to acknowledge vital knowledge that most women are assaulted by someone they know, to include intimate partner violence as a form of gendered violence, and to include realities of people of all genders who face gender-based violence and community members from marginalized groups. Gunraj describes METRAC's challenges of securing full cooperation from institutions that are conservative and hierarchical by design, since effectiveness in making campuses safer for women and others is contingent on administrations' allocation of resources for implementing the audits' recommendations.

In the next chapter, a second, more recently developed preventative program is covered. In "Theory Becomes Practice: The Bystander Initiative at the University of Windsor," Anne Forrest and Charlene Senn discuss a sexual assault prevention initiative grounded in organizational change theory and practice. Arguing that the missing element in making campuses significantly safer for women has been university administrations, the authors launched the Bystander Initiative at University of Windsor to close the gap between theory and practice that occurs when student affairs work in isolation from academic researchers. Forrest and Senn describe how over the last five years, the program has been actively reflected upon, evaluated, modified, and expanded.

Finally in this section, a report commissioned by the advocacy organization Students Nova Scotia in partnership with the province of Nova Scotia is critically discussed by Norma Jean Profitt and Nancy Ross in their chapter, "A Critical Analysis of the Report *Student Safety in Nova Scotia*: Co-creating a Vision and Language for Safer and Socially Just Campus Communities." Reminding readers that violence against women is the most pervasive yet unacknowledged human rights violation in the world, Profitt and Ross write a comprehensive critique of the Students Nova Scotia report with reference to the broader framework of sexual assault as an issue of power and structural inequalities. While commending the report for naming rape culture and acknowledging the incidence on campuses in that province, the authors take issue with the report's partial nature based on its failing to position the problem within a framework of gender-based violence against girls and women and failing to name sexism and misogyny as the common thread. Profitt and Ross examine such issues raised within the report as the discourse of risk and "responsibilization" that places onus on individuals as if they exist outside their contexts. The authors call for a social justice framework for all educational initiatives on sexual assault prevention to be solidly grounded in theory to address the social roots of rape, build a culture of community rights and responsibilities, and change social structures and everyday practices.

The fourth section, "Fighting Back: Anti-violence Activism on Campus," examines the activist groups and strategies that are taking aim at sexual violence and the inadequacies of university responses. The chapters in this section feature two differently configured activist groups: one composed of faculty, staff, and parents in addition to students, the other a solely student-run organization with some dependency on university funding. The chapters are written by representatives of these groups at different universities, yet they share a focus in pressing their respective institutions for an external audit of their campuses. The chapter by Elizabeth Quinlan and Gail Lasiuk on activism at the University of Saskatchewan spans the efforts of that university's Coalition Against Sexual Assault (CASA) since forming in 2003. York University's activist group, the Sexual Assault Survivors Support Line (SSASL), featured in the chapter authored by Jenna MacKay, Ursula Wolfe, and Alex Rutherford, has an even longer history dating back to the mid-1990s. These authors' descriptions of long-standing campus activist groups provide important historical context for the contemporary surge in widespread anti-violence activism on North American campuses.

The fifth and final section of this collection covers strategies for change. The opening chapter, "From Reacting to Preventing: Addressing Sexual Violence on Campus by Engaging Community Partners" by Julie Lalonde, explores the potentials and pitfalls of partnerships between universities and community-based agencies addressing sexual violence. Commissioned by the University of Ottawa's Task Force on Respect and Equality, Lalonde interviewed individuals from various front-line agencies working on sexual violence in conjunction with universities. The chapter's findings speak to the importance of cooperation from universities' senior administration for productive partnerships; otherwise, campus–community partnerships often result in the agency doing the heavy lifting because of the inherent power imbalances between their community groups and university personnel. The next chapter, "Why Theory Matters: Using Philosophical Resources to Develop University Practices and Policies Regarding Sexual Violence" by Ann Cahill, is a plea to universities to bring to bear the full range of intellectual resources from a variety of disciplines to develop policies and other mechanisms to address sexual violence. The benefit, Cahill argues, will be more fulsome polices that reflect a deeper understanding of the problem and do more than meet the minimum level of legal compliance. The starting point for the final chapter by Elizabeth Sheehy and Daphne Gilbert, "Responding to Sexual Assault on Campus: What Can Canadian Universities Learn from U.S. Law and Policy?" is the contrast between the United States, with its legislation regulating reporting of campus sexual assaults and the coordination between law enforcement and campus security forces, and Canada, where legislation is only very recently being introduced. The chapter sets out to answer the question of whether Canadian universities should have similar legal responsibilities to those of their counterparts in the United States. The authors survey the results of the over 30-year experience in the United States to identify thorny issues associated with legislating campus sexual violence prevention and response. The chapter's addendum brings the analysis up to date by covering recent legislative changes.

Sexual violence is one of the most pressing global problems. Its manifestation on Canadian university campuses reflects its extensive reach into all spheres of social life. While university administrations rush to develop policies and procedures to address campus sexual violence and activists continue to expose the inadequacies of these attempts and press for improved sexual assault prevention and responses on university campuses, it is vital that we explore the issue with the full breadth of available theoretical and methodological tools that interdisciplinary social scientific research affords. The editors of this collection hope that the volume is one small contribution to such a project.

NOTE

1 The exception is Brandon University, whose task force was established in the wake of a little-publicized September 2015 complaint.

REFERENCES

Ahrens, C. (2006). Being silenced: The impact of negative social reactions on the disclosure of rape. *American Journal of Community Psychology, 38,* 263–274.

Axon, R. (2016, October 19). Dept of Ed opens Title IX investigation into Baylor's handling of sexual violence. *USA Today.*

Baker, K. (2013, August 6). Student rape survivors launch much-needed know your IX campaign. *Jezebel.* Retrieved from http://jezebel.com/student-rape -survivors-launch-much-needed-know-your-ix-1041940722

Bohmer, C., & Parrot, A., (1993). *Sexual assault on campus: The problem and the solution.* New York, NY: Lexington Books.

Bolger, D. (2013, April 18). Sexual assault survivor activists launch "Know Your IX" campaign. *Huffington Post.* Retrieved from http://www.huffingtonpost.com/ dana-bolger/sexual-assault-survivor-a_b_3104714.html

Borja, S., Callahan, J., & Long, P. (2006). Positive and negative assessment and social support of sexual assault survivors. *Journal of Traumatic Stress, 19,* 905–914.

Brigden, K. (2016, July 12). Personal correspondence with Deputy Minister of Advanced Education, Saskatchewan Government.

Bill 15: The Sexual Violence Awareness and Prevention Act (Advanced Education Administration Act and Private Vocational Institutions Act Amended), 1st Sess., 41st Leg., Manitoba, 2016. Retrieved from https://web2.gov.mb.ca/bills/41-1/b015e.php

Bill 23: Sexual violence and misconduct policy act, 5th Sess., 40th Leg., British Columbia, 2016 (1st reading).

Bill 114: Safer Universities and Colleges Act., 2d. Sess., 62d Gen. Assembly, Nova Scotia, 2015. Retrieved from http://nslegislature.ca/legc/bills/62nd_2nd/1st_read/b114 .htm

Bill 132: Sexual Violence and Harassment Action Plan Act (Supporting Survivors and Challenging Sexual Violence and Harassment), S.O. 2016, c. 2, Ontario, 2016. Retrieved from http://www.ontla.on.ca/web/bills/bills_detail.do?locale=en&BillID=3535

Brownmiller, S. (1975). *Against our will: Men, women, and rape.* New York, NY: Fawcett Columbine.

Campbell, R. (2006). Rape survivors' experiences with the legal and medical systems: Do rape victim advocates make a difference? *Sociology of Health and Illness, 35*(4), 514–528.

Canada. (1985). Sexual assault. In *Criminal Code*, R.S.C. 1985, c. C-46, s. 271. Retrieved from http://www.canlii.org/en/ca/laws/stat/rsc-1985-c-c-46/113712/rsc-1985-c-c-46 .html#sec271_smooth

Canadian Press. (2016, February 15). Clarity needed in UBC system for handling sex assault allegations: Report. *CBC News.* Retrieved from http://www.cbc.ca/news/ canada/british-columbia/clarity-needed-in-ubc-system-for-handling-sex-assault -allegations-report-1.3449040

Cass, A. (2007). Routine activities and sexual assault: An analysis of individual- and school-level factors. *Violence and Victims, 22*(3), 350–364.

Crabb, J. (2016, April 5). "Behavioural contract" for sex assault victims a mistake: Brandon U president. *CTV News.* Retrieved from http://winnipeg.ctvnews.ca/ behavioural-contract-for-sex-assault-victims-a-mistake-brandon-u-president -1.2846306

Dalhousie University, Task Force on Misogyny, Sexism, and Homophobia in Dalhousie University Faculty of Dentistry. (2015, June 26). *Report of the Task Force on Misogyny, Sexism and Homophobia in Dalhousie University Faculty of Dentistry.* Retrieved from https://www.dal.ca/content/dam/dalhousie/pdf/cultureofrespect/ DalhousieDentistry-TaskForceReport-June2015.pdf

Dalhousie won't release names of dentistry Facebook scandal participants. (2015, January 15). *CBC News.* Retrieved from http://www.cbc.ca/news/canada/nova-scotia/ dalhousie-won-t-release-names-of-dentistry-facebook-scandal-participants -1.2890938

Donnelly, E. (2015, September 18). Lady Gaga's new music video is an intense PSA about campus sexual assault. *Refinery 29.* Retrieved from http://www.refinery29 .com/2015/09/94238/lady-gaga-til-it-happens-to-you-video-campus-rape

Dyck, D. (2016, October 24). UBC, former student fail to reach deal on human-rights complaint. *Canadian Press.* Retrieved from http://www.cbc.ca/news/canada/ british-columbia/ubc-and-former-student-fail-to-reach-agreement-on-human -rights-complaint-1.3819891

Firth, M. (2016, April 14). Brock prof breaks silence. *St. Catharines Standard.* Retrieved from http://www.stcatharinesstandard.ca/2016/04/14/brock-prof-breaks-silence

Fisher, B., Daigle, L., & Cullen, F. (2009). *Unsafe in the ivory tower: The sexual victimization of college women.* Thousand Oaks, CA: Sage.

Fisher, B., Daigle, L., Cullen, F., & Turner, M. (2003). Reporting sexual victimization to the police and others: Results from a national-level study of college women. *Criminal Justice and Behavior, 30,* 6–38.

Freyd, J., & Birrell, P. (2013). *Blind to betrayal.* New York, NY: Wiley.

Gavey, N. (2005). *Just sex? The cultural scaffolding of rape.* New York, NY: Routledge.

Government of Ontario. (2016). *Sexual violence and harassment action plan: Supporting survivors and challenging sexual violence and harassment.* Toronto, ON: Queen's Park Press.

Graham, K., Bernards, S., Abbey, A., Dumas, T., & Wells, S. (2010). Young women's risk of sexual aggression in bars: The roles of intoxication and peer social status. *Drug and Alcohol Review, 33,* 393–400.

Gray, M. (2015, September 25). *Opening address*. Ryled Up Counter Conference on Campus Sexual Violence, Toronto, Ontario..

Hampson, S. (2015, March 6). How the dentistry-school scandal has let loose a torrent of anger at Dalhousie. *Globe and Mail*. Retrieved from http://www .theglobeandmail.com/news/national/education/how-the-dentistry-school -scandal-has-let-loose-a-torrent-of-anger-at-dalhousie/article23344495/

Hertzog, J., & Yeiling, J. (2009). College women's rape awareness and use of commonly advocated risk reduction strategies. *College Student Journal, 43*(1), 59–73.

Hodgson, J. (2010). Policing sexual violence: A case study of Jane Doe v. the Metropolitan Toronto Police. In J. Hodgson & D. S. Kelley (Eds.), *Sexual violence: Policies, practices, and challenges in the United States and Canada* (pp. 173–190). London, UK: Lynne Rienner.

Jaschik, S., & Lederman, D. (2015). *The 2015 Insider Higher Ed Survey of College and University Presidents: Conducted by Gallup*. Washington, DC: Inside Higher Ed.

Jenkins, M., Langlais, P., Delis, D., & Cohen, R. (1998). Learning and memory in rape victims with posttraumatic stress disorder. *American Journal of Psychiatry, 155*(2), 278–279.

Jenkins, M., Langlais, P., Delis, D., & Cohen, R. (2000). Attentional dysfunction associated with posttraumatic stress disorder among rape survivors. *Clinical Neuropsychologist (Neuropsychology, Development and Cognition: Section D), 14*(1), 7–12.

Johnson, H., & Dawson, M. (2011). *Violence against women in Canada: Research and policy perspectives*. Don Mills, ON: Oxford University Press.

Johnston, A. (2016, April 7). Brandon University dodges plagiarism charges in sexual violence report. *CBC News*. Retrieved from http://www.cbc.ca/news/canada/ manitoba/brandon-university-plagiarize-sexual-violence-report-1.3525207

Jordan, C., Combs, J., & Smith, G. (2014). An exploration of sexual victimization and academic performance among college women. *Trauma, Violence, & Abuse, 15*(3), 191–200.

Kessler, R., Sonnega, A., Bromet, E., Hughes, M., & Nelson, C. (1995). Pot-traumatic stress disorder in the national comorbidity study. *Archives of General Psychiatry, 52*, 1048–1060.

Krakauer, J. (2015). *Missoula: Rape and the justice system in a college town*. New York, NY: Doubleday.

Krebs, C., Linkquist, C., Warner, T., Fisher, B., & Martin, S. (2007). *The Campus Sexual Assault Study*. Washington, DC: National Institute of Justice, U.S. Department of Justice.

Krug, E., Dahlberg, L., Mercy, J., Zwi, A., & Lozano, R. (2002). *World report on violence and health*. Geneva, Switzerland: World Health Organization.

Lakehead University, Task Force on Sexual Assault Education, Prevention and Support. (2014). *Report of Task Force on Sexual Assault Education, Prevention and Support*. Retrieved from https://www.lakeheadu.ca/sites/default/files/uploads/249/ Report,%20Sexual%20Assault%20Task%20Force.pdf

Lamb, S. (1999). Constructing the victim: Popular images and lasting labels. In S. Lamb (Ed.), *New versions of victims: Feminists struggle with the concept* (pp. 108–138). New York: New York University Press.

Lisak, D., Gardinier, L., Nicksa, S., & Cole, A. (2010). False allegations of sexual assault: An analysis of ten years of reported cases. *Violence Against Women, 16*(12), 1318–1334.

Lisak, D., & Miller, P. (2002). Repeat rape and multiple offending among undetected rapists. *Violence and Victims, 17*(1), 73–84.

MacKinnon, C. (1987). *Feminism unmodified: Discourses on life and law.* Cambridge, MA: Harvard University Press.

Macyshon, J. (2016, April 6). Second student says Brandon University silenced her after alleged sexual harassment. *CTV News.* Retrieved from http://www.ctvnews.ca/canada/second-student-says-brandon-university-silenced-her-after-alleged-sexual-harassment-1.2848909

Mathieu, E. (2014). Universities vow to "prevent and respond" to sexual assault. *Toronto Star.* Retrieved from http://www.thestar.com/news/canada/2014/11/29/universities_vow_to_prevent_and_respond_to_sexual_assault.html

Mayor, L. (2015, November 20). UBC "abandoned" women who reported sexual assaults. *CBC News.* Retrieved from http://www.cbc.ca/news/canada/ubc-sexual-assaults-complaints-expulsion-1.3328368

McGregor, M., Ericksen, J., Ronald, L., Janssen, P., Vliet, A., & Schulzer, M. (2004). Rising incidence of hospital-reported drug-facilitated sexual assault in a large urban community in Canada. *Canadian Journal of Public Health, 95*(6), 441–445.

Newton-Taylor, B., DeWit, D., & Gliksman, L. (1998). Prevalence and factors associated with physical and sexual assault of female university students in Ontario. *Health Care for Women International, 19*, 155–164.

Orchowski, L., Meyer, D., & Gidycz, C. (2009). College women's likelihood to report unwanted sexual experiences to campus agencies: Trends and correlates. *Journal of Aggression, Maltreatment and Trauma, 18*, 839–858.

Orchowski, L., & Gidycz, C. (2012). To whom do college women confide following sexual assault? A prospective study of predictors of sexual assault disclosure and social reactions. *Violence Against Women, 18*(3), 264–288.

Ormiston, S. (2014, September 29). Universities under pressure to combat sexual misconduct on campus. *CBC News.* Retrieved from http://www.cbc.ca/news/universities-under-pressure-to-combat-sexual-misconduct-on-campus-1.2781455

President's Council. (2013). *Promoting a culture of safety, respect and consent at Saint Mary's University and beyond: Report from the President's Council.* Retrieved from http://www.smu.ca/webfiles/PresidentsCouncilReport-2013.pdf

Province of Manitoba. (2015). *Province to introduce proposed groundbreaking legislation that would ensure safer campuses for students* [News release].

Quinlan, A. (Forthcoming). *The technoscientific witness of rape: Contentious histories of law, feminism, and forensic science.* Toronto, ON: University of Toronto Press.

Sabina, C., & Ho, L. (2014). Campus and college victim responses to sexual assault and dating violence: Disclosure, service utilization, and service provision. *Trauma, Violence, & Abuse, 15*(3), 201–226.

Sawa, T. (2016, March 11). Brock University tells student to keep quiet about sexual harassment. *CBC News.* Retrieved from http://www.huffingtonpost.ca/2016/03/11/brock-university-sexual-h_n_9438470.html

School of secrets. (2015, November 23). *The Fifth Estate.* Retrieved from http://www.cbc.ca/fifth/episodes/2015-2016/school-of-secrets

Senn, C., Eliasziw, M., Barata, P., Thurston, W., Newby-Clark, I. R., Radtke, L., & Hobden, K. (2014). Sexual violence in the lives of first-year university women in Canada: No improvements in the 21st century. *Women's Health, 14,* 13–38.

Sheehy, E. (Ed.). (2012). *Sexual assault in Canada: Law, legal practice and social activism.* Ottawa, ON: University of Ottawa Press.

Slater, G. (2015, September 24). *Summary of initiatives: Respect and Equality Action Team.* Ottawa, ON: University of Ottawa. Obtained via personal communication with Action Team leader.

Smith, C., & Freyd, J. (2013). Dangerous safe havens: Institutional betrayal exacerbates sexual trauma. *Journal of Traumatic Stress, 26*(1), 119–124.

Smith, P., White, J., & Holland, L. (2003). A longitudinal perspective on dating violence among adolescent and college-age women. *American Journal of Public Health, 93*(7), 1104–1109.

Statistics Canada. (2010). *The nature of sexual offenses.* Ottawa, ON: Author.

Svokos, A. (2014, October 29). Students bring out mattress in a huge carry that weight protest against sexual assault. *Huffington Post.* Retrieved from http://www.huffingtonpost.com/2014/10/29/carry-that-weight-columbia-sexual-assault_n_6069344.html

Taylor, K. (2015, May 19). Mattress protest continues at Columbia University into graduation event. *New York Times.* Retrieved from https://www.nytimes.com/2015/05/20/nyregion/mattress-protest-at-columbia-university-continues-into-graduation-event.html?_r=0

United States Department of Education Office for Civil Rights. (2011, April 4). *Dear colleague letter.* Retrieved from http://www2.ed.gov/about/offices/list/ocr/letters/colleague-201104.pdf

University of Alberta Sexual Assault Centre. (2001). A survey of unwanted sexual experience among University of Alberta Students. Retrieved from https://uofa.ualberta.ca/current-students/sexual-assault-centre/-/media/7d6cd389c2a44db5a1cbd3249dd0d49a.ashx

University of British Columbia. (2014). *Transforming UBC and developing a culture of equality and accountability: Confronting rape culture and colonist violence.* Vancouver, BC: Author.

University of British Columbia (May 13, 2014). Renewing our commitment to equity and diversity: Response to the task force recommendations. Available at: http://equity2.sites.olt.ubc.ca/files/2014/05/RENEWING-OUR-COMMITMENT-TO-EQUITY-AND-DIVERSITY-FINAL-02.pdf

University of Ottawa. (2015). *Report of the Task Force on Respect and Equality: Ending sexual violence at the University of Ottawa.* Retrieved from https://www.uottawa.ca/president/sites/www.uottawa.ca.president/files/report-of-the-task-force-on-respect-and-equality.pdf

University of Ottawa men's hockey won't ice 2015–16 team. (2015, January 16). *CBC News.* Retrieved from http://www.cbc.ca/news/canada/ottawa/university-of-ottawa-men-s-hockey-won-t-ice-2015-16-team-1.2912592

World Health Organization. (2002). Sexual violence. In *World Report on Violence and Health* (Chapter 6). Retrieved from http://www.who.int/violence_injury_prevention/violence/global_campaign/en/chap6.pdf?

Ziering, A. (Producer) & Dick, K. (Director). (2015). *The hunting ground* [Motion Picture]. United States: Weinstein Company.

PART I

CAMPUS

SEXUAL

VIOLENCE

Impacts, Voids, and Institutional Betrayals

CHAPTER 1

SEXUAL COERCION ON CAMPUS

The Impact of Victimization and Disclosure on the
Educational Experiences of Canadian Women

Lana Stermac, Sarah Horowitz, and Sheena Bance

Despite increased attention to issues around violence against women, sexual assault continues to be a serious and significant problem for women on Canadian university campuses (Belknap & Sharma, 2014; Stermac, Horowitz, & Bance, 2014). Recent media reports on sexually inappropriate behaviours in universities highlight some of the continuing controversies surrounding the scope of campus-based sexual victimization, including the accuracy of incidence and prevalence rates and the range and adequacy of responses from university administrators to address these behaviours (Chiose, 2014; Ormiston, 2014).

The best prevalence statistics we have in Canada confirm high rates of sexual victimization on university campuses (DeKeseredy & Schwartz, 1998; Schwartz & DeKeseredy, 1997; Senn et al., 2013). The most comprehensive early work in this area involving 293 female undergraduates on Canadian college campuses found that over 32% of the women surveyed reported being sexually victimized in some way (DeKeseredy & Schwartz, 1998). Other studies of Canadian regional campuses (e.g., Elliot, Odynak, & Krahn, 1992; Finkelman, 1992) support these high rates. More recently, Tremblay et al. (2008) examined a broad range of negative social experiences among students in Ontario and found that the most serious experiences, reported by over 10% of university students, involved incidents of sexual behaviours. A recent study, although not exclusive to incidents of campus-based sexual assaults, revealed that almost 60% of first-year undergraduate women in Canada had experienced some form of sexual victimization since the age of 14 (Senn et al., 2013).

Although increased focus on campus sexual assault and victimization in Canada is leading to more research as well as the development of new and promising prevention programs (Senn, 2013), much of this work to date has ignored the educational context of university attendance and the effects on student academic performance and educational experiences. In this chapter we consider some important sequelae of sexual victimization on women's education, with attention to the changing and ethnoculturally diverse population of current students in Ontario.

IMPACTS OF SEXUAL VICTIMIZATION

The negative effects of sexual behaviours on campus that include physical violence, coercion, and stalking behaviours are well documented (Jordan, Combs, & Smith, 2014; Wilcox, Jordan, & Pritchard, 2006), and a number of studies illustrate the centrality of health and mental health concerns (Amstadter et al., 2010). Sabina and Ho's (2014) recent study of service utilization on campuses found that physical and mental health services were the most commonly accessed services among sexual assault survivors.

Concern about the impact of sexual victimization on the health and well-being of students has broadened only recently to include examining effects on education and academic performance (Jordan, Combs, & Smith, 2014). Sexual victimization can influence women's education and potential career trajectories in a number of ways (Horsman, 1999; Wagner & Magnusson, 2005). Research on the learning effects of traumatic sexual behaviours in emerging adulthood supports findings of long-term impacts on academic and educational outcomes among sexually victimized women (Bremner et al., 1993; Bremner et al., 1995). In addition to memory deficits and attention problems seen among adult survivors of sexual abuse, sexual victimization is associated with psychological trauma states, which can have a profound impact on learning outcomes and academic performance (Horsman, 1999; Jenkins, Langlais, Delis, & Cohen, 1998, 2000).

Only a few studies have identified the routes by which sexual victimization may interfere directly with women students' education. Early work by DeKeseredy and Schwartz (1998) identified areas of negative impact, including the possibility of disengagement, missed classes, and potential school withdrawal. More recent research has linked various forms of sexual violence against women students, including stalking, intimate partner violence, sexual harassment, and sexual assault, to academic impacts such as moving residences, dropping classes, reduced GPA and overall performance, lower academic satisfaction, disengagement from academics, and increased likelihood of dropping out of school (Fisher, Cullen, & Turner, 2000; Huerta, Cortina,

Pang, Torges, & Magley, 2006; Jordan et al., 2014; Smith, White, & Holland, 2003). The Ontario Women's Directorate report *Developing a Response to Sexual Violence* (2013) notes several ways that sexual victimization can affect a student's academic career. Students may develop fears around areas on campus associated with the incident(s) and adopt limitations to their movements in order to avoid the perpetrator; they may even voluntarily suspend their studies or transfer campuses. Difficulties concentrating, poor mental health, and decreased engagement have been noted by clinicians and researchers alike (Ontario Women's Directorate, 2013; Stermac et al., 2014). While Jordan et al. (2014) provide some initial and compelling data linking women's experience of sexual assault to lowered GPA, researchers also note the need for further and more comprehensive investigation of factors associated with the impact of sexual victimization on academic performance.

Negative outcomes of sexual coercion and other forms of sexual victimization may be increased for some women (Ahrens, Rios-Mandel, Isas, & del Carmen Lopez, 2010; Luce, Schrager, & Gilchrist, 2010; Ontario Women's Directorate, 2013; Porter & Williams, 2011). The risk and impact of sexual victimization for racialized women and Indigenous women in Canada is only recently being investigated and understood within the context of political and economic disparity within both home and immigrant communities, as well as the legacy of colonized histories (Ahrens, Rios-Mandel et al., 2010; Ontario Women's Directorate, 2013; Porter & Williams, 2011; Quinlan, Clarke & Horsley, 2010). Research on sexual victimization of university women has generally focused on majority-culture students despite the increasing diversity of Canadian campuses, further limiting our understanding of the pathways through which sexual victimization has an impact on women's education.

The importance of disclosure on the impact of sexual victimization

A number of factors are associated with the overall effects of sexual victimization, including on women's education. One of the most important of these, arguably, is disclosure of the individual's experiences of victimization. Whether, how, and with whom sexual assault survivors talk about victimization can affect their coping, what actions they take against a perpetrator, and longer-term mental health and educational outcomes. While discussing difficult experiences is generally linked to reduced symptoms and increased well-being, sexual assault disclosure is variably associated with positive, neutral, or even negative outcomes, suggesting that the social reaction following disclosure is just as important as whether or not disclosure occurs. Examining some of the issues related to women's decisions around disclosure is important in understanding the full impact of victimization experiences on their university experiences and educational trajectory. Most literature on disclosure of sexual victimization distinguishes between formal and informal disclosure. Formal disclosure includes services such as law enforcement, medical providers, counselling, or advocacy services, whereas informal disclosure refers to friends, family members, or romantic partners. Only small numbers of university student survivors make disclosures to law enforcement or to health or victims' services (Lindquist et al., 2013). Rates of disclosure to campus services of any kind range from 3% to 20%, with a high proportion of these accounted for by psychological and counselling services (Sabina & Ho, 2014; Walsh, Banyard, Moynihan, Ward & Cohn, 2010). It is likely that this is partially accounted for by the fact that the vast majority of university students—at least in the United States—are largely unaware of campus mental health services (Sabina & Ho, 2014; Walsh et al., 2010; Yorgason, Linville, & Zitman, 2008).

The vast majority of sexual victimization disclosures are to informal supports, especially female friends, mothers, and romantic partners (Jacques-Tiura, Tkatch, Abbey, & Wegner, 2010; Sabina & Ho, 2014). This is likely because survivors most often disclose due to a need for emotional support and advice, and to feel less alone, rather than a desire for tangible aid or prosecution of the perpetrator (Jacques-Tiura et al., 2010; Moors & Webber, 2012). However, people often avoid disclosing informally for reasons such as not wanting to upset people or to be blamed for the victimization (McElvaney, Greene, & Hogan, 2014; Paul, Gray, Elhai, & Davis, 2009). Most studies on informal disclosure indicate that survivors receive a combination of largely positive reactions mixed with negative reactions; however, a large portion of survivors regret disclosing even to close friends and family, often due to feeling ashamed or blamed (e.g., Jacques-Tiura et al., 2010).

Reactions to sexual victimization disclosure received from those close to an individual (friends or family) can influence later decisions to seek counselling or take action in the criminal justice system (Fehler-Cabral & Campbell, 2013). When disclosure is received with support or encouraged by peers, young adults are more likely to disclose again in the future (McElvaney et al., 2014; Orchowski, Untied, & Gidycz, 2013). Similarly, when others react negatively to disclosure, survivors often stop disclosing altogether (Ahrens, 2006). Negative responses are associated with higher symptoms of post-traumatic stress and depression, as well as self-blame for the victimization (Ahrens, Stansell, & Jennings, 2010; Orchowski, 2009; Orchowski et al., 2013). Those who are most in need of emotional support—such as survivors with higher levels of post-traumatic stress, depression, or physical symptoms—have been found to be less likely to disclose, and nondisclosure is associated with increased distress and post-traumatic stress even many years after the victimization (Ahrens, Stansell, et al., 2010; Hébert, Tourigny, Cyr, McDuff, & Joly, 2009).

The decision to disclose or not disclose as well as the subsequent experience of disclosure may be central to women's educational outcomes. University student survivors who do not access supports or accommodations may experience greater impacts on educational performance, may become isolated on campus, and may continue to be in a dangerous environment because of continued contact with a perpetrator. The university context, which heavily emphasizes peer relationships and entails close social contact, tends to have a unique culture, services particular to the campus, and norms around reporting on-campus rather than off (Sabina & Ho, 2014).

SEXUAL COERCION AND EDUCATION RESEARCH PROGRAM

Despite abundant evidence of the negative effects of sexual victimization on women and the recent acknowledgement of the importance of examining overall educational and learning outcomes, surprisingly little research has systematically investigated this. Given the increasing diversity of Canadian universities and the possibility of interactions between racialization and sociocultural factors with victimization outcomes, it is especially important to expand our research on educational impacts and to include ethnoculturally diverse students (Kaukinen, 2014; Ontario Women's Directorate, 2013; Stermac et al., 2013). To address these gaps in the Canadian literature on campus sexual assault and education, we developed a program of research examining the impact of sexual victimization on university women's health and education.

The initial and pilot study in our research, which we report on here, examined the range of educational and academic outcomes associated with sexual coercion experiences among an ethnoculturally diverse sample of undergraduate students in Ontario universities, including a high proportion of racialized participants. We focused on the complexities of disclosure of sexual victimization and its relationship to educational outcomes. This initial qualitative study consisted of individual interviews with 15 women undergraduate students aged 19 to 27 ($M=21$) who were attending universities in southern Ontario and who experienced sexual coercion during their university enrolment (including any unwanted sexual behaviours ranging from sexual comments or pressure to touching to rape). The self-reported ethnocultural backgrounds of the majority of participants were Caribbean-Canadian, East Asian, South Asian, and mixed.

A constructivist grounded theory approach (Charmaz, 2006) was used to design the semi-structured interviews for the study. Interviews provided an in-depth understanding of women's experiences of sexual coercion during their undergraduate years. Women were asked about the nature and context of the sexually coercive experience, how they responded and coped with what occurred, their academic performance and academic and social engagement on campus, and their attitudes towards their education and career. Interview transcripts were analyzed for major themes. Constant comparison methods were used to identify similarities and differences among interviews and refine sub-categories (Charmaz, 2006).

Impacts on education

Participants in the study described unwanted sexual experiences that occurred with university peers (both acquaintances and strangers), boyfriends or partners, friends, non-student acquaintances, authority figures (e.g., employers), and non-student strangers. Experiences involved only male perpetrators. Sexual behaviours occurred in various locations, including university residences, academic settings such as classrooms and study halls, non-university social and employment settings (e.g., school-sponsored networking events), and individuals' homes.

All participants in this study felt that unwanted sexual behaviours had some impact on their education; however, this varied from self-reported minimal annoyance to significant interference both psychologically and academically. Interviews revealed that the impact of sexual victimization on women's educational experiences was associated with a number of variables. Several main themes emerged from participants' discussion of their educational experiences, as grouped and described below.

Academic performance. The majority of participants described serious impacts on their academic performance and work, including missed classes, exams, and assignments; several reported that their GPA decreased. A number of participants dropped courses and spoke of the possibility of transferring programs or even dropping out of their program after the incident. Financial concerns of retaking courses were mentioned by two students. Effects on academic performance identified by participants also included difficulty concentrating in lectures, being distracted in class or while doing schoolwork, or spending time attempting to avoid contact with perpetrators instead of focusing on schoolwork.

Safety on campus. A number of participants discussed educational impacts as changes in their feelings of safety on campus. This included where and how they studied and lived (e.g., going from having their door open in residence to closed), which classes they attended, and discomfort being in the presence of male classmates and males in general. Feeling unsafe with male classmates, professors, and teaching assistants also interfered with academic performance for some participants, who participated less in their courses and avoided seeking academic guidance from male professors or teaching assistants.

Extracurricular and social interactions. Changes in extracurricular activities and socializing were mentioned, including less social interaction with males and less participation in discipline-related professional events. Several participants noted increased isolation as a result of anxiety, low mood, and an increased focus on self-protection. One student stated that her experiences led her to less verbal interactions in male-led classes and less participation in peer groups with males.

Attitudes towards education and future careers. A number of participants stated that their attitude towards their education or careers changed after victimization experiences. One student stated she became apathetic, several questioned their choice of study field (especially those in traditionally male-dominated fields such as engineering) and considered transferring to less male-dominated fields, and another student questioned the overall value of her schooling (Bance, Stermac, & Horowitz, 2014).

Disclosure of sexual victimization

All but two of the participants in our study disclosed their unwanted sexual experiences to at least one person prior to participating in this research. However, they did so along varying timelines, to varying targets, and in differing amounts of detail. Consistent with findings of past research, the majority of study participants ($n=12$) disclosed to informal targets such as friends or family, while only a subset of six of these same participants disclosed to a more formal target, and one participant disclosed only to formal targets. Racialized women in the study all disclosed their experiences informally. Informal targets of disclosure were most commonly friends but also included romantic partners, mothers, and peers who had disclosed similar experiences. Formal disclosures included professors, school counsellors, psychiatrists, residence staff, registrars, shelter staff, hospital staff, and family doctors. One study participant disclosed victimization to law enforcement but stated this was unintentional as she had only intended to speak informally to officers.

Participants often waited to disclose their experience rather than doing so immediately after victimization, and most stated that they found it difficult to disclose and tried to avoid doing so. For example, one participant who experienced ongoing coercion for over a year told her psychiatrist about the experience only after she had left the abusive situation.

In addition to delayed disclosure, participants engaged in partial disclosures, giving some details but not others or downplaying the impact of the victimization. Some participants who were victimized by partners framed the victimization as "a bad breakup" to some friends, while sharing the full experience with others. One participant, who experienced long-term harassment at profession-related school events, asked friends to attend the events with her but did not explain why she wanted them there. Sometimes participants expressed more general concerns about sexual assault to formal university targets without talking about their own personal experience. For example, a participant asked to have general information posted about assault and consent in her residence but did not reveal her own experience of assault.

Access to university support services also played a role in participants' decisions to disclose information selectively; for example, one participant indicated that she requested academic accommodations related to anxiety rather than disclosing the victimization. Another participant opted not to disclose the details of her assault because there would not be an option for ongoing counselling or treatment. Participants who disclosed formally appreciated when others were respectful of privacy. For example, one participant found it helpful that the letters given to professors regarding accommodations were nonspecific about reasons for the request.

Cultural narratives in disclosure decisions

Findings from this preliminary study suggest that for some participants, ethnocultural and racialized background was relevant to their decision to disclose or withhold disclosure about victimization, as well as to the reactions others had to disclosures and to the impacts of those reactions. While some of the beliefs about sexual victimization, such as self-blame, victimization not being "serious enough," and a feeling of responsibility to manage any associated distress alone, were similar to concerns noted in past research on majority-culture women, other concerns not commonly addressed in largely majority-culture samples were also noted. Specifically, a prominent concern raised by racialized women with East Asian and South Asian backgrounds was that sexuality and sexual victimization were not appropriate topics of discussion within their ethnocultural group and/or within their family. Some participants indicated that ethnocultural prohibitions on discussing sexuality and sexual victimization were primary reasons for avoiding disclosure, particularly with parents but also with peers. One participant reported that in addition to acting as a barrier to disclosure, ethnocultural norms against talking about sexual victimization contributed to her sense of shock, self-blame, and isolation following an assault incident. This participant stated that she believed that sexual victimization did not happen to women in her ethnocultural group in general and as a result never expected that this could happen to her. She linked this belief to relatively more conservative norms for dating and alcohol consumption, pointing to common beliefs that victimization "only happens to a certain kind of girl." This participant reported that she experienced only negative responses following disclosure and that none of her peers whom she disclosed to (all being within her South Asian culture) were particularly supportive. Indeed, she surmised that telling a friend outside of her cultural background may have led to a more positive response.

Disclosure of sexual victimization and impact on education

The characteristics of disclosures made by participants in this study were related to academic outcomes in a number of ways. While all women reported some impact of sexual victimization on their educational experience or performance, it is notable that so few of them disclosed to formal supports within the university. Most commonly, participants experienced several days or weeks following the victimization when they had difficulty sleeping and concentrating on schoolwork, and avoided classes or certain areas of campus due to proximity to the perpetrator or reminders of the victimization. Increased isolation from peers, social activities, or family was also often noted and associated with shame, fear of judgment, low energy, and an emphasis on self-protection. Additionally, participants often indicated a sense of responsibility for coping with the aftermath of victimization on their own, rather than troubling their friends or family or even accessing support services. This sense of responsibility precluded disclosure. For example, one participant said she felt counselling was meant for students experiencing really "serious" difficulties rather than for students like her, and another participant spoke about removing herself from group work in school because of proximity to the perpetrator, saying that she felt that disclosure would have disrupted her peers' work, whereas non-disclosure would affect only her. She also spoke about disengagement from more personal academic writing assignments, explaining that she initially avoided this task but eventually was able to write about the sexually coercive experience as part of an assignment.

When participants did speak to others about their victimization experiences, how the target reacted was important to participants' continued coping, academic engagement, and willingness to access services. For example, one participant was unable to access post-victimization counselling through the university due to a cap on the number of available sessions, and found the experience of being turned down after telling her story so disheartening that she did not follow up with other potential supports. Conversely, participants who felt supported by their peers or by university staff generally spoke about being able to maintain academic performance and to continue with class and social activities.

Several participants in the present study identified impacts of disclosure as potential barriers to future academic and even career advancement. Sometimes the impacts were quite direct; for example, one participant who was concerned about getting into graduate school due to a post-victimization drop in grades approached her registrar but was told that the drop was not severe enough for accommodations. Other times the impacts were more indirect, such as for participants who shared that people they disclosed to encouraged them to accept victimization as "normal," and discouraged speaking out about it at school or work. This minimizing response led some participants to feel apathetic about academic or career success and to consider changing fields. One student discussed experiences of harassment that led her to avoid taking courses in her own program. She felt there was a culture of silence around harassment in her male-dominated future profession which was also evidenced in her classes and professional training.

The prevalence of partial disclosure among study participants indicated that many experiences of victimization may pass under the radar. Participants revealed that they found ways to avoid mentioning victimization in changing their routine or in accessing university services. Students said they were "busy," "sick," or "tired" in order to avoid classes or buildings where the perpetrator might be present or because of symptoms such as sleeplessness and low energy. Being uncomfortable working or socializing with the perpetrator or with men more generally may be explained as shyness in order to disguise women's true experiences.

Delayed disclosure sometimes interfered with participants' ability to access academic accommodations. One participant disclosed a sexual assault to her registrar several months after its occurrence when she realized that she could not bring her grades back up, but was told that she had waited too long to seek assistance. The participant explained that she had not been able to disclose earlier because she felt she needed to continue to engage in school to maintain her motivation and mental well-being. This was noted by several other participants who spoke about increased engagement in their schoolwork after victimization, using academic participation as a refuge, a means of avoiding social engagements, or a way to protect self-esteem. Some of the same participants, however, experienced a drop in grades later or experienced isolation from peers and extracurricular activities. Several were also experiencing distressing symptoms such as difficulties sleeping and concentrating, as well as low mood and hypervigilance.

DISCUSSION

The findings from our preliminary study demonstrate that sexual victimization has an impact on women's education and learning. While our study is exploratory and includes a small number of participants, the findings also indicate that the experience of disclosure is important to survivors' educational trajectories and presents some unique issues for racialized women.

Findings in the present study mirrored past preliminary research on the educational impacts of sexual victimization, with participants experiencing lower grades, missed classes, reduced participation, and reduced mobility on campus (Fisher et al., 2000; Huerta et al., 2006; Jordan et al., 2014; Smith et al., 2003). Importantly, participants in the present study also described the emotional, social, and academic trajectories that they experienced as leading to these outcomes. For example, participants described common trauma symptoms such as low mood, anxiety, preoccupation, and concentration difficulties as leading to reduced engagement in classes, difficulties completing assignments, and dropping courses. They described feeling physically unsafe—both with regards to proximity to the specific perpetrator and to males in general—as leading to missing classes; participating less in class discussions; avoiding courses, events, and social engagements involving males or occurring at night; requesting less academic help from male professors and teaching assistants; and even considering changes in study field or career. They also described important interactions among difficulties accessing support or services, stigma, increased apathy, and changed attitudes about their own educational and career futures, which in turn may also have compounded academic performance.

An extensive body of research has demonstrated the importance of disclosure of sexual victimization to both positive and negative outcomes for survivors, but little of this research has considered the university context or educational outcomes (e.g., Orchowski, 2009; Orchowski et al., 2013). As was the case in past research, participants in the present study disclosed primarily to informal supports, engaged in delayed and partial disclosures, and experienced a range of positive and negative responses. Avoiding disclosure often increased social isolation and decreased access to accommodations and services, while positive disclosure experiences were described as central to positive coping and maintaining academic performance. However, participants described some negative outcomes to disclosure, such as minimizing and blame that directly or indirectly affected their grades, finances, willingness to access services, attitudes towards education, and confidence in their ability to attain educational and career goals. In addition, participants described reasons for withholding disclosure that are more specific to the university context, such as using academic tasks as a means of coping and maintaining a sense of self-worth, leading them to avoid requesting accommodations.

Participants described the "cultural" milieu as important to both disclosure and educational outcomes, specifically giving examples of what they labelled as gendered and ethnocultural contexts. Some participants spoke about increased awareness of gender following victimization experiences, in combination with feeling unsafe around men and avoiding active participation in male-dominated classes or events. Several participants spoke about sexual victimization by men as being a common and expected experience of women in general. In conjunction with this, one participant spoke in detail about experiencing a silence regarding sexualized violence against women within the university context, and expressed concerns about managing a similar environment if she remains in her chosen career path.

Participants in the present study who named ethnocultural context as important to talking about and recovering from sexual victimization focused on whether sexuality is appropriate to discuss, and narratives about whom sexual victimization happens to, particularly in familial and peer contexts. Existing research on the ethnocultural context of disclosure has tended to focus on very specifically delineated groups, such as "Latina" or "Asian" women in the United States (e.g., Ahrens, Rios-Mandel, et al., 2010); however, one study by Foynes, Platt, Hall, and Freyd (2014) found that endorsement of what they termed "Asian values," such as the importance of group harmony and social and familial responsibility, predicted reduced disclosure above and beyond actual ethnicity. Similarly, much existing research that does not address ethnocultural background has identified the importance of shame, self-blame, and rape myths in both disclosure and outcomes following sexual victimization (e.g., Orchowski, 2009; Sabina & Ho, 2014), and it is unclear whether ethnocultural context is important above and beyond common cross-cultural values and social norms that act as barriers to disclosure.

Some studies have also begun to address social and systemic barriers to disclosure and support for racialized women, primarily focusing on African-American women with regards to perceptions of racism in the criminal justice system, a history of negative interactions with police, and a legacy of sexual victimization during slavery (Jacques-Tiura et al., 2010; Long & Ullman, 2013; Ullman and Filipas, 2001; Washington, 2001; Wyatt, 1992), and also noting a lack of community resources for Latina women (Ahrens, Rios-Mandel, et al., 2010). Unfortunately, few studies to date have addressed systemic barriers that may be specific to racialized women in the Canadian context, and our study represents one of the first exploring sexual victimization in a diverse Canadian sample. For example, very little research has been done with Indigenous women (e.g., Quinlan et al., 2010). Women in the most prevalent minority groups in Canada may have different narratives about sexual victimization and different histories with Canadian law enforcement and health care systems than those addressed in American research. Given the complexity of disclosure and nondisclosure for survivors of sexual victimization, researchers need to more fully understand the complex dynamics among ethnocultural background, racialization and systemic barriers, and disclosure from a Canadian perspective, as well as to clarify the context and directionality of the findings (Ahrens, Cabral, & Abeling, 2009; Orchowski et al., 2013; Paul et al., 2009).

CONCLUSION

This chapter examined initial research on sexual victimization impacts on education among students on university campuses in Ontario. We also highlighted the complexities of disclosure of sexual victimization within the ethnoculturally diverse context of some university campuses.

Our preliminary exploratory study on undergraduate women's educational experiences offers a deeper understanding of past findings that victimization affects grades and educational participation. However, larger samples and more extensive qualitative as well as quantitative research are required to better delineate specific impacts, for example, in investigating the extent of changes to GPA, the long-term effects on university completion and career, and the specific impact of potential factors such as trauma symptoms and social support. In particular, our findings point to the potential importance of disclosure, non-disclosure, and resultant support or lack thereof in mitigating educational impacts.

In addition, our study is one of the first to qualitatively explore sexual victimization experiences in a highly diverse Canadian sample with a high proportion of racialized women. Women in our sample identified and alluded to gendered barriers to education and career that they related to sexual victimization. Further research is needed to examine whether racial minority status and related histories may compound some of the difficulties with access to counselling and academic accommodations that participants discussed, as well as longer-term concerns about field of study, attitudes towards education, and career plans. Similarly, participants in the present study referenced a number of similar expectations, beliefs, and judgments about sexual victimization in relation to existing research with racial minority groups in the United States, as well as research regarding rape myths and self-blame with largely majority-culture samples. With the diverse makeup of many of our university campuses, the unique experiences of Canadian students are vital to understand. Research, in particular further qualitative studies, can elucidate the dynamics around both majority and minority perspectives of intrapersonal and interpersonal factors that shape women's educational trajectories (Walsh et al., 2010).

In addition to a need for future research, our study highlights considerations that are important to university administrators, faculty, and support services. Universities must be aware of the array of different beliefs about sexuality and sexual victimization—both in majority and minority cultures, as well as in the university environment broadly—that could have an impact on women students' coping, support seeking, and educational trajectories in addition to prevention efforts. Self-blame and shame are common and may be compounded with blame and ostracization from university social groups, peers, or family members who may deny the occurrence or impact of sexual victimization. Moreover, our findings indicate an interaction between disclosure and education. The common occurrence of avoidance and withholding disclosure indicates the importance of considering that students who stop participating in class or remove themselves from extracurricular activities could be struggling with concerns about sexual victimization. Similarly, in our study, students' shame and self-blame about victimization commonly occurred with a belief that resultant lowered grades or lowered school engagement was a personal failure, acting as an important barrier to asking for academic accommodations or support within a school-enforced timeline. There is a need within universities for work around stigma reduction and tailoring accommodations and support services to the common concerns and needs of students who have experienced sexual victimization.

REFERENCES

Ahrens, C., Rios-Mandel, L., Isas, L., & del Carmen Lopez, M. (2010). Talking about interpersonal violence: Cultural influences on Latinas' identification and disclosure of sexual assault and intimate partner violence. *Psychological Trauma: Theory, Research, Practice and Policy, 2*, 284–295.

Ahrens, C. E. (2006). Being silenced: The impact of negative social reactions on the disclosure of rape. *American Journal of Community Psychology, 38*, 263–274.

Ahrens, C. E., Cabral, G., & Abeling, S. (2009). Healing or hurtful: Sexual assault survivors' interpretations of social reactions from support providers. *Psychology of Women Quarterly, 33*, 81–94.

Ahrens, C. E., Stansell, J., & Jennings, A. (2010). To tell or not to tell: The impact of disclosure on sexual assault survivors' recovery. *Violence and Victims, 25*, 631–649.

Amstadter, A., Zinzow, H., McCauley, J., Strachan, M., Ruggiero, K., Resnick, H., & Kilpatrick, D. (2010). Prevalence and correlates of service utilization and help seeking in a national college sample of female rape victims. *Journal of Anxiety Disorders, 24*, 900–902.

Bance, S., Stermac, L., & Horowitz, S. (2014, June). *The educational impact of sexually coercive experiences on undergraduate women.* Presented at the Canadian Psychological Association Annual Meeting, Vancouver, BC.

Belknap, J., & Sharma, N. (2014). The significant frequency and impact of stealth (non-violent) gender-based abuse among college women. *Trauma, Violence, and Abuse, 15*, 181–190.

Bhanot, S., & Senn, S. Y. (2007). Attitudes towards violence against women in men of South Asian ancestry: Are acculturation and gender role attitudes important factors? *Journal of Family Violence, 22*, 25–31.

Bremner, J. D., Randall, P., Scott, T. M., Capelli, S., Delaney, R., McCarthy, G., & Charney, D. S. (1995). Deficits in short-term memory in adult survivors of childhood abuse. *Psychiatry Research, 59*, 97–107.

Bremner, J. D., Scott, T. M., Richard, C. D., Southwick, S. M., Mason, J. W., Johnson, D. R., Innis, R. B., McCarthy, G., & Charney, D. S. (1993). Deficits in short-term memory in posttraumatic stress disorder. *American Journal of Psychiatry, 150*, 1015–1019.

Brotto, L. A., Chik, H. M., Ryder, A. G., Gorzalka, B. B., & Seal, B. N. (2005). Acculturation and sexual function in Asian women. *Archives of Sexual Behavior, 34*(6), 613–626.

Charmaz, K. (2006). *Constructing grounded theory: A practical guide through qualitative analysis.* London, UK: Sage.

Chiose, S. (2014). University sexual assault codes of conduct could be unfair, law experts warn. *Globe and Mail.* Retrieved from http://www.theglobe andmail.com/news/national/university-sexual-assault-codes-of-conduct -could-be-unfair-law-experts-warn/article22234993/

DeKeseredy, W., & Schwartz, M. (1998). *Woman abuse on campus: Results from the Canadian National Survey.* Thousand Oaks, CA: Sage.

Elliot, S., Odynak, D., & Krahn, H. (1992). *A survey of unwanted sexual experiences among University of Alberta students* (Research report prepared for the Council on Student Life, University of Alberta). Edmonton: University of Alberta, Population Research Laboratory.

Fehler-Cabral, G., & Campbell, R. (2013). Adolescent sexual assault disclosure: The impact of peers, families, and schools. *American Journal of Community Psychology, 52,* 73–83.

Fiebert, M. S., & Osburn, K. (2001). Effect of gender and ethnicity on self reports of mild, moderate and severe sexual coercion. *Sexuality and Culture, 5*(2), 3–11.

Finkelman, L. (1992). Report of the survey of unwanted sexual experiences among students of U.N.B.-F. and S.T.U. Fredericton: University of New Brunswick, Counselling Service.

Fisher, B., Cullen, F., & Turner, M. (2000). *The sexual victimization of college women.* Washington, DC: National Institute of Justice and Bureau of Justice Statistics.

Foynes, M. M., Platt, M., Hall, G. C. N., & Freyd, J. J. (2014). The impact of Asian values and victim–perpetrator closeness on the disclosure of emotional, physical, and sexual abuse. *Psychological Trauma: Theory, Research, Practice, and Policy, 6*(2), 134–141.

Hébert, M., Tourigny, M., Cyr, M., McDuff, P., & Joly, J. (2009). Prevalence of childhood sexual abuse and timing of disclosure in a representative sample of adults from Quebec. *Canadian Journal of Psychiatry, 54,* 631–636.

Horsman, J. (1999). *Too scared to learn: Women, violence and education.* Toronto, ON: McGilligan Books.

Huerta, M., Cortina, L., Pang, J., Torges, J., & Magley, V. (2006). Sex and power in the academy: Modeling sexual harassment in the lives of college women. *Personality and Social Psychology Bulletin, 32*(5), 616–628.

Jacques-Tiura, A. J., Tkatch, R., Abbey, A., & Wegner, R. (2010). Disclosure of sexual assault: Characteristics and implications for posttraumatic stress symptoms among African American and Caucasian survivors. *Journal of Trauma & Dissociation, 11,* 174–192.

Jenkins, M. A., Langlais, P. J., Delis, D., & Cohen, R. (1998). Learning and memory in rape victims with posttraumatic stress disorder. *American Journal of Psychiatry, 155,* 278–279.

Jenkins, M. A., Langlais, P. J., Delis, D., & Cohen, R. (2000). Attentional dysfunction associated with posttraumatic stress disorder among rape survivors. *Clinical Neuropsychologist, 14,* 7–12.

Jordan, C. E., Combs, J. L., & Smith, G. T. (2014). An exploration of sexual victimization and academic performance among college women. *Trauma, Violence, & Abuse, 15,* 191–200.

Kaukinen, C. (2014). Dating violence among college students: The risk and protective factors. *Trauma, Violence, & Abuse, 15,*4, 283–296.

Lindquist, C. H., Barrick, K., Krebs, C., Crosby, C., Lockard, A. J., & Sanders-Phillips, K. (2013). The context and consequences of sexual assault among undergraduate women at historically Black colleges and universities. *Journal of Interpersonal Violence, 28*(12), 2437–2461.

Long, L., & Ullman, S. E. (2013). The impact of multiple traumatic victimization on disclosure and coping mechanisms for Black women. *Feminist Criminology, 8*(4), 295–319.

Luce, H., Schrager, S., & Gilchrist, V. (2010) Sexual assault of women. *American Family Physician, 81*(4), 489–495.

McElvaney, R., Greene, S., & Hogan, D. (2014). To tell or not to tell? Factors influencing young people's informal disclosures of child sexual abuse. *Journal of Interpersonal Violence, 29*(5), 928–947.

Moors, R., & Webber, R. (2012). The dance of disclosure: Online self-disclosure of sexual assault. *Qualitative Social Work, 12*(6), 799–815.

Ontario Women's Directorate. (2013). *Developing a response to sexual violence: A resource guide for Ontario's colleges and universities.* Ottawa, ON: Queen's Printer for Ontario.

Orchowski, L. M. (2009). *Disclosure of sexual victimization: A prospective study of social reactions and subsequent adjustment* (Doctoral dissertation). Retrieved from PsychInfo (Proquest). (UMI No. 3371587)

Orchowski, L. M., Untied, A. S., & Gidycz, C. A. (2013). Social reactions to disclosure of sexual victimization and adjustment among survivors of sexual assault. *Journal of Interpersonal Violence, 28*(10), 2005–2023.

Ormiston, S. (2014, September 29). Universities under pressure to combat sexual misconduct on campus. *CBC News.* Retrieved from http://www.cbc.ca/news/universities-under-pressure-to-combat-sexual-misconduct-on-campus-1.2781455

Paul, L. A., Gray, M. J., Elhai, J. D., & Davis, J. L. (2009). Perceptions of peer rape myth acceptance and disclosure in a sample of college sexual assault survivors. *Psychological Trauma: Theory, Research, Practice, and Policy, 1,* 231–241.

Porter, J., & Williams, L. (2011). Intimate violence among underrepresented groups on a college campus. *Journal of Interpersonal Violence, 26*(16), 3210–3224.

Quinlan, E., Clarke, A., & Horsley, J. (2010). From outrage to action: Countering the institutional response to sexualized violence on university campuses. *Canadian Woman Studies, 28*(1), 46–55. Retrieved from http://search.proquest.com/docview/755499673?accountid=14771

Sabina, C., & Ho, L. Y. (2014). Campus and college victim responses to sexual assault and dating violence: Disclosure, service utilization, and service provision. *Trauma, Violence, and Abuse, 15*(3), 201–226.

Schwartz, M. D., & DeKeseredy, W. (1997). *Sexual assault on the college campus: The role of male peer support.* Thousand Oaks, CA: Sage.

Senn, C., Eliasziw, M., Barata, P., Thurston, W., Newby-Clark, I., Radtke, H., & Hobden, K. (2013). Sexual assault resistance education for university women: Study protocol for a randomized controlled trial (SARE trial). *BMC Women's Health, 13*(1), 13–25.

Senn, C. Y. (2013). Education on resistance to acquaintance sexual assault: Preliminary promise of a new program for young women in high school and university. *Canadian Journal of Behavioural Science, 45,* 24–33.

Smith, P. H., White, J. W., & Holland, L. J. (2003). A longitudinal perspective on dating violence among adolescent and college-age women. *American Journal of Public Health, 93,* 1104–1109.

Stermac, L., Horowitz, S., & Bance, S. (2014). Sexual coercion on campus: The experiences of ethno-culturally diverse women. *Psynopsis, 36*(3). Retrieved from http://www.cpa.ca/docs/File/Psynopsis/2014/Psynopsis_Summer2014.pdf

Tremblay, P. F., Harris, R., Berman, H., MacQuarrie, B., Hutchinson, G. E., Smith, M. A., & Dearlove, K. (2008). Negative social experiences of university and college students. *Canadian Journal of Higher Education, 38,* 57–76.

Ullman, S. E., & Filipas, H. H. (2001). Predictors of PTSD symptom severity and social reactions in sexual assault victims. *Journal of Traumatic Stress, 14*(2), 369–389.

Wagner, A., & Magnusson, J. (2005). Neglected realities: Exploring the impact of women's experience of violence on learning in sites of higher education. *Gender and Education, 17,* 449–461.

Walsh, W. A., Banyard, V. L., Moynihan, M. M., Ward, S., & Cohn, E. S. (2010). Disclosure and service use on a college campus after an unwanted sexual experience. *Journal of Trauma & Dissociation, 11,* 134–151.

Washington, P. A. (2001). Disclosure patterns of Black female sexual assault survivors. *Violence Against Women, 7,* 1254–1283.

Wilcox, P., Jordan, C., & Pritchard, A. (2006). Fear of acquaintance versus stranger rape as a "master status": Towards refinement of the "shadow of sexual assault." *Violence and Victims, 21*(3), 355–370.

Wyatt, G. E. (1992). The sociocultural context of African American and White American women's rape. *Journal of Social Issues, 48,* 77–91.

Yorgason, J. B., Linville, D., & Zitman, B. (2008). Mental health among college students: Do those who need services know about them? *Journal of American College Health, 57,* 173–182.

CHAPTER 2

CAMPUS VIOLENCE, INDIGENOUS WOMEN, AND THE POLICY VOID

Carrie Bourassa, Melissa Bendig, Eric J. Oleson, Cassandra A. Ozog, Jennifer L. Billan, Natalie Owl, and Kate Ross-Hopley

The universal phenomenon of violence against women is widely known, and it is clear that certain populations of women are at greater risk for violent victimization. Age and race, particularly, influence one's risk. Recent conversations have been sparked in both Canada and the United States regarding the "culture of rape" on university campuses. Indeed, recent trends are drawing attention to the normalization of systemic misogyny and its manifestation in high rates of sexual assaults, under-reporting of such events, and an atmosphere on campuses that many women report as unsafe. Pro-rape frosh chants at both the University of British Columbia (UBC) and Saint Mary's University in the fall of 2013, and more recently the pro-rape comments on a Dalhousie dental student Facebook page, are bringing to light the culture of inequity, sexism, and rape on Canadian campuses.

The term "rape culture" is widely used by both academics and media to describe systemic attitudes and behaviours that normalize, trivialize, or encourage sexual violence. The male Dalhousie dental students posted comments expressing desires to "hate f--k" their female peers and use chloroform to render women unconscious for nonconsensual sexual acts, joking that the penis is "the tool used to wean and convert lesbians and virgins into useful, productive members of society" (Kingston, 2015; Wente, 2015b). In true rape culture fashion, some media reporting of this story trivialized these actions by describing them in a "boys will be boys" fashion and labelling them as "asinine locker room jokes" (Wente, 2015a, para. 15). Therefore, the term "rape culture" does not necessarily refer to explicit acts of rape or sexual assault, but rather draws attention to the social environments that foster the gender inequity that results in women experiencing high rates of violence.

As discussions of sexualized violence and rape culture on university campuses become more prevalent and mainstream, the lack of focus on women of colour and Indigenous[1] women emerges more clearly. Many discussions of sexualized and gendered violence acknowledge a multiplicity of intersecting factors underlying women's experiences with violence that include race, ethnicity, sexual and gender diversity, age, class, and religion. An intersectional analysis demonstrates that oppression occurs on a variety of levels, and consequently that certain populations are at greater risk of violence based on multiple intersecting oppressions. However, mainstream discussions of gendered violence on campus have largely failed to incorporate an analysis rooted in intersectionality that acknowledges other avenues of oppression than gender.

In light of the advocacy work of Indigenous communities and organizations, and the subsequent Royal Canadian Mounted Police (RCMP) report, *Missing and Murdered Aboriginal Women: A National Operational Overview* (2014), a public discussion has been sparked in mainstream media on the issue of violence against Indigenous women in Canada. However, few discussions attempt to determine how colonial violence and its intersections with gender inequity create unique risk factors for Indigenous women on university campuses. A significant disconnect seems to exist between the two conversations on missing and murdered Indigenous women (MMIW) and gendered violence on campus, even though both are now prominent in mainstream media and academia. Certainly, universities have traditionally been and still are to a significant extent largely white, colonial spaces; socialized perception may be that white, young, affluent women largely compose university populations.

This chapter aims to highlight the exclusion of Indigenous women from discourses and policy processes addressing gendered violence on campuses. After arguing for the importance of a focus on Indigenous women, and providing historical and contemporary contexts that situate Indigenous women at a greater risk for violence, we report the results of an environmental scan of sexual violence policies at Canadian universities and the collection of demographic information on the victims of campus violence. With very few campuses acknowledging the intersections of colonization, racism, and sexism in connection with sexualized violence, the chapter closes with recommendations for action.

WHY THE FOCUS ON INDIGENOUS WOMEN?

The rate of violent victimization experienced by Indigenous women is over three times higher than the rate for non-Indigenous women (Perreault, 2015). Between 2001 and 2011, Indigenous women accounted for at least 11% of dating homicide victims and at least 10% of non–intimate partner homicide victims, even though Indigenous women represent only roughly 4% of the population (Sinha, 2013). Another report reveals that between 1980 and 2012, Indigenous women represented 16% of all murdered women (a fourfold over-representation), with police-recorded incidents totalling 1181 cases of missing or murdered Indigenous women (RCMP, 2014). Amnesty International (2014) found that although Indigenous women make up only 6% of the population of Saskatchewan, 60% of missing women in the province are Indigenous.

Correlation of age and Indigenous identity is related to higher rates of self-reported violent victimization (Sinha, 2013). While less than half of the female Indigenous population is aged 15 or older, almost two-thirds of Indigenous female victims fell within this age category (Brennan, 2011). Younger Indigenous people are more likely to be victims of violence than non-Indigenous youth, as they are almost two and a half times more likely to experience a violent victimization (Brennan, 2011).

Indigenous women self-report violent victimization at a rate almost three times higher than that of non-Indigenous women; however, over three-quarters of non-spousal violent incidents involving Indigenous women were not reported to the police or any other formal support services (Perreault, 2015). Rather, most Indigenous women confided in an informal source, such as a friend or family member. Of those Indigenous women who experienced violence by a current or former partner, almost half reported the most severe forms of violence, such as being sexually assaulted, beaten, choked, or threatened with a gun or a knife (Brennan, 2011). In 2009, close to 67,000 Indigenous women aged 15 or older reported being victimized by violence in the previous 12 months (Brennan, 2011); this violence is often repeated, as more than one-third of Indigenous women who reported being victimized were subsequently victimized two or more times.

With the overwhelming data demonstrating that Indigenous women are vastly overrepresented when it comes to sexual assault, violence, violent victimization, homicide, intimate partner violence, and spousal and non-spousal violence, and beyond the fact that there are over 1200 MMIW (RCMP, 2014), it is essential to draw attention to Indigenous women in discussions of violence on campuses. We focus on Indigenous women because despite being incredibly resilient and being the life-givers in our communities—the ones who were traditionally considered the sacred and honoured mothers, grandmothers, daughters, aunties, and sisters in our communities—we are instead often seen as the most vulnerable, marginalized, and at-risk population in Canada. We experience multiple oppressions of racism, classism, and sexism not only outside but also within our own communities (Kubik, Bourassa, & Hampton, 2009, p. 18).

Mainstream media is slowly beginning to give voice to the issue of violence against Indigenous women, in particular, MMIW. Indigenous activists and feminists have highlighted this issue for a long time, but in recent years it has become notably more topical in mainstream media and political communication. Although this is a significant step, it is essential to ensure that media coverage does not treat this as a silo or "one off" issue. A point that will be discussed here is the representation of Indigenous women as passive citizens. The tragically high rates of violent victimization of Indigenous women demand that discussions of this issue occur within the context of the systemic and intergenerational roots of the epidemic of violence in all its forms. If we continue to speak about MMIW and violence on campus as separate issues, failing to acknowledge Indigenous women as a part of campus violence, we risk perpetuating the same exclusion that places them at risk for violence in the first place.

Roots of Oppressions

The roots of oppressions facing Indigenous women can be traced back to colonialism and assimilation, and the related representations of Indigenous women. The success of colonization depended on the effective depiction of Indigenous cultures as uncivilized, backwards, and in need of saving (Henry & Tator, 2009). By such distortions, the cultures of the peoples inhabiting the spaces desired by colonists were demonstrated as unworthy and not properly utilizing the resources of the land, lending support to colonists to claim the land for themselves, and to enact assimilative policies that ranged from forced schooling to the involuntary migration to reserves that were part of a policy of cultural genocide. For Indigenous women the effects of an incoming patriarchal force and assertions that Indigenous cultures were "savage" and in need of saving were to create an intersection of devaluation and invisibility unrelieved except for their portrayal in dangerous stereotypes. For generations, Indigenous women were represented in historical writings and documents as either pure "Indian princesses" or dirty "savage squaws," a reduction to sexualized binaries parallel to the "Madonna/whore" dichotomy of female representations in film and art. The historical imagery used in colonial narratives extended to fictional accounts of Indigenous peoples from black-and-white Westerns to children's movies in more recent years such as Disney's *Pocahontas*. Representations of the bodies of Indigenous women became a colonizing focus that influenced historical practices of discrimination and assimilative policies and legislation that targeted Indigenous women and their families.

Indigenous women were targeted through colonial policy and, in particular, the *Indian Act* and a process of "legislated identity." At its inception in 1876, the *Indian Act* effectively decided who could be a legal, status Indian in Canada and who could not. Although the Act has affected Indigenous men and women in Canada for generations, it has had a particular impact on women. Between 1876 and 1985, if a status Indian woman (those women who were legally status according to the government and therefore on the Indian registry) married a non-Indian (including a Métis or Inuit man), she ceased to be an Indian and so did her children. Further, up until 1960, non-status Indian women were not allowed on reserves. This was part of the government's official assimilation policy from 1876 to 1973. The same policy did not apply to status Indian men, who could marry non-Indian women and retain their status; in fact, their non-Indian wives would gain status under the *Indian Act*, along with their children.

This sexist policy had intergenerational effects on families. Patriarchal models of governance were imposed on communities where traditionally Indigenous women were granted great authority and respect, often owning the lodges and making decisions. Women were highly honoured as the givers of life and well respected in the communities. Everyone had important yet equitable roles to play, and these roles were valued, honoured, and respected by all. The *Indian Act* instituted the political structures that denied women participation in political life. Most Canadian women were able to vote in federal elections starting in 1921; however, it was not until 1951 that First Nations women were able to vote in band elections, and later still before they could vote in provincial and federal elections. Indigenous women were legally and systematically stripped of their political power and given the status of second-class citizens. The subsequent socio-economic fallout ingrained a perception of Indigenous women as second-class citizens.

The value of women as the givers of life changed with the imposition of colonization, which played a role in further marginalizing Indigenous women and changing their roles within their own communities. The removal of children through the residential school system and the "Sixties Scoop" had devastating effects on families ("Sixties Scoop," 2009). The intergenerational effects of the loss of culture and breakdown of families from the abuse suffered in residential schools and in foster homes for generations is seen in communities to this day. The assimilative tactics used by the Canadian government, provincial governments, and other institutions generated significant historical trauma among Indigenous women and fostered distrust in relation to institutions. Therefore, it is not surprising that many Indigenous women do not report violence to authorities and often do so only when forms of violence are the most severe.

The continuous devaluation of Indigenous women and their reduction to bodies to be categorized, abused, and disregarded has marked the long history of treating their lives as unimportant, rendering their oppressions invisible and their bodies disposable. Their experience in a society that does not value their lives is obscured by discriminatory narratives; Indigenous women are all too frequently reduced to the physical spaces they occupy, their bodies labelled as unworthy by the media (Razack, 2005). The stereotypic and partial representation of real Indigenous women in the media is particularly troubling because of its wide influence. Many narratives of missing and murdered Indigenous women echo long-held racist and colonial ideas on the value of Indigenous peoples in general and disregard for the lives of Indigenous women in particular.

RCMP REPORT ON MISSING AND MURDERED INDIGENOUS WOMEN

Although the report on MMIW authored by the RCMP does not specifically address campus sexual violence, it is worthy of examination in the context of our review on sexual violence against Indigenous women on Canadian campuses because it offers an example of how underlying discourses of Indigenous women as second-class citizens persist. The 2014 report, *Missing and Murdered Aboriginal Women: A National Operational Overview*, documented "risk factors" (p. 17) for Indigenous women. Although the authors assert that this report relies on data, they note, "There is insufficient data relating to currently missing Aboriginal women from which to draw reliable conclusions with respect to risk factors contributing to their disappearance" (2014, p. 17). This statement underscores a crucial disparity between the seemingly well-intentioned report as evidence-based and reliable, and the avowed insufficiency of evidence from which to set forth meaningful risk factors. It is a paradox that effectively voids the authors of the responsibility of the conclusions. It is inarguable that there are insufficient data; yet the report still offers risk factors purported to be essential to understanding Indigenous women's vulnerability to violence.

Based on the data of primarily murdered women (the homicide survey noted in the report), the authors conclude that risk factors for Indigenous women are their employment status, use of intoxicants, and involvement in the sex trade. While the preamble in the report indicates discussion of risk factors is not meant to incite victim-blaming, it is difficult not to draw this conclusion in a close reading. A key failure of the report is ignoring the historical colonial context behind the overrepresentation of Indigenous women in terms of substance use and abuse, poverty, and sex trade work; without such context, the risk factors identified seem to exist in a vacuum, implying that individual circumstances are what underlie their violent victimization, and taking attention away from the systemic societal beliefs and norms that provide perpetrators with the justification that these women are "lesser than" and can therefore be stripped of their rights to safety with impunity.

Although the caveat of "we are not victim-blaming" is included in the report, it does not negate the fact that the inclusion of discussions that represent Indigenous women as being disempowered, suffering from high rates of addictions and poverty, having limited education, and being likely to work in the sex trade will necessarily influence the public discourse in normalizing this view. These are perceptions that are related in the public domain to the nearly 1200 Indigenous women who have gone missing. It is not until the discourse shifts to outline risks as systemic inequities, colonial history, social environments that foster sexism and racism, and exclusion of Indigenous culture in institutions that we can truly stop victim-blaming. Indigenous women continue to be seen as second-class, passive citizens whose power in Canadian society is insubstantial (Kubik et al., 2009).

It is this expanded context for analysis that must be brought to bear when turning our focus to Indigenous women and policies addressing sexual violence on campuses. When over 1200 Indigenous women are missing or murdered across Canada, and taking into account the rates of other forms of violence discussed in this chapter, can we possibly believe that violence in places of higher learning will not disproportionately affect Indigenous women? Many questions flow from this one, for instance, Do Indigenous women assume that the space in post-secondary education is safe for them? If Indigenous women are assaulted, do they report it? As many universities begin to address the need for safe space for women, the unique challenges and oppressions facing Indigenous women must be acknowledged and accounted for in the development of inclusive policies to make all women safer on post-secondary campuses.

ON-CAMPUS VIOLENCE

The University of Alberta (2001) surveyed undergraduate students on campus and found that over 20% of students reported having at least one unwanted sexual experience in their life. Of those reported, almost half took place while the participants were registered at the University of Alberta, with 54% occurring in their first year of university, and 26% occurring in their second year. According to the Canadian Federation of Students Ontario (2013), although university campuses are meant to be safe learning environments, women face sexual violence on campus, and many events occur during the first eight weeks of classes. Furthermore, over 80% of rapes on university campuses are committed by someone known to the victim, and four out of five female undergraduate students reported being victims of violence in dating relationships.

When *CBC News* investigated sexual assault reports at 87 Canadian post-secondary institutions, it came to light that that institutions differ in how they report data and respond to sexual assaults (Sawa & Ward, 2015). Over the last five years, only 727 sexual assaults were reported, while 16 schools said there were no reports. According to *CBC News*, "experts say the number of sexual assaults reported to Canadian post-secondary schools is surprisingly low, and an indication that they are doing a poor job of encouraging students to come forward" (Sawa & Ward, 2015, para. 1). As noted in the 2001 survey done at the University of Alberta, there are significantly more sexual assaults occurring on campus than what is officially reported.

Perry (2011) examined hate crimes on Canadian campuses and identified that "Aboriginal people, Afro-Caribbean, Muslims, and Jews, bisexuals especially were overrepresented as reported victims" (p. 335), illustrating that particular cultural groups are subject to disproportionate rates of victimization on campus. Perry notes, "The groups over represented here are vulnerable to discrimination and violence beyond institutes of higher education," including systemic violence (p. 333). A study in Alberta found that Indigenous university students face increased racial discrimination, and that risks may increase for those who participate in their culture in comparison to those that do not (Currie, Wild, Schopflocher, Laing, & Veugelers, 2012).

Additionally, in recent years, campus culture has been criticized for fostering colonial violence, in particular through the trivialization of Indigenous identities. In the fall of 2013, UBC students were challenged in the media for inappropriate Pocahontas-themed chants ("Insulting Pocahontas Chant," 2013), and more recently, in 2014 the University of Regina cheerleading team dressed up as "cowboys and Indians" to have "battle" at practice ("'Cowboys and Indians,'" 2014). Although these are only two specific events, one only needs to look to the Twitter hashtag of #Pocahotass (Poca-hot-ass) or #Poc-a-hottie around Halloween to see the rampant sexualization of Indigenous women's bodies that relies on historical stereotypes. Like the above-mentioned pro-rape stories, these two campus events sparked "debate" questioning why so much attention was given to these occurrences, and many arguments aimed to diminish the impacts, citing that the students involved did not intend harm. What is concerning about these reactions is the lack of understanding, if genuine, of why such behaviours and attitudes are inappropriate, and the need to trivialize them that may point to the defensiveness that comes from understanding their harm all too well. In all instances, students expressed these attitudes through group bonding activities designed to initiate them into the dominant campus culture through the oppression of women, Indigenous populations, and many others who fall outside of social norms (such as people of colour, people living with disabilities, those who do not identify with gender or sexuality norms, and so forth).

It is striking that discussions of campus sexual assault have paid only limited attention to Indigenous women, and in fact to intersections of women's experiences or identity outside of their gender, relying on a simulated representation of "generic" women. At the same time, analyses of cultural violence on campuses tend to focus on genderless racialized groups. As such, a focus on Indigenous women's experience of campus violence is missed.

Cultures of gender and colonial violence are fostered on multifaceted levels. Post-secondary institutions play a key role when articulating expectations of students on their arrival to campus. Without clear policies on gendered and colonial violence communicated widely, even well-meaning institutions are complicit with systemic sexism and racism. Further, post-secondary institutions are still lagging in education on Indigenous peoples and issues, and while there has been significant progress in this regard, inclusion of Indigenous histories and ways of knowing in university curricula is not uniformly offered. In general, campuses reflect the attitudes of the greater community, and in Canada, Indigenous people continue to be marginalized through systemic racism and social perceptions (Reading & Wien, 2009).

How are universities addressing violence on campus?

The 2014 review by the Metropolitan Action Committee on Violence Against Women and Children (METRAC) of relevant policy documents in 15 post-secondary institutions illustrates that most post-secondary institutions do not have a sexual assault–specific policy. Most campuses include sexual assault behaviours under harassment, discrimination, or student misconduct policies. Similarly, *The Star*'s survey of over 100 Canadian universities reveals that only 9 of 78 Canadian universities have created a special sexual assault policy, while the experiences of sexual assault victims on campus have "derailed the academic careers of women attending top institutions across the country and left them shaken, confused, anxious and depressed" (Mathieu & Poisson, 2014, "A Person I Know," para. 1).

We know that sound policies are an essential element of any university's ability to address violence. The Ontario Women's Directorate outline that well-communicated policies create "an environment where everyone on campus knows that sexual violence is unacceptable, victims receive the services they need, and perpetrators are held accountable" (2013, p. 11). Policies require monitoring and ongoing evaluation of interventions to ensure they evolve as social landscapes shift. The push for post-secondary institutions to develop policies specific to sexual assault stems from the reality that sexual violence is not a neutral sociological phenomenon, but one that is deeply rooted in gender inequity situated in larger community contexts, thereby presenting unique challenges for victims. Policies need to focus on these unique challenges and work to foster a culture of equity. In a parallel way, as we have argued, violence against Indigenous populations and Indigenous women in particular is entrenched in a larger historical and social context that presents particular challenges on university campuses for Indigenous victims of sexual assault. There is limited literature and a paucity of media coverage that speaks to the pressing need to develop policies specific to violence against Indigenous populations on campus, as in the wider social milieu.

METHODOLOGY

In line with the review completed by METRAC and *The Star*, we conducted an environmental scan of 44 English-speaking Canadian universities. The environmental scan was completed in January and February 2015. The scan was designed to search out the following two items:

- A reporting system that identifies demographic information, including Indigenous identity, for victims of violence on campus; and

- Institutional policies on campus violence, sexual violence, and colonial violence.

The scan was completed through two phases. The first phase reviewed the websites of all 44 universities to identify publicly reported statistics on campus violence. The websites were also scanned for policy documents on violence.

In addition to the website scans, phone calls were placed to each of the 44 universities. Soliciting policymakers and security departments, in situations where materials were not found online, researchers inquired about the two items noted above, and in situations where materials were found online, confirmed what was found and inquired if there were any additional materials not posted online or in the development stage.

FINDINGS

Of the 44 institutions contacted, 15 responded that they did have a campus policy that addressed violent incidents on institutional grounds, and 7 more indicated that they had policy under review or in development. Only 6 of the universities indicated that they collected ethnicity and/or gender demographic information from victims, and these data were not distributed publicly. Ten institutions indicated that their campus security had received at least some sexual assault response training, but many indicated that the training was minimal or was currently under review.

Ontario is currently at the forefront of policy development in the realm of sexual violence on university campuses with the introduction of the 2013 document *Developing a Response to Sexual Violence: A Resource Guide for Ontario's Colleges and Universities* (Ontario Women's Directorate, 2013). The document highlights the importance of prevention of sexual violence on campuses and dispels myths about sexual assault and consent; it sets out guidelines and best practices for developing an institutional strategy for prevention and handling of sexual assaults. However, this document does not address the relationship of ethnicity to vulnerability, but rather addresses the general university population as if it were homogeneous, with policy aimed at the student body as a whole.

The only public documents that addressed both violence against women and violence against Indigenous populations (or women) were found at the University of British Columbia. At the end of 2013, the president of the university created the Intersectional Gender-Based Violence and Aboriginal Stereotypes Task Force. This task force generated recommendations[2] to combat systemic attitudes and a lack of understanding related to gender-based violence and violence against Indigenous people. The recommendations stressed the need for shared responsibility and multi-level accountability and included an audit and update of policies in cooperation with subject matter experts that outlined accountability mechanisms to hold people accountable. The recommendations also addressed the need for locating leadership and responsibility in these areas, urging the university to take the lead in promoting equity at the provincial level. Additionally, curriculum development review and assessment activities were included in the recommendations. Although some Aboriginal student centres throughout Canada are working to combat violence, the UBC policy was the only campus-wide initiative located in the scan that addressed colonial violence or violence against Indigenous populations.

Our research team found no statistics on the rates of violence against Indigenous women on Canadian university and college campuses. Additionally, our informal review indicated that overall the data simply do not exist that would allow conclusions to be drawn regarding violence against Indigenous women on campuses. Small local studies, such as the one done by Currie et al. (2012), indicate that Indigenous students face racial discrimination on campuses. Risks associated with violence and sexualized violence are not solely based on singular elements of identity; in fact, various elements of Indigenous identities, such as gender, age, race, or ability (to name a few), intersect to create unique social environments of risk. As high rates of violence against Indigenous women exist throughout Canada, and campuses are often a microcosm that reflects the larger community, it is reasonable to make the assumption that Indigenous women on campus would be at particular risk for violence on campuses. Unfortunately, the data are not collected to validate this assumption.

RECOMMENDATIONS FOR ACTION

Universities as institutions have responsibilities to prevent and address violence on campus. If they fail to create safe spaces, this amounts to an institutional breach of trust. Students attend post-secondary institutions with the expectation that they house opportunities for learning, self-betterment, growth, and social justice, and they place their trust in the institution on this basis. When these opportunities are not awarded to select groups of people on the bases of their gender, ethnicity, race, or sexual orientation, this trust is diminished. Experience demonstrates that the fundamental missions of post-secondary institutions only apply to some, and therefore the institution may not act in the best interest of all students.

The UBC Intersectional Gender-Based Violence and Aboriginal Stereotypes Task Force (2014) calls upon the university to create a culture of equity. This culture of equity ensures that all students and members of the campus community can participate fully in what the university has to offer, thereby acknowledging that oppression may take the form of exclusion. In order to address underlying root causes of gender- and colonial-based violence, campuses must acknowledge and respect the contributions of Indigenous women.

As new gender-based violence strategies begin to roll out across Canada, it is not apparent that consideration is being given to the inclusion of Indigenous women. If we want to create effective and equitable policy, this must start with inclusive, safe processes. The current strategies generate basic policies and then consult special interest groups later. It is how things have always been done, but we would encourage university administrations across Canada to give pause to this course of action. From where we are sitting, Indigenous people grow weary of being asked for their consent or advice after the fact. Process is crucial to building the trust that is essential to enlightened and inclusive policies on violence. Engaging stakeholders is a fundamental element in policy development and, when it comes to Indigenous women, a necessary component of rebuilding relationships damaged by colonial policy that continues to affect Indigenous women today.

Given our history, Indigenous women may have very different needs from other women stakeholder groups, particularly in terms of racialized violence. Colonization aimed to render Indigenous women invisible; we must not repeat this exclusion by sustaining policies that once again treat them as invisible through a lack of consultation upfront.

Without data pertaining to violence against Indigenous women on campus, it is difficult to demand accountability from the campus community; information voids limit the action possible and make it easier for leaders in the campus community to turn a blind eye. An essential element of any policy is monitoring, but particularly in a situation where collection of demographic information on victims of sexual violence is missing, there is an urgent need to address this gap in order to target prevention efforts more specifically to include the experiences of Indigenous women.

Until we collectively understand the seriousness and reach of the issue of violence against Indigenous women on campus, our hands are tied in developing appropriate policy and protocol to confront this violence and ensure the safety of the growing number of Indigenous women pursuing post-secondary education. It is the responsibility of post-secondary institutions to pursue solutions that are guided by those who are directly affected. The experience of oppression and devastating loss that Indigenous women have historically experienced continues, and yet we are still here: Indigenous women *are* resilient. It is on this note that we move forward, advocating for acknowledgement of this policy gap and for action to address it.

NOTES

1   The term "Indigenous" is used because it is inclusive of status and non status First Nations, Inuit, and Métis people in Canada and is also often used to include First People from around the world. We use the term "Aboriginal," which is legally defined in Section 35.1 of the Canadian Constitution (1982) as "Indian, Inuit and Métis people of Canada," when that is the term used by Statistics Canada or for data collection purposes.

2   Available from https://equity2.sites.olt.ubc.ca/files/2014/05/Task-Force-on-IGBVAS -Final-Report-March-28-2014.pdf.

REFERENCES

Amnesty International. (2014). *Violence against Indigenous women and girls in Canada: A summary of Amnesty International's concerns and call to action.* Retrieved from http://www.amnesty.ca/sites/default/files/iwfa_submission_amnesty_international_february_2014_-_final.pdf

Bourassa, C., McKay-McNabb, K., & Hampton, M. (2004). Racism, sexism and colonialism: The impact on the health of Aboriginal women in Canada. *Canadian Woman Studies, 24*(1), 23–29.

Brennan, S. (2011, May 17). Violent victimization of Aboriginal women in the Canadian provinces, 2009. *Juristat* (Statistics Canada Catalogue no. 85-002-X). Retrieved from http://www.statcan.gc.ca/pub/85-002-x/2011001/article/11439-eng.htm

Brzozowski, J.-A., Taylor-Butts, A., & Johnson, S. (2006). Victimization and offending among the Aboriginal population in Canada. *Juristat, 26*(3) (Statistics Canada Catalogue no. 85-002-XIE). Retrieved from http://publications.gc.ca/Collection-R/Statcan/85-002-XIE/85-002-XIE2006003.pdf

Canadian Federation of Students Ontario. (2013). *Fact sheet: Sexual violence on campuses*. Retrieved from http://cfsontario.ca/downloads/CFS_factsheet antiviolence.pdf

"Cowboys and Indians" cheerleader photo sparks Regina furor. (2014, March 16). *CBC News*. Retrieved from http://www.cbc.ca/news/canada/saskatchewan/cowboys-and-indians-cheerleaders-photo-sparks-regina-furor-1.2574979

Currie, C., Wild, T., Schopflocher, D., Laing, L., & Veugelers, P. (2012). Racial discrimination experienced by Aboriginal university students in Canada. *Canadian Journal of Psychiatry, 57*, 617–625.

Drees, L. M. (2013). *Healing histories: Stories from Canada's Indian hospitals*. Edmonton: University of Alberta Press.

Ermine, W. (2007). The ethical space of engagement. *Indigenous Law Journal, 6*(1), 193–203.

Grekul, J., Krahn, A., & Odynak, D. (2004). Sterilizing the "feeble-minded": Eugenics in Alberta, Canada, 1929–1972. *Journal of Historical Sociology, 17*(4), 358–384.

Henry, R. & Tator, C. (Eds.). (2009). *Racism in Canadian university: Demanding social justice, inclusion, and equity*. Toronto: University of Toronto Press.

Insulting Pocahontas chant sparks change at UBC. (2013, October 21). *CBC News*. Retrieved from http://www.cbc.ca/news/canada/british-columbia/insulting-pocahontas-chant-sparks-changes-at-ubc-1.2129023

Kingston, A. (2015, January 14). Thank you, Margaret Wente, for exposing rape culture. *Maclean's*. Retrieved from http://www.macleans.ca/society/thank-you-margaret-wente-for-exposing-rape-culture/

Kubic, W., Bourassa, C., & Hampton, M. (2009). Stolen sisters, second class citizens, poor health: The legacy of colonization in Canada. *Humanity and Society, 33*(1–2), 18–34.

Lux, M. (2010). Care for the "racially careless": Indian hospitals in the Canadian West, 1920–1950s. *Canadian Historical Review, 91*, 407–434.

Mathieu, E., & Poisson, J. (2014, November 20). Canadian post-secondary schools failing sex assault victims. *The Star*. Retrieved from http://www.thestar.com/news/canada/2014/11/20/canadian_postsecondary_schools_failing_sex_assault_victims.html

McKenzie, H. A., Bourassa, C., Kubik, W., Strathy, K., & McKenna, B. (2010). Aboriginal grandmothers caring for grandchildren: Located in a policy gap. *Indigenous Policy Journal, 21*(3), 1–18.

METRAC. (2014). *Sexual assault policies on campus: A discussion paper*. Retrieved from http://www.metrac.org/wp-content/uploads/2014/11/final.formatted.campus.discussion.paper_.26sept14.pdf

Mosby, I. (2013). Administering colonial science: Nutrition research and human biomedical experimentation in Aboriginal communities and residential schools, 1942–1952. *Histoire sociale/Social history, 46*(1), 145–172.

Ontario Women's Directorate. (2013). *Developing a response to sexual violence: A resource guide for Ontario's colleges and universities*. Ottawa, ON: Queen's Printer for Ontario.

Perreault, S. (2015). Criminal victimization in Canada, 2014. *Juristat* (Statistics Canada Catalogue no. 85-002-X). Retrieved from http://www.statcan.gc.ca/pub/85-002-x/2015001/article/14241-eng.pdf

Perry, B. (2011). Identity and hate crime on Canadian campuses. *Race and Justice*, *1*(4), 321–340.

Razack, S. H. (2002). Gendered racial violence and spatialized justice: The murder of Pamela George. In S. H. Razack (Ed.), *Race, space, and the law: Unmapping a white settler society* (pp. 121–278). Toronto, ON: Between the Lines.

Reading, C. L., & Wien, F. (2009). *Health inequalities and the social determinants of Aboriginal peoples' health*. Prince George, BC: National Collaborating Centre for Aboriginal Health.

Royal Canadian Mounted Police. (2014). *Missing and murdered Aboriginal women: A national operational overview*. Retrieved from http://www.rcmp-grc.gc.ca/pubs/mmaw-faapd-eng.htm

Sawa, T., & Ward, L. (2015, February 9). Sex assault reporting on Canadian campuses worryingly low, expert says. *CBC News*. Retrieved from http://www.cbc.ca/m/touch/canada/story/1.2948321

Sinha, M. (Ed.). (2013). Measuring violence against women: Statistical trends. *Juristat* (Statistics Canada Catalogue no. 85-002-X). Retrieved from http://www.statcan.gc.ca/pub/85-002-x/2013001/article/11766-eng.pdf

Sixties Scoop. (2009). Indigenous foundations [Website]. Retrieved from http://indigenousfoundations.arts.ubc.ca/home/government-policy/sixties-scoop.html

Statistics Canada. (2013). *NHS in brief: The educational attainment of Aboriginal peoples in Canada—National Household Survey (NHS), 2011* (Statistics Canada Catalogue no. 99-012-X2011003). Retrieved from http://www12.statcan.gc.ca/nhs-enm/2011/as-sa/99-012-x/99-012-x2011003_3-eng.pdf

UBC President's Task Force on Gender-based Violence and Aboriginal Stereotypes. (2014, March 28). *Transforming UBC and developing a culture of equality and accountability: Confronting rape culture and colonialist violence*. Retrieved from https://equity2.sites.olt.ubc.ca/files/2014/05/Task-Force-on-IGBVAS-Final-Report-March-28-2014.pdf

University of Alberta. (2001). A survey of unwanted sexual experience among University of Alberta students. Retrieved from http://uofa.ualberta.ca/current-students/sexual-assault-centre/-/media/7d6cd389c2a44db5a1cbd3249dd0d49a.ashx

Wente, M. (2015, January 6). Dalhousie's dental hysteria. *Globe and Mail*. Retrieved from http://www.theglobeandmail.com/globe-debate/dalhousies-dental-hysteria/article22310028/

Wente, M. (2015, January 10). Advice to younger women: Practice manning up. *Globe and Mail*. Retrieved from http://www.theglobeandmail.com/globe-debate/advice-to-younger-women-practise-manning-up/article22383707/

CHAPTER 3

INSTITUTIONAL BETRAYAL AND SEXUAL VIOLENCE IN THE CORPORATE UNIVERSITY

Elizabeth Quinlan

When survivors of sexual violence turn to their institutions for accommodations and support, they are often disappointed by the disbelief, blame, and stigmatization. The sense of betrayal, often called the second assault, exacerbates the post-traumatic reactions to the initial assault (Borja, Callahan, & Long, 2006; Campbell, 2006; Esposito, 2005; Martin & Powell, 1994). Several of the survivors of the campus sexual violence in the stories described in the introductory chapter of this collection reported to the media that they felt more victimized by the institutional response to their disclosure than the assault itself. This chapter explores the connection between institutional betrayal and the increased corporatization of universities, characterized by market branding, high-fee boutique programs, and mass advertising campaigns that encourage students to make economically rational purchases of education. I argue that corporatization has contradictory effects on universities' response to the problem of sexual violence, simultaneously suppressing and motivating initiatives to address sexual violence on university campuses. The closing section of the chapter relies on results from two recently conducted empirical studies on sexual violence resources at Canadian universities to consider the nature and extent of collective institutional betrayal.

THE GROWING CORPORATIZATION OF CANADIAN UNIVERSITIES

In the 1950s and early 1960s, universities received substantial post–World War II investment to deliver on the promise of educational opportunities made to returning veterans. Then, in the 1960s, universities were further expanded to meet the growth in demand for undergraduate programs. Beginning in the 1970s, higher education institutions in Canada intensified relationships with the corporate world, a trend that continues today (Newson, 2015b).

Government funding to universities has been sharply reduced beginning with the cuts to the federal-to-provincial transfer payments in the mid-1990s, but especially since the 2008 financial crisis (Newson, 2015b). To make up the budgetary deficits left by shrinking government funding, universities have turned to funders in the private sector. With core funding being all but substituted by specialized funding programs from the federal government (e.g., the Canadian Millennium Scholarship and the Canadian Research Chairs Program), universities are pressed into an increased reliance on private funding in the form of higher tuition fees and privately sponsored research.

Associated with this new form of funding are lean management, continuous improvement, and other corporate philosophies and practices. Imported from business schools, these corporate practices often collide with the governance structures that have been the cornerstone of universities for centuries in which faculty members participate in the determination of conditions of their work (Newson, 2015c). In response, there is a growing militancy among the university faculty, and the structure of interest representation and collective bargaining has become progressively more complex and volatile. Strikes have become more common, and issues of performance indicators and other mechanisms of managerial oversight of faculty's work are points of contention ("University of Manitoba," 2016).

The research-intensification agenda now pursued by most universities reflects a narrow conceptualization of "innovation" and privileges commercial application of knowledge over curiosity-driven inquiry. In "corporate" universities, competition abounds: competition between faculty vying for the limited number of research grants; competition between internal university units for resources; and competition between universities for "market share" (Findlay, 2010). Each university communications department mounts large-scale, expensive advertising campaigns to increase their "market share" of students, branding themselves as offering the fastest ticket to high-paying, secure jobs.

In the process of corporatizing education, students are characterized as revenue-generating units (or RGUs) rather than as learners who have the capacity to shape the content, context, and outcomes of their learning (Newson, 2015a). Instead of social, political members of an academic community, students become economically "rational" actors, making decisions to "purchase" their education. To support students' selection of institutions from which they make their purchases, assessments, ratings, and rankings of universities on a variety of scales are provided by media outlets such as *Maclean's* and *The Globe and Mail*. Education is converted to a service with measureable outcomes contracted by students and formalized through course outlines and university policies such as codes of conduct. The result is that democratic rights of citizens are substituted for contractual rights of consumers (Newson, 2015a).

Knowledge is transformed from a public to a private good to be evaluated on its economic return rather than its ethical dimensions and its social and political applicability. In doing so, the grounds of students' agency have shifted away from demands that education entail envisioning alternatives to existing realities and noticing what has not been noticed before (Greene, 2007). Instead, students' pressure points become litigations involving breaches of contracts when their classes are disrupted or altered. In the consumption model of education, there is little room for students to influence the nature of their education by debating questions such as how education can help build imagination, social responsibility, and critical capacities for active citizenship.

Although some universities express strong civic mandates—for instance, the University of Saskatchewan's mission statement includes "to help society to become more just and culturally enriched"[1]—these mandates stand in contrast to a style of governance that prioritizes fiscal imperatives.

SEXUAL VIOLENCE AT CORPORATIZED UNIVERSITIES: CONTRADICTORY TENDENCIES

Sexual violence is most commonly understood as an individualized problem, rather than as a political, social phenomenon, and is often attributable to certain traits and behaviours of offenders or victims. In this view, sexual violence prevention programming is directed to changing victims' behaviour through resistance training (Senn et al., 2015), deterring potential perpetrators (Foubert & McEwan, 1998; Gidycy, Orchowski, & Berkowitz, 2011), or motivating bystanders (Banyard, Maynihan, & Plante, 2007; Coker et al, 2015; Salazar, Vivolo-Kanor, Hardin, & Berkowitz, 2015). These psycho-behavioural programs are being introduced on Canadian campuses (Concordia University, 2016; StFX Students' Union, 2016; University of Manitoba, 2016; University of Prince Edward Island, 2015; Wilfrid Laurier University, 2016). In contrast, if sexual violence was recognized as a social problem, the nature and extent of the programs would necessarily be different from those presently being adopted, with outcomes that cannot all be quantified and measured against their cost of implementation.

Where cost efficiency is a guiding principle applied to campus programs, quantified outcomes are compared and cost-benefit metrics are used to evaluate potential "returns." Most programs and services are not easily quantified, but it is an especially problematic approach when applied to sexual violence prevention, for instance, comparing the number of sexual assaults before and after the implementation of prevention programs. First, such metrics assume all assaults are reported, when in fact reporting rates are known to be very low (Sabina & Ho, 2014). Further, an increase in reporting rates can be an indication of an increased perception of safety among survivors, rather than an increase in the actual number of incidents. Given the difficulties in such a calculus, it is not surprising that universities are reluctant to invest in preventative initiatives.

The calculus of corporatization both encourages and dissuades universities from implementing the necessarily sweeping sexual violence prevention and response initiatives. While the cost-benefit logic dissuades universities from implementing the wide-ranging prevention training and response supports, there is also a countervailing force that predisposes universities to address sexual violence. As the commodification of education takes further hold, media stories covering various aspects of university life gain a heightened importance to administrators. Unfavourable reports, such as incidents of campus sexual violence, are blemishes on universities' images as good corporate citizens. Alliances with commercial partners and expansive market share of students are both compromised by high-profile media stories of inadequately resourced prevention programs and robotic, inhuman responses to disclosures of sexual violence—ranging from behavioural contracts that silence reporting survivors to pressure on survivors by administrators to pursue restorative justice resolutions rather than formal investigations and adjudications. Indeed, very quickly after the *Toronto Star*'s investigative journalists reported that only slightly less than 10% of English-speaking universities and colleges had specific sexual assault policies, the Council of Ontario Universities publicly promised better resources for survivors (Mathieu & Poisson, 2014). After the CBC contacted Brock University concerning sexual harassment of a student in the fall of 2015, the university promised to change its procedures so that complainants will learn what action is taken following the university's investigations (Sawa, 2016). The chapters in Part IV of this collection explore various activists' strategies that rely on their understanding of the media as the Achilles heel of the corporate university.

The fall of 2016 saw widespread media coverage of the sexual violence case at the University of British Columbia involving creative writing professor Steven Galloway. An open letter signed by many Canadian literary luminaries, including Madeleine Thien, Joseph Boyden, and Margaret Atwood, which defended Galloway and criticized the university for ignoring due process, was covered extensively in *The Globe and Mail* (Lederman, 2016). In the weeks following, a counterletter, drawing attention to the silencing effect of the open letter on other survivors, circulated on social media and garnered close to 1000 signatures. The mainstream media continue to cover the case, despite the fact that there are very few primary sources on the specifics of the case available for public scrutiny due to the privacy requirements of the signed confidentiality agreements and union grievance procedures. In the fullness of time, when the facts of the Galloway case are known, it will be an important case to assess the extent of improvements made to university sexual violence procedures and protocols as a result of media coverage.

INSTITUTIONAL BETRAYAL BY THE CORPORATE UNIVERSITY

Survivors of sexual violence suffer immediate and long-term health consequences, including HIV infection, post-traumatic stress disorder, suicide, depression, and social isolation (Jenkins, Langlais, Delis, & Cohen, 2010; Zinzow et al., 2011). Students who survive sexual violence tend to have lower grades compared to those who did not experience sexual violence (Jordan, Combs, & Smith, 2014). The impact of sexual violence on students' academic experience is explored in depth by Lana Stermac, Sarah Horowitz, and Sheena Bance in this collection.

Compounding the deleterious health consequences of sexual violence is the blame and further stigmatization—often described as a "second assault"—endured by victims who reach out for help within institutional structures (Ahrens, 2006; Campbell, 2006; Esposito, 2005; Martin & Powell, 1994). Explanations for the inherent unreliability of women's allegations of sexual violence (e.g., because she asked for it, because all women have masochistic rape fantasies, just because) are recycled in everyday conversations, courtrooms, forensic medical examinations, and public policy (Gavey, 2005). Similar to other contexts, when students disclose to campus officials, they are often met with suspicion and blame. Yet, the rates of false allegations are found to be exceptionally low: somewhere between 2% and 10% of campus reports are unfounded (Lisak, 2010). Negative reactions from the recipient of disclosure have been shown to increase post-traumatic stress in reporting survivors (Borja et al., 2006).

The reporting of sexual violence to campus authorities or other formal channels (e.g., professors and campus health services) varies across studies from 0% to 16%, depending on how campus authorities are defined (Sabina & Ho, 2014). Research that examines trends in disclosure shows that friends are the primary confidantes because they tend to keep confidences (Fisher, Daigle, Cullen, & Turner, 2003; Orchowski & Gidycz, 2012; Orchowski, Meyer, & Gidycz, 2009). Rather than reporting to campus officials, victims of campus sexual violence simply try to avoid the perpetrator, and the next two most common reactions are to seek psychological counselling and to move residence (Krebs, Linkquist, Warner, Fisher, & Martin, 2007). Least common is to file a complaint or initiate other disciplinary action with university officials.

Survivors who find satisfaction in formal mechanisms of redress and sanctions against perpetrators are rare. Less than 1% of perpetrators receive any disciplinary action by their universities (Krebs et al., 2007), a sharp contrast to the rates of disciplinary action taken against students who commit other offences. The documentary *The Hunting Ground* (Ziering, 2015) reveals the astonishing ratio of 200 expulsions for plagiarism to every one expulsion for sexual assault.

The sense of being betrayed by their institution adds another element of trauma for survivors. As one UBC student told the interviewer in the 2015 CBC *Fifth Estate* program "School of Secrets," the effect of her interactions with the university officials following her assault was more injurious than the assault itself: "The assault itself didn't make me a victim, it's the procedures, or lack thereof, on the part of the university that made me a victim." Blogging about the same incident, a UBC professor wrote, "The damage is that we send out a signal that we have abandoned [the students], that we don't care about them. And that the corporate brand of UBC and of the care that we give to it in the public arena is more important than signaling to our students, we care about you, we're going to make sure you have a safe place" (Mayor, 2015, para. 13).

Another student at Brock University expressed her sense of betrayal after being warned by the university to keep confidential the findings of an internal investigation that confirmed she was sexually harassed by a professor, who was also an acting associate dean at the time of the assault in 2015: "It's really changed my opinion [of Brock], from being this safe place where you go and professors are there to help foster your career and your academics, to a place where ... it's in the university's best interest to keep their reputation as a company intact and that I was just a problem" (Sawa, 2016, para. 17).

Close to half of campus survivors report at least one of the following forms of institutional betrayal: academically punishing the survivor for reporting, covering up the report, dismissing the survivor's experience, taking no proactive steps, or making it difficult to further report the experience (Smith, 2014; Smith & Freyd, 2013). Importantly, sexual assault victims who feel betrayed by their college or university have more severe trauma-related outcomes, such as disassociation, anxiety, and depression (Smith & Freyd, 2013).

Beyond these forms of reported betrayal, fundamentally, sexual violence undermines survivors' academic freedom. As Dianne Miller (2016) challenges, how can there be freedom to study when students are not free of sexual violence? Yet, universities are often more concerned with perpetrators who have been disciplined as a result of their actions than with survivors because perpetrators are more likely to litigate. For instance, the UofO men's hockey players launched a class-action lawsuit against the university for their suspension of the hockey team. Claiming they were not involved in the assault, the 24 members of the team are seeking $6 million in damages.

The UofO case and others in similar legal proceedings are giving rise to a larger debate about whether universities should be conducting investigations and disciplinary hearings pertaining to actions otherwise handled in the criminal justice system. Whether the standards of evidence for campus investigations should be lower than for criminal investigations is one of the questions central to the debate. A majority of surveyed university presidents in the United States believe they are entitled to conduct their own investigations and that the higher standard of "guilt beyond a reasonable doubt" used in criminal proceedings is inappropriate for their adjudication of sexual assault complaints because the consequences of suspension or expulsion are not nearly as severe as sanctions for criminal behaviour (Jaschik & Lederman, 2015).[2]

These debates, however interesting and important, are all too often grounded in the assumption that safeguarding the rights of suspects is at odds with believing survivors. A further premise is that the former trumps the latter. The corporatist rubric dictates that the expenditures for legal fees to ensure a victory against litigating perpetrators outweigh concerns for the long- and short-term effects of institutional betrayal felt by reporting survivors.

INSTITUTIONAL BETRAYAL IN AGGREGATE

In the fall of 2016, *Maclean's* released their annual university rankings. New to their methodology this year was the inclusion of tailored questions to augment the standardized battery of questions. These tailored questions include a single question on sexual violence, which addresses the institutions' steps to prevent it.[3] Western University, University of Windsor, and Mount Saint Vincent topped the rankings in each of the three categories: Medical/Doctoral, Comprehensive, and Primarily Undergraduate universities, respectively (Schwartz, 2016). The addition of a measure of sexual violence prevention initiatives is a notable achievement for student activists and other advocacy organizations that have lobbied for many years to include a rating on sexual violence prevention and response. While this is a move in the right direction, it is woefully inadequate. As a singular question, this new addition to the rankings does little to capture the complexity inherent in the practices, procedures, and policies governing the prevention of and response to sexual violence by universities.

A more expansive survey of students' perceptions of their institution's response to sexual violence was conducted by the Coalition Against Sexual Assault–University of Saskatchewan during the summer of 2016 (see Chapter 11 in this collection). The coalition's survey consists of eight closed questions concerning the measures to prevent and respond to sexual violence taken by the respondents' universities, including policies, training on sexual consent and how to support a disclosing survivor, and behavioural contracts issued to reporting survivors. The survey results indicate a pronounced level of student dissatisfaction with the institutions' resources directed to sexual violence (CASA–UofS, 2016). Remarkably, 40% of surveyed students (N=202) from 33 Canadian universities consider the resources for prevention of and response to campus sexual violence to be "moderately inadequate" or "very inadequate." Close to half of the survey respondents consider their university's policies and procedures for prevention and response to sexual violence to be "moderately inadequate" or "very inadequate." Roughly half of the 202 respondents rated their university's measures to *reduce* incidents of sexual violence as either "poor" or "terrible." A similar proportion rated their university's effort to *respond* to sexual violence as either "poor" or "terrible."

Further investigation of these results reveals a significant relationship between the perceptions of its students and the type of university, using *Maclean's* three-way categorization of universities (Medical/Doctoral, Comprehensive, and Primarily Undergraduate). For instance, students at Primarily Undergraduate universities are far more likely to be satisfied with the institutional supports and resources dedicated to sexual violence. That is, there is a smaller proportion of students at those universities who rate their university's policies and procedures as inadequate compared to the proportion of students at Comprehensive or Medical/Doctoral universities, 6.7% versus 50.9% and 51.1%, respectively (X^2 (24, N = 202) = 182.8, p <.01). Similarly, when asked about prevention, students at Primarily Undergraduate universities are far less likely to rate their university's measures to reduce incidents of sexual violence as inadequate, compared to those at Comprehensive or Medical/Doctoral universities: X^2 (16, N = 202) = 87.4, p <.01 (23.3% versus 54.6% and 57.2%, respectively).

In general, students at Primarily Undergraduate universities rate their institutions more favourably than those at Comprehensive and Medical/Doctoral universities. Moreover, responses from students at Comprehensive and Medical/Doctoral universities were quite similar, and together these two categories sharply differ from the Primarily Undergraduate category.

The results from the student survey deviate from the results of a second study co-conducted by the chapter's author (Brigden & Quinlan, 2016). An environmental scan of English-speaking universities' resources and supports for sexual assault prevention and response was executed by scoping universities' websites. Dimensions of the scan's rating include presence and quality of policies, incident reporting, support/centre, webpage resources, counselling and security services, and educational resources (see Appendix for the rating scheme). Our environmental scan shows that the Medical/Doctoral universities have a higher median rating compared to those in the Comprehensive category, which in turn has a higher median rating than the Primarily

Undergraduate universities. Ratings range from 91% for the University of British Columbia, a Medical/Doctoral university, to 29% for the University of Northern British Columbia, a Primarily Undergraduate university (for a full set of results, see Brigden & Quinlan, 2016).

The descending order of the scan's ratings by category (described above) corresponds to the size of the institutions, with the Medical/Doctoral the largest (averaging 26,448 full-time undergraduate students),[4] followed by the average size of institution in the Comprehensive category (18,047), then the Primarily Undergraduate category (4230). We might well speculate that institutional budgets dedicated to student resources and supports are ordered accordingly, which would readily account, at least in part, for the higher ratings by students at the larger institutions.

What do these results say about the corporatization of our public education institutions? Do the scan results suggest a sorting of "winners" from "losers," as the neo-liberal doctrine would propose? Perhaps the educational market is dividing institutions into the "haves" and "have-nots," but like all markets, it does not ensure that such inequality between institutions is in any way just or virtuous. Further, not all would agree that the larger institutions do in fact provide superior sexual violence resources and supports, as the student perception survey results reveal that students at the smaller Primarily Undergraduate universities rate the resources and supports more highly than their counterparts at the larger Comprehensive and Medical/Doctoral universities.

Before drawing the two sets of empirical results together in a commentary, it is worth noting that the survey results are subjective measures of university resources and supports, whereas the environmental scan is an objective assessment using standardized procedures, albeit based on subjectively devised indicators. So, while it might seem like a contradiction between the two sets of results, the survey measures perceptions of the resources and supports, whereas the environmental scan ranks the actual resources and supports themselves. Taken together, the survey and scan results suggest that students attending Primarily Undergraduate universities, which have a reputation of being student-centred, feel a greater connection to their institutions and rate all student services more favourably (including those directed to sexual violence), regardless of the actual resources and supports.

Although the relationship between actual resources and supports and students' perceptions of them needs to be explored more fully before any sturdy conclusions can be drawn, there are some possible interpretations of these initial results. We might surmise that the high approval ratings by students at Primarily Undergraduate universities point to effective promotional messages directed to students and parents of their improved efforts to address sexual violence. This line of speculation takes us to the tentative conclusion that with their student-friendly branding, these universities are more efficacious than their market rivals in the Comprehensive and Medical/Doctoral categories. Put in terms of the corporate rhetoric, the Primarily Undergraduate universities are gaining a competitive advantage in their image management on the issue of sexual violence.

CONCLUSION

The chapter argues that while the inner logic of corporatization has a suppressive effect on genuine initiatives to address sexual violence, it also disposes universities to respond to the problem, if for no other reason than to preserve their reputation. In response to the recent media reports, the public outcry, and the legislation introduced in a number of provinces, universities are busily drafting sexual violence policies, implementing reporting protocols, and developing preventative programs. Yet, the environmental scan of sexual violence resources and supports at Canadian universities reported in this chapter indicates that only limited resources have been devoted to implementing the policies and procedures (Brigden & Quinlan, 2016). Further results of a national survey, also discussed in the chapter, suggest marked levels of student dissatisfaction with the available resources and measures taken by their universities to reduce sexual violence. Thus, the emerging system-level reforms of legislation and campus policies and programs appear to be top-down solutions developed by politicians and university administrators, neglecting crucial aspects of students' everyday realities.

Sexual violence on university campuses is a serious and timely social problem that requires innovative and effective interventions. But, as long as corporatization on our campuses continues, the prospects for such interventions are limited. Undoubtedly, we have yet to see the full wrath of students generated by their sense of betrayal.

Appendix: Rating Scheme for Environmental Scan of Sexual Assault Resources and Supports at Canadian Universities

POLICY	INCIDENT REPORTING
1. Sexual assault implied to fall under another policy	1. No reports available
2. Sexual assault mentioned in another policy	2.
3. Sexual assault included as a section of another policy	3. Reports are available but are outdated
4. Standalone sexual assault policy in process of being created	4.
5. Complete standalone sexual assault policy	5. Reports are available and are updated regularly

SEXUAL ASSAULT SUPPORT / CENTRE	WEBPAGE
1. Referred to services off campus 2. Referred to support centre/services on campus that are not specifically for sexual assault 3. Volunteer group/team created for sexual assault support 4. University-hired person specifically for sexual assault support 5. Sexual assault centre located on campus	0.5 points (up to 5 points) for various features such as: • Definitions • FAQ/Myths & Misconceptions • Informational videos • Brochures/pamphlets produced by the university • Contact information for support resources • What to do (survivor/as a friend) • Reporting information • How to get involved

COUNSELLING & SECURITY SERVICES	EDUCATIONAL RESOURCES
1. No mention of sexual assault 2. No mention of sexual assault but list emergency services 3. Referred to off-campus resources 4. Sexual assault listed as a service offered 5. Sexual assault support listed as a service offered and extra information is available	0.5 points (up to 5 points) for various factors such as: • Basic definitions • Statistics • Awareness campaigns (i.e., #ConsentMattersSFU) • Awareness day/week • Use of external programs (i.e., Bringing in the Bystander) • Workshops • Provincially instated programs • University-developed programs

NOTES

1 Available at http://policies.usask.ca/policies/general/the-university-of-saskatchewan -mission-statement.php.
2 In the United States, Title IX legislation mandates that universities and colleges operate on a lower standard when investigating complaints. Known as the basis of "preponderance of evidence," if it is more likely than not that a sexual assault took place, the appropriate consequences must be enacted.
3 At the time of writing, the exact wording of the question was not yet made available by *Maclean's*.
4 The most consistent measure for tracking student population across all categories.

REFERENCES

Ahrens, C. (2006). Being silenced: The impact of negative social reactions on the disclosure of rape. *American Journal of Community Psychology, 38,* 263–274.

Banyard, V., Maynihan, M., & Plante, E. (2007). Sexual violence prevention through bystander education: An experimental evaluation. *Journal of Community Psychology, 35*(4), 463–481.

Borja, S., Callahan, J., & Long, P. (2006). Positive and negative assessment and social support of sexual assault survivors. *Journal of Traumatic Stress, 19,* 905–914.

Brigden, K., & Quinlan, E. (2016). *Environmental scan of sexual assault resources and supports at Canadian universities.* Retrieved from http://www.elizabethquinlan .ca/projects/env-scan/

Campbell, R. (2006). Rape survivors' experiences with the legal and medical systems: Do rape victim advocates make a difference? *Sociology of Health and Illness, 35*(4), 514–528.

Choise, S. (2014, December 30). University sexual assault codes of conduct could be unfair, law experts warn. *Globe and Mail.* Retrieved from http://www.theglobeandmail.com/news/national/university-sexual-assault-codes-of-conduct-could-be-unfair-law-experts-warn/article22234993/

Coalition Against Sexual Assault–University of Saskatchewan (CASA–UofS). (2016). Results from the survey on institutional response to sexual violence on Canadian campuses. Retrieved from http://tinyurl.com/jte8vr7

Coker, A. L., Fisher, B. S., Bush, H. M., Swan, S. C., Williams, C. M., Clear, E. R., & DeGue, S. (2015). Evaluation of the green dot bystander intervention to reduce interpersonal violence among college students across three campuses. *Violence Against Women, 21*(12), 1507–1527.

Concordia University. (2016). Bystander intervention campaign. Retrieved from https://www.concordia.ca/students/sexual-assault/bystander.html

Esposito, N. (2005). Manifestations of enduring during interviews with sexual assault victims. *Qualitative Health Research, 15*(7), 912–927.

Findlay, L. (2010). Academic freedom, institutional autonomy, and the co-operative university. In J. Newson & C. Polster (Eds), *Academic callings* (pp. 212–218). Toronto, ON: Canadian Scholars' Press.

Fisher, B., Daigle, L., Cullen, F., & Turner, M. (2003). Reporting sexual victimization to the police and others: Results from a national-level study of college women. *Criminal Justice and Behavior, 30,* 6–38.

Foubert, J. D., & McEwan, M. K. (1998). An all-male rape prevention peer education program: Decreasing fraternity men's behavioural intent to rape. *Journal of College Student Development, 39*(6), 548–556.

Gavey, N. (2005). *Just sex? The cultural scaffolding of rape.* New York, NY: Routledge.

Gidycz, C. A., Orchowski, L. M., & Berkowitz, A. D. (2011). Preventing sexual aggression among college men: An evaluation of a social norms and bystander intervention program. *Violence Against Women, 17*(6), 720–742.

Greene, M. (2007). *Democratic vistas: Renewing a perspective.* Maxine Greene Foundation. Retrieved from https://maxinegreene.org/uploads/library/democratic_v.pdf

Jaschik, S., & Lederman, D. (2015). *The 2015 Insider Higher Ed Survey of College and University Presidents: Conducted by Gallup.* Washington, DC: Inside Higher Ed.

Jenkins, M. A., Langlais, P. J., Delis, D., & Cohen, R. A. (2010). Attentional dysfunction associated with posttraumatic stress disorder among rape survivors. *Clinical Neuropsychologist, 14*(1), 7–12.

Jordan, C., Combs, J., & Smith, G. (2014). Exploration of sexual victimization and academic performance among college women. *Trauma, Violence, and Abuse, 15*(3), 191–200.

Krebs, C., Linkquist, C., Warner, T., Fisher, B., & Martin, S. (2007). *The Campus Sexual Assault Study.* Washington, DC: National Institute of Justice, U.S. Department of Justice.

Krug, E., Dahlberg, L., Mercy, J., Zwi, A., & Lozano, R. (Eds.). (2002). Violence: A global public health problem. *World report on violence and health* (pp. 1–22). Geneva, Switzerland: World Health Organization.

Lederman, M. (2016, November 18). Under a cloud: How UBC's Steven Galloway affair has haunted a campus and changed lives. *Globe and Mail.* Retrieved from http://www.theglobeandmail.com/news/british-columbia/ubc-and-the-steven-galloway-affair/article32562653/

Lisak, D., Gardinier, L., Nicksa, S., & Cote, A. (2010). False allegations of sexual assault: An analysis of ten years of reported cases. *Violence Against Women, 16*(12), 1318–1334.

Martin, P. Y., & Powell, R. M. (1994). Accounting for the "second assault": Legal organizations' framing of rape victims. *American Bar Foundation, 19*(4), 853–890.

Mathieu, E. (2014). Universities vow to "prevent and respond" to sexual assault. *Toronto Star.* Retrieved from http://www.thestar.com/news/canada/2014/11/29/universities_vow_to_prevent_and_respond_to_sexual_assault.html

Mayor, L. (2015, November 20). UBC "abandoned" women who reported sexual assaults. *CBC News.* Retrieved from http://www.cbc.ca/news/canada/ubc-sexual-assaults-complaints-expulsion-1.3328368

Miller, D. (2016). Academic freedom and freedom from sexual assault. *VOX.* Saskatoon: University of Saskatchewan Faculty Association.

Newson, J. (2015a). Disrupting the "student as consumer" model: The new emancipatory project. In C. Polster & J. Newson (Eds.), *Our Schools/Our Selves: Vol. 9. A penny for your thoughts: How corporatization devalues teaching, research, and public service in Canada's universities* (pp. 197–212). Ottawa, ON: Canadian Centre for Policy Alternatives.

Newson, J. (2015b). Introduction. In C. Polster & J. Newson (Eds.), *Our Schools/Our Selves: Vol. 9. A penny for your thoughts: How corporatization devalues teaching, research, and public service in Canada's universities* (pp. 1–26). Ottawa, ON: Canadian Centre for Policy Alternatives.

Newson, J. (2015c). The university under reconstruction: How budget-based rationalization and corporate linking are transforming Canadian universities. In C. Polster & J. Newson (Eds.), *Our Schools/Our Selves: Vol. 9. A penny for your thoughts: How corporatization devalues teaching, research, and public service in Canada's universities* (pp. 33–54). Ottawa, ON: Canadian Centre for Policy Alternatives.

Orchowski, L., & Gidycz, C. (2012). To whom do college women confide following sexual assault? A prospective study of predictors of sexual assault disclosure and social reactions. *Violence Against Women, 18*(3), 264–288.

Orchowski, L., Meyer, D., & Gidycz, C. (2009). College women's likelihood to report unwanted sexual experiences to campus agencies: Trends and correlates. *Journal of Aggression, Maltreatment and Trauma, 18*, 839–858.

Sabina, C., & Ho, L. Y. (2014). Campus and college victim responses to sexual assault and dating violence: Disclosure, service utilization, and service provision. *Trauma, Violence, and Abuse, 15*(3), 201–226.

Salazar, L., Vivolo-Kanor, A., Hardin, J., & Berkowitz, A. (2015). A web-based violence bystander intervention for male college students: A randomized control trial. *Journal of Medical Internet Research, 16*(9), 1–16.

Sawa, T. (2016, March 11). Brock University tells student to keep quiet about sexual harassment. *CBC News*. Retrieved from http://www.huffingtonpost.ca/2016/03/11/brock-university-sexual-h_n_9438470.html

School of secrets. (2015, November 23). *The Fifth Estate*. Retrieved from http://www.cbc.ca/fifth/episodes/2015-2016/school-of-secrets

Schwartz, Z. (2016). Students' choice: Introducing *Maclean's* student satisfaction rankings. *Maclean's*. Retrieved from http://www.macleans.ca/education/http://www.macleans.ca/education/students-choice-introducing-macleans-student-satisfaction-rankings/

Senn, C., Eliasziw, M., Barata, P. C., Thurston, W. E., Newby-Clark, I. R., Radtke, L., & Hobden, K. (2015). Efficacy of a sexual assault resistance program for university women. *New England Journal of Medicine, 372*(24), 2326–2335.

Smith, C. (2014). Institutional betrayal. *American Psychologist, 69*(6), 575–587.

Smith, C., & Freyd, J. (2013). Dangerous safe havens: Institutional betrayal exacerbates sexual trauma. *Journal of Traumatic Stress, 26*(1), 119–124.

StFX Students' Union. (2016). Bringing in the bystander. Retrieved from http://www.theu.ca?q=bystander

University of Manitoba. (2016). Sexual assault: Prevention. Retrieved from http://umanitoba.ca/student/sexual-assault/prevention.html

University of Manitoba, faculty association hit impasse in mediation. (2016, October 31). *CBC News*. Retrieved from http://www.cbc.ca/news/canada/manitoba/university-manitoba-strike-impasse-mediation-1.3828888

University of Prince Edward Island. (2015). Bringing in the bystander (BITB) training. Retrieved from http://www.upei.ca/communications/campus-notice/2015/11/bringing-bystander-bitb-training

University of Windsor. (2016). Empowering student bystanders. Retrieved from http://www1.uwindsor.ca/bystander

Wilfrid Laurier University. (2016). Bringing in the bystander Laurier. Retrieved from https://legacy.wlu.ca/news_detail.php?grp_id=1331&nws_id=13443

Ziering, A. (Producer) & Dick, K. (Director). (2015). *The hunting ground* [Motion picture]. United States: Weinstein Company.

Zinzow, H., Amstadter, A., McCauley, J., Ruggiero, K., Resnik, H., & Kilpatrick, D. (2011). Self-rated health in relation to rape and mental health disorders in a national sample of college women. *Journal of American College Health, 59,* 588–594.

PART II

VIOLENT SPACES

ON CANADIAN UNIVERSITY

CAMPUSES

CHAPTER 4

"IT'S NOT ABOUT ONE BAD APPLE"
The 2007 York University Vanier Residence Rapes

Madison Trusolino

In August 2007 I moved into York University's Vanier Residence, which houses about 200 new and continuing undergraduates. One week later, on September 7, two men, Daniel Katsnelson and Justin Connort, entered the building and raped two female first-year students. The safety afforded through the transitional lodging of residence, between living with one's parents or guardians and independent living, vanished. The aftermath revealed the role universities play in perpetuating a culture of fear and securitization on campuses across North America.

This profoundly disturbing event is my starting point for an investigation of the conflicts, resistance, and discourse surrounding sexual assault on Canadian university campuses. I argue that this case demonstrates that the contemporary university, while a promoter of neo-liberal and post-feminist discourse, remains a key site of feminist struggle. Neo-liberalism, a political-economic institutional framework, envisions human well-being as being best achieved through the liberation of private and individual interests (Harvey, 2007, p. 2). Similarly, post-feminism, according to feminist sociologist Angela McRobbie (2009), takes into account the vocabulary of feminism, such as "choice" and "empowerment," applying these terms to the needs of individuals instead of collectives. Both post-feminism and neo-liberalism are based on the idea that competition, individualism, and entrepreneurialism should be valued over solidarity, collectivism, and community.

In order to further examine this case study of the 2007 assaults as York University, I have developed two contrasting subjectivities using Michel Foucault's conception of the active subject as outlined in his essay "The Subject and

Power" (1982), who, while implicated by the social forces and institutions from above, is also capable of resistance from below. Alongside this "active" reading of Foucault, I draw on the work of autonomist Marxists who use resistance as their theoretical starting point in their investigations of power relations. The first subject, the "self-securitized woman," is born out of the post-feminist and neo-liberal discourse of the university. She is considered responsible for her own safety and security, not relying on external protection, internalizing the constant fear of bodily harm. I contrast the self-securitized female subject with what I call the "autonomous woman," a subject who promotes and utilizes the collective power of women's movements to resist violence and the imposition of fear, control, and self-securitization. I explore this resistant subjectivity by looking at the response by feminist campus organizations to the security discourse promoted by the media and the public after the rapes. I conclude by investigating the formation of the SlutWalk, an annual march against victim-blaming and slut-shaming formed by current and past York University students, which addresses the persistent discourse of self-securitization.

Before delving into my case study, I provide here some context of sexual assaults in North America to help further illustrate the urgent need for a feminist response to sexual assaults of women on university campuses. Several studies have been conducted over the last 30 years on the rates of sexual assault on university campuses in North America. The studies surveyed in the introductory chapter in this collection offer a statistical review of the rates of sexual victimization of women on university campuses. In addition, studies have shown an intense perpetuation of rape myths. Rape myths work to excuse the perpetrator and/or attempt to justify assault by placing blame on the survivor, for example, the myth that women at university are "too educated" to not realize when they have been raped (Schwartz & Leggett, 1999, p. 252). Talbot, Neill, and Rankin's 2010 study found that 22% of people surveyed thought a woman was partially or totally responsible for rape if she was in a deserted space, 33% if she was drunk, and 37% if she did not say no clearly enough (Barnett, 2013). There is also ample evidence that survivors internalize these myths—for example, Martin D. Schwartz and Molly S. Leggett's (1999) study on the emotional trauma of rape survivors found that 79.3% of women who were raped while intoxicated blamed themselves.

Taken together, these studies demonstrate a consistent, even structural pattern of victimization of women at post-secondary institutions on North American campuses. The case study of the Vanier Residence rapes is ideal not only because of the resistance that followed, but also because it allows me to work through the events that destabilized my first "home away from home."

FEAR, SECURITY, AND SELF-SECURITIZATION ON UNIVERSITY CAMPUSES

Women on university campuses are the subjects of intense regulation through both external and internal forces, which has only increased because of a slew of sexual assaults on university campuses reported in the mainstream media. Feminist sociologist Angela McRobbie argues that women's self-regulation is a central tenet of post-feminism. In *The Aftermath of Feminism: Gender, Culture and Social Change* (2009), McRobbie argues that within post-feminism, young women are "offered a notional form of equality, concretized in education and employment, and through participation in consumer culture and civil society, in place of what a reinvented feminist politics might have to offer" (p. 1). Patriarchal authority and norms are internalized within what McRobbie calls a "regime of self-policing" whereby young women are "congratulated, reprimanded and encouraged to embark on a new regime of self-perfectability" (p. 63).

Post-feminism is an inherently neo-liberal response to the feminist movements of the 1960s and 1970s, and one, as we shall see, that has found an ideal setting in the contemporary academy. Feminist sociologists Rosalind Gill and Christina Scharff identify three ways that neo-liberalism and post-feminism overlap: they are structured by individualism, undermining the social or political; they both rely on self-regulating subjects; and they both call upon women to "work on and transform the self, to regulate every aspect of their conduct, and to present all their actions as freely chosen" (quoted in Butler, 2013, p. 45).

The focus on self-regulation is intimately tied to neo-liberal strategies of crime prevention. Criminologists such as Pat O'Malley (2013) and David Garland (1996) suggest that crime is no longer taken as an abnormality, but rather as an inevitability. Both O'Malley and Garland propose that, under neo-liberalism, the responsibility of managing risks is transferred from the state to the individual (p. 183). O'Malley argues that this creates what Foucault originally called an entrepreneur of one's self who must take responsibility, and be held accountable, for creating and assessing the risks in one's life in order to be self-sufficient, relying as little on the state, or even other members of society, as possible.

In the case of the York University rapes, this regulation of one's self manifested in the self-securitization of women's bodies. Sociologists Elizabeth Comack and Tracey Peter (2005) argue that the responsibility to keep one's self safe, or as Garland calls it, "responsibilitization," can be used as a tool by the criminal justice system to blame the victim in cases of sexual assault and rape. Comack and Peter contend that survivors must present themselves to show that they are the ideal victim who "lives up to the neo-liberal ethos: she is reasonable, rational, and responsible and demonstrates that she can make the 'right' choices in her own self-governance" (p. 298). While everyone is subject to responsibilitization, in the case of sexual assault and rape, women are particularly affected by a surveillance regime where the criminal justice system, while intimately interfering with their lives, also holds them responsible for "their own self-governance" (p. 309).

Autonomist Marxists Michael Hardt and Antonio Negri (2012) suggest that fear, most of all, is what drives people to be complicit in a surveillance regime, accepting the role of "watcher and watched" (p. 24). The authors emphasize that the fear of the police or the state is not as strong as the fear of "dangerous others and unknown threats," or what they call a "generalized social fear" (p. 24). Generalized social fear acts as a way to gain complicity and legitimacy from the public in the construction of a tighter and more prominent security regime.

Communication scholar Fiona Jeffries (2013) argues that separating the personal experience of fear and the politics that contribute to the construction of that fear delinks it from more systemic problems of oppression. Jeffries cites urban scholar Stephen Graham, who suggests that everyday spaces that have high "circuits of movement" are being touted as "zones of threat" (p. 335). Graham believes that this is used as a justification for increased security and police presence in areas that have higher concentration of people. Given the high-profile events outlined in the previous section, I argue that the university can be considered one of these "zones of threat," where the fear of violence is used to regulate the movement of bodies through the process of external and internal securitization. This internalization is facilitated by the individualization of security and responsibility whereby university administrators defer their obligation of creating a safe campus onto their students. This sentiment permeated the discourse from York University administrators after the rapes were committed in Vanier Residence.

CASE STUDY: THE 2007 VANIER RESIDENCE RAPES

As the previous sections suggest, sexual assault and violence against women are endemic on Canadian campuses. While the bulk of sexual violence against women on campuses occurs under a veil of silence, the 2007 rapes at York University garnered a plethora of media coverage. Two short weeks after committing the rapes, and facing eleven charges including five counts of break and enter, two counts of sexual assault, and two counts of forcible confinement, Katsnelson and Connort turned themselves into the police (Makin, 2010). The weeks leading up to the arrests were tense, and while it was confirmed that the perpetrators were not residents of Vanier, we were, nonetheless, constantly looking over our shoulders, suspicious of everyone.

The attacks happened on the first pub night of the year shortly after the conclusion of frosh week. Our names were still on our dorm room doors, originally intended as a way for new residents to get to know each other; Katsnelson and Connort used them to track down female residents. The fear after the assaults was palpable. We were told that the security guards who strolled our hallways at all hours were there to protect us, yet encountering a group of big men in big boots in the dark was anything but reassuring. Houry Sekunian, a 19-year-old resident at Vanier at the time of the rapes, described the general feeling amid the student population: "I'm scared to go to the bathroom by myself. We go in packs. I knew our campus wasn't safe, but you can walk around outside with people. You're not going to have people sleep next to you in bed because you're scared" (Henry, 2007).

During reading week that same year, when most students were back home, I did ask a friend to sleep in my room with me after a group of us thought we saw a large figure in one of our floor's bathroom stalls. We told each other it was a ghost; we made up stories about our fears rather than naming them. No one wanted to say, "I'm afraid of getting raped at the library, in my residence, walking home from the bus stop." The non-corporal image of a ghost was a perfect manifestation of the fear that haunted us on campus. As one third-year student who lived in Vanier at the time of the rapes, Morrisa Silvert, stated a full year after the attacks, "I feel even worse now. When it happened, I tried really hard not to think about it a lot. As it went later and later through the year, I started to think about it more and more" (Yutangco, 2008). Like Silvert, I tried to pretend that the rapes no longer bothered me. Despite the extra security measures the university took following the assaults, I could never calm my heartbeat when I worked late in the library, or when I walked across campus at dusk.

The extra security measures implemented by the university included doubling York security patrols; increasing staff at Vanier and other residences on campus; heightening the presence of the Toronto Police Service on campus; issuing security alerts through the university website and student emails; and putting up posters across the campus that reminded students to stay vigilant ("York Adds Extra Security," 2007). These practices were in addition to York's existing 24/7 campus security patrols and monitored CCTV coverage, foot patrols, and network of emergency "blue light" telephones. Despite the heightened security measures, York graduate Rebecca Hall (2007) wrote to the *Toronto Star* critiquing the York University administration's efforts to create a safe campus: "York tends to increase safety measures only when incidents are brought to the media's attention, rather than taking preventative measures all the time" (p. A4). Only after persistent demands from the York Federation of Students, York's largest student union, did the school agree to hire an independent safety audit company, METRAC, to perform a safety audit that included long-term suggestions for creating a safe campus (Yuntangco, 2008).

In addition to ramping up security on campus, York administrators and police officials promoted self-securitizing practices for students. York University's director of media relations, Alex Bilyk, continually urged students to remain "vigilant." Detective Kim Hancock said that students needed to be cautious not only after dark but "at all times"; she advised that "if you have a lock on your [dorm] door, use it at night" (Henry, 2007). This discourse perpetuated victim-blaming, where the survivor of an assault is seen as somehow to blame for the attack, and the internalization of self-blame and securitization. For example, the *Toronto Star* reported that after the sexual assaults there was a spike in women registering in self-defence classes, claiming to be taking charge of their own safety. Deb Chard, an instructor of Wen-Do, stated, "All the statistics show that women who fight back or make scenes are more likely to survive [an attack]" (Gordon, 2007, p. L3). Chard continued, "If you walk with a certain type of confidence, you're less attractive to an attacker. You don't seem like a victim."

Interestingly, everyone from the university, to the police, to the rapist himself in comments made after his arrest used the same discourse of victim-blaming. The fact that the actual perpetrators of rape often use the same rape myths to justify their actions became evident when, in court, Daniel Katsnelson's lawyer wrote that Katsnelson hoped that "some day the victim would be able to take something positive away from this, such as ... that maybe she will know to keep her doors locked" (Freed, 2010, p. 8). Although Katsnelson's remark was markedly repellent, it fits in with a larger discourse of victim-blaming where the actions, personality, and morals of the survivor are scrutinized, particularly when the case does not support the traditionally held definition of rape where, as former law professor Susan Estrich explains, the "perpetrator is a stranger; the act is committed in a public setting; [and] the victim shows signs of resistance or being overpowered" (Fisher, Daigle, & Cullen, 2010, p. 4).

Victim-blaming discourses have the effect of downplaying the severity and frequency of acquaintance rape while shifting the focus onto stranger rape. The focus on stranger rape that occurs in the discussion of campus sexual assault is disproportionate to the statistics. A 2011 Statistics Canada report on sexual assault found that in three-quarters of incidents, perpetrators of reported sexual assaults were known to the survivors (Sinha, 2013). Because of the stigmatization of, in particular, acquaintance rape, Schwartz and Leggett (1999) argue that many women will not reach out to rape counsellors or mental health services. In a *Toronto Star* timeline of York University campus assaults, for example, no instances of acquaintance rape were listed (Casey & Aulakh, 2011). The constant discussion of stranger rape in the media, public institutions, and governmental campaigns serves to displace attention from the systematic causes of violence onto a foreboding "other." In these depictions, feminist legal scholar Kristin Bumiller (2008) argues that perpetrators of sexual violence are often portrayed as "driven by sadistic impulses" and the genesis of sexual violence is found in "sites of excess, such as racial hatred, open borders, and sexual perversion" (p. 20). Bumiller asserts that the majority of cases that reach the public sustain "excessive fears among women about the potential threat of violence from dangerous (usually dark-skinned) strangers" (p. 19). This was no different in this particular case with the fear of violence being projected onto the north Toronto area of Jane and Finch, the neighbourhood that surrounds the campus.

Jane and Finch is a low-income, racialized area that is often at the centre of "sensationalized media reports on crime, gun violence, and poverty" (Ikeda & Rosser, 2009, p. 38). It was not uncommon at York for people to make covertly racist comments about the Jane and Finch neighbourhood couched in concerns for their own and others' safety. In a Ryerson University student publication, *RyersOnline* (2007), the author compares the surrounding area of Ryerson to that of York: "Women complained [that] there are no boundaries between [York's] vast campus and the surrounding neighbourhoods.... This leaves the campus wide open to whoever wants to stroll through York's forest-filled, and often poorly-lit grounds—including 'sketchy' people wearing gang colours" (p. 38). Invoking such images of people clad in "gang colours" suggests a racialized and dangerous other lurking in the shadows of the campus. Such stereotypes clash with the reality of the 2007 rapes. Katsnelson was a York alumnus who not only "came from a good family" and "had a good background" but also worked for the Responsible Business Group with former Toronto Mayor David Miller after the rapes (Freed, 2010). Although Katsnelson was a stranger to the two women, he does not embody the image of the dangerous other that the student journalist evokes. As two York University graduate students, Naoko Ikeda and Emily Rosser (2009), wrote in response to the article, separating the campus from its surrounding community works to dispel the fact that the campus itself is "deeply implicated and constituted through particular social relations of power, including gender and racial hierarchy" (p. 38), not to mention the community in which it is located.

Moreover, the fear of the other that is encouraged often creates the conditions for enacting increasingly stringent security measures. Bumiller (2008) suggests that this process produces a "culture of control" grounded in "conceptions of essential 'otherness' of the criminal and highly dependent on mechanisms of social segregation" (p. 6). This kind of reaction, Bumiller argues, criminalizes and pathologizes offenders while obscuring the root causes of violence against women. The resistance to this process of securitization and self-securitization on York campus effectively repoliticized the problem of sexual violence on university campuses.

Resisting self-securitization: The emergence of the autonomous woman

The incidents at York University sparked feminist discussions and actions that brought a resistant subjectivity to the forefront, one that I call "the autonomous feminist." Foucault (1982) describes subjectivity as a condition of being both "subject to someone else by control and dependence" and "tied to his own identity by a conscience or self-knowledge (p. 781). This understanding of subjectivity is an active one, shaped from above by domination, as is evident by the internalization of securitization, but also capable of resistance from below, in the case of the autonomist woman.

My discussion of the autonomous woman draws on the theory and activism of autonomist feminism, which has a history that stretches back to the Wages for Housework (WFH) movement, founded by Italian scholars and activists such as Silvia Federici and Mariarosa Dalla Costa in 1972. WFH looked at reproductive work, the unpaid labour of women within the home, identifying the family as the "other factory," where women were "caged in a form of labour—housework—with an unlimited working-day, no wage, no vacation and no social assistance" (Dalla Costa, 1988, p. 25). Feminist autonomists not only acknowledged women's work within the home, but also set the stage for the analysis of unwaged labour and the exploitation of subjects, including students, beyond the confines of traditional workplaces.

Federici (Carlin & Federici, 2014) explains that autonomy in the women's liberation movement originally meant that women could organize and live autonomously from men. In this context, autonomy is the capacity for women's self-determination or self-governance. The conception of autonomy markedly contrasts and is in opposition to neo-liberal individualism, which is about furthering one's own individual interests rather than the reciprocal relationship between the individual and the collective. Individualizing the problem of sexual violence through the discourse of self-securitization works to dismantle the collective response. Rather than being bound to the individualizing practices of self-securitization, the autonomist feminist practices collective responsibility over individual responsibility.

The autonomous woman works to change what Jeffries (2013) calls the negative conception of security as "security *from* crime, harassment, threat to property etc." to the positive "security *of* housing, healthcare, transportation and so on" (p. 335). Fear and insecurity become the terrain of struggle, and collective resistance to fear has the potential of producing "alternative social forms" (p. 337). The response that began within the York University community but reached well beyond the walls of the campus worked to not only unpack and resist the language of securitization, but also create a new subjectivity that openly addressed the external and internal powers that work to control the minds and bodies of women.

This subjectivity emerged from an ongoing process to create a safe and healthy environment for all students led by students, faculty, and other members of the York University community. At the forefront of this process were the York Federation of Students and the Graduate Student Association, who pushed for the York University administration to appoint METRAC to perform an external safety audit (Massa, 2008). This ultimately led to York commissioning a lengthy report from METRAC on practical ways in which to address systemic oppression on campus.

In addition, the York University Graduate Women's Studies Student Association (GWSSA), frustrated with the discourse of securitization that emerged on campus in response to the rapes, worked to discursively change the conversation around how best to stop violence on campus. Naoko Ikeda and Emily Rosser (2009), members of the GWSSA, wrote about the administration's response post-attack, "It was frustrating to be framed as potential victims who must watch out to prevent our own assaults, but at the same time having all the appropriate responses to violence already scripted out for us through the security apparatus" (p. 39). In an open letter that was distributed across campus and in the York University campus newspaper *The Excalibur*, the GWSSA wrote about the danger of the use of security language, such as being "vigilant":

> We're angry because instead of hearing a loud and repeated condemnation of sexual assault, we're told how to avoid being raped. York administration's security bulletin calls on us to be "vigilant" about our safety. Women have heard this before: don't make the same mistakes as 'those' women; don't go out alone at night; don't be in the wrong place at the wrong time; basically don't get raped. (p. 40)

The letter also called upon others to recognize the interconnectedness of rape with larger systemic problems. "Rape is not accidental, and it is not isolated. It thrives in a culture that is tolerant of violence, especially violence against women. Currently it thrives here, at York" (p. 40). The GWSSA dispelled the idea that rape is an individual problem and by doing so called for the York University administration to take responsibility for a culture of violence and sexism on campus.

Utilizing an intersectional feminist approach to violence on campus, the GWSSA partnered with a class of undergraduate women's studies students to co-write a letter of solidarity for the York University Black Students' Association (YUBSA) after white supremacist graffiti was found across campus.

Creating this connection demonstrated the GWSSA's position that all move-ments against violence should also be fundamentally anti-racist. The GWSSA also encouraged its members to discuss these issues in their classrooms, using, for example, York Campus alerts as pieces for critical analysis. Finally, the GWSSA began a guerilla postering campaign crossing out the phrase "Don't Get Raped" with "Don't Rape," rhetorically redirecting the responsibility away from survivors and onto the perpetrators (Ikeda & Rosser, 2009, p. 40). Ikeda and Rosser believe that the GWSSA's actions contributed to an "increase in discussion and student involvement in resisting securitization on York's terms" (p. 41), showing what a community response to the rapes, rooted in justice for all, could look like.

Despite the continued efforts of the York student and faculty community, York once again found itself immersed in a media frenzy on January 24, 2011—just three years after the rapes in Vanier Residence—when two male police officers and two school security guards spoke on a safety panel at York's Osgoode Hall Law School. In response to a question asking how women could protect themselves from being sexually assaulted, Constable Michael San-guinetti responded, "I've been told I shouldn't say this [but] women should avoid dressing like sluts in order not to be victimized" (Morrow, 2011). San-guinetti later apologized to the university and was disciplined internally (although the details of how he was disciplined were not released to the pub-lic). While Toronto Police Chief Bill Blair condemned the remarks, saying that they "place[d] the blame upon the victims, and that's not where the blame should ever be placed" (Thomas, 2011), Sanguinetti's remarks were a reminder of how rape myths persist within law enforcement and sparked the beginning of the SlutWalk movement.

The first SlutWalk took place on April 3, 2011, at Queen's Park in Toronto and was attended by between 3000 and 5000 people, just "ten short weeks" (O'Reilly, 2012, p. 245) after the original comment was made to a group of ten people. The original SlutWalk was organized by a core group of women including Heather Jarvis, Sonya Barnett, Alyssa Teckah, Jeanette Janzen, and Erika Jane Scholz, most of whom were either current or past York University students. After Jarvis, a former Torontonian attending Guelph University, read about the incident in *The Excalibur*, she contacted Barnett, a York alumna, and together they decided to "have a walk to express our frustrations and demand better" (Miller, 2011, p. A7). Rather than merely having a campus-centred event, the organizers decided to take the opportunity to reach out to the greater Toronto community through social media, asking people to join them to

make a unified statement about sexual assault and victims' rights and to demand respect for all. Whether a fellow slut or simply an ally, *you don't have to wear your sexual proclivities on your sleeve,* we just ask that you come. *Any* gender-identification, any age. Singles, couples, parents, sisters, brothers, children, friends. Come walk or roll or strut or holler or stomp with us. (SlutWalk, n.d.)

The invitation to all people broke down the individualizing barriers that are erected both physically and psychologically through securitization.

The SlutWalk directly addressed both victim-blaming and the use of the word "slut." The SlutWalk Toronto website states that SlutWalk is reappropriating the term "slut," a word that has historically had a negative connotation: "Aimed at those who are sexually promiscuous, be it for work or pleasure, it has primarily been women who have suffered under the burden of this label" (SlutWalk, n.d.). The fear of the free movement of women's bodies, as feminist-autonomists have pointed out, is part of a long history of the female body being regulated by the state and capital in order to be utilized for its productive and reproductive capacities (Echeverria & Sernatinger, 2014). The restriction on the movement of women's bodies works to strip away practices of self-determination. Through the reappropriation of the term, the organizers attempted to shrug off its power to insult and control women.

Heather Mallick, a journalist writing in support of the SlutWalk for the *Toronto Star,* wrote that it is not "what you're wearing that matters, it's that cops, and indeed rapists, will assess you whatever you wear" (Mallick, 2011, p. A16). SlutWalk points to the larger institutional problem of ingrained patriarchy. "It's not about one bad apple cop," said Jane Doe, an activist who sued the police after she was used as bait to catch a serial rapist—one of the speakers at the first Toronto SlutWalk—"it's about an institution that is permeated with these kind of notions and beliefs" (Thomas, 2011). Doe demonstrated that it is the very institutions that we rely on for protection on our campuses, whether the state and/or capital through the form of private security, increased police presence, and surveillance technology, that perpetuate shame and fear that fracture our communities.

The SlutWalk was not without critique from other feminists. Feminist scholar Kathy Miriam (2012) pointed towards critiques from women of colour, who she notes "have been historically configured and concretely exploited as always already sluts and thus unrapeable" (p. 264). The "reclaiming" of the term "slut" wasn't seen as a core element to some of the movements. For example, founder of the Philadelphia SlutWalk Hannah Altman (2012), having read previous critiques, decided to focus on "blaming the perpetrator and not the victim" (p. 251). Altman, understanding the importance of recognizing her privilege so as to make sure the movement was not just "another white heterosexual movement" (p. 252), invited speakers that included people of colour and members of the LGBTQ+ community, and acknowledged the history of violence against people of colour and transgendered individuals in Philadelphia. While SlutWalk is still in the process of changing and improving as it enters its fifth year, it has demonstrated that what might start as a campus issue can connect communities within and outside of the walls of the university.

CONCLUSION

Self-securitization has become common practice for most women on and off university campuses. These practices have the effect of individualizing rather than politicizing the problem of sexual violence, as was evident in the responses from the York University administration and Toronto police in the aftermath of the 2007 rapes. The forceful critique of the language of victim-blaming and self-securitization from feminist groups, the student union, and undergraduate and graduate anti-oppression organizations at York University, as well as the creation of the SlutWalk, brought to the forefront the subject of the autonomous woman. By reframing sexual assault as a political rather than an individual issue, these campus organizers demonstrated the importance of creating a collective feminist movement.

It was these organizers that inspired me to write this chapter, which was both an emotionally demanding and rewarding exercise for me. For years I pushed this incident to the back of my mind, and pulling these memories to the forefront allowed for a working-through of previously suppressed memories and anxieties. Throughout the process of writing I felt burdened, wondering if this was my story to tell, asking myself if the weight of memory and the reliving of the past was worth it. In the end contextualizing and intertwining my fears, anxieties, and memories with the economic, political, and social history of campus sexual assaults has allowed me to recognize the importance of sharing our stories. In sharing our stories we are not alone; we have power and agency to name and address the systemic problems that perpetuate violence against women on our campuses and in our communities.

REFERENCES

Altman, H. (2012). SlutWalk Philadelphia. *Feminist Studies, 38*(1), 251–253.

Arrest made in Vanier Residence sexual assaults. (2007, September 21). *Yfile*. Retrieved from http://yfile.news.yorku.ca/2007/09/21/arrest-made-in-vanier-residence-sexual-assaults/

Barnett, B. (2013). How newspapers frame rape allegations: The Duke University case. *Women and Language, 35*(2), 11–33.

Brennan, S., & Taylor-Butts, A. (2008). *Sexual assault in Canada 2004 and 2007. Canadian Centre for Justice Statistics Profile Series*. Ottawa, ON: Canadian Centre for Justice Statistics.

Bumiller, K. (2008). *In an abusive state: How neoliberalism appropriated the feminist movement against sexual violence*. London, UK: Duke University Press.

Butler, J. (2013). For white girls only? Postfeminism and the politics of inclusion. *Feminist Formations, 25*(1), 35–58.

Carlin, M., & Federici, S. (2014). The exploitation of women, social reproduction, and the struggle against global capital. *Theory & Event, 17*(3).

Casey, L., & Aulakh, R. (2011, July 19). The university must warn of assaults, students say: York under fire for lack of information about alleged assaults. *Toronto Star*, p. A1.

Comack, E., & Peter, T. (2005). How the criminal justice system responds to sexual assault survivors: The slippage between "responsibilization" and "blaming the victim." *Canadian Journal of Women and the Law, 17*(2), 283–309.

Dalla Costa, M. (1988). Domestic labour and the feminist movement in Italy since the 1970s. *International Sociology, 3*(3), 23–34.

DeKeseredy, W., & Kelly, K. (1993). The incidence and prevalence of women abuse in Canadian university and college dating relationships. *Canadian Journal of Sociology, 18*(2), 137–159.

Echeverria, T., & Sernatinger, A. (2014, February 24). The making of capitalist patriarchy: Interview with Silvia Federici. *North Star*. Retrieved from http://www.the northstar.info/?p=11947

Federici, S. (1984). Putting feminism back on its feet. *Social Text, 9*(10), 338–346.

Fisher, B. S., Daigle, L. E., & Cullen, F. T. (2010). *Unsafe in the ivory tower: The sexual victimization of college women*. Thousand Oaks, CA: Sage.

Foucault, M. (1982). The subject and power. *Critical Inquiry, 8*(3), 777–795.

Freed, D. A. (2010, March 27). Rapist hopes teen sees the "positive" as court hears about York U nightmare, assailant says ordeal may teach victim to lock door. *Toronto Star*, p. 8.

Garland, D. (1996). The limits of the sovereign state: Strategies of crime control in contemporary society. *British Journal of Criminology, 36*(4), 445–471.

Gill, R., & Scharff, C. (2011). Introduction. In R. Gill & C. Scharff (Eds.), *New femininities: Postfeminism, neoliberalism and subjectivity* (pp. 1–20). New York, NY: Palgrave Macmillan.

Gordon, D. (2007, September 20). Women learn to fight back: Campus attacks in Toronto prompting higher enrolment in self-defense classes, organizers say. *Toronto Star*, p. L3.

Hall, R. (2007, September 11). Security lacking at York. *Toronto Star*, p. A7.

Hardt, M., & Negri, A. (2012). *Declaration*. New York, NY: Argo-Navis.

Harvey, D. (2007). *A brief history of neoliberalism*. New York, NY: Oxford University Press.

Henry, M. (2007, September 9). Dorm room rapes stun York U: "We go in packs" to the bathroom, students say after 2 men enter 6 rooms and attack sleeping women. *Toronto Star*, p. A1.

Ikeda, N., & Rosser, E. (2009). "You be vigilant! Don't rape!": Reclaiming space and security at York University. *Canadian Women Studies, 28*(1), 37–43.

Jeffries, F. (2012). Mediating fear. *Global Media and Communication, 9*(1), 37–52.

Jeffries, F. (2013). Fear disarmed. *Perspectives on Global Development and Technology, 12*, 332–339.

Makin, K. (2010, April 15). York University rapist jailed for eight years. *Globe and Mail*, p. A12.

Mallick, H. (2011, March 30). Why SlutWalk? Because women don't ask for it. *Toronto Star*, p. A16.

Massa, G. (2008, June 4). York students respond to the selection of METRAC as York University external auditor. *CNW*.

McRobbie, A. (2009). *The aftermath of feminism: Gender, culture and social change.* London, UK: Sage.

Morrow, A. (2011, February 18). Police officer's sex-assault remarks prompt reprimand. *Globe and Mail*, p. A7.

Miller, S. (2011, March 17). Police officer's remarks at York inspire "SlutWalk." *Toronto Star*, p. A7.

Miriam, K. (2012). Feminism, neoliberalism, and SlutWalk. *Feminist Studies, 38*(1), 262–266.

O'Malley, P. (2013). Uncertain governance and resilient subjects in the risk society. *Onati Socio-Legal Series, 3*(2), 180–195.

O'Reilly, A. (2012). Slut pride: A tribute to SlutWalk Toronto. *Feminist Studies, 38*(1), 245–250.

Schwartz, D., & Leggett, M. S. (1999). Bad dates or emotional trauma? The aftermath of campus sexual assault. *Violence Against Women, 5*(3), 251–271.

Sinha, M. (Ed.). (2013). Measuring violence against women: Statistical trends. *Juristat* (Statistics Canada Catalogue no. 85-002-X). Retrieved from http://www.statcan .gc.ca/pub/85-002-x/2013001/article/11766-eng.pdf

SlutWalk Toronto. (n.d.). Retrieved from http://slutwalktoronto.com

Talbot, K., Neill, K. S., & Rankin, L. L. (2010). Rape-accepting attitudes of university undergraduate students. *Journal of Forensic Nursing, 35*(2), 170–179.

Thomas, N. (2011, April 3). Women rally against "slut" stereotypes. *Toronto Star*, p. GT1.

van Wormer, K. (2008). Anti-feminist backlash and violence against women worldwide. *Social Work and Society International Online Journal, 6*(2).

York adds extra security in wake of sexual assaults in Vanier. (2007, September 10). *Yfile*. Retrieved from http://yfile-archive.news.yorku.ca/2007/09/10/ york-adds-extra-security-in-wake-of-sexual-assaults-in-vanier/

Yutangco, P. (2008, September 3). York attack memories still fresh: A year after rapes were reported in dorms, university has beefed up security to keep students safe. *Toronto Star*, p. A17.

CHAPTER 5

RAPE CHANT AT SAINT MARY'S UNIVERSITY

A Convergence of Business School Ethics, Alcohol Consumption, and Varsity Sport

Judy Haiven

In the first week of September 2013, Saint Mary's University (SMU) in Halifax made national news when a video showed student leaders encouraging up to 400 hundred first-year students to sing a "rape chant" during university orientation. Not special to SMU students, these catchy rhymes and songs were meant to boost student spirit and focused on degrading women and promoting nonconsensual sex.

> "Y is for your sister
> O is for oh so tight
> U is for underage
> N is for no consent
> G is for grab that ass
> SMU boys we like them young!"
> ("Saint Mary's University Unveils," 2014; "Sexist Frosh Chant," 2013;
> Tamburri & Samson, 2014)

A short four months later, in January 2014, members of the SMU football team (the Huskies) were caught tweeting hate, racism, and sexism online (Jeffrey, 2014a). Despite being "outed," some players continued to tweet messages including this one: "That bitch bit me last night. Hope your [sic] dead in a ditch, you are scum" ("Saint Mary's Athletes," 2014). Also, "Cut your face off and wear it while I'm fucking your mother" and "See a girl who's feeling down? Feel her up" (Wong, 2014). And "b**tch get on yo knees" (Thomson, 2014). Another was a retweet from another twitter account: "School is like a boner. It's long and hard unless you're Asian" (Wong, 2014). Media reports say the university reacted by suspending between six and ten players from the team, but not from the university (Jeffrey, 2014a; Thomson, 2014).

This chapter focuses on the culture that led to the infamous rape chant and other events at Saint Mary's University. It puts forward the idea that the norms operating in the male-dominated discipline of business along with a culture of heavy drinking contributed to the rape chant. This chapter situates the discussion by taking a historic look at events in the male-dominated discipline of engineering at Canadian universities—once renowned for creating a misogynist climate on campus. In doing so, the chapter demonstrates that yesterday's engineering students seem to have passed the misogynist baton to today's business school students. Of course, there is no denying that sports teams played a role in the mistreatment of women, but that will be dealt with in another chapter in this book (see Fogel's "Precarious Masculinity and Rape Culture in Canadian University Sport").

More than three years have passed since the infamous rape chant at SMU. In order to explain what happened at SMU, two things need to be understood. First—the chants, the hazing, and the sexist behaviour occur at many universities across Canada, in the United Kingdom, and in the United States (Barness 2014; Bates, 2014; National Union of Students, 2013). Second, these events grow out of a history and pattern that is contemporary yet decades old.

SMU's rape chant is not necessarily the worst example of sexist behaviour. For example, Dalhousie, the Maritimes' largest university, also in Halifax, received national attention when the Class of DDS 2015 Gentlemen, a Facebook page set up by 13 male dental students, posted misogynist comments and threats against women students (Backhouse, McRae, & Iyer, 2015). We have all heard about sexism and misogyny on campuses across Canada and the United States. Every autumn the media gets wind of rape chants, initiation rites, underage drinking, cruel party games, and sexual assault and splashes the news across the front pages. The articles are sometimes accompanied by the warning that four out of five female students will become victims of violence in a dating relationship while at university and that one woman in five will be sexually assaulted during her four years of university (Canadian Federation of Students, 2015). I am writing about SMU because I teach at the university and have witnessed much of what has gone on.

But that is not the only reason I am writing about the rape chant and the football tweets at Saint Mary's University. I became a university business school professor at the age of 50. Before that time, I was a successful freelance writer and filmmaker. My "beat" was social justice—or rather injustice. Over the years I have been involved in many activities, including strike support, backing civil liberties cases, and working against social inequality, to name a few. I serve as the Nova Scotia chair of the Canadian Centre for Policy Alternatives, a left-of-centre think tank. Even after becoming an academic, I worked on behalf of many individuals to assist them with problems in employment and issues of human rights and to expose lack of equal opportunity dealt to women and minorities in our country. Part of my life continues in the role of activist and civil libertarian, and it is from this perspective that I write this reflective chapter. I deliberately draw on sources that are reliable but rarely cited by academics. These sources lend an immediacy and an alternative flavour to the subject of sexual assault on Canadian university campuses.

I start the chapter by reviewing recent data from other universities, followed by a brief discussion of rape culture. I then link historical events such as the Godiva ride and the Montreal Massacre to misogyny in the male-dominated discipline of engineering so that the examination of what took place at SMU can be set against the historic backdrop of rape culture at universities. The chapter addresses the culture at SMU, the administration's response to the crises that occurred, and my own response to the crises: a button campaign to challenge rape culture.

THE CULTURE OF RAPE: A BROADER CONTEXT

In February 2015, a *CBC News* investigation looked at the last five years of sexual assaults on campuses across the country (Sawa &Ward, 2015). The CBC found that from 2009 to 2014, more than 700 sexual assaults were reported to Canadian universities and colleges. While Toronto's Ryerson University (with nearly 24,000 students) had more reports of sexual assault than any of the 87 institutions contacted, small Acadia University in Wolfville, Nova Scotia, had the highest rate of sexual assault—when adjusted for student population. Clearly, there could have been problems with the CBC's methodology (most noteworthy is the voluntary nature of the institutions' inclusion in the sample), but at least it made efforts in the right direction.

In autumn 2014, the University of Ottawa was in the spotlight as the first university in Canada to conduct a survey of its students on their experiences of harassment (UofO, 2015) The survey revealed that 44% of female students experienced some form of sexual violence or unwanted sexual touching. More than 52% of women students found themselves harassed or threatened because of what they posted online. Yet the *CBC News* investigation found that over five years, only ten students reported an assault at the University of Ottawa (Sawa & Ward, 2015). The discrepancy is explained, at least in part, by virtue of the underreporting of sexual violence: less than 10% of sexual assaults are reported (Brennan & Taylor-Butts, 2008; Sinha, 2013).

For years, men (and women) equivocated about what to call sexual violence against women—spoken, threatened, or executed. Rape was not classified as "culture." Rape was an individual action such as an assault, an attack, sexual violence. It was a result of male aggression. Elsewhere in this book there are other definitions of rape culture, but this chapter defines it in 16 succinct words: "It is a complex of beliefs that encourages male sexual aggression and supports violence against women" (Buchwald, Fletcher, & Roth, 2005, p. xi).

Melissa McEwan, a feminist blogger on the site Shakesville, posted "Rape Culture 101" (2009). She lists many well-worn notions that our society puts forward to excuse sexual assault, including the premise that "boys will be boys," a sort of "jocular apologia" for rapists; that only certain people rape; that only certain people get raped (one in six women will be sexually assaulted in their lifetimes); and that rape may be viewed as a compliment. In other words, a man could rape a woman if she was sufficiently attractive. She also sums up the lengths women must go to in order to prevent being victimized by men. The list strikes home to women on or off campus:

> Rape culture is not even talking about the reality that many women are sexually assaulted multiple times in their lives. Rape culture is the way in which the constant threat of sexual assault affects women's daily movements. Rape culture is telling girls and women to be careful about what you wear, how you wear it, how you carry yourself, where you walk, when you walk there, with whom you walk, whom you trust, what you do, where you do it, with whom you do it, what you drink, how much you drink, whether you make eye contact, if you're alone, if you're with a stranger, if you're in a group, if you're in a group of strangers, if it's dark, if the area is unfamiliar, if you're carrying something, how you carry it, what kind of shoes you're wearing in case you have to run, what kind of purse you carry … to get a roommate, to take self-defense, to always be alert, always pay attention, always watch your back always be aware of your surroundings and never let your guard down for a moment lest you be sexually assaulted and if you are and didn't follow all the rules *it's your fault.* (McEwan, 2009, para. 10)

Despite this daunting task list, many women still feel they must adhere to it—or feel guilty and responsible for letting down their guard. The strategy for women who want to be safe is to always be aware, always be on their toes, never trust a man, and never take chances. This is the cautious, individual response to rape culture. Is there something wrong with being cautious? No, of course not. But every time a woman has to be cautious to be safe, it underscores men's privilege. Men rarely have to exercise caution in their daily activities.

A new study of more than 900 first-year female students at three Canadian universities shows that when the young women receive training in avoiding sexually compromising situations and resisting sexual attacks, their risk of rape decreases dramatically (Senn et al., 2015). A control group of half the participants in the study received a 12-hour training session in which they learned to refuse offers of a car ride home after drinking and to slap away a man's hand when groped in a bar. The other half who did not take the training received only the standard brochures that warn of sexual assault. At the end of the year, there were 23 rapes in the group that received the training and 42 in the one that received the brochures.

Though some have praised the training for demonstrating that young women do not have to be "helpless and vulnerable" ("Sexual-Assault Prevention," 2015), one wonders where men's responsibilities lie. As the quotation by McEwan (2009) demonstrates, women have been trained to be full of self-doubt and polite when dealing with potential attackers. Building women's self-esteem is always a useful first step. But women are fighting a systemic battle, in which institutions such as universities systemically deny that rape and sexual attacks go on, and frequently excuse men on campus who do it (Krakauer, 2015).

Terrence Crowley, who was trained in a U.S. social movement called Men Stopping Violence, wrote about his personal responsibility in stopping rape (Crowley, 2011). He believed his master's degree in psychology trained him to be sympathetic and useful in helping women. But what he still had to learn was different. The training he received showed him he had to be accountable and answerable to women, something he had never thought about before. If he denied or brushed over his male privilege, Crowley understood he was helping to keep rape culture in place. As he explains, "as a man, I accrue privilege simply by remaining silent, accepting this legacy, and saying nothing about its cost in terms of women's lives" (Crowley, 2011).

What is the institutional strategy to combat rape culture? It is not usually a legal strategy—or else a large number of male university students (plus some male faculty members) would be routinely arrested. It is not a policy- or program-based strategy, because of the more than 100 universities across Canada, fewer than 10 have sexual assault policies (Browne, 2014). Where there are policies on paper, do those policies effectively shut down rape culture? There does not seem to be evidence of that. Then what is it that perpetuates rape culture on campus—how can it be, when women are more than half of undergraduate and master's students, when women account for 41.5% of university professors (Canadian Association of University Teachers, 2015)? Clearly, the answer is located in a very different place, as the historical tour in the next section demonstrates.

HISTORICAL DIMENSIONS OF MISOGYNY IN MALE-DOMINATED DISCIPLINES

On the wall in my office is a copy of a painting of Lady Godiva, by the British pre-Raphaelite artist John Collier. Painted at the end of the 1800s, the picture depicts a beautiful, dark-haired young woman riding on a white horse through a street in medieval Coventry, England, in approximately AD 1050. Legend has it that the peasants on the Earl of Mercia's estates near Coventry could no longer afford to pay the high taxes demanded by Lord Leofric (Coe, 2003). The peasants asked Godiva, Leofric's wife, to intercede. The lord agreed to lower the taxes on the condition that Godiva ride naked through the busy town marketplace. She did—the painting shows her in profile, her long hair covering all but her legs.

Fast-forward 900 years to the mid-20th century. In the 1980s, women students at many Canadian university campuses with engineering schools witnessed the Lady Godiva ride. For example, at the University of Saskatchewan, engineering students paraded a half-clothed woman on horseback around the centre of the campus (Drolet, 2011; University of Saskatchewan, n.d.). At the University of British Columbia, up to 1990, a naked woman cloaked in an academic robe sat on a horse that was led through the campus—to howls of engineering students (Banham, 1981).

On December 6, 1989, 14 women engineering students were massacred at l'École Polytechnique in Montreal. Twenty-five-year-old, unemployed Marc Lépine gunned down the women before taking his own life. A short time later, police discovered a letter from Lépine stating he "hated feminists" (Diebel, 2014). Lépine had also kept an "annex," a written list of 19 "radical feminists" (his words) whom he planned to kill. The list included names of women journalists, politicians, and even a police officer. In his suicide note, Lépine wrote that he wanted to "send the feminists who have always ruined my life to their maker" (Eglin & Hester, 1999, p. 256).

Across Canada the night of the massacre in Montreal, thousands of women (and some men) honoured the murdered women by protesting violence against women. I attended a candlelight vigil at the University of Saskatchewan. Despite Lépine's suicide note, the majority of journalists and politicians insisted the killer was simply mentally ill (Eglin & Hester, 1999, p. 258; Grey, 2011).

February 1990, barely two months later, engineering week was celebrated at universities across Canada. CBC-TV's national news program *Sunday Report* (Webb, 1990) produced a three-minute news item about the Godiva ride, in the wake of the Montreal Massacre. Reporter Karen Webb (1990) conceded that because 3% of professional engineers were women, and only 10% of engineering students were female, sexism might play a role in the Godiva ride.

Webb interviewed the University of British Columbia's engineering student council president, who wanted to maintain the tradition of the Godiva ride on campus. He lamented the loss of a school ritual and good fun, if the ride were to be cancelled. At the University of Saskatchewan, Webb interviewed one male engineering student who said nothing needed to change as the Godiva ride would die out eventually.

The engineering students interviewed did not want to link the Godiva ride to the Montreal Massacre. Journalist Karen Webb was, like many of her male colleagues, ambivalent about what drove Lépine (Grey, 2014). However, Webb (1990) ended her TV report by suggesting that he was less than sane: "Many engineering students say that they resent being put under a microscope just because a madman chose women in their faculty as his targets."

While many in the mainstream media called Lépine a madman (but interestingly, never a terrorist, as they might have done today), Canadian feminists saw that something more sinister and more systemic had happened (Page, 2014).

Leading Quebec journalist Francine Pelletier, whose name appeared on Lépine's "annex" of feminists, claimed that the massacre was a political act (Pelletier, 2014). According to her, it was not simply about women but rather about women who were threatening men's power by entering male professions: "If he had wanted to target women, he would have gone to a nursing school. He was targeting women who had the audacity to want to do a man's job" (quoted in Rebick, 2009, para. 6; see also Alam, 2014).

The registrar at l'École Polytechnique confirmed this years later when asked why Marc Lépine had never been admitted to the school, despite having applied twice: "I was surprised by the way he spoke about women, about how they were taking over the job market. He thought there was something wrong with that" (Gagné & Lépine, 2008, p. 171).

Sea change?

It could be said that the Montreal Massacre ended the Godiva rides. In the 1990s, across Canada, engineering school students returned to doing other practical jokes, such as dangling Volkswagen Beetle cars from the Golden Gate Bridge (Rosenfeld, 2014). At the same time, more women started to enter professions such as law, pharmacy, and medicine (Canadian Press, 2013b; Turcotte, 2013). The numbers of women entering engineering school edged up, though they fared less well than at other professional schools. Recent Canadian statistics collected by Engineers Canada (2013, p. 22) reveal that women are fewer than 18% of total undergraduate engineering school enrolments, with a similar percentage in Nova Scotia universities. That number has not increased appreciably in 20 years (Presse, 2014).

In the 1990s, at the same time that more women started to enter the professional schools such as law, medicine, and dentistry, they also entered university business schools (Canadian Press, 2013b). Women became a prime focus for recruitment (Gellman, 2015; Moneo, 2014). Suddenly, enrolment at business schools boomed. It started with the post-graduate master of business administration (MBA) degree designed for students who wanted "specialized training in the functions of business" (Mintzberg, 2004, p. 5). By 2010 women were at least half of all business school students at Canadian universities, and just about half of students in MBA and business school Ph.D. programs (AUCC, 2011). But, is an increased number of women enough to affect rape culture? The recent events at SMU suggest not, as discussed in the next section.

SEXISM AT SAINT MARY'S UNIVERSITY

Sexism and misogyny at SMU predates the rape chant scandal. At the end of 2004, 24-year-old commerce student Paul Pedersen, as part of an entrepreneurship class assignment, published the 2005 Halifax University Girls Calendar (Pedersen, 2005). The calendar featured SMU women students, some in provocative poses and others in bikinis or sexy outfits. For example, Ms. February was Jackie, a third-year student dressed in a tight purple sweater and high heels who suggestively pulled down the edge of her white stretchy underpants in her photo. Pedersen sold nearly 500 copies of the calendar in the last few days of classes before the Christmas break (Gillis, 2005). He proudly admitted that he got an A on the assignment because he had started with $10 from his own pocket (Ozano, 2005) and made close to $4000 (Gillis, 2004; Power, 2005).

Sally Whitman, in a front-page article about the calendar in the SMU student newspaper *The Journal*, wrote,

> Has there been no consideration by the faculty and administration as to what this calendar suggests to the men and women attending this school? Or what it suggests to those looking to come here? ... It suggests to me that women, even though making up roughly half of the university students these days, are not given the respect and equality of citizenship that they have fought so long for. (2004)

Due to complaints from some members of the faculty, students, and the SMU Women's Centre, Pedersen wasn't allowed to sell the calendar on campus in the new term starting January, which prompted his response, "The main problem with university is a lot of times a lot of the stuff that's taught isn't really practical. With something like this, the good thing about it was everyone involved got a taste of doing something that you can't learn in a classroom"

(Gillis, 2005). Pedersen agreed to change the calendar name from The Girls of Saint Mary's to the Halifax University Girls Calendar, so as not to refer to SMU directly (Gillis, 2004).

Fast-forward eight years to 2012: walking across the quadrangle at SMU, on a cheery September morning in the first week of school, I noticed two women students standing on a picnic table dancing. The first thing I saw was their short skirts, and then I saw their shin pads and sneakers. A gaggle of other young women stood watching, all similarly dressed. As I got closer, I heard the two dancing on the table shout out, "Fuck you!" to anyone within earshot.

It was a busy day, with students rushing by carrying teetering piles of textbooks and overstuffed backpacks. A daycare teacher shepherded six pre-schoolers, clinging to a skipping rope so as not to get lost, past the chanters. The "fuck you" became more rhythmic and louder.

When I reached the picnic table, I stopped. "What are you doing?" I must have sounded angry. Suddenly a white male student appeared. "We're not doing anything wrong," he told me. "We have a right to do this." "Who are you?" I asked. One woman answered, "This is the initiation for the women's soccer." The young man claimed he was the assistant coach of the SMU women's soccer team. He told me it was the "girls' right" to participate and it was "none of my business." Several of the young women loudly insisted they "wanted" to do this.

I told the two to get down from the table; it was dangerous. I also said hazing was not allowed. "This isn't hazing," said the young man aggressively. "Initiation is not hazing. We can do this." The two women stopped chanting as they watched me go into the Loyola building, but as the door closed after me, I heard them start the drill again. It shocked me that a male student was organizing it; it surprised me that the women went along. I sent an email of complaint to the director of athletics, an email to the person in charge of student services, and an email to the university's conflict resolution officer. I heard that a couple of other faculty members and one person from the administration had complained too.

A few days later I got an email from the woman assistant coach of the women's soccer team. She wanted to meet with me at my office to try to explain what had happened. The coach was an attractive fourth-year political science student. She apologized and said she didn't mean for me or any other faculty person to see the initiation ritual—it was nothing more, she stressed. The young woman said she came to see me merely to deliver an apology for "any offence caused." Within three minutes she had left my office. A day or two later I received a generic "I'm sorry" email from her on behalf of the team. The perfunctory, lacklustre response by those receiving my complaint sowed the seeds of my button campaign, which I describe later in the chapter.

Frosh week 2013

At least one SMU student took a cellphone video of first-year orientation activities showing students and their student leaders singing and clapping a spirited chant condoning rape and nonconsensual sex. The video was uploaded to social media and went viral ("Sexist Frosh Chant," 2013; Sullivan, 2013).

Also at the orientation, hundreds of students chanted and sang words such as "No means yes, and yes means anal" (Lostracco, Ward, & Colbourne, 2014). Some thought this event was harmless "lad culture." Others saw it as a sign of a rape culture at the university, a culture fanned by the goings-on at fraternity or sports team house parties where it was usual to have drinking and sex. The media reported that hundreds of first-year students and the 80-plus frosh leaders, recruited and trained by the Saint Mary's University Students' Association (SMUSA), were shouting the offensive words (Bousquet, 2013; Mann, 2013).

These chants have been used across Canada on many campuses (Sullivan, 2013). However, chanting about the "benefits" of rape and nonconsensual sex at this time seemed rawer for people, especially in Halifax. This is because only six months before, 17-year-old Rehtaeh Parsons had taken her own life after a naked and sexually exploitative photo of her appeared on the Internet (Kingston, 2015). The photo showed one youth appearing to have intercourse with an underage, very drunk Parsons at a party. On a phone-in radio program in the aftermath of Parsons' death, a caller said, "It's not rape if she's asleep (or drunk)." The issue about whether or not Parsons had consented to the photo being taken in the first place remain unanswered. Clearly, she never expected it to be posted publicly. Still, the family and the broader community have been left with a damning photo and the tragic and senseless death of a child.

This was also the summer of the blockbuster YouTube video of Robin Thicke performing "Blurred Lines," a hit tune that emphasizes nonconsensual sex. Some DJs called it "the hottest song of the summer" (Trust, 2013). Feminists in Halifax made their own parody of the song, "Ask First," by inventing new lyrics about consensual sex being sexy (Burnet & Trace, n.d.; Grant, 2013). Consent became a serious topic.

During classes that fall, female students sat quietly or teared up when I raised the issue of the rape chant in class. Excuses from both sexes came quickly: "They didn't know what they were chanting," "They said it to be part of a group and to have a little fun," "It's what happens when there is too much to drink." The vice-president academic and research at SMU warned some faculty members not to raise the situation in class because it could inspire bullying and harassment:

> My office has been receiving reports of harassment and bullying behaviour
> directed against students alleged to have been involved in the chant incident

that occurred during Orientation Week. Some of these reports refer to harassment and bullying from other students, *but have included reference to unnamed faculty members* at Saint Mary's University. (D. Gauthier, personal communication, September 10, 2013, author's emphasis)

The media had a field day. The local papers and the national media drew attention to SMU and other campuses where the rape chants happened ("UBC Promises," 2013). Saint Mary's decided to take action, though predictably, control of the message rested with SMU's president.

The SMU President's Council and SMUSA

In September 2013, just after the news came out about the rape chant, SMU president J. Colin Dodds established the independent President's Council, which was "charged to provide recommendations to the President to foster a cultural change that prevents sexualized violence, and inspires respectful behaviour and a safe learning environment within the Saint Mary's Community" (President's Council, 2013, p.16). He named six faculty, administrative, and community people, plus four students, to the committee. Its chair was Wayne MacKay, a professor at the Schulich School of Law at Dalhousie University and former director of the Nova Scotia Human Rights Commission (Schulich School of Law, n.d.). In the SMU President Council's report, *Promoting a Culture of Safety, Respect and Consent at Saint Mary's University and Beyond*, the council made 20 recommendations, which were thoughtful attempts to change the culture at the university (President's Council, 2013).

Recommendations included increasing students' understanding of consent, promoting a culture of equity on campus, and gathering data to shed light on sexual assault and other issues (President's Council, 2013). At the same time, the council acknowledged the most difficult task for them was to try to change the culture and addressed two major pressures. The first was the problem of excessive student drinking. The report noted that the "vast majority of sexual assault cases involve alcohol," and further that women, who are more "vulnerable to … alcohol" than men, face greater danger of sexual assault when drinking excessively (President's Council, 2013, p. 22). Second, there was the problem of varsity sports teams, which encourage "pro-sexual violence … and a culture that promotes, or at least does not discourage, sexualized violence" (President's Council, 2013, pp. 35–36). In terms of male varsity sports teams, the report cites three factors that establish a "'rape-supportive culture' [including] sex segregation, tolerance for violence and male dominance" (President's Council, 2013, p. 35).

The SMU President's Council report was followed by the appointment of an "Action Team" tasked to implement the recommendations. In December

2014, the *Update from the President's Council Action Team* (President's Council Action Team, 2014) revealed which tasks, or recommendations, had been
completed. These included revising SMU's sexual assault policy, developing
a university-wide code of conduct, gathering data on the problem of sexual
assaults on campus, and reclaiming and redesigning orientation week, now
renamed welcome week (President's Council Action Team, 2014, p. 5).

Orientation week, which used to be organized by SMUSA, was now taken
over by the SMU administration (J. Patriquin, personal communication,
March 31, 2015). This was a slap in the face to SMUSA. As James Patriquin,
former SMUSA president (2014–2015) notes, the biggest change he saw had to
do with the newly titled welcome week: it was "as if someone's parents were trying to plan an event. SMUSA was diminished, we had two seats on a committee
of 30 people" (J. Patriquin, personal communication, March 31, 2015). SMUSA
had also taken steps to change the culture on campus. Patriquin recalls,

> Right after the chant we had a society expo,[1] and people were afraid to stand
> with SMUSA shirts though some students were supportive. I had profs [all
> men] come up and say I was disgusting, that I should resign, sharp criticisms
> on social media, death threats—we were disgusting. It was unfortunate.
> (J. Patriquin, personal communication, March 31, 2015)

Patriquin maintains that SMUSA did not get the recognition it deserved for
a series of initiatives to change the culture at SMU in the wake of the rape
chant debacle. Patriquin says that SMUSA has appointed its first student
equity officer,[2] who campaigns for Indigenous students and hosts workshops
with Mi'kmaq elders. In addition, SMUSA has provided bystander training[3]
to more than 200 students, including varsity athletes, the athletic councils,
and the student bar's bouncers, as recommended by the President's Council
report. SMUSA also commissioned two reports on student safety, as well as
a campaign called More than Yes, which promotes a better understanding of
consent (J. Patriquin, personal communication, March 31, 2015).

By January 2014, the buzz had died down. In the third week of January,
news broke on UNews.ca, a website staffed by senior students in the journal-
ism program at the University of King's College in Halifax (Lostracco et al.,
2014). Members of the SMU Huskies football team were tweeting messages
that were hateful and misogynist, such as "bitch get on yo knees," "See a girl
who's feeling down? Feel her up," and "No means yes and yes means anal"
(Lostracco et al., 2014).

The director of athletics and recreation at SMU, David Murphy, insisted he
couldn't be responsible for what the team members did in their spare time; he
was not monitoring their tweets. He admitted, "I'm falling behind in my due

diligence and my ability to teach these kids. Maybe that's a breakdown in the communication. You have an older person who is not savvy to all that … you have to be very, very careful with social media" ("Saint Mary's Athletes," 2014).

Up to ten members of the team were suspended, and Murphy resigned early from his contract with the university ("David Murphy Steps Down," 2014). The footballers were suspended from practice, but it was the dead of winter and there were no games scheduled for months. Also, the suspensions did not affect the students' academic studies. Many in the Halifax university community found this too little, too late, especially in comparison to what had happened to the women's hockey team at Dalhousie University a year before.

In December 2012, Dalhousie University president Tom Traves suspended most of the members of the Dalhousie women's hockey team, which meant they forfeited playing for a year (Canadian Press, 2013a). This was after the media reported on a sexist and anti-lesbian hazing ritual (Taber, 2013) and "cases of intimidation, excessive drinking, personal disrespect, humiliation—in short, bullying" (Dhillon, 2013, para. 3). In light of the action taken by Dalhousie, a term's suspension for the SMU team did not seem too serious.

The button campaign

The football tweets at SMU in February 2014 were a significant catalyst for the step I took towards changing the culture at the university. I borrowed a button-making machine and began to make buttons that read, "I'm at SMU, and I'm against Sexism." Another one said, "I'm at SMU, and I'm against Racism," and the third one read, "I'm at SMU and I'm against Homophobia." That night my husband (also a professor at SMU) and I made about 100 buttons.

I soon realized it would take hours to churn out the numbers we needed. I contracted making the buttons to a novelty firm, which quickly couriered 500 buttons. Meanwhile, my husband and I were giving out what we had made in all the high-student-traffic areas on campus. Most young people cheerily took them and some politely declined; others were not so polite. Some professors and support staff began to wear them. Then people off campus started to wear them.

Encouraged, I asked my union, the SMU Faculty Union (SMUFU), if they would help pay for the next order. In an email, they flatly refused.

> The Union Executive has considered your request for financial support for the button campaign you initiated recently. We appreciate the fact that you are making an effort to make a difference on our campus. However, we have decided not to participate in this particular campaign. We are not opposed to members wearing your buttons should they so wish, but we would like to tackle the issue by communicating our concerns to the Administration

Positively pinning. Photo by Jeff Harper/Metro. Reproduced with permission from Metro and Torstar Corporation

> directly. We appreciate your having contacted us, and we invite you to keep the Union in mind with future ideas/concerns. (M. Lamoureux, private communication, February 12, 2014)

Marc Lamoureux, SMUFU president, writing on behalf of the executive, had the gall to tell me they would not *oppose* members wearing the button, *if they so chose!*[4] I was furious! The issue of sexual violence is so powerful, so brutal, and so common, yet it lies so deeply buried beneath the surface—especially for men with power. The executive of the union was almost all male, but even the women on the executive went along with the decision, which was never brought to a general membership meeting. The union clearly revelled in its role as supporter of the status quo—essentially, supporter of the university administration. During this whole time I heard not a word, and not one media outlet revealed any bumps in the friendly bond the administration had either with my union or with the students' association (as you'll see below). It was clear the dominant culture at university spoke with one voice. In fact, my union commanded so little respect that not one member of the union's executive sat on the SMU President's Council, nor on the Action Team.

SMUSA, the students' association, was no better. After avoiding meetings with me, two members of the council executive looked at the buttons and complained that the yellow background and black type were Dalhousie University colours. They told me if I made buttons in SMU colours, they would *consider* helping to pay for them. I ordered another thousand in white letters with a maroon background—the SMU colours. I squeezed all the words onto one button: "I'm at SMU & I'm against Racism, Sexism & Homophobia." Still, SMUSA would have nothing to do with the buttons. I was more disappointed with the students' association than the faculty union, probably because I had hope that younger people would be more sensitive to sexual violence and more horrified by the rape chant than university profs who were older and less involved. But SMUSA was also infected with the culture at SMU—the association's then-president, Jared Perry, was a business school student.

In the wider community, when young people popped up around Halifax wearing the buttons, the media contacted me. I appeared with the buttons on the front page of the free newspaper *Metro*, and in a story without a photo, in *The Chronicle Herald* (Davenport, 2014; Jeffrey, 2014b).

The campaign was financially supported by the Nova Scotia Union of Public Employees (NSUPE), which represented 60 custodians and security people at Saint Mary's—the lowest-paid workers on campus—and by the Nova Scotia Public Interest Group (NSPIRG).[5] In the next couple of weeks, we distributed close to 1000 buttons. But, stubbornly, only a handful of students and even fewer fellow professors volunteered to help. I wondered why that was.

THE CULTURE AT SAINT MARY'S UNIVERSITY

The culture at SMU is not much different from that of other universities in the Maritimes, or even across Canada. It started as a Catholic boys' high school, and in 1970 became a fully co-ed university. With about 8000 students, SMU is the second-largest university in Nova Scotia ("About Saint Mary's," 2013, para. 7). I believe three phenomena have converged at Saint Mary's to open the door to sexism and misogyny: the pre-eminence of the business school, the sports culture, and the drinking culture.

Business school culture

Today the Sobey School of Business at SMU is the largest business school east of Montreal (Sobey School of Business, 2015c) with 75 professors (Sobey School of Business, 2015b) and 3500 students (Sobey School of Business, 2015a). The problem with most business schools and business school education is that they tend to focus on teaching students how to make profits and prop up the capitalist system. Lately, many business schools have been promoting an entrepreneurial culture (Baluja, 2014; Cid, 2013). In other words, the "business of business is business" (Marsden, 2002; Wladawsky-Berger, 2013). In business school there is little emphasis on the common good, group solutions, or questioning authority. Rather, thousands of business school students graduate from programs that are geared toward individual solutions and greediness (Marsden, 2002; Walker, 2009). "A menace to society," is what renowned Canadian business studies professor Henry Mintzberg calls business school–trained MBAs (Gutterplan, 2012, para. 4).

Business school education can contribute to a competitive and winner-take-all type of thinking, or the "pedagogy of the privileged" (Schumpeter, 2009). Privilege is often accorded to men in the dominant ethnic group (McIntosh, 2013)—but what about women? Women held only 15.9% of seats on corporate boards in Canada in 2013, which was 1.5% more than in 2011 (Catalyst Inc., 2013). In 2013, only 40% of boards had any women on them at all. Australia also has a dearth of women on boards; however, an industry group says chief executives "should be challenged for explanations and even have their pay cut if they fail to appoint women to senior positions" (Milman, 2013). But Canadian business, unlike its Australian counterpart, has taken little initiative. According to the Government of Canada's Advisory Council for Promoting Women on Boards (2014), the problem is not "supply side" but rather "demand side" in that there are plenty of women qualified and capable of being on boards or heading Crown corporations, but few are selected. Of course, nowhere in this report is there a mention of target figures or quotas, which are the first steps in changing the situation. The fact that women are still under-represented on boards and in public appointments demonstrates that business education's message to women students is, you probably won't make it to the top. Women are second rate.

Sports culture

SMU is known for its football team, the Huskies. Over a period of 20 years, the Huskies have won the Vanier Cup[6] twice (Canadian Interuniversity Sport, 2014). Football and other team sports are used as a major tool for student recruitment at SMU. However, the SMU President's Council report (2013) notes that widespread academic research suggests that male varsity team membership "may be consistent with pro-sexual violence attitudes and a culture that promotes, or at least does not discourage, sexualized violence" (p. 35). The report cites anthropologist Peggy Reeves-Sanday, who says that key elements of rape culture are "sex segregation, tolerance for violence and male dominance" (p. 35). A recent book, *Missoula*, by Jon Krakauer (2015) examines this issue in depth, as does the next chapter in this collection. The established link between varsity sport and sexual violence is concerning because SMU has 13 varsity teams.

Drinking culture

Another point in the triangle at SMU is the students' tendency to abuse alcohol. Some would say that SMU has a drinking culture. Though not markedly different in this respect from other universities, drinking is allowed in the student residence rooms and at the Gorsebrook, the student bar on campus. The Gorsebrook is open most days from 11 a.m. until well after midnight. Saint Patrick's Day is a major celebration at SMU—and it is more or less accepted that many students take the day off classes, and take the next day to sober up. Alcohol is served and freely available at many functions and events.

The SMU President's Council report (2013) notes that "the vast majority of sexual assault cases involve alcohol" (p. 21). One estimate is that almost 90% of Canadian university students drink alcohol, while 32% report drinking heavily at least once a month; in Nova Scotia, 51% report drinking heavily at least once a month (Tamburri, 2012). Underage drinking is common: 77% of Canadians over age 15 report drinking in the last year and heavy drinking is common among 20-to-24-year-olds (President's Council, 2013, p. 21). Binge drinking by students is also part of their culture. Some young people now mix alcohol with heavily caffeinated energy drinks, which can lead to more "negative alcohol related consequences" (President's Council, 2013, p. 22) than using alcohol alone. As researchers Warkentin and Gidycz (2007) note, "when combined, the use of alcohol and/or drugs not only increases the likelihood of a sexual assault occurring but also works to decrease the perpetrator's feelings of responsibility" (pp. 830–831).

Still, excessive drinking remains a persistent problem, in part because policing is difficult. To combat this, SMUSA has committed to hosting more events with limited access to alcohol and even alcohol-free events (President's Council, 2013, p. 12). The President's Action Team has established an Alcohol Advisory Committee, which came out with an update from the President's Action Team in mid-2016 (President's Council Action Team, 2016, p. 9).

CONCLUSION

The incidents at SMU in September 2013 arose from a culture that seeks to privilege power that accompanies maleness over everything else. While the SMU President's Council, established in the wake of the incidents, was investigating how to change the culture at SMU, I started a button campaign to try to change the culture with buttons that read, "I'm at Saint Mary's University and I'm against Racism, Sexism and Homophobia." The buttons captured the imagination of hundreds of students and the attention of the local media. However, SMUSA and my union, SMUFU, refused to support the initiative. Both groups insisted on waiting for the university to take action before doing anything.

At SMU there is a new level of awareness of the issue of sexual violence on campus. However, despite bystander training, lectures, and in-service courses and training, what has changed? And how can we tell? A lot of change seems to be driven by the media. Each time there is a new story, the administration sits up and takes some action. More action is driven by numbers; currently, SMU, like most Maritime universities, is facing a serious drop in enrolment over the coming years (Tamburri, 2014). This has pushed the universities to recruit more international students and initiate more graduate programs. At the Sobey School of Business, 50% of students are international students. We might hope that the drinking and the sports culture are not so attractive to the international students as they are to the home students.

Issues such as gender, race, and misogyny are endemic to all universities in Canada. Being organized and being vigilant are two ways forward.

NOTES

1   Society expo is an open forum in which campus clubs can recruit student members.
2   SMU's administration structure makes the director of human resources also wear the hat of equity officer.
3   "Bystander education programs teach potential witnesses safe and positive ways that they can act to prevent or intervene when there is a risk for sexual violence. This approach gives community members specific roles that they can use in preventing sexual violence" (New York State Dept. of Health, 2013, p. 3).
4   Full disclosure: I have been active in the union and a member of the executive for about ten years. I even served as union president from 2011 to 2012.
5   "The Nova Scotia Public Interest Research Group, or NSPIRG, ... is a non-profit, non-partisan and non-governmental organization. Our mandate is to link research with action for social and environmental within an anti-oppressive framework" (NSPIRG, n.d.).
6   The Vanier Cup is the top award for Canadian inter-university football; see https://en.wikipedia.org/wiki/Vanier_Cup.

REFERENCES

About Saint Mary's: History. (2013). Retrieved from http://www.smu.ca/about/history.html

Alam, T. (2014, December 6). Misogyny kills: Remember the Montreal Massacre. NATO Association of Canada. Retrieved from http://natoassociation.ca/misogyny-kills-remember-the-montreal-massacre/

Association of Universities and Colleges of Canada. (2011). *Trends in Higher Education: Vol. 1. Enrolment.* Ottawa, ON: Author.

Backhouse, C., McRae, D., & Iyer, N. (2015). *Report of the Task Force on Misogyny, Sexism, and Homophobia in Dalhousie University Faculty of Dentistry.* Retrieved

from Dalhousie University: https://www.dal.ca/content/dam/dalhousie/pdf /
cultureofrespect/DalhousieDentistry-TaskForceReport-June2015.pdf

Baluja, T. (2014, March 13). MBA entrepreneurs: Dragon's Den enthusiasts
or realists? *Globe and Mail.* Retrieved from http://www.theglobeandmail
.com/report-on-business/careers/business-education/mba-entrepreneurs
-dragons-den-enthusiasts-or-realists/article17451242/

Banham, J. *Godiva ride* [Photograph]. (1981). UBC Archives Photograph Collection,
Vancouver, BC. Retrieved from http://digitalcollections.library.ubc.ca/cdm/
search/collection/arphotos/searchterm/Godiva

Barness, S. (2014, September 6). Columbia University student will drag her mattress around campus until her rapist is gone. *Huffington Post.* Retrieved from
http://www.huffingtonpost.com/2014/09/03/emma-sulkowicz-mattress-rape
-columbia-university_n_5755612.html

Bates, L. (2014, October 10). 10 things female students shouldn't have
to go through at university. *The Guardian.* Retrieved from http://
www.theguardian.com/lifeandstyle/womens-blog/2014/oct/10/10-things
-female-students-face-university-misogyny-banter

Bennis, W. G., & O'Toole, J. (2005, May 1). How business schools lost their
way. *Harvard Business Review.* Retrieved from https://hbr.org/2005/05/
how-business-schools-lost-their-way

Boeringer, S. B. (1996, June). Influences of fraternity membership, athletics, and
male living arrangements on sexual aggression. *Violence Against Women, 2*(2),
134–147.

Bousquet, T. (2013, September 5). SMU's pro-rape chant: A teachable moment. *The
Coast.* Retrieved from http://www.thecoast.ca/RealityBites/archives/2013/09/05/
smus-pro-rape-chant-a-teachable-moment

Brennan, S., & Taylor-Butts, A. (2008). *Canadian Centre for Justice Statistics Profile
Series: Sexual assault in Canada 2004 and 2007.* Ottawa, ON: Statistics Canada.

Browne, R. (2014, October 30). Why don't Canadian universities want to talk about
sexual assault? *Maclean's.* Retrieved from http://www.macleans.ca/education/
unirankings/why-dont-canadian-universities-want-to-talk-about-sexual-assault/

Buchwald, E., Fletcher, P. R., & Roth, M. (2005). *Transforming a rape culture* (Rev. ed.).
Minneapolis, MN: Milkweed.

Burnet, J. M., & Kaleigh, T. (n.d.). *Ask first* [Video file]. Retrieved from https://vimeo
.com/70304632

Cabrera, A., & Bowen, D. (2005). Professionalizing global management for the twenty-
first century. *Journal of Management Development, 24*(9), 781–805.

Canadian Association of University Teachers. (2015). *CAUT almanac of post-secondary
education in Canada, 2014–2015.* Retrieved from http://almanac.caut.ca/#/en/
academic-staff

Canadian Federation of Students. (n.d.). *Sexual violence on campuses.* Retrieved from
http://cfsontario.ca/downloads/CFS_factsheet_antiviolence.pdf

Canadian Interuniversity Sport. (2014). Vanier Cup winners. Retrieved from http://
www.cfhof.ca/museum/canadian-interuniversity-sport/

Canadian Press. (2013a, January 16). Suspension of Dalhousie women's hockey
team stands after alleged hazing incident. *Globe and Mail.* Retrieved from
http://www.theglobeandmail.com/sports/hockey/suspension-of-dalhousie
-womens-hockey-team-stands-after-alleged-hazing-incident/article7428171/

Canadian Press. (2013b, June 26). Women in Canada embrace higher education: Statcan. *Maclean's*. Retrieved from http://www.macleans.ca/education/uniandcollege/women-in-canada-embrace-higher-education-statcan-survey/

Catalyst Inc. (n.d.). Catalyst Accord: Women on corporate boards in Canada. Call to action. Retrieved from http://www.catalyst.org/catalyst-accord-women-corporate-boards-canada

Chat transcript: Future of business school. (2009, May 29). *Bloomberg*. Retrieved from http://www.bloomberg.com/bschools/content/may2009/bs20090526_498100.htm

Cid, V. (2013, September 17). In defence of Sauder: Behind the business school stereotypes. *The Ubyssey*. Retrieved from http://ubyssey.ca/features/defense-sauder-stereotypes992/

Coe, C. (2003, July–August). Lady Godiva: The naked truth. *Harvard Business Magazine*. Retrieved from http://harvardmagazine.com/2003/07/lady-godiva-the-naked-tr.html

Crowley, T. (2011). The lie of entitlement. Retrieved from http://www.culturalbridges tojustice.org/resources/written/the-lie-of-entitlement

Dalhousie suspends 13 dentistry students from clinic amid Facebook scandal. (2015, January 5). *CBC News*. Retrieved from http://www.cbc.ca/news/canada/nova-scotia/dalhousie-suspends-13-dentistry-students-from-clinic-amid-facebook-scandal-1.2889635

Davenport, R. (2014, February 5). Anti-intolerance message pushing the right buttons at Saint Mary's University. *Metronews*.

David Murphy steps down as Saint Mary's AD early. (2014, March 28). *Chronicle Herald*. Retrieved from http://thechronicleherald.ca/sports/1196727-david-murphy-steps-down-as-saint-mary's-ad-early

Dhillon, S. (2013, January 3). Dalhousie women's hockey team forfeits season for hazing. *Globe and Mail*. Retrieved from http://www.theglobeandmail.com/sports/hockey/dalhousie-womens-hockey-team-forfeits-season-for-hazing/article6929809/

Diebel, L. (2014, December 6). Two women on Marc Lepine's death list speak out: Mass murderer Marc Lepine had a list of 19 women he wanted to kill. *Toronto Star*. Retrieved from http://www.thestar.com/news/insight/2014/12/06/two_women_on_marc_lpines_death_list_speak_out.html

Drolet, D. (2011, January 12). Campus traditions. *University Affairs*.

Eglin, P., & Hester, S. (1999). "You're all a bunch of feminists": Categorization and the politics of terror in the Montreal Massacre. *Human Studies, 22*(2/4), 253–272.

Engineers Canada. (2012). *Canadian engineers for tomorrow: Trends in engineering enrolment and degrees awarded 2008–2011*. Retrieved from http://www.engineers canada.ca/sites/default/files/w_report_enrolment_eng.pdf

Gagné, H., & Lépine, M. (2008). *Aftermath*. Toronto, ON: Viking Canada.

Gellman, L. (2015, May 6). Business schools are fighting to recruit top women. *Wall Street Journal*. Retrieved from http://www.wsj.com/articles/why-business-schools-are-fighting-over-top-women-1430957422

Gillis, J. (2004, November 26). Checking a date at Saint Mary's: 21 female SMU students pose for "Girls Calendar." *Chronicle Herald*, p. B1.

Gillis, J. (2005, January 6). SMU bans campus sales of pinup calendar. *Chronicle Herald*, p. B4.

Government of Canada's Advisory Council for Promoting Women on Boards. (2014). *Good for business: A plan to promote the participation of more women on Canadian boards*. Ottawa, ON: Status of Women Canada.

Grant, J. (2013, July 16). Ask first: Haligonians respond to Robin Thicke with sexy-but-consensual video of their own. *Halifax Media Co-op*. Retrieved from http://halifax .mediacoop.ca/video/ask-first-haligonians-respond-robin-thicke-sexy-co/18284

Grey, S. (2014, May 29). The motive is misogyny: The Montreal Massacre and the Santa Barbara shooting. *Georgia Strait*. Retrieved from http://www.straight.com/ news/86331/motive-misogyny-montreal-massacre-and-santa-barbara-shooting

Gutterplan, D. D. (2012, May 20). The anti-MBA. *New York Times*. Retrieved from http://www.nytimes.com/2012/05/21/world/europe/21iht-educlede21.html?_r=0

Jeffrey, D. (2014a, January 27). SMU to suspend football players after tweets of "hate, racism and sexism." *Chronicle Herald*.

Jeffrey, D. (2014b, February 7). SMU profs take aim at negative attitudes. *Chronicle Herald*, p. A10.

Kingston, A. (2015, April 15). Rehtaeh Parsons, Dalhousie and the wait for justice in Nova Scotia. *Maclean's*. Retrieved from http://www.macleans.ca/society/rehtaeh -parsons-the-dds-2015-scandal-and-the-wait-for-justice-in-nova-scotia/

Krakauer, J. (2015). *Missoula: Rape and the justice system in a college town*. New York, NY: Doubleday.

Lostracco, D., Ward, J., & Colbourne, K. (2014, January 27). SMU football team members' posts mock consent. *Unews.ca*. Retrieved from http://unews.ca/smu -football-team-members-posts-mock-consent

Mann, A. (2013, September 4). Halifax university under fire for sexist chant at frosh event. *Toronto Star*. Retrieved from http://www.thestar.com/news/ canada/2013/09/04/halifax_university_under_fire_for_sexist_chant_at_frosh _event.html

Marsden, C. (2002). The new corporate citizenship of big business: Part of the solution to sustainability? *Business and Society Review, 105*(1), 8–25.

McCray, K. L. (2014). Intercollegiate athletes and sexual violence: A review of literature and recommendations for future study. *Trauma, Violence, & Abuse, 1–6*.

McEwan, M. (2009, October 9). Rape culture 101 [Blog post]. Retrieved from http:// www.shakesville.com/2009/10/rape-culture-101.html

McIntosh, P. (2013). Unpacking the invisible knapsack. In M. L. Andersen & P. Hill Collins (Eds.), *Race, class, and gender* (pp. 74–78). Boston, MA: Cengage Learning.

Milman, O. (2013, November 6). Business Council: CEOs accountable for failure to promote women. *The Guardian*. Retrieved from http://www.theguardian.com/ world/2013/nov/06/business-council-women-on-boards

Mintzberg, H. (2004). *Managers not MBAs: A hard look at the soft practices of managing and management development*. San Francisco, CA: Berrett-Koehler.

Moneo, S. (2014, December 23). Seven business school deans reflect on 2014— and look ahead to 2015. *Globe and Mail*. Retrieved from http://www.the globeandmail.com/report-on-business/careers/business-education/seven -business-school-deans-reflect-on-2014/article22187143/

National Union of Students. (2013). *That's what she said: Women students' experiences of "lad culture" in higher education. Summary report*. Retrieved from http:// www.nus.org.uk/Global/Campaigns/That's%20what%20she%20said%20full%20 report%20Final%20web.pdf

Nova Scotia Public Interest Group. (n.d.). We speak out against oppression in all its forms. Retrieved from http://www.nspirg.org

Ozano, N. (2005, September 12). Calendar with "push the envelope." *Daily News.*

Page, S. (2014, December 6). How I sanitized the feminist outrage over the Montreal massacre. *Ottawa Citizen.* Retrieved from http://ottawacitizen.com/news/national/page-how-i-sanitized-the-feminist-outrage-over-the-montreal-massacre

Pedersen, P. (2005). Halifax university girls calendar 2005 [Calendar]. Halifax, NS.

Pelletier, F. (2014, December 5). What hasn't yet been said about the Polytechnique massacre. *Montreal Gazette.* Retrieved from http://montrealgazette.com/news/local-news/what-hasnt-yet-been-said-about-the-polytechnique-massacre

Power, B. (2005, September 13). It must be that time again: Campus calendar back for another round of criticism. *Chronicle Herald,* p. B3.

President's Council. (2013). *Promoting a culture of safety, respect and consent at Saint Mary's University and beyond: Report from the President's Council.* Retrieved from http://www.smu.ca/webfiles/PresidentsCouncilReport-2013.pdf

President's Council Action Team. (2014, December). An update from the President's Council Action Team. Retrieved from http://www.smu.ca/webfiles/ActionTeam Report-December.pdf

President's Council Action Team. (2016, June). An update from the President's Council Action Team. Retrieved from http://www.smu.ca/webfiles/ActionTeam Update-June2016.pdf

Presse, M. (2014, October 24–30). Gender gap in Dal Engineering unchanged for 20 years. *Dalhousie Gazette.* Retrieved from http://dalgazette.com/arts-culture/gender-gap-in-dal-engineering-unchanged-for-20-years/

Rebick, J. (2009, December 6). What was the impact of the Montreal Massacre? Remembering from Montreal at feminist gathering. *Rabble.* Retrieved from http://rabble.ca/blogs/bloggers/judes/2009/12/what-was-impact-montreal-massacre-remembering-montreal-feminist-gatheri

Rosenfeld, A. (2014, February 7). If you think the clock tower was impressive, check out what the engineers did in 2001 [Blog post]. Retrieved from http://ubyssey.ca/blog/engineers-san-francisco-car-001/

Saint Mary's athletes lock down social media accounts after sexist tweets. (2014, January 28). *CBC News.* Retrieved from http://www.cbc.ca/news/canada/nova-scotia/saint-mary-s-athletes-lock-down-social-media-accounts-after-sexist-tweets-1.2513962

Saint Mary's University unveils frosh week changes in wake of rape chant. (2014, August 27). *CBC News.* Retrieved from http://www.cbc.ca/news/canada/nova-scotia/saint-mary-s-university-unveils-frosh-week-changes-in-wake-of-rape-chant-1.2748017

Sawa, T., & Ward, L. (2015, February 6). Sex assault reporting on Canadian campuses worryingly low, says experts. *CBC News.* Retrieved from http://www.cbc.ca/m/touch/news/story/1.2948321

Schulich School of Law at Dalhousie University. (n.d.). A Wayne MacKay, CM, QC. Retrieved from http://www.dal.ca/faculty/law/faculty-staff/our-faculty/wayne-mackay.html

Schumpeter. (2009, September 24). The pedagogy of the privileged. *The Economist.* Retrieved from http://www.economist.com/node/14493183

Senn, C. Y., Eliasziw, M., Barata, P., Thurston, W. E., Newby-Clark, I., Radtke, L., & Hobden, K. L. (2015). Efficacy of a sexual assault resistance program for university women. *New England Journal of Medicine, 372*(24), 2326–2335. doi:10.1056/ NEJMsa1411131

Sexist Frosh Chant [Video file]. (2013, September 6). *Global News*. Retrieved from https://www.youtube.com/watch?v=cSkuLsiI3I0

Sexual-assault prevention program cut rape rate nearly in half. (2015, June 11). *CBC News*. Retrieved from http://www.cbc.ca/news/health/sexual-assault -prevention-program-cut-rape-rate-nearly-in-half-1.3109186

Sinha, M. (Ed.). (2013). Measuring violence against women: Statistical trends. *Juristat* (Statistics Canada Catalogue no. 85-002-X). Ottawa, ON: Minister of Industry.

Sobey School of Business. (2015a). Explore our programs. Retrieved from http://www .smu.ca/academics/sobey/academic-programs.html

Sobey School of Business. (2015b). Faculty and research. Retrieved from http://www .smu.ca/academics/sobey/sobey-faculty-and-research.html

Sobey School of Business. (2015c). Master of business administration, MBA. Retrieved from http://www.smu.ca/academics/sobey/sobey-mba.html

Staley, O. (2010, May 20). Goldman Harvard recruit pledges to do no harm, fights for oath. *Bloomberg Business*. Retrieved from http://www.bloomberg.com/apps/ news?pid=newsarchive&sid=a1lZrOzMxnMM

Stop Sexual Violence: A sexual violence bystander intervention toolkit [Brochure]. (n.d.). Retrieved from https://www.health.ny.gov/publications/2040.pdf

Sullivan, P. (2013, September 11). U is for underage, N is for no consent—SMU rape chant an embarrassment to higher education. *Metro Canada*.

Taber, J. (2013, March 1). Hazing probe left Dalhousie women's hockey players feeling bullied. *Globe and Mail*. Retrieved from http://www.theglobeandmail.com/news/ national/hazing-probe-left-dalhousie-womens-hockey-players-feeling-bullied/ article9237797/

Tam, C. (2013, October 22). UBC investigates chant encouraging rape of underage girls. *Global News*. Retrieved from http://globalnews.ca/news/825544/ubc -investigates-after-students-led-in-chant-encouraging-rape-of-underage-girls/

Tamburri, R. (2012, August 29). Heavy drinking a problem at most Canadian campuses: Report. *University Affairs*. Retrieved from http://www.universityaffairs.ca/news/ news-article/heavy-drinking-a-problem-at-most-canadian-campuses-report/

Tamburri, R. (2014, April 9). Atlantic universities try to boost enrolment amid a declining university-aged cohort. *University Affairs*. Retrieved from http://www .universityaffairs.ca/features/feature-article/crunch-time-in-atlantic-canada/

Tamburri, R., & Samson, N. (2014, October 20). Ending sexual violence on campus. *University Affairs*. Retrieved from http://www.universityaffairs.ca/features/ feature-article/ending-sexual-violence-campus/

Thicke, R. (n.d.). *Blurred lines* [Video file]. Retrieved from https://www.youtube.com/ watch?v=yyDUC1LUXSU

Thomson, A. (2014, January 28). SMU under another cloud of controversy over hateful tweets. *CTV News*. Retrieved from http://www.ctvnews.ca/canada/ smu-under-another-cloud-of-controversy-over-hateful-tweets-1.1659450

Trust, G. (2013, September 5). Robin Thicke's "Blurred Lines" is *Billboard*'s song of the summer. *Billboard*. Retrieved from http://www.billboard.com/articles/ news/5687036/robin-thickes-blurred-lines-is-billboards-song-of-the-summer

Turcotte, M. (2013). Women and education. In *Women in Canada: A gender-based statistical report* (Statistics Canada Catalogue no. 89-503-X). Ottawa, ON: Minister of Industry.

UBC promises "lasting change" following rape chant. (2013, September 18). *CBC News British Columbia*. Retrieved from http://www.cbc.ca/news/canada/british-columbia/ubc-promises-lasting-change-following-rape-chant-1.1859234

University of Ottawa. (2015). *Report of the Task Force on Respect and Equality: Ending sexual violence at the University of Ottawa*. Retrieved from https://www.uottawa.ca/president/sites/www.uottawa.ca.president/files/report-of-the-task-force-on-respect-and-equality.pdf

University of Saskatchewan, College of Engineering. (n.d.). History: Formative years. Retrieved from http://engineering.usask.ca/about-us/history.php

Walker, P. (2009, May 8). Who taught them greed is good? *The Guardian*. Retrieved from http://www.theguardian.com/business/2009/mar/08/credit-crunch-mbas

Warkentin, J. B., & Gidycz, C. A. (2007). The use and acceptance of sexually aggressive tactics in college men. *Journal of Interpersonal Violence, 22*, 829–850.

Webb, K. (1990, February 4). Students scrutinize Lady Godiva ride after Montreal Massacre. *Sunday Report* [Television series]. Retrieved from http://www.cbc.ca/archives/entry/students-scrutinize-lady-godiva-ride-after-montreal-massacre

Whitman, S. (2004, December 1). Halifax University Girls: A step back. *The Journal, 70*(12), 1.

Wladawsky-Berger, I. (2013). Reshaping business and capitalism for the 21st century. *Wall Street Journal*. Retrieved from http://blogs.wsj.com/cio/2013/10/11/reshaping-business-and-capitalism-for-the-21st-century/

Wong, J. (2014, January. 29). "They made a mistake. They feel really bad about it": SMU football players on offensive tweets. *Global News*. Retrieved from http://globalnews.ca/news/1110768/smu-to-suspend-football-players-following-offensive-tweets/

CHAPTER 6

VIOLENT BODIES IN CAMPUS CYBERSPACES

Andrea Quinlan

"The celebration of rape on the Internet is one of the most insidious instruments of violence against women." (Visano, 2010, p. 51)

In 2014, both Dalhousie University and the University of Ottawa were pushed into mainstream media's spotlight when news broke that male students on their campuses had been using Facebook to discuss sexually violent acts against their female classmates. In the wake of previous public outcry in 2013 over the sexually violent orientation chants at Saint Mary's University and the University of British Columbia, the Facebook groups at Dalhousie and the University of Ottawa further propelled the wave of public controversy and debate about rape culture and misogyny on Canadian university campuses. In mainstream media, some activists, scholars, and commentators argued that the male students' sexually violent remarks on Facebook reflected the pervasive rape culture on university campuses. Others claimed that both cases were merely examples of inappropriate comments made by immature male students. Although they disagreed on the significance of what was posted on Facebook, both groups framed the Facebook posts as *talk* about violence and bodies, and not as a form of bodily violence in its own right.

The public debates about these two Facebook groups raise some pressing questions about violence and the relationships between the online world and physical university campuses. While some commentators claimed that online spaces reflected the gendered relations that already existed on university campuses, others contended that they were largely unrelated to anything that occurred on physical campuses. The online world appeared in these debates as a space where sexual violence was talked about but not perpetrated. This chapter examines the Facebook groups involved in these incidents at Dalhousie University and the University of Ottawa to explore online forms of campus sexual violence. Through this analysis, I propose that what occurred on Facebook at these universities was not simply *talk* that reflected gendered, raced, and classed relations on campus. Rather, it was a form of sexual violence that was fundamentally embodied and had material consequences for those on university campuses.

With the increasing presence of Internet technologies in social life, criminologists and other social scientists have taken significant interest in technology-facilitated crime (Cornelius & Hermann, 2011; Jewkes, 2007; Jewkes & Yar, 2010; Wall, 2001, 2010). Online sexual violence, however, has remained largely unexplored, save for a few notable exceptions (Henry & Powell, 2015; Powell, 2009, 2010). In one recent article, Henry and Powell (2015) argue that gender hierarchies are reproduced online in what they call "technology-facilitated sexual violence (TFSV)" (p. 759). By challenging what they see as a false dualism between online and offline spaces, Henry and Powell suggest that TFSV causes distinct "embodied harms" (p. 758) that have yet to be adequately acknowledged and understood in scholarly literature and criminal law. Their work opens up important empirical and theoretical questions about the relations between bodies and online spaces, and how both the harms *and* perpetration of online sexual violence can be conceptualized as embodied. Through an empirical examination of the Facebook groups at Dalhousie and UofO, this chapter takes up these questions in a Canadian university campus context.

This chapter begins by examining the increasing role of online spaces on Canadian university campuses and proposes that the body is crucial to understanding online forms of sexual violence. Building on Henry and Powell's (2015) work, I draw on Anne Balsamo's (1996) writing on cyberspace and Ann Cahill's (2001, 2011) work on sexual violence as an intersubjective embodied experience to explore how online sexual violence is embodied. I then describe the cases of online sexual violence at Dalhousie and the University of Ottawa and trace the resulting media scrutiny on both universities, as well as the public controversies that were sparked over the universities' responses. I examine how these cases of online sexual violence were minimized and normalized by some commentators who cast them as merely examples of inappropriate, immature online comments that would have no material effects on university campuses. Problematizing this simplistic view, I then draw on Don Ihde's (2002) theorizing on bodies and technology, and return to Ann Cahill's (2001, 2011) work on bodies, sexual violence, and subjectivity to explore the role of embodied subjectivities and technology in the two cases of online sexual violence. I suggest that cyberspace is a site where violent embodied subjectivities are formulated and campus rape culture and sexual violence are (re)created and resisted. I conclude that an appreciation for the relations between bodies and technologies opens a path to understanding the material consequences of online sexual violence.

VIOLENT CYBERSPACES: BLURRING THE BOUNDARIES OF THE UNIVERSITY CAMPUS

The boundaries of university campuses are becoming increasingly blurred. In 2002, David Noble argued that Canadian universities were turning to online education to increase enrolments, reduce labour costs, and de-skill university education. He saw this turn as part of a widespread move to commodify and automate higher education. Janice Newson's (2015) analysis of the continued use of online technology in universities suggests that little has changed since Noble penned his critique of online education over ten years ago. In fact, Newson's work illustrates how universities have been expanding their use of online spaces to dissolve the boundaries between their campuses and prospective "consumers" of education, while reducing the costs of education delivery. (For more discussion on the corporatization of universities and its effects on higher education, see Elizabeth Quinlan's chapter in this collection.)

In this context, the definition of *the university campus* is shifting. No longer just a physical space made up of campus buildings, classrooms, and libraries, the campus is now a space that simultaneously occupies virtual and physical worlds. Blurring university campus boundaries has consequences for how we conceptualize rape culture *on* the university campus. Much of the public debate and discussion about sexual violence on university campuses to date has focused on physical forms of sexual violence that occurs in libraries, hallways, and classrooms of the university. However, in a context in which campus life is increasingly online, there is a pressing need to understand online forms of campus sexual violence. Feminist theoretical work on cyberspace and rape offers some important insights for this project.

Cyberspace, according to Anne Balsamo (1996), is commonly thought of as a non-material world where physical bodies are largely absent. The Internet appears to transcend the material, physical world, and be a realm that is not tied to any geographical, temporal, or physical location. Balsamo suggests, however, that this view of cyberspace mistakenly masks the role of the body in virtual spaces. It obscures the fact that the online world is created by embodied beings who are socially, temporally, and geographically located. It also conceals how embodied acts in the online realm can have material consequences offline. By seeing the Internet as an embodied world that is intricately connected to the material world of the university campus, it becomes possible to see online sexual violence and its material consequences for people on university campuses.

Balsamo (1996) suggests that shedding light on the role of body in cyberspace reveals how cyberspace is not merely a representation of reality, but instead is a site where reality can be (re)created. The conversations on Facebook at Dalhousie and the University of Ottawa were not merely comments that discursively *represented* rape culture on campus, but instead, were conversations in which rape culture and sexual violence were *(re)created* and *(re)-produced*. Here, I argue that these conversations were examples of an embodied perpetration of sexual violence. This understanding brings into view the harms of online sexual violence (Henry & Powell, 2015) and the ways in which online sexual violence perpetuates rape culture on campus. To explore the body in the perpetration of online sexual violence, I draw on Cahill's (2001, 2011) understanding of sexual violence as an intersubjective embodied experience. (See Cahill's chapter in this collection for more discussion of her work on sexual violence.)

Cahill (2001) proposes that feminist analyses of rape and sexual violence have largely ignored and misunderstood the significance of the material body. Feminist theorists such as Susan Brownmiller and Catharine MacKinnon, according to Cahill, missed the opportunity to understand rape as a sexually violent act between two sexed bodies. Instead, these theorists, in her view, oversimplified the body as either a purely biological entity or a site of essential dominance and powerlessness. In contrast to these two theoretical models, Cahill argues for a more complex view of the body in feminist analyses of sexual violence. The body, she proposes, is an entity that is inscribed with power relations and marked by social, political, and material forces; it is a site where power is produced and where resistance is possible. Human subjects are not defined solely by their bodies, but are also brought into being through their relations with other embodied human subjects. Subjectivity is therefore, in Cahill's view, co-constituted.

This understanding of bodies and subjectivity helps shed a new critical light on sexual violence. Rape, Cahill suggests, is an intersubjective embodied experience involving the assault of one sexually specific, marked body by another. In a sexually violent encounter, the subjectivities of the victim and the perpetrator are co-constituted: he[1] becomes a perpetrator and she the victim when he forces his body, will, and sexuality on her. Through this bodily violence, her subjectivity becomes overwhelmed and obscured by his. Understanding rape as intersubjective and embodied draws attention to both the role of the material body in the perpetration and experience of sexual violence and the interrelationship between material bodies. Seeing sexual violence in this light, according to Cahill, makes its material effects on victims'/survivors' lives far more visible.

While Cahill (2001, 2011) is primarily concerned with physical forms of sexual violence, her analysis of sexual violence as an intersubjective, embodied experience has relevance for the online realm. To build on Henry and Powell's (2015) contention that online sexual violence produces embodied harms, I take up Cahill's work on embodiment and sexual violence to explore how the perpetration and victimization of online sexual violence is intersubjective and embodied, despite the fact that it occurs in a virtual space that is commonly thought of as disembodied and disconnected from the material world. By doing so, I draw attention to the role of the body and technology in the perpetration and experience of online sexual violence and bring the material consequences of online sexual violence on campus communities more clearly into view. Here, I deliberately use the term "online sexual violence"[2] to draw attention to the fact that what occurred at Dalhousie and the University of Ottawa was more than just a few misguided comments in the disembodied world of cyberspace. Instead, it was the perpetration of a material form of violence that had material consequences for people in these campus communities.

ONLINE SEXUAL VIOLENCE AT THE UNIVERSITY OF OTTAWA

In February 2014, during the election campaign for the Student Federation of the University of Ottawa (SFUO), the student federation president received an anonymous email. The email contained screen shots of a sexually violent Facebook conversation about her between five male students, four of whom were in leadership positions in the SFUO. The five students had been using the Facebook group to share sexually violent fantasies of orally and anally raping the female student president. The "president will suck me off in her office chair and after I will fuck her in the ass on Pat's desk," one of the male students wrote online (as quoted in Feibel, 2014, para. 9). Two others followed by saying, "Someone punish her with their shaft," and "I do believe that with my reputation I would destroy her" (as quoted in "uOttawa Student Leader," 2014, para. 9). The male students encouraged each other with gifts of beer if they succeeded in carrying out these violent acts: "If you fuck [name of president], I will definitely buy you a beer" and "[I'll] get a 24 for Bart if he does it" (as quoted in Feibel, 2014, para. 11). These comments were part of an ongoing dialogue between the male students in which the female student presidents' body became the target of imagined violence and conquest. The male students' own bodies became tools of aggression and dominance that would be rewarded if they succeeded in sexually violating their female colleague. By collectively imagining and describing this sexual violence, the male students in the Facebook group perpetrated a form of sexual violence in which they were envisioning their bodies violently and sexually attacking another.

Not long after receiving the anonymous email, the female student president bravely took these online conversations to the media. She asserted that they were reflective of misogyny and rape culture at the University of Ottawa. Her positioning as a woman in a leadership role at the university, she argued, was a large part of why she was targeted (Levinson, 2014a). In an open letter to the university, 28 professors at UofO came out in her support, stating that she had "courageously shone a light on the everyday misogyny that infects our campus and hinders real leadership" (Levinson, 2014b, para. 10). Under significant public pressure from the media scrutiny, the president of the University of Ottawa, Alan Rock, stated publicly, "The comments demonstrate attitudes about women and sexual aggression that have no place on campus, or anywhere else in Canadian society" (as quoted in Clim, 2014, para. 4). He vowed to address the situation properly. Despite this apparent support from the university's leadership, the SFUO Board of Administration refused to publicly condemn the online conversation. To the media, the student president described her frustration with the board's response:

> It was kind of like getting a double whammy, you get put in a very difficult situation and to have these men try to take all power away from me by telling me that I need to be censored and that I can't take action.... This is also incredibly frustrating and I think speaks to the fact that rape culture does not get challenged enough. (as quoted in "uOttawa Student Leader," 2014, para. 22)

In the weeks following, the university president announced a task force to address sexism and violence against women on the university campus ("uOttawa Student Leader," 2014).[3] Over the course of the next nine months, the task force conducted a campus climate survey, in addition to holding consultations and working groups. It found that 30% of the female students and 14% of male students surveyed had experienced online harassment involving sexist comments or sexualized insults, and 16% of female students and 8% of male students reported that they had experienced at least one incident of sexual violence (University of Ottawa, 2015). What became clear was that the Facebook group at the University of Ottawa was not an isolated incident, but instead was part of a wide-sweeping phenomenon of sexualized violence on- and offline at the university.

ONLINE SEXUAL VIOLENCE AT DALHOUSIE UNIVERSITY

Near the end of 2014, the media spotlight shifted to a second Facebook group, this time one organized by several male dentistry students at Dalhousie University. The students had been using the online group to share sexual fantasies and jest about rape and violence against women. They called themselves the Class of DDS [Dalhousie Dentistry Students] 2015 Gentlemen. Online, they wrote about using chloroform to drug women, described imagined rape and sexual violence against their female classmates, and took polls on whom of their classmates they most wanted to "hate fuck" (as quoted in Backhouse, McRae, & Iyer, 2015, p. 10). In these discussions, their female classmates' bodies became the subject of scrutiny and jeer: "Two reasons why I like girls in Dentistry: 1 mm looks big to them and it normally only takes less than 10 mm to enter a canal!" (as quoted in Backhouse et al., 2015, p. 8). Similar to the male students at the University of Ottawa, the male students at Dalhousie also made references to their own body parts as violent weapons to be used against women. One described the penis as "the tool used to wean and convert lesbians and virgins into useful, productive members of society" (as quoted in "Françoise Baylis Pans Dalhousie Dentistry," 2015, para. 7). Another clarified this further, "and by productive I'm assuming you mean it inspires them [the women] to become chefs, housekeepers, babysitters, etc." (as quoted in Haiven, 2014, para. 3).

One of the male students in the Facebook group showed a female classmate the Facebook posts.[4] She alerted the university administration and indicated that she wanted to file a formal complaint. The university administrators were quick to try to control and contain the news of the Facebook group. They encouraged the female student not to file a formal complaint through the Student Code of Conduct and opt instead for an informal process of conflict resolution. The university assembled a crisis team to assess the safety risks that the Facebook group members posed to female students on campus, and quickly concluded that there were none. These initial responses of the university, which left the female student reportedly feeling isolated and unsupported, would quickly become the subject of national scrutiny.

Despite attempts to contain the story, a week later, the Facebook conversations of the DSS group were leaked to CBC News and a widespread national debate ensued on the university's responsibility to respond to the online sexual violence. Some urged the university to initiate an independent investigation and expel the students involved in the Facebook group, while others claimed that the male students were being unfairly targeted for thoughtless comments that indicated no more than a lack of judgment. Provincial licensing bodies in Ontario and Alberta demanded that Dalhousie reveal the names of the male students involved and argued that their behaviour warranted denying them professional accreditation. Dalhousie administrators refused to reveal the students' names and claimed that doing so would violate laws guaranteeing student privacy. As more complaints from female students at Dalhousie flooded into the university administrators' offices, the university president met with some of the female students and later announced that they had chosen to pursue an informal restorative justice process. However, the university's attempt to cast the restorative justice process as productive and voluntary was met with heavy criticism. Many of the female students involved reported feeling pressured by the administration to participate in the process, and some spoke publicly about the inadequacy of restorative justice models for dealing effectively with sexual violence. In an open letter to the president, some of these students wrote that "the university is pressuring us into this process, silencing our views, isolating us from our peers, and discouraging us from choosing to proceed formally" ("4 Women from the DSS Class of 2015," 2015, p. 1). They asserted that by not formally investigating the Facebook group, the university was "send[ing] the message that there is no penalty for harming its female students in this way. You will be telling us we don't matter" (p. 1).

In response to mounting public pressure, the university suspended the male students in the DSS group from clinical duties, on the grounds of concerns for patient safety and evident violations of professional standards. These suspensions were, however, later revoked in March 2015, after the male and female students who had participated in the restorative justice process released statements about it. The male students outlined their remorse for their actions and the female students said that as a result of the process, they no longer felt threatened by the male students. The male students in the DSS group returned to their clinical duties, which allowed them to obtain the necessary credits to graduate in May 2015. The university president applauded the restorative justice process, claiming that as a result, "the men have taken ownership of their actions ... [and] gained a deep understanding of the harm that was caused" (as quoted in Backhouse et al., 2015, p. 26). He claimed that the process could serve as a model for other universities. But provincial crediting bodies in Ontario and Nova Scotia were not as convinced. They announced that as a result of the events at Dalhousie, they would now be requiring applicants to answer questions about whether they had been the subject of an inquiry, complaint, or investigation at their post-secondary institution ("Dalhousie Students Disciplined," 2015).

While the events at Dalhousie University and the University of Ottawa both revolved around online sexual violence involving male students targeting their female classmates, the two cases were distinct in the level of public outcry they produced. The events at Dalhousie University garnered substantial media attention in comparison with the incident at the University of Ottawa. Unlike the events at University of Ottawa, the Dalhousie Facebook group sparked a national public controversy among activists, university administrators, and professional associations regarding universities' failures to adequately respond to sexual violence. The level of media scrutiny that fell on the Dalhousie Facebook group in 2015 was perhaps fuelled by the events that had previously occurred at the University of Ottawa, as well as other cases of campus sexual violence that had been publicized at the time. When the news emerged of the Dalhousie Facebook group, the national media and the public were primed for launching into a national debate about sexual violence on campus and universities' responsibility to respond. Despite the differing levels of media attention the two cases received, both provoked many attempts to deny and minimize online forms of sexual violence as merely inappropriate comments by a few "bad apples" with immaterial consequences on the campus community. In these discussions, the sexual violence that occurred in these Facebook groups and its embodied effects on the targeted female students and their allies at Dalhousie University and the University of Ottawa were rendered largely invisible.

"MISGUIDED AND IMMATERIAL": THE NORMALIZATION OF ONLINE SEXUAL VIOLENCE

Mainstream media featured many quotes from columnists, students, and members of the public who collectively cast the sexually violent online conversations at Dalhousie and the University of Ottawa as misguided comments that were disconnected from the "real-life" behaviours of the male students involved and the material lives of the female students and their campus communities. By casting the online sexual violence in this way, these commentators transformed the online violence into something that was seemingly innocuous and natural. Their comments reveal how online sexual violence is often minimized, obscured, and made to seem normal in dominant discourse.

Championing this view of online sexual violence, *Globe and Mail* columnist Margaret Wente (2015) described the activity on the Dalhousie Class of DDS 2015 Gentlemen Facebook group as an example of immaturity and bad behaviour among a group of boys. Diminishing both the severity of the online sexual violence and its effect on the female students, Wente wrote, "Such coarse talk is not atypical of young male group behaviour. It does not mean that they actually wanted to assault chloroformed women" (p. 1). For Wente, the male Dalhousie students joking about drugging and having "hate sex" with their female classmates was normal, albeit "juvenile," male behaviour that reflected neither intention nor desire. Their words were, in Wente's view, abstract, disembodied, and largely harmless. It was all merely an incident of online misbehaviour among a group of boys who were, as she said, simply in need of "a sharp smack across the chops from a respected elder" (p. 1).

Wente was not the only voice in mainstream media dismissing the online violence as just typical bad behaviour among boys. One patient of the Dalhousie dentistry school was quoted in the media as saying that "it sounds like they're all made to suffer for a couple of idiotic actions. They need to grow up" ("Dalhousie Dentistry Students," 2015, p. 20). The Facebook group at the University of Ottawa was similarly described. One of the male students involved in the violent online conversations reflected back on his involvement and said, "There's a lot of *boys'* talk and locker room talk that can seem pretty normal at the time, but then when you actually look back at it, it can be offensive" (emphasis added; as quoted in "uOttawa Student Leader," 2014, para. 27). The online sexual violence at Dalhousie and the University of Ottawa was thus reduced to normal young male *mis*behaviour that, at worst, offended some people's sensibilities. Some public figures tried to challenge this framing of the Facebook groups. The Nova Scotia Minister of Women, Joanne Bernard, said in reference to the Dalhousie group, "These aren't boys. These are men and they're very well aware of what the repercussions are for their actions" ("Dalhousie Dentistry Facebook," 2014, para. 9). Despite attempts like these, the dismissal of the online violence as juvenile mischief served as a rhetorical tool to mask the violence and depreciate its severity and consequences for both the targeted female students and their campus communities.

In addition to the argument that the Facebook groups were juvenile, some suggested that the Facebook conversations were intended to be private, and therefore did not warrant or justify scrutiny or reprimand. Not long after the student president at the University of Ottawa spoke publicly about the violent online conservation about her, the male students responsible retaliated with a threat of legal action on the grounds that their conversation was intended to be private and therefore could not be publicized or distributed ("uOttawa Student Leader," 2014). Not dissuaded, she distributed copies of the conversation to the SFUO Board of Administration and used them in the media to illustrate the systemic rape culture at her university. Although many applauded her courage and argued alongside her that the male students' conversation was indicative of a rape culture on campus (Levinson, 2014b), others seemed more preoccupied by the fact that a private conversation on Facebook had been publicized than by the contents of the conversation. Following an online article about the University of Ottawa Facebook group, CBC News created an online poll where almost 40% of respondents (8576 votes) agreed with the statement that private Facebook messages should stay private because "everyone talks about things they shouldn't" ("uOttawa Student Leader," 2014, para. 43). For these survey respondents, the imperative of privacy seemingly superseded any imperative to publicize and problematize online forms of sexual violence. The Facebook comments were not seen as inherently problematic; what made them so was that they had been made public. Reflecting this sentiment, one of the Facebook group members explained, "I would never say that kind of thing out in the public but when it was a private conversation I guess it slipped my mind that that's really not acceptable" ("uOttawa Student Leader," 2014, para. 29). The insinuation that sexual violence is excusable so long as it is not publicized was yet another tool to trivialize and normalize the online sexual violence and its effects on the campus community.

BODIES IN CYBERSPACE AND EMBODIED (ONLINE) SEXUAL VIOLENCE

The attempts to dismiss the online sexual violence at Dalhousie University and the University of Ottawa glossed over how these online conversations were fundamentally embodied and had real, material, embodied consequences for everyone on campus, including the male students involved, the female students who were targeted, and their campus communities. The male students used the online space to explore, enact, and experience sexual violence. In both Facebook groups, female bodies were used in sexually violent fantasies, and male bodies were used to denote power, control, and dominance. In this way, bodies were at the centre of what occurred on Facebook.

Don Ihde (2002) has written extensively on the relationship between bodies and technologies. He suggests that through technological artifacts, individuals can experience aspects of the world and come to experience and know themselves as bodies. He calls this "the embodiment relation," which he defines as "the relation of experiencing something in the world through an artifact, a technology" (p. xi). Through the Internet and the vividly violent conversations that were held online, the male students in the two Facebook groups could experience their own bodies as dominant, violent, and powerful, while constructing female bodies as inherently submissive and powerless. Through the Internet, they could imagine and virtually experience acts of sexual domination and violence. Although the acts of online violence were not physically embodied in the same way as forms of sexual violence that involve physical contact, the online sexual violence was embodied nonetheless. These online conversations constructed male and female bodies as dominant and passive, respectively, and created a space in which violence between these gendered and sexed bodies was collectively witnessed and experienced.

Although the conversations occurred online, they had embodied consequences. Henry and Powell (2015) assert that the effects of online sexual violence can be both psychical and physical. This idea was reflected in the media coverage of the University of Ottawa and Dalhousie Facebook groups. The female student president at the University of Ottawa described her embodied reaction in the media after she read the violent online conversation about her. She said that she felt "shocked and a little nauseous" after reading the online dialogue, and described it as "very scary" and "violent" (Levinson, 2014a, para. 2). In a similar way, the vice-president of the student union at Dalhousie described the effects that the online sexual violence had on the female students' concentration and ability to participate in the classroom. She said, "Imagine sitting in a classroom and trying to focus on studying—because that's what you're there for—when you're sitting in a room with people that have talked about raping you" (as quoted in "Dalhousie Dentistry Complaints," 2014, para. 11). Feeling nauseous, shocked, scared, unsafe, and distracted are feelings that are deeply rooted in the body.

As evidenced in these quotes, the consequences of the online sexual violence were not limited to the online realm. Rather, the sexual violence transcended the apparent barrier between cyberspace and the material world, and acted directly on the targeted female students in very real, physical ways. As Henry and Powell (2015) argue, the harms of online sexual violence can also extend beyond individuals to the social groups of which they are a part. The effects of the online sexual violence extended to other students who were not the explicit targets of the Facebook discussions. The student president at the University of Ottawa described this by saying, "This kind of behavior has clear impacts on women ... it creates an environment that is intimidating, threatening, and toxic" (as quoted in Feibel, 2014, para. 4). In her view, the online sexual violence contributed to creating a world in which women felt physically threatened and unsafe. To suggest that the Facebook conservations between the male students at both universities were simply misguided comments without material effects on students or campus environments seriously underestimates and discounts the embodied nature of the online sexual violence and its effects.

OBJECTIFIED BODIES?

In the media, some scholars and activists drew attention to the material consequences of the online sexual violence by arguing that the Facebook groups at Dalhousie and the University of Ottawa were examples of male objectification of women. On Facebook, the male students, they suggested, had abhorrently turned the female students' bodies into objects to be used and abused. One faculty member at the University of Ottawa said in a media interview, "That's what rape culture does, women no longer count as people, they're *objects* to be derided, discarded, and to be destroyed" (emphasis added; as quoted in

Levinson, 2014b, para. 13). Another from Dalhousie used similar words to denounce the Dalhousie Facebook group. She said, "It is never OK to discriminate or sexually *objectify* people around you" (emphasis added; "Dalhousie Dentistry Complaints," 2014, para. 16). The concept of objectification was thus used to emphasize both the wrongs of the online sexual violence and its consequences on women. The online sexual violence was reprehensible *because* it involved and resulted in the objectification of women. This framing of online sexual violence as a form of objectification has been a relatively common one in academic literature (DeKeseredy & Olsson, 2011; Henry & Powell, 2015; Nussbaum, 2010). The apparent popularity of the concept of objectification to explain the harms of online sexual violence in both mainstream media and academic literature raises some interesting questions: Why is the concept of objectification so often used to understand online sexual violence? What aspects of the violence does it help to reveal? What aspects of the violence does it perhaps obscure, if any?

Framing violence against women as a form of objectification has a long history in feminist scholarship (Cahill, 2011). Many second-wave feminists argued that the male gaze strips women's power by turning them into objects or non-humans to be used by men. Dworkin's (1987) and MacKinnon's (1987, 2005) well-known critiques of pornography suggested that pornography reproduces gendered inequality by objectifying women's bodies for male sexual pleasure. The faculty who commented on the Dalhousie and University of Ottawa incidents were drawing on this rich intellectual history when they described the Facebook groups as the objectification of women. Similar to feminist critiques of pornography, these scholars used the concept of objectification to draw attention to how male students used sexual imagery and descriptions of sexual violence to turn their female classmates into sexualized objects to be "derided, discarded, and to be destroyed" (as quoted in Levinson, 2014b, para. 13). This objectification, in their eyes, was a reflection of a rape culture rooted in gendered inequality. While the concept of objectification usefully draws attention to how the male students discursively and visually portrayed female students' bodies online, it arguably obscures some of the embodied aspects of the online violence. More specifically, it does little to reveal the specific role the male students' bodies played in the online sexual violence and offers little insight into the specific embodied consequences of the violence for the male and female students at both universities.

Cahill (2011) proposes that the concept of objectification has some notable limitations for understanding violence against women, which feminist scholarship on the topic has largely ignored. She argues that objectification, while useful in some respects, obscures the role of the body in violence against women, and therefore does little to reveal the embodied nature and consequences of violence. By challenging a concept that has been so well used in the past few decades of feminist writing on violence, Cahill's critique undoubtedly shakes conventional feminist thinking on violence. However, given the unique nature of online sexual violence and the virtual space in which it is perpetrated, it is worthwhile to think critically about well-used theoretical concepts and to consider what possible alternatives might offer. Here, I take up Cahill's critique of objectification to open up some new avenues for understanding the embodied nature of online sexual violence.

The feminist concept of objectification, according to Cahill (2001), rests on a problematic notion that to be seen as "just" a body, or a material object, is to be reduced to something that is less than human. When women are discursively or visually turned into objects, so it is commonly understood, they lose their identity as human subjects and instead become objects or things to be used by others. This perspective, Cahill argues, stems from a theoretical model that is based on a "mind/body hierarchy" (p. 25), in which the intellectual mind is privileged over the material body. It relies on an understanding of the body as being an object without subjectivity, and the person as being predominantly intellectual, disembodied, and autonomous from others. Cahill suggests that this is a limited understanding of personhood that ignores the importance of the body and masks how subjectivities are constructed in relation to one another. By proposing instead that the self is intersubjective, embodied, and in constant relation with other bodies, she offers a new set of theoretical tools to understand the complex nature of online sexual violence and its material consequences.

Cahill argues that the concept of objectification offers little insight into the inherent harms of sexual violence. She proposes that most forms of sexuality, regardless of whether they are healthy or violent, involve being an object of another's gaze. Being seen as a sexual body, or an object for sex, is therefore not inherently harmful, as the common feminist understanding of objectification might imply. Instead, what is harmful, according to Cahill, is when women are reduced to being a particular kind of subject whose desires and actions are forced to reflect those of men. Acts in which women's subjectivities are "derivatized" (p. 33), or made derivative in relation to male desires, are inherently harmful and reproduce gendered relations of power. Cahill sees derivatization as "an act, a way of framing or constructing the feminine in terms of the masculine" (p. 50), where the feminine subject is constructed as merely a projection of masculine desire. She explains:

> To derivatize is to portray, render, understand or approach a being solely or primarily as a reflection, projection, or expression of another being's identity, fears, etc. The derivatized subject becomes reducible in all relevant ways to

the derivatizing subject's existence—other elements of her being or subjectivity are disregarded, ignored, or undervalued. (p. 32)

The concept of derivatization casts sexual violence as an intersubjective, embodied act in which a victim's subjectivity is overwhelmed by a perpetrator's. The perpetrator imposes his body and will on the victim, and her will becomes overshadowed and derivatived by his. In this sexually violent encounter, the subjectivities of the victim and the perpetrator are co-constructed. The perpetrator uses his body to situate himself as dominant and the victim as derivative. In this encounter, the perpetrator of sexual violence does not see the victim as merely an *object*, according to Cahill. Instead, he sees her as a particular kind of *subject*, who can be dominated, controlled, and victimized. In order for the perpetrator to be able to assert his power and dominance, in his eyes the victim needs to be a *subject* who can be dominated and "who is capable of experiencing the horrors of being victimized" (p. 134).

While Cahill's analysis focuses on physical forms of sexual violence, it has relevance for understanding sexual violence in online spaces. With Cahill's concept of derivatization, online sexual violence can be understood as an embodied act in which two subjectivities are co-constructed: a dominant subject, whose will can be imposed *on* another body, and a derivatized subject, whose will can be imposed *upon* by another body. Casting this view onto the Facebook groups at the UofO and Dalhousie, it could be argued that in those online conversations, the female students were not simply treated as objects by the male students, but instead as particular kinds of subjects who could be dominated, controlled, and victimized by male bodies.

The technology of the Internet played an enabling role in the construction of these subjectivities. Since these conversations occurred in semi-private online spaces that the female students could not directly access, the male students could more easily turn the women into derivatized subjects without their consent, their knowledge, or the possibility of their resistance. In these violent online conversations, the male students were simultaneously constructing their own subjectivities as dominating and powerful. The technology of the Internet facilitated the collective fostering of this male subjectivity. By understanding how the male and female students' subjectivities were co-constituted online, the material, embodied consequences of the online sexual violence come into clearer view.

Subjectivities constituted online can shape, inform, and reflect relations of power on campus. If female students are constituted as derivatized subjects and male students as dominating subjects in the online realm, female-identified students will never be equal members of the campus community—not because some male students see them as bodily sexed objects, but because they see female students as subjects whose will can be ignored and overpowered. The Facebook groups were online spaces where violent male subjectivities were constructed and rehearsed and derivative female subjectivities were envisioned.

The targeted female students at Dalhousie and the University of Ottawa shared the unique status of occupying realms in the university that have historically been dominated by men. Student governance positions and professional programs, such as dentistry and engineering, have historically been occupied almost exclusively by male students. Perhaps it is not surprising that it is in these programs and areas of the university where students who identify as women continue to struggle to gain entry and legitimacy that the backlash against their presence is most fierce. By rendering female students as derivative subjects who can be dominated and controlled by male students, these online conversations not only *reflect* a campus culture of continued gendered inequality. They also have the potential to *inform* a campus culture in which female-identified students are not valued or recognized as fully legitimate, contributing members of the campus community. Online sexual violence is thus both a barometer and a breeding ground for unequal gendered relations in university classrooms, hallways, dorm rooms, cafeterias, and other campus spaces.

A SPACE FOR RESISTANCE

Built into Cahill's (2001) understanding of derivatization is the possibility of resistance. Just because an individual attempts to derivatize another does not mean that that attempt is successful, nor does it necessarily determine relations of power thereafter. The Facebook groups at Dalhousie and the University of Ottawa helped spark a surge of online activism around rape culture on Canadian university campuses. The women who had been targets of the online sexual violence used online media to voice their anger and frustration about sexual violence on campus and made a clarion call to their universities to respond. Activists from across Canada joined them in online spaces to publicly denounce misogyny and rape culture on Canadian university campuses and put pressure on universities to be accountable for it. The online realm became a space for collective resistance to online sexual violence.

Just a few weeks after the news broke of the sexually violent Facebook group at the University of Ottawa, a new Facebook group formed denouncing the rape culture at the university and calling for the resignation of the male students involved from the student federation. By March 2, 2014, the group had over 1300 members (Levinson, 2014b). One member of the federation commented on the wave of online support for the student president: "I don't think I've honestly seen so many students united in rallying against something" (as cited in Levinson, 2014a, para. 17). The news at Dalhousie also sparked an online petition to encourage the university to expel the male students involved in the Facebook group. The petition garnered 1000 signatures in one afternoon, 40,000 signatures in a week, and 50,000 signatures by the middle of January (Backhouse et al., 2015). Alongside the petition, the Twitter hashtag #dalhateswomen attracted over 60,000 tweets. Online news media forums featured many calls to action. Saint Mary's University professor Judy Haiven's 2014 article in rabble.ca titled "The 'Middle Road' Won't Do for Dalhousie's 'Gentlemen' Dentists" featured such a call, which read as follows:

> While some of the women featured on the Gentlemen's site may settle for a glorified apology for the miscreant soon-to-be dentists, how will this help to solve the problem of misogyny, power and privilege? It will not. Frequently women who suffer at the hands of men are told "education will help." Will it? We've seen all the education and training available at universities across this country have not turned the tide against misogyny. The education almost never zeroes in on men, race, class, power and privilege, which are the underpinnings of misogyny. The education never tackles our misogynist culture. Only by making serious examples can institutions curb this sort of behaviour.... When are we going to get sick of being forced down the middle road of apology and fake contrition? A slap on the wrists merely enables repetition. When are we going to act? (paras. 8–9)

Alongside the wave of critical online media, twitter posts, and online petitions, the Dalhousie Gender and Women's Studies program organized and aired a Forum on Misogyny that was streamed across the country. The forum featured a panel of scholars and activists who discussed strategies for resisting rape culture and misogyny on campus. While these online forms of resistance likely did not radically transform the deeply entrenched gendered relations or any other forms of oppression on campus, they symbolized a collective effort to resist online sexual violence and recognize its broader harms on campus communities. With these efforts, the Internet was transformed from being a tool for perpetrating sexual violence to a tool for resisting it.

CONCLUSION

Online forms of sexual violence are embodied. Through the technology of the Internet, these forms of sexual violence act on and through bodies with material consequences for everyone on university campuses. What occurred on Facebook at Dalhousie and the University of Ottawa cannot be dismissed as merely misguided comments made in a world disconnected from "real life."

Nor can it be explained as purely a reflection of typical, and largely harmless, juvenile behaviour of adult male students. Instead, it must be understood as a form of sexual violence that both reflects and perpetuates rape culture on campus. Sexual violence in online spaces is not disembodied and disconnected from the material world, but is instead embodied in ways that produce very real effects on victims/survivors, perpetrators, and their campus communities.

Given these very real effects of online sexual violence on university campuses, university administrators need to take greater responsibility for what occurs in online spaces and institute and resource strategies for reducing these forms of sexual violence. While university administrators are devoting much attention to the question of how they can use online spaces to increase enrolments and profits (Newson, 2015; Noble, 2002), they are largely ignoring more pressing questions of how to address the violence that occurs in these online spaces. Under the weight of public pressure and legislation in a growing number of jurisdictions, many Canadian universities have recently developed sexual assault policies. However, few if any of these policies have included specific references to online forms of sexual violence and strategies for reducing it. This absence of specific measures suggests a blind spot in university administrators' understanding of campus rape culture and the mechanisms through which it is perpetuated. Combating sexual violence on campus will require the recognition of all its forms in both the virtual and material worlds, and will involve addressing its embodied, material consequences for all members of campus communities.

NOTES

1 My gendered language here reflects current data on sexual assault perpetration and victimization, which suggest that male-identified people are far more likely to perpetrate sexual violence than any other social group, and that women are more commonly the victims/survivors of their violence (Brennan & Taylor-Butts, 2008; Sinha, 2013). This gendered language, however, is not meant to deny that men and people who identify as trans and non-binary can be and are victims/survivors of sexual violence.

2 In this chapter, I have opted to use the phrase "online sexual violence" instead of "technology-facilitated sexual violence" (Henry & Powell, 2015, p. 759), as it offers greater specificity and more accurately describes the forms of violence that occurred at Dalhousie and the University of Ottawa.

3 This announcement followed another high-profile story of campus sexual violence that garnered national attention, in which members of the university hockey team sexually assaulted a woman in Thunder Bay (see Fogel's chapter in this collection for further discussion). The task force's mandate was to provide the university president with recommendations on how to foster a respectful campus culture free from sexual violence and violence against women (University of Ottawa, 2015).

4 Details in this summary of events at Dalhousie are drawn from Backhouse, McRae, and Iyer's (2015) formal report on Dalhousie University's handling of the Dentistry Facebook group. In response to significant media scrutiny, the university commissioned the independent report in January 2015.

REFERENCES

Backhouse, C., McRae, D., & Iyer, N. (2015). *Report of the Task Force on Misogyny, Sexism, and Homophobia in Dalhousie University Faculty of Dentistry.* Retrieved from Dalhousie University: https://www.dal.ca/content/dam/dalhousie/pdf/cultureofrespect/DalhousieDentistry-TaskForceReport-June2015.pdf

Balsamo, A. (1996). *Technologies of the gendered body.* London, UK: Duke University Press.

Brennan, S., & Taylor-Butts, A. (2008). *Sexual assault in Canada* (Catalogue 85F0033M no. 19). Ottawa, ON: Canadian Centre for Justice Statistics Profile Series, Statistics Canada.

Brownmiller, S. (1975). *Against our will: Men, women, and rape.* New York, NY: Bantam Books.

Cahill, A. (2001). *Rethinking rape.* Ithaca, NY: Cornell University Press.

Cahill, A. (2011). *Overcoming objectification: A carnal ethics.* New York, NY: Routledge.

Clim, B. (2014, March 3). Leaked Facebook conversation sparks controversy at uOttawa. *StudentUnion.ca: Covering student politics in Canada.* Retrieved from http://www.studentunion.ca/2014/03/leaked-facebook-conversation-sparks-controversy-at-uottawa/

Cornelius, K., & Hermann, D. (2011). *Virtual worlds and criminality.* Dordrecht, The Netherlands: Springer.

Dalhousie dentistry complaints date back to the summer, student says. (2014, December 16). *CBC News.* Retrieved from http://www.cbc.ca/news/canada/nova-scotia/dalhousie-dentistry-complaints-date-back-to-summer-student-says-1.2875507

Dalhousie dentistry Facebook posts not "boys being boys," says minister. (2014, December 17). *CBC News.* Retrieved from http://www.cbc.ca/news/canada/nova-scotia/dalhousie-dentistry-facebook-posts-not-boys-being-boys-says-minister-1.2876547

Dalhousie dentistry students return to class; will be taught separately. (2015, January 12). *CBC News.* Retrieved from http://www.cbc.ca/news/canada/nova-scotia/dalhousie-dentistry-students-taught-separately-senate-mulls-review-1.2897477

Dalhousie students disciplined for Facebook group finding dentistry work: Lawyer. (2015, July 10). *The Globe and Mail.* Retrieved from http://www.theglobeandmail.com/news/national/dalhousie-students-disciplined-for-misogynistic-facebook-group-finding-dentistry-work-lawyer says/article25409831/

DeKeseredy, W., & Olsson, P. (2011). Adult pornography, male peer support, and violence against women: The contribution of the "dark side" of the Internet. In M. Vargas Martin, M. Garcia-Ruiz, & A. Edwards (Eds.), *Technology for facilitating humanity and combating social deviations: Interdisciplinary perspectives* (pp. 34–50). Hershey, PA: Information Science Reference.

Dworkin, A. (1987). *Intercourse.* New York, NY: Basic Books.

Feibel, A. (2014, February 28). Sexually graphic group chat between student officials posted online. *Fulcrum: The University of Ottawa's Independent Student Newspaper.* Retrieved from http://thefulcrum.ca/news/sexually-violent-conversation-between-student-officials-leaked-online/

4 Women from the DSS Class of 2015. (2015, January 6). [Letter to Dr. Richard Florizone, President of Dalhousie University]. Retrieved fromhttps://www.documentcloud.org/documents/1391799-letter-to-dr-richard-florizone-president.html

Françoise Baylis pans Dalhousie dentistry men's apology. (2015, March 6). *CBC News*. Retrieved from http://www.cbc.ca/news/canada/nova-scotia/françoise-baylis-pans-dalhousie-dentistry-men-s-apology-1.2984202

Haiven, J. (2014, December 19). Misogyny at Dal: When we are sick of being forced down the middle road of apology and contrition. Retrieved from http://halifax.mediacoop.ca/story/misogyny-dal-when-are-we-sick-being-forced-down-mi/32524

Henry, N., & Powell, A. (2015). Embodied harms: Gender, shame, and technology-facilitated sexual violence. *Violence Against Women, 21*(6), 758–779.

Jewkes, Y. (Ed.). (2007). *Crime online*. New York, NY: Routledge.

Jewkes, Y., & Yar, M. (2010). Introduction: The Internet, cybercrime, and the challenges of the 21st century. In Y. Jewkes & M. Yar (Eds.), *Handbook of Internet crime* (pp. 1–8). Portland, OR: Willan.

Ihde, D. (2002). *Bodies in technology*. Minneapolis: University of Minnesota Press.

Levinson, R. (2014a, March 2). "Rape culture" signifies deeply rooted attitudes: Professor. *Ottawa Citizen*. Retrieved from http://ottawacitizen.com/news/local-news/rape-culture-signifies-deeply-rooted-attitudes-professor

Levinson, R. (2014b, March 3). Students quit U of O board after making sex comments about student federation president. *Ottawa Citizen*. Retrieved from http://ottawacitizen.com/news/local-news/students-quit-u-of-o-board-after-making-sex-comments-about-student-federation-president

MacKinnon, C. (1987). *Feminism unmodified: Discourses on life and law*. Cambridge, MA: Harvard University Press.

MacKinnon, C. (2005). *Women's lives: Men's laws*. Cambridge, MA: Belknap Press of Harvard University Press.

Newson, J. (2015). The turn to technology in higher education. In C. Polster & J. Newson (Eds.), *A penny for your thoughts: How corporatization devalues teaching, research, and public service in Canada's universities* (pp. 117–136). Ottawa, ON: Canadian Centre for Policy Alternatives.

Noble, D. (2002). *Digital diploma mills: The automation of higher education*. Toronto, ON: Between the Lines.

Nussbaum, M. (2010). Objectification and Internet misogyny. In S. Levmore & M. Nussbaum (Eds.), *The offensive Internet: Speech, privacy, and reputation* (pp. 68–90). Cambridge, MA: Harvard University Press.

Powell, A. (2009). New technologies, unauthorised visual images and sexual assault. *ACSSA Aware, 23*, 6–12.

Powell, A. (2010). Configuring consent: Emerging technologies, unauthorised sexual images and sexual assault. *Australian and New Zealand Journal of Criminology, 43*, 76–90.

Sinha, M. (Ed.). (2013). Measuring violence against women: Statistical trends. *Juristat* (Statistics Canada Catalogue no. 85-002-X). Retrieved from http://www.statcan.gc.ca/pub/85-002-x/2013001/article/11766-eng.pdf

University of Ottawa. (2015). *Report of the Task Force on Respect and Equality: Ending sexual violence at the University of Ottawa*. Retrieved from https://www.uottawa.ca/president/sites/www.uottawa.ca.president/files/report-of-the-task-force-on-respect-and-equality.pdf

uOttawa student leader, subject of explicit online chat. (2014, March 2). *CBC News*. Retrieved from http://www.cbc.ca/news/canada/ottawa/anne-marie-roy-uottawa-student-leader-subject-of-explicit-online-chat-1.2556948

Visano, L. (2010). A critical critique of the cultures of control: A case study of cyber rape. In J. Jodgson & D. Kelley (Eds.), *Sexual violence: Policies, practices, and challenges in the United States and Canada* (pp. 51–71). London, UK: Lynne Rienner.

Wall, D. (Ed.). (2001). *Crime and the Internet*. London, UK: Routledge.

Wall, D. (2010). Criminalising cyberspace: The rise of the Internet as a "crime problem." In Y. Jewkes & M. Yar (Eds.), *Handbook of Internet crime* (pp. 88–103). Portland, OR: Willan.

Wente, M. (2015, January 6). Dalhousie's dental hysteria. *Globe and Mail*. Retrieved from http://www.theglobeandmail.com/globe-debate/dalhousies-dental-hysteria/article22310028/

CHAPTER 7

PRECARIOUS MASCULINITY AND RAPE CULTURE IN CANADIAN UNIVERSITY SPORT

Curtis Fogel

In a 2014 news conference, University of Ottawa chancellor Michaëlle Jean proclaimed that the university, and its hockey team in particular, had what she characterized as a rape culture. On a road trip to Thunder Bay, where the University of Ottawa Gee-Gees took on the Lakehead University Thunder-wolves men's hockey team in a back-to-back weekend double-header, hockey players from the Gee-Gees allegedly sexually assaulted a Thunder Bay woman. The Gee-Gees coach, Real Paiement, was reportedly aware of the incident and did not report it to university officials. University of Ottawa president Alan Rock stated that the behaviour was "disreputable and unbecoming of representatives of uOttawa and suggested an unhealthy climate surrounding the team" (Ditchburn, 2015, para. 9). The coach was fired and the Gee-Gees hockey team was suspended indefinitely.

Two players from the Gee-Gees hockey team, Guillaume Donovan and David Foucher, were criminally charged with sexual assault. An internal investigation by the University of Ottawa revealed that "team members, in various states of undress, watched while Foucher and Donovan engaged in sexual activity with Doe, or were present in the room while sexual activity was occurring. Some of these players may have played a role in the activity or touched Doe. Other players overheard the sexual activity through the open connecting door to the adjoining hotel room" (*Creppin v. University of Ottawa*, 2015). The two criminally charged players, Donovan and Foucher, are awaiting trial at the time of this writing.

While the University of Ottawa sexual assault scandal has received significant media attention, it is one of many cases in recent history involving sexual
violence perpetrated by Canadian university athletes. In this chapter, I explore
several recent cases of athlete-perpetrated sexual violence in university sport
before identifying common themes and examining why competitive university sport appears to be a "hot spot" for sexual violence in North America
(Ratcliffe, 2004, p. 5).

UNIVERSITY SPORT AS AN INSTITUTIONAL HOT SPOT OF SEXUAL VIOLENCE

The term "hot spot" is traditionally used in criminology in geo-mapping of
specific geographic locations that show high crime rates. These geographic
areas with a high density of crime are also sometimes termed "hot zones"
or "hot places." I am using the term in a somewhat different sense to refer
to an "institutional hot spot" rather than a geographic one. That is, it is my
contention that a high density of sexually violent activity characterizes the
institution of competitive North American sport, which is not easily denoted
on a geographic map.

The precise density of sexual violence in the social institution of sport is not
known, particularly in a Canadian university context. This is due to a number
of factors, including, but not limited to, low rates of sexual assault reporting
by survivors, no Uniform Crime Report (UCR)[1] data on sport participation
of offenders, and no mechanism to consistently record and report incidents
of sexual violence on university campuses in Canada. Anecdotally, looking at
media reports of sexual violence on university campuses in Canada, it can be
identified that athletes do appear frequently as accused perpetrators. In fact,
the results of my recent review of media files on reports of sexual violence
on Canadian university campuses from the past ten years indicate that of the
over 100 cases, 23% involved university athletes as alleged perpetrators. Given
that competitive athletes compose about 1% to 3% of the university student
population in Canada, this number of alleged perpetrators is largely out of
proportion.

These informal findings should not be seen as definitive. The articles were
collected on various media databases, such as Newstand Major Dailies, and
included any articles that discussed sexual violence at Canadian universities.
Drawing statistical conclusions about criminal behaviour purely from media
reports is problematic. First, the vast majority of crimes of a sexually violent
nature go unreported. Second, those that are reported to police or university
officials will not necessarily lead to media reports. Third, it can also be argued
that athlete-perpetrated sexual violence on university campuses is perceived as

more newsworthy, and therefore receives more coverage than sexual assaults committed by non-athletes.

A final challenge in using media reports is that universities in Canada often refuse to include the full details on cases involving athletes and rumoured sexual misconduct. For example, in 2013 the Dalhousie University women's hockey team was suspended for hazing activities, followed by the men's rugby team in 2014. In both cases, the facts have not been made public in the media despite ongoing rumours that the acts involved sexual misconduct (Auld, 2014). As such, the 23% figure could actually be an underestimate due to potential heightened secrecy surrounding athlete-perpetrated sexual violence, although it is fairly consistent with existing research on sexual violence in sport that has been conducted in the United States. While the 23% figure is not to be taken as scientifically precise, it remains alarming and hints at a serious problem in Canadian university sport.

Researchers at the Center for the Study of Sport in Society at Northeastern University were commissioned to conduct a pioneering study of sexual violence in university sport in the 1990s. Their task was to show that athletes are no more likely than non-athletes to commit sexual assault. For the study, they collected reports of sexual assault at 20 National Collegiate Athletic Association (NCAA) universities with football and basketball programs perennially ranked in the top 20 of the United States. They found that male athletes were responsible for nearly 20% of reported sexual assaults on the university campuses, despite making up only 3% of the student population at these universities (Crosset, Benedict, & McDonald, 1995). According to Benedict (1997), the centre would not allow the researchers to publish their findings out of fear of damaging the relationships with sports organizations that funded the centre. Benedict left the centre and published the work, and continues to do important research on athlete-perpetrated violence against women at all levels of competitive sport.

Other research on university sport in the United States has revealed that university athletes commonly react positively to derogatory, violent, and sexist remarks about women. In one study, 27% of university athletes reported positive reactions to such behaviours (Volkwein, Schnell, Sherwood, & Livezey, 1997). Similarly, Boeringer (1999) surveyed 113 fraternity members, 52 athletes, and a control group of 312 males at an American university and found that students who were members of a fraternity or an athletic team were significantly more likely to have attitudes that support rape. Research by Peggy Sanday (1981, 1990) suggests that where sexist attitudes and tolerance are high, a high frequency of sexual violence is likely to occur. Likewise, Warshaw (1988) argues, "athletic teams are breeding grounds for rape [because they] are often populated by men who are steeped in sexist, rape-supportive beliefs" (p. 112).

Chandler, Johnson, and Carroll (1999) conducted a study of 342 college students in the United States, and found that student athletes were significantly more likely to engage in sexual behaviour, as well as to perpetrate sexual violence, than non-athletes. Forbes, Adams-Curtis, Pakalka, and White (2006) sampled a group of college freshmen in the United States and found that men who played contact sports in high school were significantly more likely to condone rape, sexist attitudes, and violence, and to have negative views of gay men. Using a meta-analytic review approach, Murnen and Kohlman (2007) determined that a strong relationship exists between athletic participation, hyper-masculinity, and sexually aggressive attitudes and behaviours.

In sum, there is significant research evidence to show that the institution of sport, particularly university sport in North America, is a hot spot of sexual violence. These studies can be criticized for focusing largely on self-reports, with limited samples focused on one or a few universities, and with statistical analyses that do not control for certain variables such as race and ethnicity. However, research results across different universities, with different racial and ethnic compositions, and with different sample sizes and approaches consistently show a significant link between sport participation and sexual violence. There is little reason to believe that such a link is not present at Canadian universities, despite a current lack of quantitative research on the issue.

SEXUAL VIOLENCE IN CANADIAN UNIVERSITY SPORT

In this chapter I do not seek to fill the quantitative research void on sexual violence in Canadian university sport. My research follows a case-study approach focusing on a small sample of cases of sexual violence that have occurred in the context of Canadian university sport. The cases were chosen based on the availability of information on the cases, and because they are representative of common themes across incidents of sexual violence in Canadian university sport. This approach allows for a more detailed understanding of the different forms that sexual violence in university sport often takes and the common threads between them, as well as elucidating why university sport is an institutional hot spot for sexual violence. In this section I will briefly describe three cases representing three main forms of sexual violence in university sport: (1) athlete-perpetrated sexual violence against women, (2) gang rapes perpetrated by athletes against women, and (3) athlete-on-athlete sexual violence in the course of hazing rituals. These do not compose the only forms of sexual violence occurring in Canadian university sport, but they appear to be the most prevalent forms in Canadian university sport.[2]

Athlete-perpetrated sexual violence against women

Mark Yetman, a goaltender for the Brock University Badgers hockey team, was convicted of sexually assaulting three women in December 2009 and January 2010. One December evening, Yetman and a teammate met two women at a St. Catharines bar and they all went back to Yetman's residence. Breaking off into two rooms, Yetman's teammate and one of the women engaged in consensual sex, while Yetman and the other woman began consensual sexual activity in a separate room. However, the sexual activity between Yetman and the woman became increasingly violent and the woman pleaded with Yetman to stop (Walter, 2012).

After this assault, he entered the other room, asked his teammate to leave, and proceeded to violently choke, hit, and sexually assault the other woman. In her testimony she stated, "I couldn't breathe at all ... I couldn't see straight. My vision was spotty. I was really scared. I didn't know if he was going to let up" (Walter, 2012, para. 5). By all media accounts, he remained a member of the Brock hockey team throughout the investigation of the first two reported sexual assaults.

In the following January, he was accused of a third sexual assault. Yetman was drinking and socializing with a group of three teammates and two women at a St. Catharines bar. Yetman and the two women went back to their apartment. One of the women went to sleep, while Yetman made sexual advances on the other, who refused and fled the apartment. She tried calling and texting her sleeping friend to warn her that Yetman was still in the apartment, but it was too late as he had entered the sleeping woman's room, removed her pyjamas and underwear, and had nonconsensual sex with her (Dakin, 2013).

In a 2012 jury trial for the first two sexual assaults, Yetman argued that although the sex was "rough" with the first two women, it was consensual (Dakin, 2012). The members of the jury disagreed and found Yetman guilty of both counts of sexual assault. Released on bail while awaiting sentencing, Yetman returned to his home province of Newfoundland and continued to play hockey, winning a senior men's league championship in the days before his sentencing. He was sentenced to two years less a day, with strong encouragement to pursue anger management counselling while incarcerated. Shortly thereafter he faced a second trial for the third sexual assault. This time he pleaded guilty to the sexual assault. Over 40 coaches, teachers, and acquaintances wrote character references for Yetman claiming him to be of good character. He was sentenced to three years to be served concurrently with the previous sentence he received (Dakin, 2013).

Gang rapes perpetrated by athletes against women

On September 10, 2011, several members of the McGill University Redmen football team allegedly drugged, confined, and sexually assaulted an 18-year-old Concordia University student. The survivor and her friend met some football players at a Montreal bar. They went back to the residence of the players, where the survivor was offered an open beer. She alleges that she must have been drugged via the open beer, as her next memory was waking up on a bed being sexually violated by several men whom she was telling to stop. Her next memory was waking up in the morning by getting her clothes thrown at her as the football players wanted her to leave because they had a practice to attend (Fazioli, 2014).

After an investigation by Montreal police, three players were charged with sexual assault against the Concordia student in April 2012. Two of the players were also charged with forcible confinement (Shields, 2013). The athletes were allowed to remain enrolled at McGill University and were able to continue playing for the university football team. Julie Michaud, of the Centre for Gender Advocacy at Concordia University, lamented this decision by McGill University, stating, "This incident happened a long time ago, McGill has known about it for a long time, and there was absolutely no consequence to the people who have been accused of a really serious crime" (Shields, 2013, para. 2). In the fall of 2013, over two years after the alleged sexual assault, the three charged players voluntarily quit the team. Later reports suggest that they may have been suspended due to public outcry.

In the fall of 2014, all charges against the three McGill University football players were dropped in the moments before their trial was set to begin (Montgomery, 2014). According to one of the player's lawyers, charges were dropped due to insufficient evidence. He stated, "When the Crown attorney, who has a particular role to play in prosecutions, examined his entire file, he concluded that with the evidence he had he should not go forward with his prosecution" (as cited in Bachelder, 2014, para. 3). Other accounts indicate that a new witness was located at the last moment, a resident student advisor at Concordia University whom the survivor confided in after the alleged assault, and who claimed in an email that the group sex was consensual (Montgomery, 2014). The survivor in the alleged gang assault by the football players reportedly remains traumatized by her experiences that night, as well as by the outcome of the pre-empted trial (Fazioli, 2014).

Athlete-on-athlete sexual violence

Well before the other well-publicized McGill University football sexual violence scandal dubbed the "Mr. Broomstick incident," which involved "nudity, degrading positions and behaviours, gagging, touching in inappropriate manners with a broomstick, as well as verbal and physical intimidation of rookies by a large portion of the team" (Drolet, 2006, p. 1), the University of Guelph Gryphons hockey program became embroiled in a hazing scandal. Unlike McGill University, which suspended its entire football program after the Mr. Broomstick hazing ritual was reported, the 1996 University of Guelph hockey coach, Marlin Muylaert, took the position that players who refuse to participate in a sexual hazing, and who are not willing to apologize to teammates for refusing to participate in the hazing, should be cut from the team (MacGregor, 1996).

The veterans of the Gryphons hockey team notified players of an upcoming party where they should "bring condoms, booze, and wear loose-fitting clothes, because they wouldn't be wearing them long" (Lannon, as cited in Robinson, 1998, p. 84). One of the rookie players, Robert Boyko, was hesitant to participate but went anyway. However, on entering the room he saw other rookies lying naked on the floor and left immediately to report the incident to his coach, Marlin Muylaert. Boyko and two other rookie members from the team who refused to be sexually hazed were reportedly cut from the team in response (MacGregor, 1996).

In a letter to the players and University of Guelph administration, the coach explained his decision, stating, "The bottom line is there are two kinds of hazing rituals, one is the degrading, damaging type, the other is fun and enjoyable. This was the fun and enjoyable type" (Muylaert, as cited in Bryshun, 1997, p. 41). The "fun and enjoyable" hazing acts in question reportedly involved heavy drinking, forced nudity, passing eggs mouth-to-mouth between rookie teammates, and eating marshmallows out of players' anuses (Bryshun, 1997). After an investigation, the University of Guelph gave the coach a one-game suspension for his conduct. Robert Boyko subsequently sued the University of Guelph for $1 million, claiming psychological damages and harassment that forced him to leave the school and his hockey career (McCarthy, 1997). No criminal charges have been reported in the incident.

MAKING SENSE OF ATHLETE-PERPETRATED SEXUAL VIOLENCE

Looking at the case studies of Mark Yetman, the alleged McGill gang rape, and the Guelph hazing suspensions, along with countless other cases I have been researching and the existing research on sexual violence in sport, several overarching elements emerge that appear to foster, support, and sustain a rape culture in Canadian university sport. I describe each of the three elements in the sections below. The first is that university sport is, arguably, a total institution. Second, institutional structures in university sport and Canadian society more generally, such as the legal system, commonly tolerate and potentially even promote sexual violence in and around sport; that is, a rape culture exists in the total institution of university sport. Third, many of the values and norms within the institution of sport, as well as the power dynamics that play out, cultivate a dangerous form of masculine identity formation that is precarious and relies heavily on violence, including violence against women, for identity stability.

Sport as a total institution

The institution of sport, particularly at the competitive university level, is of a totalizing nature. In a previous study I conducted, university football players described their involvement in the sport as all-encompassing, as time-consuming, and even as a prison sentence (Fogel, 2013). There are times in a university season when an athlete may have up to three practices in a single day, in addition to team sessions reviewing plays and strategies in a classroom, watching game footage with the team, eating meals with the team, and weight-lifting with teammates. Not unlike in the military, in competitive sport athletes are organized, regimented, and trained to fulfill a largely singular purpose: winning athletic contests.

The concept of the total institution has been popularized by Erving Goffman (1961), who describes the characteristics as follows:

> First, all aspects of life are conducted in the same place and under the same single authority. Second, each phase of the member's daily activity is carried on in the immediate company of a large batch of others, all of whom are treated alike and required to do the same thing together. Third, all phases of the day's activities are tightly scheduled, with one activity leading at a prearranged time into the next, the whole system being imposed from above by a system of explicit formal rulings and a body of officials. Finally, the various enforced activities are brought together into a single rational plan purportedly designed to fulfill the official aims of the institution. (p. 6)

This description is very fitting of the totalizing nature of many competitive sports on university campuses in Canada. Competitive sport differs from the total institutions that Goffman visited and researched in the 1950s, in that there are no high walls, fences, or forests that surround sport and make it nearly impossible to leave. However, I would argue that these walls are largely symbolic and mobile in the context of sport; while an athlete could conceivably decide not to follow along with the deeply prescribed training schedule and meeting times, this would lead to suspension or removal from the team.

For Goffman (1961), totalistic institutions serve to resocialize individuals, stripping their individual identities, values, and beliefs, and building up new desirable behaviours, attitudes, and identities. This concept is similar to Foucault's (1975) notion of modern prisons as "complete and austere institutions"

(p. 231) that serve to make the body and mind "docile" (p. 135) and therefore malleable to being shaped in desirable ways. Just as in prisons or the military and other total institutions, the total institution of competitive sport strips athletes of much of their individual identities, and socializes and resocializes them in ways that make them tough, strong, hard, and likely to win in their athletic endeavours. When a competitive team enters the field, rink, or hardwood, they enter in unison like marching military troops, the warm-up choreographed as tightly as an elite dance troupe, and when the whistle blows to start the game they fight in unity to punish and outscore their opponents.

While total institutions can be very effective in achieving their desired results of reshaping individuals to be winners or whatever the goal of the institution happens to be, it is my contention that they are also breeding grounds for violent and destructive behaviours, often fostering cultures of rape and other forms of interpersonal violence.

It has recently been reported that approximately 26,000 people in the American military experienced unwanted sexual contact in 2012 alone (Burris, 2014). The United States Department of Justice estimated that 216,600 sexual assaults occurred in American prisons in 2008 (Kaiser & Stannow, 2011). These are serious institutional hot spots for sexual violence. These are also institutions where violent attitudes, beliefs, and behaviours are socialized and often promoted, just as they are in many competitive sports where high rates of sexual violence appear to exist.

Social, legal, and institutional tolerance of sexual violence in sport

These total institutions with rape cultures are also largely ineffective in acknowledging and taking the necessary steps to address serious problems related to sexual violence, which is part of what perpetuates rape culture in total institutions. Kirby, Greaves, and Hankivsky (2000) argue that when athletes are sexually assaulted by other athletes or by coaches or administrators of sport, little viable redress is available. They write,

> Structurally, high performance sport is essentially an unregulated workplace where athletes are expected to devote themselves to the goal and demonstrate a strong work ethic. Yet they remain ill-protected by regulations, laws and policies that normally offer workers rights and avenues of redress. This disempowering structure sets the stage for exploitation and silence. If and when sexual abuse occurs [in sport], the structure does not assist the athlete in speaking out, seeking redress or righting situations. (p. 26)

Part of what makes some total institutions breeding grounds for sexual violence is that sexual violence and the attitudes, values, and beliefs that support it are rendered "tolerable" deviance.

Robert Stebbins (1996) defines tolerable deviance as behaviours that "occupy a middle ground, both attitudinally and emotionally, between acceptable, normative practices and disdainful, criminal practices" (p. xi). For Stebbins, deviance is defined in relation to the moral norms of the community, a conception similar to the one proposed by Émile Durkheim (1893/1968), and later by Kai Erikson (1966). In the Durkheimian sense, when the "collective conscience" is morally offended, a community unites, a crime is socially defined, and the society seeks retribution through the punishment of the offender (1893/1968, p. 80). Through this process, moral boundaries are defined, clarified, and redefined within the community (Erikson, 1966). Building on this, Stebbins (1996) explains that tolerable deviance occurs when individuals cause a slight, but not major, offence against the collective morality of a community. In the context of competitive university sport, sexual violence is often considered tolerable deviance by coaches, university administrators, the sports community, and legal officials; it is rarely treated as disdainful, criminal behaviour.

In the case of Mark Yetman, he was able to continue playing hockey, guiding his team to a league championship, even after he had been convicted of three brutally violent sexual assaults while he awaited his sentencing hearing. And, over 40 community members wrote letters to the sentencing judge encouraging a non-custodial sentence because of the great person they thought Mark Yetman to be. At McGill University, the three football players accused of drugging, forcibly confining, and gang raping an 18-year-old Concordia University student were able to continue playing for their university football team and attending university classes while they awaited their trial. At the University of Guelph, the hockey players were suspended not for forcing rookie athletes to participate in nonconsensual sex hazing rituals, but for refusing to be the victims of those sexual activities. This tolerance of sexual violence, in the total institution of competitive university sport, propagates a rape culture. Accusations and even convictions for sexual assault and other forms of interpersonal violence are often not seen as problematic by some coaches, and are often viewed positively as a character trait that might help a team in their quest to win games and championships. As former National Football League (NFL) coach Forrest Gregg (2009) writes prescriptively on building a winning football team, "you don't want choir boys on your side" (p. 310).

Dangerous masculinities in sport

Forrest Gregg's "choir boy" quote points to a second important element of the formation and maintenance of a rape culture in competitive sports. A significant aspect of the socialization and resocialization processes that occurs in sport, as with many other total institutions, is masculine identity formation.

All things seen to be feminine, weak, or soft are treated with contempt in the highly misogynistic and homophobic world of competitive men's sports (see Forbes et al., 2006). To be a "choir boy" is to be too nice, too fragile, and too delicate; it is an ultimate insult in many competitive male sports cultures.

Nancy Theberge (1981) contends that competitive sport is "a fundamentally sexist institution that is male dominated and masculine in orientation" (p. 342). Male athletes are socialized to aspire towards masculine identities that exude toughness, strength, power, and dominance. This is understood as part of the blueprint for assembling competitive athletes and winning teams. Michael Messner (1992) makes the important observation that sport is an arena not only where violent, dominant forms of masculinity are taught to boys and young men, but also where constant masculinity struggles between men occur. He argues, "Sport must be viewed as an institution through which domination is not only imposed, but also contested; an institution within which power is constantly at play" (p. 13).

Connell and Messerschmidt (2005) assert that masculinities are part of a highly complex gender hierarchy. There are hierarchies of masculinities within social institutions, characterized by complex power struggles, with dominant and subordinate forms. Masculinities are "multiple" with power relations of gender operating between men, particularly in the context of male-oriented total institutions (Carrigan, Connell, & Lee, 1985, p. 551). Competitive male university sport is an arena for hotly contested masculinity, power relations, and dominance. This, in turn, can lead to a high risk for the occurrence of sexual violence. As Volkwein-Caplan and Sankaran (2002) argue, "Sexual harassment and sexual assault are particularly likely to occur in tightly knit competitive male groups (e.g. military units, gangs, college fraternities, sport) that bind men emotionally to one another and contribute to their seeing sex relations from a position of power and status" (p. 11). Burton-Nelson (1994) writes,

> Nowhere are masculinity and misogyny so entwined as on the rugby field. At the post-game parties that are an integral part of the rugby culture, drunken men sing songs that depict women as loathsome creatures with insatiable sexual appetites and dangerous sexual organs. Men sing of raping other men's girlfriends and mothers. Rape is also depicted as a joke. (p. 88)

Messner (2002) characterizes the "athletic masculinity" that is constructed in sport as dangerous, leading to what he terms "the triad of violence" whereby masculine ideals lead athletes to commit violence against opponents, against themselves in the form of playing through injuries, and against women in the form of sexual and physical violence (p. 27). Masculinity becomes a competition within sport, where these three forms of violence become mechanisms by which male athletes climb the rungs of the hierarchy of athletic masculinity.

It is my view that the competition for masculine identity acknowledgement and dominance is particularly dangerous in the context of sport because of the precariousness of athletic or sporting masculinities. Masculine status in sports is highly unstable and constantly under threat, requiring continued identity work. An athlete might have a poor performance on the field of play, receive condemnation from the crowd and coaches, and be shunned by teammates, even if a few days earlier the athlete hit a game-winning shot and was celebrated as a hero by coaches, teammates, and fans. Likewise, injuries can take athletes out of competitions and have the potential to end their athletic careers in an instant. This notion is expressed well by a junior Canadian football player I interviewed in a previous study who stated, "We are all aware of the potential that your career could be over [with] the next snap because some guy rolls up on you from behind and you blow every ligament in your knee" (Fogel, 2013, p. 39).

This precariousness of masculine status has dangerous implications, as male athletes may engage in harmful behaviours to stabilize their masculine dominance. One way in which this is accomplished is through the sexual conquest of women. Sexual intercourse becomes a masculine competition, with women as the trophies. One athlete interviewed by Michael Messner (1992) describes this as follows: "We were like wolves hunting down prey.... If a girl doesn't give it up in 60 seconds, drop her!" (p. 101). In one of the many sexual assaults perpetrated by current and former male athletes described in Krakauer's (2015) recent study, one young male stole the pants and underwear of a woman after he allegedly sexually assaulted her. He explained to the police that they were "proof for his friends" that he had engaged in sexual intercourse with the young woman. Former basketball player Wilt Chamberlain (1991) infamously boasted that he had engaged in sexual intercourse with over 20,000 women. Describing an athlete's approach to sex as masculine identity confirmation and competition, Laura Robinson (1998) writes, "His actions have nothing to do with providing sexual pleasure and respect for a woman and everything to do with being seen as a man in his world" (p. 118).

Sex competitions in university sport can be even more literal than male predators seeking out sexual conquests and bringing back trophies to prove their conquests or boasting about them in autobiographies. Some athletic teams set up formal competitions that assign points for accomplishing sexual acts. One example of such a competition, referred to as the "LAD Point System," awards points for sexual acts with women, such as three points to "slip a finger in on the dance floor" or receive a "BJ [fellatio] in public," or other obscene behaviours, such as four points to "photobomb with your balls out," and with points deducted for preventing others from engaging in sexual acts, for example, "Minus two points for every time you cock block" (Bates, 2012).

Another sex competition documented in sport is what is termed a "Fantasy Slut League" (Leff, 2012). In such "leagues" female students are drafted, largely unknown to them, by male athletes. The draft determines an order or rank of girls at the particular school. Points are then awarded to the male athletes "for documented engagement in sexual activities with female students" (Leff, 2012, para. 4).

Whether sex competitions are laid out in specific rules or are part of the culture of particular sports teams, sexual intercourse with women appears to be a significant way that male athletes present and stabilize masculine identities in the context of sport, where masculinity is highly unstable. In such a context, where women are perceived as objects of a masculine competition, the occurrence of sexual assaults seems very likely.

Furthermore, athletes are trained to understand that consent in the context of competition is largely irrelevant (see Fogel, 2013, for a lengthy discussion on consent, or lack thereof, in competitive sports). If a competitive university football player is told by a coach to tackle an opposing player with as much force as possible and he says no, he will likely be required to sit on the bench or be cut from the team. Likewise, a competitive hockey player cannot say to a player on the opposing team that he does not want to be body-checked in a particular game and therefore not get body-checked in that game. When athletes enter competition, consent becomes largely irrelevant. Their bodies inflict pain and injury, and have pain and injury inflicted upon them, whether they are consenting to such violence or not. This understanding of consent by competitive athletes is problematic in a context where sexual intercourse becomes a competition.

Sexual violence perpetrated in university sport also often takes the form of gang rapes, involving multiple male athletes and a single victim. The majority of reported sexual assault cases in Canadian university sport are what could be called gang rapes, including the alleged McGill football sexual assault and Guelph hazing sexual assaults previously described. Based on a study of athlete-perpetrated sexual assaults at U.S. colleges and universities, Jeffrey Benedict (1997) notes that 33% of reported sexual assault cases involving athletes have multiple athletes as perpetrators. I think this is an understated number, as Benedict looked only at cases of male athletes assaulting women; had he considered that nonconsensual sexual hazing rituals could be considered gang rapes, that number would have increased exponentially.

Part of the performance of masculinity in sport appears to be a willingness to engage in sexual acts in front of teammates, and participate in shared violations of women's and rookie athlete's bodies. One university hockey player interviewed by Laura Robinson (1998) details a teammate's experience with being involved in a gang rape of a woman:

> [He] told me about an initiation where they had to have sex with this one girl in a hotel room ... she told them to stop it. They were hurting her. [He] knew she didn't want it. There were eight guys altogether. He didn't want to do it, because he knew he was about to rape a girl, and he knew he wasn't a rapist. But he knew what the team would do to him if he didn't rape her, so he did. He feels so terrible about it.... But the girls are seen as the fresh meat, and these guys are the wolves. (p. 122)

While deeply disturbing, this quote provides some insight into the inner workings of a sexual perpetrator in sport who does not have a biological drive or impulse to commit sexual assault, but rather feels that he must do so to maintain his status and place on his university hockey team.

CONCLUSION

I do not contend that all university athletes are perpetrators of sexual violence. In fact, it is quite possible that the vast majority of university athletes—including athletes in highly aggressive team sports like football, rugby, and hockey that appear to have the highest reported rates of sexual violence—are not rapists, are able to resist the misogynistic socializing characteristics of elite male sports, and do not use sexual intercourse, with or without consent, to establish and stabilize their precarious masculine identities. My argument is that various factors in competitive university sport coalesce to create a high-risk environment for the perpetration of sexual assault, which is characterized by misogynistic and sexist attitudes, objectification of women, defensive homophobia, sexually aggressive definitions of manhood, pressures for men to "score," and tolerance and promotion of sexual violence. These are the basic characteristics of a "rape culture" (Herman, 1984, p. 20).

This chapter represents a preliminary inquiry into sexual assault in Canadian university sport. One important step towards addressing the serious social problem of athlete-perpetrated sexual violence is increased research on the topic, including quantitative studies to allow for a better understanding of prevalence, and qualitative studies that include the voices of athletes themselves who witness, perpetrate, and are victimized by sexual violence. Increased research should also be done to explore the structures and cultures within the total institutions of competitive sport that serve to tolerate, and potentially promote, athlete-perpetrated sexual violence.

Existing research points to a need for universities to take a hard look at their athletic programs, with an eye to structural changes to reduce the totalizing nature of university sport by restricting time involvement on competitive teams to four days per week and no more than two hours per day plus travel times to allow for a well-rounded life outside of sport; providing athlete-specific training workshops on consent and healthy, lawful sexual relations; providing diversity training to university coaches; involving male athletes in public and campus campaigns to end violence against women; establishing clear and effective sexual assault reporting structures in university athletic departments and on university campuses more generally; and holding perpetrators to account by using internal disciplinary mechanisms to swiftly review and suspend guilty athletes from play and university campuses, rather than waiting for the often slow decisions to be made by legal officials who work within a system that requires a higher burden of proof that strongly advantages the offender in sexual assault cases.

NOTES

1 UCR data reflect reported crime that has been substantiated by police in Canada. It is not an accurate measure of all crimes in Canada, as some crimes are never detected or brought to the attention of the police, which is often referred to as the "dark figure of crime" (Maxfield, Weiler, & Widom, 2000). Sexual assault has a high dark figure, with low reporting rates, as identified in Chapter 1.

2 Other documented forms of sexual assault in sport include athlete-on-athlete sexual assault on the field of play, coach-on-athlete sexual exploitation and abuse, sexual assaults involving training and medical staff, and administrator-on-athlete sexual assaults.

REFERENCES

Auld, A. (2014, September 30). Dalhousie men's rugby club suspended over hazing allegations. *Globe and Mail*. Retrieved from http://www.theglobeandmail.com/sports/more-sports/dalhousie-mens-rugby-club-suspended-over-hazing-allegations/article20853127/

Bachelder, J. (2014, November 19). Sexual assault charges against former Redmen football players dropped: Prosecution cites insufficient evidence as reason for withdrawal. *McGill Daily*. Retrieved from http://www.mcgilldaily.com/2014/11/sexual-assault-charges-former-redmen-football-players-dropped/

Bates, L. (2012, November 27). Sites like Uni Lad only act to support our everyday rape culture. *Independent*. Retrieved from http://www.independent.co.uk/voices/comment/sites-like-uni-lad-only-act-to-support-our-everyday-rape-culture-8360109.html

Benedict, J. (1997). *Public heroes, private felons: Athletes and crimes against women*. Boston, MA: Northeastern University Press.

Boeringer, S. B. (1999). Associations of rape-supportive attitudes with fraternal and athletic participation. *Violence Against Women, 5*(1), 81–90.

Bryshun, J. (1997). *Hazing in sport: An exploratory study of veteran/rookie relations* (Master's thesis). University of Calgary, Alberta.

Burris, M. (2014). Thinking slow about sexual assault in the military. *Buffalo Journal of Gender, Law, and Social Policy, 23*, 21–72.

Burton-Nelson, M. (1994). *The stronger women get, the more men love football: Sexism and the American culture of sport.* New York, NY: Harcourt Brace.

Carrigan, T., Connell, R., & Lee, J. (1985). Toward a new sociology of masculinity. *Theory and Society, 14*(5), 551–604.

Chamberlain, W. (1991). *A view from above: The life of a legend in his own words.* New York, NY: Villard.

Chandler, S. B., Johnson, D. J., & Carroll, P. S. (1999). Abusive behaviors of college athletes. *College Student Journal, 33*(4), 638–645.

Connell, R., & Messerschmidt, J. (2005). Hegemonic masculinity: Rethinking the concept. *Gender & Society, 19*, 829–859.

Creppin v. University of Ottawa. (2015). Statement of defence. Court File No. 15-63058.

Crosset, T., Benedict, J. R., & McDonald, M. A. (1995). Male student-athletes reported for sexual assault: A survey of campus police departments and judicial affairs offices. *Journal of Sport and Social Issues, 19*(2), 126–140.

Dakin, D. (2012, October 24). Jury finds Yetman guilty of sexual assaults. *Niagara Falls Review.* Retrieved from http://www.niagarafallsreview.ca/2012/10/23/jury-finds-yetman-guilty-of-sexual-assaults

Dakin, D. (2013, April 5). Mark Yetman pleads to sexual assault. *Niagara Falls Review.* Retrieved from http://www.niagarafallsreview.ca/2013/04/05/mark-yetman-pleads-to-sexual-assault

Ditchburn, J. (2015, January 21). Ottawa Gee-Gees hockey saga takes another turn. *Toronto Star.* Retrieved from http://www.thestar.com/sports/hockey/2015/01/21/ottawa-gee-gees-hockey-saga-takes-another-turn.html

Drolet, D. (2006, October 10). When rites go wrong. *University Affairs.* Retrieved from http://www.universityaffairs.ca/when- rites-go-wrong.aspx

Durkheim, É. (1968). *The division of labor in society* (George Sampson, Trans.). New York, NY: Free Press. (Original work published 1893)

Erikson, K. (1966). *Wayward puritans: A study in the sociology of deviance.* New York, NY: Wiley.

Fazioli, D. (2014, November 18). "It's hard to move on": Alleged victim in McGill sex scandal speaks out. *Global News.* Retrieved from http://globalnews.ca/news/1679223/its-hard-to-move-on-alleged-victim-in-mcgill-sex-scandal-speaks-out/

Fogel, C. (2013). *Game-day gangsters: Crime and deviance in Canadian football.* Edmonton, AB: Athabasca University Press.

Forbes, G., Adams-Curtis, L., Pakalka, A., & White, K. (2006). Dating aggression, sexual coercion, and aggression-supporting attitudes among college men as a function of participation in aggressive high school sports. *Violence Against Women, 12*, 441–455.

Foucault, M. (1975). *Discipline and punish: The birth of the prison.* New York, NY: Vintage Books.

Gage, E. (2008). Gender attitudes and sexual behaviors: Comparing center and marginal athletes and non-athletes in a collegiate setting. *Violence Against Women, 14*(9), 1014–1032.

Goffman, E. (1961). *Asylums.* New York, NY: First Anchor Books.

Gregg, F. (2009). *Winning in the trenches.* Covington, KY: Clerisy Press.

Herman, D. (1984). The rape culture. In J. Freeman (Ed.), *Women: A feminist perspective* (3rd ed., pp. 20–38). Mountain View, CA: Mayfield.

Kaiser, D., & Stannow, L. (2011). Prison rape and the government. *New York Review of Books*. Retrieved from http://www.nybooks.com/articles/2011/03/24/prison-rape-and-government/?pagination=false

Kirby, S., Greaves, L., & Hankivsky, O. (2000). *The dome of silence: Sexual harassment and abuse in sport*. Halifax, NS: Fernwood.

Krakauer, J. (2015). *Missoula: Rape and the justice system in a college town*. New York, NY: Doubleday.

Leff, L. (2012). High school's athletes formed "Fantasy Slut League," awarding points for sex. *Toronto Star*. Retrieved from http://www.thestar.com/news/world/2012/10/23/high_schools_athletes_formed_fantasy_slut_league_awarding_points_for_sex.html

MacGregor, R. (1996, October 30). Time to admit problems in our game. *StarPhoenix*, pp. B1–B2.

Maxfield, M. G., Weiler, B. L., & Widom, C. S. (2000). Comparing self-reports and official records of arrests. *Journal of Quantitative Criminology, 16*(1), 87–110.

McCarthy, E. (1997, January 29). Former player sues team, university for negligence. *Ottawa Citizen*, p. D3.

Mehta, D. (2013, March 3). Legal threats dropped against Ottawa student leader after "rape culture" remarks. *Globe and Mail*. Retrieved from http://www.theglobeandmail.com/news/national/education/legal-threats-dropped-against-ottawa-student-leader-after-rape-culture-remarks/article17222104/

Messner, M. (1992). *Power at play: Sports and the problem of masculinity*. Boston, MA: Beacon Press.

Messner, M. (2002). *Taking the field: Women, men, and sport*. Minneapolis: University of Minnesota Press.

Montgomery, S. (2014, November 17). Sexual assault charges dropped against McGill Redmen. *Montreal Gazette*. Retrieved from http://montrealgazette.com/news/local-news/sexual-assault-charges-dropped-against-mcgill-redmen

Murnen, S., & Kohlman, M. (2007). Athletic participation, fraternity membership, and sexual aggression among college men: A meta-analytic review. *Sex Roles, 57*(1/2), 145–157.

Ratcliffe, J. H. (2004). The hotspot matrix: A framework for the spatio-temporal targeting of crime reduction. *Police Practice and Research, 5*(1), 5–23.

Robinson, L. (1998). *Crossing the line: Sexual harassment and abuse in Canada's national sport*. Toronto, ON: McClelland and Stewart.

Sanday, P. (1981). The socio-cultural context of rape: A cross-cultural study. *Journal of Social Issues, 37*, 5–27.

Sanday, P. (1990). *Fraternity gang rapes: Sex, brotherhood, and privilege on campus*. New York: New York University Press.

Shields, B. (2013, November 22). McGill campus football team at centre of sex assault controversy. *Global News*. Retrieved from http://globalnews.ca/news/985364/mcgill-campus-football-team-the-centre-of-sex-assault-controversy/

Stebbins, R. A. (1996). *Tolerable differences: Living with deviance*. Toronto, ON: McGraw-Hill Ryerson.

Theberge, N. (1981). A critique of critiques: Radical and feminist writings on sport. *Social Forces, 60*(2), 341–353.

Volkwein, K., Schnell, F., Sherwood, D., & Livezey, A. (1997). Sexual harassment in sport: Perceptions and experiences of American female student-athletes. *International Review for the Sociology of Sport, 32*(3), 283–295.

Volkwein-Caplan, K., & Sankaran, G. (2002). *Sexual harassment in sport: Impact, issues, and challenges.* Oxford, UK: Meyer and Meyer Sport.

Walter, K. (2012, October 18). Second woman testifies ex-Brock goalie assaulted her. *Niagara Falls Review.* Retrieved from http://www.niagarafallsreview.ca/2012/10/17/second-woman-testifies-ex-brock-goalie-assaulted-her

Warshaw, R. (1988). *I never called it rape.* New York, NY: Harper and Row.

PART III

INSTITUTIONAL PREVENTION

AND RESPONSES

TO SEXUAL VIOLENCE

CHAPTER 8

WOMEN AS EXPERTS
Origins and Developments of METRAC's Campus Safety Audit

Andrea Gunraj

When the Metropolitan Action Committee on Violence Against Women and Children (METRAC) launched its safety audit in 1989 and adapted it for use in post-secondary educational spaces, the idea that women were experts on their own sense of safety was still considered novel. The audit became an important catalyst to identify learning spaces that were hostile to women, as well as validating their safety concerns and proposing appropriate solutions. Yet gaps remained. The audit focused on public, stranger-perpetrated violence, and in focusing on women, it often missed the ever-shifting experiences of gender-based violence involving multiple identity factors. To address this issue, METRAC updated its campus audit to integrate a gender-aware, intersectional analysis shaped by multiple levels of social influence.

This chapter summarizes the evolution of METRAC's Campus Safety Audit Process as it incorporated the complexities of an intersectional analysis of victimization and employed a social-ecological model where critical reflection on policies and practices, and the involvement of all stakeholders—students, administrators, faculty, and surrounding communities—are essential for change. I provide a brief review of the origins of the audit process and its underlying "women-as-experts" principle, followed by a discussion of the audit's application to post-secondary institutional spaces. Then I address its "growing pains" as a tool that necessarily evolved to suit the diverse realities and needs of campus communities. The chapter concludes with a discussion of common tensions and challenges inherent in a community development model, with the purpose of building safer and more inclusive post-secondary institutional learning environments.

THE EVOLUTION OF METRAC'S SAFETY AUDIT

METRAC first developed its Women's Safety Audit in 1989 soon after women founded the organization in response to sexual assaults against women in Toronto public spaces in 1984. Formerly known as the Metropolitan Action Committee on Public Violence Against Women and Children, METRAC first focused on implementing the recommendations of the Metro Toronto Task Force on Public Violence Against Women and Children. Today, the organization continues to work with individuals, communities, and institutions to make the changes needed to prevent violence against diverse women and youth. Its programs serve communities across Canada, and its reach extends to global partnerships. METRAC's work promotes safety, increases access to justice, builds youth leadership, promotes equity and inclusion, and builds knowledge and awareness to reduce gender-based violence and its negative impacts.

In 1989, when it was first developed, METRAC's Women's Safety Audit Process was based on women's common stories and experiences of assault, as well as their fear of victimization, particularly gendered victimization, in public and semi-public places. As Guberman (2002) writes:

> Women described where they were afraid to go, the characteristics of those areas, and when they were afraid to go there. They talked about what they did to protect themselves, and what they didn't do for fear for their safety. Most significantly, some talked about not going out at all for fear for their safety. (p. 2)

The audit centred on assessing the physical environment and design elements that have an impact on women's sense of fear and safety in public spaces, such as inadequate lighting, isolated areas, lack of clear signage, low visibility and sightlines, and limited access to emergency services. It was designed to respond to these lived realities and centred on improvements that could be made to the physical environment that would reduce opportunities for assault.

In contrast to other types of safety audits, METRAC's safety audit centres on perceptions of safety in public spaces and includes fear of sexual assault and harassment. Many other audits rely on the principles of Crime Prevention Through Environmental Design (CPTED), an approach that "considers environmental conditions and the opportunities they offer for crime or other unintended and undesirable behaviors" (Zahm, 2007, pp. 5–6). This kind of model seeks to eliminate opportunities for crime and unwanted behaviour by using elements of the environment to control access, provide opportunities to see and be seen, define ownership, and encourage maintenance of territory (Zahm, 2007). But audits based purely on CPTED principles cannot necessarily respond to the unique dynamics of gender-based violence where women are most often at risk from men they know, violence frequently happens behind closed doors, and the "site" of crime is the victimized individual's body (DeKeseredy, Shahid, Renzetti, & Schwartz, 2005, pp. 29–30).

The audit is also informed by community development principles. While the term is often ill-defined, the definition of community development used by Ontario Healthy Communities Coalition (n.d.) aligns well with METRAC's audit approach. The coalition writes that community development is an approach to build economic and social progress for a whole community with active participation and reliance upon the community's agency. It works best when democracy, inclusivity and social justice, integrated services and enhancement of natural networks and capacities, non-authoritarianism, and preventative approaches are valued and applied. Bhattacharyya's (2004) theory of community development is also useful; she characterizes community development as "a positive response to the historic process of erosion of solidarity and agency," based on the "premise … that people have an inalienable right to agency and that solidarity is a necessity for a satisfying life" (p. 14). Appropriate methods of practice in community development that follow from this approach would be overlapping principles of self-help, felt needs, and participation, and action outcomes on both the micro and macro level (pp. 21, 24). In this respect, the METRAC audit relies fundamentally on the agency of community members to identify spaces that feel unsafe, and on their drive to create more safety.

Within the 12 years following its launch, METRAC revised its audit to address the social environment in addition to the physical environment and design elements. As such, the audit grew to include attitudes and behaviours, policies and practices, and availability of services to bolster personal safety in everyday life for women and others who feel vulnerable (Guberman, 2012, p. 1). The audit tool was further expanded to include the realities of people of all genders who face the risk of gender-based violence, discrimination, and harassment, thereby recognizing the importance of including all community members in the safety-building process, in particular those who are the most marginalized.

METRAC's Women's Safety Audit Process has been used extensively across Canada since its inception in 1989 and has been adapted for use around the world as a "dynamic participatory concept that exists in a constant state of modification and improvement" (Women in Cities International, 2008, p. 8). Notably, the Women's Safety Audit Process was named a best practice in 2008 by the UN-HABITAT Safer Cities Programme. The story of its development is one of ever more flexibility, inclusiveness, and effectiveness, from the initial application in community spaces such as neighbourhood streets, parks, playgrounds, and established housing complexes, to its application in semi-public and private spaces, including transit systems, hospitals, shopping malls, underground garages, workplaces, educational institutions, and new developments in the pre-build stage.

HOW THE AUDIT PROCESS WORKS

The safety audit process is made up of several steps. To begin, METRAC representatives train a group of community members and users of a space on key basics of community safety and violence issues and how to conduct the audit. They review the audit checklist that covers areas such as lighting, sightlines, maintenance, and past incidents of violence. This training process is designed to build community capacity and enable community members to conduct audits on their own in the future. While it should be led by participants who live, work, play, and learn in the area, the audit process may be attended by local stakeholders such as politicians, municipal staff, representatives of community organizations and faith groups, and nearby business owners.

METRAC representatives assist audit participants in identifying a route and area to audit that is based on what is relevant and important to their lives (for instance, prevention or intervention at sites identified by residents as fraught with danger). They collectively conduct a site tour of the space and complete a survey on what they felt and noticed, identifying their primary physical and social safety concerns. They discuss these concerns and decide on three or four priorities on which to focus. All the data gathered during the site tour (surveys, notes, and pictures) is collected for analysis by METRAC representatives, who prepare a report with recommendations that can number between 10 and 50.

The group uses the recommendations to discuss and negotiate with relevant decision makers such as landlords, municipal government representatives, and building administration. As Guberman (2012) notes, "the audits that result in the most effective changes are those that are a partnership from the start between the women who have local safety concerns and key stakeholders such as elected representatives, city officials or the police, who have the authority to implement recommended changes" (p. 2). As one might expect, those recommendations that are easily implemented, such as repairs to lights and installation of signage, are most often swiftly acted on, while complex recommendations requiring greater financial and systemic resources can take longer to implement and their fulfillment is less certain as they require greater levels of deliberation, advocacy, planning, development, and evaluation by community members and decision makers. These larger-scale recommendations may include creating prevention resources, developing new support services for victims/survivors of violence, and allocating additional security measures to monitor an area.

UNIQUE FOUNDING PRINCIPLE

In relaying her experiences leading to a 1989 audit project of Toronto's public transit system, Wekerle (2005) explains:

> It was critical that one of the [auditing team members] was a woman familiar with issues of violence against women since her perceptions of the transit environment were often at variance with the responses of the two male representatives from the [Toronto Transit Commission (TTC)] and the police department. It was also critical that the report ... was written by METRAC from the perspective of women's experiences and with the goal of making women's realities of using public transit more visible.... This framing of the problem would not have occurred if the report had been written by either the TTC or the Metropolitan Police Department. (p. 283)

Wekerle's experience of advocating for women's involvement in transit audits reflects the core principle of METRAC's safety work and the safety audit approach: women are experts on their sense of safety and must therefore be closely consulted when it comes to planning and policy.

The design of the audit is therefore to engage as leaders those who live, work, play, and go to school in an area, with the caveat that "no professional training is necessary" (Guberman, 2012, p. 1). Rather, METRAC audits are informed by participatory action research methodologies that promote shared ownership of the research process through a community-based analysis of social problems that is oriented to community action (Kemmis & McTaggart, 2008).

METRAC founded the women's audit to give priority and legitimacy to women's perspective as space users, a unique conceptualizing of women as experts on their own safety by virtue of their knowledge, experiences, and organizing (Andrew, 2000, p. 163). As METRAC's original Women's Safety Audit Guide put it, a degree in architecture or urban planning was not needed for an individual to express "what works and what doesn't work" in terms of a personal sense of safety (METRAC, 1989, p. 5). The audit process validated women's negotiation with their environments by acknowledging that "living as a woman ... has given each of us a lifetime of experience and knowledge" in relation to matters of safety (METRAC, 1989, p. 5). It was precisely this lived knowledge and expertise on gender-based violence that professional space planners often lacked.

The "women-as-experts" position in METRAC's audit follows a path forged since the 1970s in Canada by feminist space planners, academics, and activists who "critically [analyzed] the role of the built environment in the perpetration of gender inequality and other forms of social and environmental injustice" and attended to gender bias in the way spaces are designed and managed (MacGregor, 1995, p. 26). In general terms, feminist critiques of mainstream space planning and management helped to formulate the understanding that a "sense of insecurity affects women's everyday life, restricting their personal freedom and access to public and private spaces," promoting efforts to make women's safety and security fit their own experiences (Moser, 2012, p. 437). As critiques of broad-strokes issues emerged on the differentiation of women's and men's access to public spaces and economic compensation for women's labour, feminist scholars and activists began to recognize that some women—for instance, poor women, racialized women, and single mothers—have always had to negotiate the public sphere in situations of high risk just to survive. There emerged an anti-oppressive, intersectional feminist perspective that sought to incorporate women as a diverse group who share some experiences but face varying risks and opportunities in public space that are based on social identity factors such as race, class, sexuality, ability, and age (Dumbrill, 2003, pp. 102–104; Mattsson, 2014, pp. 9–10; Sandercock & Forsyth, 2005, pp. 68–70).

Consequently, it was the range of feminist critique that contributed to the emergence of "gendered spatial planning" for different uses and experiences of space, emphasizing that space planning must serve the diverse needs in any community that includes women (Royal Town Planning Institute, 2007, p. 4). Although more women are entering the field of space planning now, Sandercock and Forsyth (2005) note that male dominance in perspectives, approaches, standards, and theory prevails (pp. 77–78). In light of this reality, safety audits that rely on women's voices serve an important counterbalancing function as one key method of promoting the perspective of women's safety in public spaces that were designed without their input (Moser, 2012, p. 438).

UNIQUENESS AND COMPLEXITY OF CAMPUS SPACES

Promoting safety with the goal of reducing gendered violence can be a complicated matter in any public space; however, the complexity and variability in post-secondary institutional contexts pose special challenges because, for one thing, campuses are mixed-use complexes that include public areas such as quads, public roads, and shops; semi-public areas like classrooms and libraries; and private places like dorm rooms. One building alone might contain spaces that fall along many degrees of the public–private spectrum, and buildings are

utilized for a wide array of purposes—scientific research, living quarters, technological development, and quiet study, to name a few. Campuses sometimes
constitute self-contained mini-cities, neighbourhoods, or clusters of neighbourhoods with all the necessities for daily living: food services, home areas,
retail complexes, sports facilities, workplaces, spiritual centres, civic engagement sites, childcare sites, and entertainment, art, and recreational spaces.
Furthermore, one post-secondary institution can consist of several campuses
that are miles apart from each other, and with the advent of distance-learning
and online courses, post-secondary sites are increasingly digital, operating in
the elusive domain of cyberspace.

Structurally, campus communities are also diverse in terms of social identities, backgrounds, and the institutional positions and needs of their members.
The people who work, live, and learn on campus can represent any number
of intersections of gender and sexuality, ethno-racial backgrounds, languages,
abilities, immigration statuses, faiths and beliefs, income levels, and ages. Even
in cases where members share key identity factors such as race, ethnicity, and
income level, a campus is distinctively positioned to host a greater diversity
than its surrounding neighbourhoods and communities due to the population
of students and faculty it attracts in an increasingly transnational world.

Taking into account the multiple features that make campus spaces unique
called for the development of a special type of audit to move beyond the more
generalized community process, and in 1991 METRAC launched its Campus
Safety Audit Process (CSAP) in partnership with the Council of Ontario Universities' Committee on the Status of Women. This version of the audit com-
bines the elements of training, site visits, and space tours that were endemic
to the community-based audit, but with the added feature of broader safety
surveys, focus groups, and interviews with the campus population (both students and faculty) to yield a more comprehensive understanding of "campus
culture" and community dynamics (METRAC, 1991). Significantly, the CSAP
also includes an analysis of relevant institutional policies and practices, as well
as campus programming and off-campus services that are accessible to campus
community members. Consequently, this audit entails a more comprehensive
process that as such is more heavily facilitated by a team of METRAC representatives working in close partnership with campus stakeholders: student
government representatives, union bodies, institutional leaders, and administration and/or security departments. Since its launch more than 20 years
ago, the CSAP has been used in 22 universities and colleges across Canada.

GROWING PAINS

For reasons discussed above, the Women's Safety Audit Process has appealed to those searching for a systematic approach to address the experience of gender-based violence, a problem all too often normalized as constituting the "burden" of being a woman (Garcia-Moreno, Heise, Jansen, Ellsberg, & Watts, 2005, p. 1283). In the years following its inception, the audit became a catalyst for identifying spaces that at the very least were unequal to women's needs, and at the most, presented formidable barriers to women's inclusion, access, and fulfillment of human rights. In the case of METRAC's campus-specific audit, the momentum was to identify hostile learning environments for women and build the case for educational institutions to understand their lack of prevention and intervention policies in terms of an "institutional breach of trust" (Marshall, 1991, p. 76).

However, there were anomalies in the design of METRAC's early campus audit, which was focused on stranger-perpetrated violence against women in public areas of the institution. For instance, although the original audit guide acknowledged that most sexual assaults are committed by someone known to the survivor/victim, checklist questions did not include private or quasi-private sites where sexual assaults would tend to take place (METRAC, 1991, pp. 8–9). Given that 68% of aggravated sexual assaults occur in and around residential settings, the original audit checklist failed to include questions about on-campus student dorms and their unique features as living spaces embedded in learning sites (Brennan & Taylor-Butts, 2008, p. 14).

Similarly, the original campus audit guide and checklist did not acknowledge intimate partner violence as a form of gendered violence that can occur on campuses and contribute to the sense of risk that women and other vulnerable groups may experience. As such, the audit was prone to miss data on the forms of gender-based violence that are most often perpetrated by partners and ex-partners, namely criminal harassment or stalking (Sinha, 2013, p. 23).

Moreover, the original Campus Safety Audit Guide was ill-equipped to address multiple identities. It did not strongly reflect the risks that different women and vulnerable people face, depending on the social identities that determine oppression and privilege, for instance, focusing as it did on women as an underserved group in campus planning and management. An example of an unintended contradiction in this regard is in the original guide, which specified that the auditing team "should reflect the range of racial and cultural diversity on campus" while there was no cross-checking mechanism in the audit to reveal how inclusive the team really was (METRAC, 1991, pp. 14, 34). So while the guide asked participants to note whether clear, effective policies on racism and homophobia existed, the questions that would cull this kind of data in other sections were not present, nor were participants asked to identify their own social locations. The audit was therefore subject to such pitfalls as non-racialized and heterosexual auditors being asked to evaluate policies that did not strongly reflect the realities of their day-to-day lives and of which they were not aware. Added to this, the original guide was not inclusive of transgendered campus community members despite their high rates of multiple forms of victimization, including sexual violence (Faulkner, 2006, p. 157; Longman Marcellin, Scheim, Bauer, & Redman, 2013; Scheim, Bauer, & Pyne, 2014).

A MORE INTEGRATED APPROACH TO CAMPUS AUDITS

By the early 2000s, elements that were missing in the original campus audit guide were recognized in no small part by a complement of staff with expertise who advocated for adoption of an anti-oppressive, intersectional feminist framework for programs and practices at METRAC.

Accordingly, by 2002 METRAC had overhauled its entire Campus Safety Audit Process to better meet the needs of diverse women and people at risk in relation to the complexities of post-secondary institutional life. The new process captured specific metrics to identify how intimate partner violence contributes to a lack of safety in post-secondary spaces, and importantly, the audit adopted an integrated anti-oppression framework. For example, audit participants were asked to respond to questions on identify factors such as ethno-racial background, sexuality, age, and abilities. Capturing the elements of "social location" was an integral step to making the campus audit more inclusive and meaningful, locating participants along the social matrix of power, privilege, and oppression that determines access to social respect and resources (Kondrat, 1999, p. 464). Not only does this framework allow for analysis of diverse perspectives, but it can now identify the gaps in audits where voices might be missing. Another significant change in the new campus audit was the introduction of expanded methods for engagement such as reaching out to the student groups and clubs that serve those who are marginalized, for instance, ethno-specific groups and LGBTTIQQ2S[1] students. Another addition to the audit was the inclusion of questions and metrics addressing the incidence of intimate partner violence, which heightens fear and a sense of risk on campus, as elsewhere.

Further, the revised Campus Safety Audit Process addressed such relevant features of contemporary campus life as the prevalence of hate-based crimes and gender-based harassment as it might play out in distance learning and digital course work. More complex and comprehensive data were thereby incorporated into the overall analysis and crafting of safety recommendations.

All these changes have contributed to making METRAC's campus audit a more integrated, inclusive, and powerful tool. While still incorporating elements of "traditional" crime prevention approaches such as Crime Prevention Through Environmental Design and a gender analysis framework, the audit now reflects a social-ecological model of violence prevention where all elements of a community can be explored, from individual to community relationships, to governing policies and practices, to cultural norms (Centers for Disease Control and Prevention, 2013; Jeffery, 1971; Warren, 2007).

ONGOING CHALLENGES

In 2016, StrategiSense Consulting undertook a preliminary evaluation of METRAC's neighbourhood-level audit to assess its impact and identify areas for improvement. The audit was found to be effective in empowering participants to take action on local safety issues, as it increased their skill and confidence in the civic process. The audit was also found to build participant awareness of community safety issues and a sense of community among those who used it. By way of improvement, StrategiSense Consulting identified that the neighbourhood audit process needs to be more accessible for people who use languages other than English and French; include mechanisms for more diverse community engagement; and have more robust follow-up and collaborative supports to ensure that safety changes actually happen after the audit is completed. Even though this evaluation focused on the neighbourhood audit, it is likely that these strengths and improvements can be adapted and applied to fit the campus audit.

Beyond the findings of this external evaluation, while the Campus Safety Audit Process has undergone a significant transformation, its effectiveness in reducing gendered violence and building inclusive, safe learning environments is affected by tensions inherent in contemporary post-secondary environments. The model of community development is widely recognized as an effective approach to address root causes of social problems such as gender-based violence prevention and intervention, but this approach for campus audits must contend with the considerable challenges of working within an institutional setting.

As discussed above, post-secondary institutions are increasingly complicated entities where even a relatively small institution may consist of several competing interests and groups. Moreover, the success of implementing safety-inducing changes following an audit will depend on campus stakeholders with the greatest degree of decision-making power (such as executives, governors, and administrators) endorsing recommendations that require significant internal change, and committing appropriate resources to the project of reducing gendered violence. In order for effective community development to occur on campuses, there must be strong commitment on the part of institutional leaders to flattening hierarchies and supporting the marginalized campus voices of women; transgender, racialized, and Indigenous individuals; and people with disabilities. However, given the tendency of educational institutions to be characterized by impression management, self-preservation, and conservatism in their practices and objectives, they are particularly resistant to change (Lane, 2007, p. 86). The nature of conservatism mitigates against changing the status quo of power dynamics in which women's safety needs are relegated to a secondary position, and discriminatory practices, stereotyping attitudes, and inherent biases tend to go unchallenged. Resistance to change is especially detrimental to the implementation of integrated, multifaceted safety-enhancing policy, practice, and program changes that touch the root causes of violence and extend beyond surface improvements such as the installation of new lighting on dim pathways.

Moreover, there are other, broader considerations that influence the implementation of recommendations from a safety audit, including a university's strategic goals, public relations, and legislative and fiscal management pressures. For instance, the American Federation of Teachers Higher Education (n.d.) notes a growing trend of campus corporatization where high-level decisions are made from a political and financial perspective rather than an academic or educational-value perspective, weakening democratic governance on campus. These realities hinder community development initiatives contingent on the participation of all stakeholders to build safety and enhance and protect human rights, equity, and inclusion within campus environments.

Monitoring and evaluation also pose a challenge following an audit process. The most far-reaching safety-enhancing recommendations require a phased, multi-year implementation process, and are best served by a robust feedback loop where those most affected by violence, harassment, and exclusion can express what is and is not working. However, this kind of project requires the investment of significant financial and human resources from post-secondary institutions, which may preclude the quick wins sought by administration. It is again incumbent upon campus stakeholders with the most access to power and resources to create room for long-term development and systemic change over time.

It is clear that the support of high-level on-campus change makers who hold power in the institution and have the trust of other power holders will be absolutely essential to overcoming these challenges. When they are well placed within institutions and buy into the audit project and its philosophy and methods, such change makers can be invaluable in getting buy-in and allocation of resources for implementing, monitoring, and evaluating recommendations. From audit inception to planning and wrap-up, the facilitation of internal change makers is critical to the audit's outcomes, especially when they come up against the counterforces of institutional conservatism and corporatization.

For example, after an incident of sexual assault that garnered media attention for a relatively small campus environment, METRAC was contacted by the head of security. This trusted director reported to high-level administration and was eager to advocate for the audit with decision makers from a security perspective. The director was able to get buy-in to do the audit and then to allocate significant resources towards implementation of audit recommendations over a period of several years. As a result, most recommendations were implemented long after the audit was completed, including the establishment of new services for students at risk of sexual violence.

On another larger and more complex campus, the audit was led by a multi-disciplinary team of administrators, staff, faculty, and students, a model that was powerful precisely because the team was set up to report directly to the highest levels of the institution who were openly committed to the audit's equity-based perspectives and community-building philosophy. It was the structure of this audit, with buy-in from the start from leaders empowered to follow up recommendations, that enabled safety outcomes that could have been stalled, if only because of the size and complexity of this campus environment.

CONCLUSION

Clearly, the METRAC Campus Safety Audit Process has undergone significant evolution in theory and practice since its inception over 20 years ago, developing to reflect the realities of gender-based violence and discrimination against women, as well as other groups at high risk in contemporary post-secondary spaces. It will necessarily continue to exist as a shifting, fluid, and flexible tool in pursuit of innovative ways to build safer, more inclusive spaces for higher learning.

Nonetheless, the audit's effectiveness in transforming unsafe campuses and triggering equity-building change must have the commitment and collaboration of institutions that launch the process to buy into its community development and participatory approach. Post-secondary institutional leaders must commit to flattening hierarchies, countering the tendency towards conservatism in attitudes and practices that impede deep change. They must be willing to engage marginalized community members within the campus and surrounding areas by using methods that capture the "felt needs" of these participants.

Further, the identification of internal institutional change makers in positions of authority to advocate for the audit's methods and recommendations will continue to be critical to success. And finally, campuses need to allocate adequate planning and resources to implement, monitor, and meaningfully evaluate audit recommendations. It will be this level of commitment that ensures a change process that produces relief for women and other vulnerable campus members who are most affected by all forms of violence.

ACKNOWLEDGEMENTS

Thank you to Wendy Komiotis (executive director, METRAC) for her editing support; Jessica Mustachi (safety coordinator, METRAC) for her editing and research support; and METRAC volunteers Ceila Wandio and Daisy Kling for their research support.

NOTE

1 Lesbian, gay, bisexual, transgender, transsexual, intersex, queer, questioning and two-spirit.

REFERENCES

American Federation of Teachers Higher Education. (n.d.). *Shared governance in colleges and universities: A statement by the Higher Education Program and Policy Council*. Washington, DC: Author.

Andrew, C. (2000). Resisting boundaries? Using safety audits for women. In K. B. Marianne & A. H. Young (Eds.), *Gendering the city: Women, boundaries, and visions of urban life* (pp. 157–168). Lanham, MD: Rowman & Littlefield.

Baum, F., MacDougall, C., & Smith, D. (2006). Participatory action research. *Journal of Epidemiology and Community Health, 60*(10), 854–857.

Bhattacharyya, J. (2004). Theorizing community development. *Journal of the Community Development Society, 34*(2), 5–34.

Brennan, S., & Taylor-Butts, A. (2008). *Sexual assault in Canada: 2004 and 2007*. Ottawa, ON: Minister of Industry.

Centers for Disease Control and Prevention. (2013, December 27). *The social-ecological model: A framework for prevention*. Retrieved from http://www.cdc.gov/violence prevention/overview/social-ecologicalmodel.html

DeKeseredy, S., Shahid, A., Renzetti, C. M., & Schwartz, M. D. (2005). Reducing private violence against women in public housing: Can second generation CPTED make a difference? *CRVAW Faculty Journal Articles*, Paper 300.

Dumbrill, G. C. (2003). Child welfare: AOP's nemesis? In W. Shera (Ed.), *Emerging perspectives on anti-oppressive practice* (pp. 101–119). Toronto, ON: Canadian Scholars' Press.

Faulkner, E. (2006). Homophobic sexist violence in Canada: Trends in the experiences of lesbian and bisexual women in Canada. *Canadian Woman Studies, 25*(1/2), 154–161.

Garcia-Moreno, C., Heise L., Jansen, H. A. F. M., Ellsberg, M., & Watts, C. (2005). Violence against women. *Science, 310*(5752), 1282–1283.

Guberman, C. (2002). *Empowerment strategies for women: The safety audit: What's next?* First International Seminar on Women's Safety, Montreal, QC.

Guberman, C. (2012). Safety audits: A catalyst for change. *Universitas Forum, 3*(1), 1–3.

Jeffery, C. (1971). Crime prevention through environmental design. *American Behavioral Scientist, 14*(4), 598–598.

Kemmis, S., & McTaggart, R. (2008). Participatory action research: Communicative action and the public sphere. In N. K. Denzin & Y. S. Lincoln (Eds.), *Strategies of qualitative inquiry* (3rd ed., pp. 271–330). Thousand Oaks, CA: Sage.

Kondrat, M. E. (1999). Who is the "self" in self-aware: Professional self-awareness from a critical theory perspective. *Social Service Review, 73*(4), 451–477.

Lane, I. F. (2007). Change in higher education: Understanding and responding to individual and organizational resistance. *Journal of Veterinary Medical Education, 34*(2), 85–92.

Longman Marcellin, R., Scheim, A., Bauer, G., & Redman, N. (2013). Experiences of transphobia among trans Ontarians. *Trans PULSE e-Bulletin, 3*(2). Retrieved from http://transpulseproject.ca/wp-content/uploads/2013/03/Transphobia-E-Bulletin-6-vFinal-English.pdf

MacGregor, S. (1995). Deconstructing the man made city: Feminist critiques of planning thought and action. In M. Eichler (Ed.), *Change of plans: Towards a nonsexist sustainable city* (pp. 25–49). Toronto, ON: Garamond Press.

Marshall, P. (1991). Sexual abuse involving breach of trust: A barrier to equality in the administration of justice. *Canadian Women's Studies Journal, 11*(4), 73–77.

Mattsson, T. (2014). Intersectionality as a useful tool: Anti-oppressive social work and critical reflection. *Journal of Women and Social Work, 29*(1), 8–17.

METRAC. (1989). *Women's Safety Audit Guide.* Toronto, ON: Author.

METRAC. (1990). METRAC: A catalyst for change. *Women & Environments, 12*(1), 4–5.

METRAC. (1991). *Women's Campus Safety Audit Guide.* Toronto, ON: Author.

Moser, C. (2012). Mainstreaming women's safety in cities into gender-based policy and programmes. *Gender & Development, 20*(3), 435–452.

National Institutes of Health. (2014, September 26). Cultural competency. Retrieved from http://www.nih.gov/clearcommunication/culturalcompetency.htm

Ontario Healthy Communities Coalition. (n.d.). Values and principles of community development. Retrieved from http://www.ohcc-ccso.ca/en/courses/community-development-for-health-promoters/module-one-concepts-values-and-principles/values-

Royal Town Planning Institute. (2007). *Gender and spatial planning: RTPI good practice note 7.* London, UK: Author.

Sandercock, L., & Forsyth, A. (2005). A gender agenda: New directions for planning theory. In S. S. Fainstein & L. J. Servon (Eds.), *Gender and planning: A reader* (pp. 67–85). New Brunswick, NJ: Rutgers University Press.

Scheim, A., Bauer, G., & Pyne, J. (2014). Avoidance of public spaces by trans Ontarians: The impact of transphobia on daily life. *Trans PULSE e-Bulletin, 4*(1). Retrieved from http://transpulseproject.ca/wp-content/uploads/2014 /01/Trans-PULSE-E-Bulletin-8-English.pdf

Sinha, M. (Ed.). (2013). *Measuring violence against women: Statistical trends.* Ottawa, ON: Minister of Industry.

StrategiSense Consulting. (2016). *Evaluation of the METRAC safety audit.* Toronto, ON: Author.

Warren, H. (2007). Using gender-analysis frameworks: Theoretical and practical reflections. *Gender & Development, 15*(2), 187–198.

Wekerle, G. R. (2005). Gender planning in public transit: Institutionalizing feminist policies, changing discourse, and practices. In S. S. Fainstein & L. J. Servon (Eds.), *Gender and planning: A reader* (pp. 275–295). New Brunswick, NJ: Rutgers University Press.

Women in Cities International. (2008). *Women's safety audits: What works and where?* Nairobi, Kenya: United Nations Human Settlements Programme (UN-HABITAT).

Zahm, D. (2007). *Using Crime Prevention Through Environmental Design in problem-solving.* Washington, DC: U.S. Department of Justice.

CHAPTER 9

THEORY BECOMES PRACTICE
The Bystander Initiative at the University of Windsor

Anne Forrest and Charlene Y. Senn

This is the story of the first five years (2010–2015) of the University of Windsor's Bystander Initiative to Mitigate the Incidence of Sexual Assault (BI). UWindsor's BI is one piece of an urgently needed, national effort to improve campus safety for women students. Across North America, a startling number of women experience sexual assault during their post-secondary education, yet until recently there has been little progress towards effective and sustainable sexual assault prevention education. Our particular contribution to this effort is our focus on organizational change. We adopt a multi-pronged approach to achieve what we refer to as "institutionalization." The BI's long-term goal is the creation of an anti-rape campus ethos supported by students who are willing and able to intervene and disrupt sexual assaults in the making, and our principal tool is the undergraduate curriculum. To this end, we created two undergraduate courses to educate male and female students about sexual assault and to train peer facilitators who deliver a three-hour sexual assault prevention workshop to students in a range of other undergraduate courses and to students in first-year law. The workshop is now available to 1200 to 1500 students a year.

The UWindsor BI is designed to produce a series of small but persistent changes in students' thinking and behaviour that, over time, will shift the campus climate towards one that is less tolerant of sexual assault and more supportive of students who take action when intervention is called for. Students engaged with the BI learn to identify potentially dangerous situations, determine that help is needed, take responsibility for providing assistance, and intervene while keeping themselves safe. Our model applies tipping point theory (Allsop, Bassett, & Hoskins, 2007; Cooke & Buckley, 2008; Gladwell, 2006), which hypothesizes that a marked shift in attitudes or behaviours within an organization can be accomplished if as few as 10% to 15% of its members are influenced, then choose to become influencers. Achieving and maintaining this critical mass is challenging on university campuses, which, by nature, are "leaky" organizations.

Our story begins in 2008 and remains unfinished business. This is the story of our first five years.

It is a story of good luck, good strategy, and synergy; importantly, for us, it is also a story of feminist-inspired social change. We see progress on this issue to be a matter of gender equity, as well as campus safety and student health. The authors are academic activists and friends who share values and a vision of a more equitable campus. In other ways we are quite different: Charlene Senn is a feminist applied social psychologist whose research and activism focus on male violence against women, particularly on education that leads to individual and social change; Anne Forrest is a feminist labour relations researcher embedded in Women's and Gender Studies, whose union activism and scholarship focus on organizational change and social justice.

This chapter begins by positioning the UWindsor BI in the context of sexual assault prevention efforts, and then describes and analyzes our progress towards institutionalization. From the outset, we applied four working principles:

- Utilize expertise;
- Embed sexual assault prevention education in the curriculum;
- Engage students—most importantly, men—as change agents; and
- Cultivate a spirit of mutuality.

These principles guided the BI plan of action we put to the administration for funding in 2010 and our subsequent modifications of that plan. Each iteration is grounded in feminist sexual assault prevention research or organizational-change theory and practice. Essential to our process has been the practice of self-critique and program modification to overcome the obstacles we encountered. We are hopeful that our guiding principles and our experience with implementation will assist colleagues on other campuses who are engaged in this important work.

THE UWINDSOR BI IN CONTEXT

Sexual violence against women is commonplace across North America. In Canada, one in two women experiences sexual assault or attempted sexual assault at some point in her life (Canadian Panel on Violence Against Women,

1993; Randall & Haskell, 1995). Access to women's bodies is a deeply ingrained aspect of male privilege in the wider culture (Belknap & Erez, 1995; Breitenbecher, 2000; Carr, 2005; Katz, Heisterkamp, & Fleming, 2011), and the behaviours involved are widely accepted as normal in heterosexual relationships (Buchwald, Fletcher, & Roth, 1993; Herman, 1979; Kelly, 1987, 2012). On university and college campuses, as many as one in four women students experiences rape or attempted rape during her post-secondary education (Fisher, Cullen, & Turner, 2000). While there is evidence that sexual assault rates can differ across campuses (Krebs et al., 2016), no one is exempt. Social events—parties, dating, and pub nights—provide the context for these encounters; the most common locations are the home, apartment, or dorm of the perpetrator or victim or their friends and family (Fisher et al., 2000; Tjaden & Thoennes, 2000). Contrary to popular perception, the perpetrators are commonly men who are known to the women, close in age, and often friends or friends of friends (DeKeseredy & Kelly, 1993, 1995; Fisher et al., 2000; Krebs et al., 2016). The history of campus sexual assault prevention activism has been ongoing since the early 1980s, and the interventions have been many (for reviews, e.g., Basile et al., 2016; DeGue et al., 2014; Gidycz & Dardis, 2014; Lonsway et al., 2009; Morrison, Hardison, Mathew, & O'Neil, 2004). Nonetheless, 30 years later, the incidence of sexual assault and attempted sexual assault remains stubbornly unchanged.

A key reason why campuses remain unsafe for women is the absence of administration-led systemic change. The University of New Hampshire (UNH), the home of Bringing in the Bystander (BITB), was one of the few exceptions. The negative media coverage and legal liability that followed a group rape in a campus dorm in 1987 induced the sense of urgency UNH administrators needed to create a policy, victim support, and prevention infrastructure (Keegan, 1988). The University of Windsor had no such awakening; our beginning was much less dramatic. In a chance discussion, the university lawyer was shocked to learn that the oft-cited one-in-four statistic applied to our campus (Alksnis, Desmarais, Senn, & Hunter, 2000; Senn et al., 2014; Simpson & Senn, 2003). Duly informed, he was alarmed by potential liability issues and asked us for a plan of action. Some time later, this plan was considered by senior administrators. Yet, even then, when everyone in upper management agreed that "something should be done," our proposal was found to be in no one's remit: too activist for some, too academic for others, too broad to fit the responsibility categories of the university, and so it languished for more than two years. In the end, the sense of urgency that fuels organizational change (Kotter, 2011) came from a new administration's call for renewal projects—projects that would assist the university to achieve its strategic objectives. Ours attracted resources because it addressed a social problem the administration could no longer ignore and because it promised students opportunities for practical learning. In 2010, we were awarded the funds needed to offer the two BI courses, plus one-time funds to evaluate the effectiveness of our BI program over a four-year period. Two years later, we fundraised for a one-year post-doctoral fellowship to support the BI's pedagogical goals, and subsequently secured a limited-term position. Recently, we were granted a third tranche of funding for a tenure-track learning specialist dedicated to the Bystander Initiative.

Our institutionalization model is a novel application of sexual assault prevention programming. Until now, academic research has centred primarily on the development of prevention interventions that change individual attitudes and behaviours. In theory, these programs can reduce the incidence of sexual assault on campus by activating student bystanders to speak out against social norms that support sexual assault and coercion or act to prevent a sexual assault in the making. To date, however, this connection has not been demonstrated, we think, because no one has attempted to deliver prevention programming, year after year, to the large number of students required to change a campus culture.[1] We sought to address this important limitation by offering the administration a well-thought-out program of (gradual) institutional change that operationalizes the four principles stated above. Administrative support for this project was essential because external research funding is not available for interventions once their effectiveness has been established.

OUR FIRST PRINCIPLE: UTILIZE EXPERTISE

Advising universities to utilize available expertise may seem trite, yet the history of sexual assault prevention efforts reveals a disconnect on this point. The use of poorly designed, ineffective, or untested programming offered by inexperienced facilitators under less-than-ideal conditions remains common (Lonsway et al., 2009; Morrison et al., 2004; Schewe, 2002), even though evidence-based educational materials and best-practice implementation guidelines are available. This gulf between theory and practice results, in part, because sexual assault prevention education is commonly the responsibility of student affairs staff who work in isolation from the academic researchers who develop and evaluate prevention programming and, in part, because student affairs staff are not schooled in the application of research-based educational materials. The result is that staff sometimes confuse sex education—a good thing in itself—with prevention education or select a recommended but untested program that has little or no impact on prevention or, worse, a program that inadvertently increases men's likelihood of perpetration (e.g., Berg, Lonsway, & Fitzgerald, 1999).

We chose Bringing in the Bystander as our prevention module precisely because it is theoretically sound, proven to be effective for both women and men, and codified for consistent delivery. Bystander-type interventions have emerged as one of the most effective forms of campus sexual assault prevention education (Basile et al., 2016; Flood, 2011; Lonsway et al., 2009) and were specifically endorsed by the Obama Task Force Report (White House Task Force to Protect Students from Sexual Assault, 2014). BITB is one of the best known and most effective programs. Created by researcher-activists at the University of New Hampshire, both versions of their BITB (ninety minutes and four and a half hours) are designed to help students understand the importance of speaking out against social norms that support sexual assault and coercion, recognize and safely interrupt situations that could lead to sexual assault, and be an effective and supportive ally to rape survivors (Banyard, Eckstein, Plante, & Moynihan, 2007; Banyard, Plante, & Moynihan, 2004; Moynihan et al., 2014). In a number of studies of undergraduates, athletes, fraternities and sororities, BITB has increased participants' intentions and capacity to act, improved their sexual assault knowledge and attitudes, and enhanced students' readiness to change (Banyard et al., 2007; Banyard, Eckstein, & Moynihan, 2010; Cares et al., 2015; Moynihan, Banyard, Arnold, Eckstein, & Stapleton, 2010). On its own, without a booster intervention, bystander knowledge and efficacy were sustained for two months; with a booster session, improvements were sustained for up to twelve months (Banyard et al., 2007; Moynihan et al., 2014).

The BITB workshop joins the social psychology of bystander behaviour with a gendered analysis of sexual assault. Preparing participants to overcome the emotional and social barriers that inhibit individuals from stepping forward in a crisis is a key element of Darley and Latané's (1968) theoretical model, which BITB applies (Moynihan, Eckstein, Banyard, & Plante, 2010). Participants learn to notice situations that could lead to sexual assault, identify the risks involved, take responsibility for changing the situation, figure out what they could do, and take action; they are also encouraged to see sexual assault as one form of sexual violence against women and to empathize with and offer appropriate support to victims/survivors. Workshop delivery embeds best-practice guidelines for sexual assault prevention education, such as well-trained students engaged in peer-to-peer facilitation (similarity and expertise as per Eagly & Chaiken, 1984; Schewe, 2002); single-gender[2] groups of 20 to 25, which are more effective for men (Brecklin & Forde, 2001; Lonsway et al., 2009; Schewe, 2002); and mixed-gender leader pairs, which sends the message that men can and should collaborate with women on an issue that is commonly thought to be a "women's issue" (Casey & Lindhorst, 2009; Flood, 2011; Schewe, 2007). Workshops also include active pedagogy such as a visualization exercise and small-group discussions of scenarios. The result is practical education that encourages participant engagement and deep (rather than surface) learning (Biggs & Tang, 2011).

For our purposes, BITB was a clear choice because it can be delivered over and over again without loss of consistency, it is scalable without loss of effectiveness, and it is supported by a strong and helpful team at Prevention Innovations. Importantly, its solid research credentials have helped us protect the integrity of our program in the face of challenges from administration and students. We have been asked why the program focuses on sexual assault prevention—Why not include anti-homophobia or anti-racism education, as well?—and asked to defend its focus on men's violence against women—What about the sexual violence experienced by men or in lesbian and gay relationships? From time to time, students have argued against separate workshops for men and women—Wouldn't women and men benefit from listening to each other? they asked—and others have challenged the rule that workshop facilitators must be peers of year-one and year-two students, in other words, aged 30 or younger. In these situations, the long intellectual history of the BITB has allowed us to argue with confidence that these elements of structure and delivery are not weaknesses, as some believe, but strengths that bolster overall effectiveness.

OUR SECOND PRINCIPLE: USE THE CURRICULUM

The decision to embed sexual assault prevention education into the undergraduate curriculum is both our most significant innovation and our most important lesson learned. No other delivery method could reliably train sufficient numbers of peer educators or reach the number of students—most particularly male students—needed to approach the 10% to 15% of students required for our tipping point model. Even more important is the cognitive authority of course-based prevention education. For students, the curriculum defines the university and its purpose; hence, embedding prevention education in courses both commands students' attention and respect, and offers an effective counterweight to the dominant discourse that inoculates students— men in particular (Crooks, Goodall, Hughes, Jaffe, & Baker, 2007)—against thinking deeply and personally about sexual assault.

Traditionally, prevention education has been offered outside of class time to students who volunteer their participation. The literature points to many challenges in this method of delivery. To be effective, prevention education requires regular and consistent program delivery; yet we know that priorities shift and funding for this issue waxes and wanes. Effectiveness also depends on well-trained peer (i.e., student) educators; yet the reality is that even committed, well-intentioned student volunteers get busy and cannot complete the training or prioritize their paid work and so are unavailable to deliver workshops when they are scheduled. For these reasons, the plan we put to our administration in 2010 created two upper-year, social science BI courses to recruit, educate, and train peer educators, who then lead BITB workshops for other undergraduates. Students must apply for admission—we look for a serious, good-faith purpose—and be the age peers of those in first- and second-year courses (age 17 to 30). Half the seats in both courses are reserved for men.

In course 1, students learn the social psychology of bystander behaviour and sexual violence from a feminist perspective; they also receive the BITB workshop as participants. This course is classroom based and the pedagogy is instructor led, with a focus on the application of theory. To make the issues concrete and personal—particularly important for men (Katz et al., 2011)—considerable class time is devoted to developing the skill of self-reflection. Individually and collectively, students deconstruct rape myths and trace how these ideas have come to have such a hold on their thinking. Exercises require students to employ the new analysis, for example, by creating social media messages and participating in role play that develops students' capacity for empathy and stretches their arsenal of intervention strategies. Student evaluation involves analyzing and applying course readings and videos, identifying and reflecting on the power of rape myths, interrogating the social norms associated with masculinity, and completing a final take-home exam. Roughly half the students in course 1 go on to course 2, where they deepen their knowledge of sexual violence, learn to deliver the BITB workshop, and lead workshops for other undergraduates under the course instructor's supervision.

Course 2 requires active student participation in every class and a commitment to working with presentation partners outside of class. To intensify their knowledge and develop their capacity to respond thoughtfully to questions or challenges from workshop participants, students dissect and reconstruct elements of BITB, rehearse their delivery, and receive feedback from their peers, teaching assistants, volunteers from previous years, and the course instructor. Working in mixed-gender pairs where possible, students deliver the three-hour workshop to other undergraduates. The course instructor is on hand to provide guidance and support when difficulties arise—in one instance, significant pushback from a men's group—and for post-workshop debriefing. For practical reasons, students are not evaluated on their BITB workshop delivery—this is simply not possible given multiple, concurrent workshops—but on a set of critical-reflection assignments designed to build and hone their capacity to lead BITB workshops.

An unforeseen crisis in year one led us to broaden and deepen our use of the undergraduate curriculum. Following standard practice, we initially chose to deliver the BITB workshop to students living in residence and quickly discovered that buy-in was very limited. This led to our most important modification of the BI to date: the creation of a UWindsor three-hour version of BITB and its integration into undergraduate courses, where it replaced or was an additional three-hour class. We looked for courses in which the learning outcomes are aligned with the values and content of BITB, and we now collaborate with four programs that value the moral reasoning and leadership development the workshop offers their students. In our second year, BITB workshops were offered to students enrolled in two second-year courses, one in criminology and one in social psychology; in fall term of our fourth year, workshops were also offered to students enrolled in the required introductory business course. A collaboration with the Faculty of Law has extended the BITB workshop to all year-one law students as well.

A further development in our use of the curriculum—the cross-listing of the two BI courses—resulted from another practical problem. Every term, we need to recruit 50 to 60 students to course 1, ideally, half men, to make sure we will have enough facilitators in course 2. We naively assumed that word of mouth would become sufficient to fill course 1, but turnover in the student body means there is a new cohort to be reached every year. The students we attract are enthusiastic about the practicum aspect of these courses and become passionate advocates for the BI. Even so, recruitment remains a challenge, and one that grew more pressing as the number of workshops on offer increased. When the number of facilitator pairs falls short, we must supplement by hiring students from the previous term (without additional funding for this purpose) or relax the best practice that workshops be delivered by men and women working in pairs. This dilemma has been eased, but not eliminated, by the adoption of both BI courses by Psychology, Social Work, Sociology-Criminology, and Women's and Gender Studies, which allows students in these programs to count these courses towards their major.

OUR THIRD PRINCIPLE: ENGAGE STUDENTS AS CHANGE AGENTS

The importance of engaging students as change agents cannot be overstated: only students can reshape the social norms that prevail in settings likely to lead to sexual assault. The bystander message—"You have the capacity and the responsibility to stop a sexual assault before it happens"—can be effective whenever it is practised, but has the capacity to reduce the incidence of sexual assault only when it is practised widely and consistently. Our institutionalization model aims for the latter: we hypothesize that training 10% to 15%

of the student body will generate sufficient numbers of students who, acting together, can close off opportunities for would-be rapists to act with impunity. Achieving this outcome is possible only with significant student engagement.

The gendered nature of sexual assault makes it imperative that men support the goals of the BI; yet efforts to draw men into the conversation are often shunned (Lonsway et al., 2009). The literature is replete with attempts to educate in which the participation of men was extremely low, in part, because workshops directed at men, for example, to athletic teams and fraternities, are often seen as punitive or as unfairly assuming that all men are potential perpetrators (e.g., Casey & Lindhorst, 2009, on peer networks). The bystander model of prevention, which positions men as potential pro-social bystanders to a sexual assault, not potential perpetrators, overcomes the male-bashing stigma attached to other forms of programming. Workshops such as BITB approach men as good citizens who have a responsibility and the strength of character to lend a helping hand to a woman in need, even when doing so entails pushing against generally accepted male behaviour (Stein, 2007).

In this way, the bystander message reinforces what the majority of men believe about themselves. Recent research tells us that most men are caring and protective of the women in their lives. Many reject violence against women, but actively block messages about its scale and significance by presuming that its incidence and harm are exaggerated (Crooks et al., 2007). And while men may not condone violence, they often do not speak out or act on their beliefs (Berkowitz, 2002; Katz, 1995) because they (falsely) believe other men condone sexually aggressive behaviour (Bohner, Jarvis, Eyssel, & Siebler, 2005) or because they buy into or are pressured into supporting attitudes and beliefs that blame women for their victimization (for a study of the impact of rape-supportive social norms, see Eyssel, Bohner, & Siebler, 2006). Crooks et al. (2007) call this the "well-meaning man" problem: these are good men at heart but hesitant to intervene and distrustful of their skills to do so (Amar, Sutherland, & Laughon, 2014).

To be effective, prevention education must move this majority of men from passive to active, as the UWindsor BI seeks to do. In both the BI courses and BITB workshop, men are challenged to see the issue in personal terms and encouraged to find their own motivation for helping end violence against women (Katz, 1995). They learn that sexual assault is a common occurrence, which means the woman at risk could be a sister, cousin, or girlfriend. And they learn about "Frank," an undetected rapist (Lisak, n.d.), who looks like a buddy but deliberately sets women up for assault by getting them drunk and isolating them from friends. Both of these messages help men connect with, rather than judge, women who are victimized and open them up to the message that they have a responsibility to help. The BI also offers men the tools they need to identify and interrupt situations that could lead to sexual assault. With others, they brainstorm a range of intervention strategies for a variety of settings, and are urged to choose methods that would deflect and de-escalate the situation while protecting their physical safety and their social reputation.

The universal message of the bystander approach also meets the needs of women students who are, in any event, more likely than men to both see a sexual assault in the making and intervene to help the intended victim. The oppositional perpetrator–victim model that unintentionally underlies some sexual assault prevention education alienates those young women who reject the supposed weakness associated with the "victim" label, while others feel compelled to defend men against what they see as a blanket condemnation of all men as potential perpetrators. The dualistic model also invites judgmental attitudes towards women who have experienced sexual assault and feeds the divisive, woman-blaming messages—"She should have known better"; "I would never put myself in that situation"—so prominent in the wider culture. The bystander model, by contrast, offers women something to be for, not just against. It addresses women as caring and concerned for the welfare of others and teaches a problem-solving approach—see the problem, take responsibility, attempt to help—which connects with their greater predisposition to intervene and builds the skills they need to act on these good intentions (Amar, Sutherland, & Kesler, 2012).

OUR FOURTH PRINCIPLE: CULTIVATE A SPIRIT OF MUTUALITY

Our fourth principle—mutuality—also emerged over time and in light of experience with implementation. Mutuality in the sense of reciprocity was part of our vision from the start: simply put, we needed university resources to implement our plan of action, so offered the administration the promise of value for money. The broader vision of mutuality—mutuality as interdependence and reciprocity—grew out of our decision to embed the BITB workshop in the curriculum. Taking this step brought to the fore our need for faculty allies. The BI now epitomizes mutuality in both senses, and is unique on our campus because it is a collaboration of three faculties—the Faculty of Arts, Humanities, and Social Science, the Odette School of Business, and the Faculty of Law—and an alliance between academic faculty and student affairs staff.

In our view, the value-for-money proposition we put to the administration in 2010 was appropriately mindful of the university's tight financial situation, on the one hand, and our need for substantial and ongoing funding, on the other. For these reasons, we chose a demonstration-project approach, with the tacit understanding that the BI would be modified as needed or abandoned in the event that it was ineffective. Recognizing the risk the administration was taking, we submitted a slim, detailed budget with our base funding application and included a rigorous four-year evaluation of the project. We can now report that, using well-established social psychology measures and methodology (pre- and post-intervention surveys with a control group), the UWindsor BI did increase participants' willingness to intervene in situations that could lead to sexual assault and that those attitudes and skills translated into changes in behaviour (Senn & Forrest, 2016). With these findings in hand, we applied for and received additional funding for a tenure-track learning specialist, an appointment that will secure the program's future.

In post-workshop surveys administered one week and sixteen weeks after the intervention, participants reported increased readiness to change, greater willingness to take action, and an increased intention to help others in the future; they were also more confident that they had the skills needed to intervene and reported fewer concerns about what others would think if they took action. Importantly, we also found that change moved beyond attitudes and beliefs to the domain of behaviour. Where participants in our study had or could create opportunities for taking action, they reported increased proactive bystander behaviour towards both friends and strangers. For example, they developed a plan for how to intervene should they witness sexual assault or raised the issue in conversations with friends. By contrast, as the study progressed, students in the control group described themselves as being less likely to assume responsibility to intervene, facing more barriers related to skills deficit, and experiencing heightened worry about what others would think if they did act.

Three of our findings are particularly noteworthy. First, the positive effect on bystander intentions to assist strangers, as well as friends, is significant because others have demonstrated that helping behaviour is lower for strangers (Burn, 2009; Levine & Crowther, 2008), and many analyses of bystander interventions focus on friends or show no effectiveness for strangers (e.g., Cares et al., 2015). Second, we found that all the positive outcomes we describe above applied to both men and women, a most reassuring result given the well-documented challenges of reaching men (e.g., Cares et al., 2015). In fact, in one important dimension—bystander behaviour in risky situations—our BITB workshop had a higher impact on men than women at the 16-week follow-up; overall, women increased their bystander intervention with strangers but not with friends, whereas men dramatically increased their bystander intervention with both friends and strangers, even though they reported lower intent and higher barriers to intervention at the outset. And third, our effects—heightened bystander efficacy, increased intentions, and more prosocial bystander behaviour—are more robust than reported by other researchers. In those evaluations, bystander efficacy was always influenced (Banyard et al., 2007; Moynihan & Banyard, 2008; Moynihan, Banyard, et al., 2010; Moynihan, Banyard, & Plante, 2007), and intentions (Moynihan, Banyard, et al., 2010) and behaviour (Banyard et al., 2007) were sometimes influenced, but never all three. Whether the increased impact of our intervention is due to a larger sample (which may have increased our power to detect effects) or to the two-semester training program for peer educators and the added legitimacy of sexual assault education and prevention when it is embedded in the curriculum and endorsed by professors, we cannot know.

Our value-for-money claim was dramatically enhanced by the unexpected explosion of media interest in sexual assault during 2014. A series of incidents in Canada and the report of the Obama task force drew public attention to the high incidence of sexual assault on campuses and the lack of adequate response by administrators. The result has been a wave of good press for the University of Windsor and its ahead-of-the-curve Bystander Initiative. The university's willingness to invest in sexual assault prevention education has identified us as a leader on this issue in Canada and generated many calls for advice and help from colleagues across the country. At the same time, the university has yet to take full pride of ownership. Despite our requests and offers of help, the administration has not adopted the BI as a signature program and only now (five years later) is including the BI in recruitment events or materials distributed to prospective students and their families.

The extension of mutuality to include interdependence followed our decision to incorporate the BITB workshop into undergraduate courses. The original plan—to deliver the workshop to first-year students living in residence—proved unworkable with only 70 students recruited in our first year. It was clear that relying on volunteer participants would put the entire project at risk. To test our tipping point hypothesis, we needed to educate hundreds of students every year, and the only way this could be accomplished was to incorporate the workshop into the undergraduate curriculum. We were not in a position to command this to happen, but as senior faculty members with strong service, research, and administrative profiles, we had considerable social capital. But no matter how enthusiastic we were about our project, we needed the cooperation of our colleagues more than our colleagues needed the workshop for their courses; indeed, without their collaboration our BI would certainly have failed. At the same time, the BI offered instructors the opportunity to incorporate three hours of practical learning and skills building into their courses and to simultaneously contribute to the solution of a gender inequity.

We benefited significantly from the support of two part-time teaching faculty[3] whose courses served as our proving ground. With their cooperation we learned how to offer four workshops simultaneously without disrupting their classes, which, in turn, allowed us to collaborate with Business where BITB is now incorporated into year-one professional development and leadership education. To ensure positive outcomes for everyone, we adjusted workshop delivery to meet the needs of individual instructors while maintaining critical elements of best practice. In the process, the number of undergraduates offered the workshop each year has increased manyfold, and we have gained the vocal support of full- and part-time colleagues. Their collaboration has been invaluable.

Similarly, our collaboration with student services staff and administrators has grown from one that was essentially practical—we needed a vice-president to sponsor our application for funding—to one that is deeper and mutually rewarding with exciting synergy. They recently spearheaded a funding application to provide training in sexual violence to all front-line staff—this time with our support—and we worked with them (and others) to develop the sexual violence policy and protocol when, five years ago, we would likely not have been included. This collaboration is an unanticipated benefit for us and for the campus.

CONCLUSION

The UWindsor Bystander Initiative is unique in Canada because we seek to reduce the incidence of sexual assault by institutionalizing prevention education. Our long-term goal is organizational change. A safer campus for women requires a marked shift in campus attitudes and behaviours related to sexual assault. The BI supports the emergence of these new social norms by offering high-quality sexual assault prevention education to significant numbers of students each year. We chose the bystander model of prevention education because of its community-minded ethos, its message of personal responsibility, and its proven effectiveness with both men and women, and we ensure consistent, best-practice delivery by providing workshop leaders with two terms of education and training.

In this chapter, we have described and analyzed the four principles that informed our plan of action. All guided our vision from the outset, and all contributed to the success of the BI. But our experience has not been seamless. Through trial and error, the application of each of these principles has been rethought, modified, or expanded over the course of the last five years. We believe our current plan is a strong basis for continuing into the future, but recognize that we must continue to practise critical self-reflection and carefully monitor successes and failures.

We believe these principles are transferable to other campuses, that is to say, we believe that, properly adapted to local circumstances and resources, these principles would enhance the delivery of prevention efforts elsewhere.

We invite others to build on or modify what we have learned, and trust that these efforts will bring us closer to our shared goal of heightened campus safety for women, lower rates of victimization, and greater educational equity.

ACKNOWLEDGEMENTS

The Bystander Initiative (BI) team began formally in 2010 with two members (the co-authors). Dusty Johnstone was a valuable member of the BI team from 2011 to 2015, first as an intern, then as a post-doctoral fellow working on pedagogy and course development, and most recently as a limited-term learning specialist. Emily Rosser joined the team in July 2015 as the tenure-track BI learning specialist. Our sincere thanks to Prevention Innovations for permission to adapt and use the BITB workshop and to R. Eckstein and A. Borges for their help with adaptation and training. We thank Betty Barrett, who taught the first BI course, and Jessica Penwell Barnett, Michele Gnanamuttu, Chelsea McClellan, Mia Sisic, and Stephanie Craig for their varied contributions to BI research. We acknowledge the many student peer facilitators who have delivered the workshops with passion and enthusiasm over the years.

NOTES

1   Green Dot uses a different model (peer diffusion) to influence community change; they have not yet been able to demonstrate campus-level changes in sexual assault rates (Coker et al., 2014), although there is some evidence that a Green Dot campus has a lower incidence of sexual harassment and stalking.
2   At the University of Windsor, students are advised, "Participants who identify as trans or genderqueer can join the workshop of their choice. The Bystander Initiative's approach to gender is rooted in intervention research. If you have thoughts or questions about this issue, please feel free to contact the coordinator at erosser@uwindsor.ca."
3   Our thanks to Scott Mattson and Tom Groulx.

REFERENCES

Alksnis, C., Desmarais, S., Senn, C. Y., & Hunter, N. (2000). Methodologic concerns regarding estimates of physical violence in sexual coercion: Overstatement or understatement? *Archives of Sexual Behavior, 29*(4), 141–152.

Allsop, D. T., Bassett, B. R., & Hoskins, J. A. (2007). Word-of-mouth research: Principles and applications. *Journal of Advertising Research, 47*(4), 398.

Amar, A. F., Sutherland, M., & Kesler, E. (2012). Evaluation of a Bystander Education Program. *Issues in Mental Health Nursing, 33*(12), 851–857. doi:10.3109/016128 40.2012.709915

Amar, A. F., Sutherland, M., & Laughon, K. (2014). Gender differences in attitudes and beliefs associated with bystander behavior and sexual assault. *Journal of Forensic Nursing, 10*(2), 84–91.

Banyard, V. L., Eckstein, R., Plante, E. G., & Moynihan, M. M. (2007). Sexual violence prevention through bystander education: An experimental evaluation. *Journal of Community Psychology, 35*(4), 463–481. doi:10.1002/jcop.20159

Banyard, V. L., Eckstein, R. P., & Moynihan, M. (2010). Sexual violence prevention: The role of stages of change. *Journal of Interpersonal Violence, 25*(1), 111–135. doi:10.1177/0886260508329123

Banyard, V. L., Plante, E. G., & Moynihan, M. M. (2004). Bystander education: Bringing a broader community perspective to sexual violence prevention. *Journal of Community Psychology, 32*(1), 61–79.

Basile, K. C., DeGue, S., Jones, K., Freire, K., Dills, J., Smith, S. G., & Raiford, J. L. (2016). *STOP SV: A technical package to prevent sexual violence*. Atlanta, GA: National Center for Injury Prevention and Control, Centers for Disease Control and Prevention.

Belknap, J., & Erez, E. (1995). The victimization of women on college campuses: Courtship violence, date rape, and sexual harassment. In B. S. Fisher & J. J. Sloan (Eds.), *Campus crime: Legal, social and policy perspectives* (pp. 156–178). Springfield, IL: Charles G. Thomas.

Berg, D. R., Lonsway, K. A., & Fitzgerald, L. F. (1999). Rape prevention education for men: The effectiveness of empathy-induction techniques. *Journal of College Student Development, 40*(3), 219–234.

Berkowitz, A. D. (2002). Fostering men's responsibility for preventing sexual assault. In P. A. Schewe (Ed.), *Preventing violence in relationships* (pp. 163–196). Washington, DC: American Psychological Association.

Biggs, J., & Tang, C. (2011). *Teaching for quality learning at university: What the student does*. Berkshire, UK: McGraw-Hill Education.

Bohner, G., Jarvis, C. I., Eyssel, F., & Siebler, F. (2005). The causal impact of rape myth acceptance on men's rape proclivity: Comparing sexually coercive and noncoercive men. *European Journal of Social Psychology, 35*(6), 819–828. doi:10.1002/ejsp.284

Brecklin, L. R., & Forde, D. R. (2001). A meta-analysis of rape education programs. *Violence and victims, 16*(3), 303–321.

Breitenbecher, K. H. (2000). Sexual assault on college campuses: Is an ounce of prevention enough. *Applied and Preventative Psychology, 9*, 23–52.

Buchwald, E., Fletcher, P., & Roth, M. (1993). *Transforming a rape culture*. Minneapolis, MN: Milkweed Editions.

Burn, S. M. (2009). A situational model of sexual assault prevention through bystander intervention. *Sex Roles, 60*(11–12), 779–792.

Canadian Panel on Violence Against Women. (1993). *Changing the landscape: Ending violence, achieving equality*. Ottawa, ON: Minister of Supply and Services Canada.

Cares, A. C., Banyard, V. L., Moynihan, M. M., Williams, L. M., Potter, S. J., & Stapleton, J. G. (2015). Changing attitudes about being a bystander to violence translating an in-person sexual violence prevention program to a new campus. *Violence Against Women, 21*(2), 165–187.

Carr, J. L. (2005). *American College Health Association campus violence white paper*. Baltimore, MD: American College Health Association.

Casey, E. A., & Lindhorst, T. (2009). Toward a multi-level, ecological approach to the primary prevention of sexual assault: Prevention in peer and community contexts. *Trauma, Violence, and Abuse, 10*, 91–114. doi:10.1177/1524838009334129

Coker, A. L., Fisher, B. S., Bush, H. M., Swan, S. C., Williams, C. M., Clear, E. R., & DeGue, S. (2014). Evaluation of the Green Dot bystander intervention to reduce interpersonal violence among college students across three campuses. *Violence Against Women, 21*(12), 1507–1527. doi:1077801214545284

Cooke, M., & Buckley, N. (2008). Web 2.0, social networks and the future of market research. *International Journal of Market Research, 50*(2), 267.

Crooks, C. V., Goodall, G. R., Hughes, R., Jaffe, P. G., & Baker, L. L. (2007). Engaging men and boys in preventing violence against women applying a cognitive–behavioral model. *Violence Against Women, 13*(3), 217–239.

Darley, J., & Latané, B. (1968). Bystander intervention in emergencies: Diffusion of responsibility. *Journal of Personality and Social Psychology, 8*(4), 377–383.

DeGue, S., Valle, L. A., Holt, M. K., Massetti, G. M., Matjasko, J. L., & Tharp, A. T. (2014). A systematic review of primary prevention strategies for sexual violence perpetration. *Aggression and Violent Behavior, 19*(4), 346–362.

DeKeseredy, W. S., & Kelly, K. (1993). The incidence and prevalence of woman abuse in Canadian university and college dating relationships. *Canadian Journal of Sociology, 18*(2), 137–159.

DeKeseredy, W. S., & Kelly, K. (1995). Sexual abuse in Canadian university and college dating relationships: The contribution of male peer support. *Journal of Family Violence, 10*(1), 41–53.

Eagly, A. H., & Chaiken, S. (1984). Cognitive theories of persuasion. In L. Berkowitz (Ed.), *Advances in experimental social psychology* (Vol. 12, pp. 267–359). San Diego, CA: Academic Press.

Eyssel, F., Bohner, G., & Siebler, F. (2006). Perceived rape myth acceptance of others predicts rape proclivity: Social norm or judgmental anchoring? *Swiss Journal of Psychology, 65*(2), 93–99. doi:10.1024/1421-0185.65.2.93

Fisher, B. S., Cullen, F. T., & Turner, M. (2000). *The sexual victimization of college women: Findings from two national-level studies.* Washington, DC: National Institute of Justice and Bureau of Justice Statistics.

Flood, M. (2011). Involving men in efforts to end violence against women. *Men and Masculinities, 14*(3), 358–377. doi:10.1177/1097184X10363995

Gidycz, C. A., & Dardis, C. M. (2014). Feminist self-defense and resistance training for college students: A critical review and recommendations for the future. *Trauma, Violence, and Abuse, 15*(4), 322–333. doi:10.1177/1524838014521026

Gladwell, M. (2006). *The tipping point: How little things can make a big difference.* New York, NY: Little, Brown.

Herman, D. (1979). The rape culture. In J. Freeman (Ed.), *Women: A feminist perspective* (pp. 41–63). Palo Alto, CA: Mayfield.

Katz, J. T. (1995). Reconstructing masculinity in the locker room: The Mentors in Violence Prevention Project. *Harvard Educational Review, 65*(2), 163–175.

Katz, J. T., Heisterkamp, H. A., & Fleming, W. M. (2011). The social justice roots of the Mentors in Violence Prevention model and its application in a high school setting. *Violence Against Women, 17*(6), 684–702. doi:10.1177/1077801211409725

Keegan, P. (1988, February). Dangerous parties. *New England Monthly,* 52–93.

Kelly, L. (1987). The continuum of sexual violence. In J. Hanmer & M. Maynard (Eds.), *Women, violence and social control* (pp. 46–60). Basingstoke, UK: Macmillan.

Kelly, L. (2012). Standing the test of time? Reflections on the concept of the continuum of sexual violence. In J. M. Brown & S. L. Walklate (Eds.), *Handbook on sexual violence* (pp. xvii–xxvi). London, UK: Routledge.

Kotter, J. P. (2011). *Leading change: Why transformation efforts fail.* Boston, MA: Harvard Business Review Press.

Krebs, C., Lindquist, C., Berzofsky, M., Shook-Sa, B., Peterson, K., Planty, M., … Stroop, J. (2016). *Campus Climate Survey Validation Study final technical report.* Retrieved from http://www.bjs.gov/content/pub/pdf/ccsvsftr.pdf

Levine, M., & Crowther, S. (2008). The responsive bystander: How social group membership and group size can encourage as well as inhibit bystander intervention. *Journal of Personality and Social Psychology, 95*(6), 1429.

Lisak, D. (Writer). (n.d.). The undetected rapist [DVD]. New York, NY: National Judicial Education Program, Legal Momentum.

Lisak, D., & Miller, P. M. (2002). Repeat rape and multiple offending among undetected rapists. *Violence Against Women, 17*(1), 73–84.

Lonsway, K. A., Banyard, V. L., Berkowitz, A. D., Gidycz, C. A., Katz, J. T., Koss, M. P., ... Ullman, S. E. (2009, January). Rape prevention and risk reduction: Review of the research literature for practitioners. *VAWnet: The national online resource center on violence against women*, 1–20.

Morrison, S., Hardison, J., Mathew, A., & O'Neil, J. (2004). *An evidence-based review of sexual assault preventive intervention programs: Technical report*. Washington, DC: National Institute of Justice.

Moynihan, M. M., & Banyard, V. L. (2008). Community responsibility for preventing sexual violence: A pilot study with campus Greeks and intercollegiate athletes. *Journal of Prevention and Intervention in the Community, 36*(1), 23–38. doi:10.1177/0886109909331702

Moynihan, M. M., Banyard, V. L., Arnold, J. S., Eckstein, R. P., & Stapleton, J. G. (2010). Engaging intercollegiate athletes in preventing and intervening in sexual and intimate partner violence. *Journal of American College Health, 59*(3), 197–204. doi: 10.1080/07448481.2010.502195

Moynihan, M. M., Banyard, V. L., Cares, A. C., Potter, S. J., Williams, L. M., & Stapleton, J. G. (2014). Encouraging responses in sexual and relationship violence prevention: What program effects remain 1 year later? *Journal of Interpersonal Violence*, 1–23. doi:10.1177/0887260514532719

Moynihan, M. M., Banyard, V. L., & Plante, E. G. (2007). Preventing dating violence: A university example of community approaches. In K. A. Kendall-Tackett & S. M. Giacomoni (Eds.), *Intimate partner violence* (pp. 17.11–17.15). Kingston, NJ: Civic Research Center.

Moynihan, M. M., Eckstein, R. P., Banyard, V. L., & Plante, E. G. (2010). *Facilitator's guide: Bringing in the bystander—A prevention workshop for establishing a community of responsibility* (Revised version). Durham: University of New Hampshire.

Randall, M., & Haskell, L. (1995). Sexual violence in women's lives: Findings from the Women's Safety Project, a community-based survey. *Violence Against Women, 1*(1), 6–31.

Schewe, P. A. (2002). Guidelines for developing rape prevention and risk reduction interventions. In P. A. Schewe (Ed.), *Preventing violence in relationships* (pp. 107–136). Washington, DC: American Psychological Association.

Schewe, P. A. (2007). Interventions to prevent sexual violence. In L. Doll, E. N. Haas, S. Bonzo, D. Sleet, & J. Mercy (Eds.), *Handbook of injury and violence prevention* (pp. 223–240). Atlanta, GA: Springer Science + Business Media.

Senn, C. Y., Eliasziw, M., Barata, P. C., Thurston, W. E., Newby-Clark, I. R., Radtke, H. L., ... SARE Study Team. (2014). Sexual violence in the lives of first-year university women in Canada: No improvements in the 21st century. *BMC Women's Health, 14*(135), 1–8.

Senn, C. Y., & Forrest, A. (2016). "And then one night when I went to class ...": The impact of sexual assault bystander intervention workshops incorporated in academic courses. *Psychology of Violence, 6*(4), 607–618. doi:10.1037/a0039660

Simpson, A., & Senn, C. Y. (2003). Sexual coercion and sexual assault: Are the effects on hostility gender specific? *Guidance & Counselling, 18*(3), 111–117.

Stein, J. L. (2007). Peer educators and close friends as predictors of male college students' willingness to prevent rape. *Journal of College Student Development, 48*(1), 75–89.

Tjaden, P., & Thoennes, N. (2000). *Full report of the prevalence, incidence, and consequences of violence against women: Findings from the National Violence Against Women Survey.* Retrieved from https://www.ncjrs.gov/pdffiles1/nij/183781.pdf

White House Task Force to Protect Students from Sexual Assault. (2014). *Not alone.* Retrieved from https://www.justice.gov/ovw/page/file/905942/download/

CHAPTER 10

A CRITICAL ANALYSIS OF THE REPORT *STUDENT SAFETY IN NOVA SCOTIA*

Co-creating a Vision and Language for Safer and Socially Just Campus Communities

Norma Jean Profitt and Nancy Ross

exualized violence against women has been making news in Nova Scotia. On April 7, 2013, Rehtaeh Parsons was taken off life support after hanging herself. Seventeen months prior, she alleged that four young men had sexually assaulted her; her aggressors had circulated a photograph of the rape on social media. During frosh week of 2013, we became privy to the Saint Mary's University pro-rape chants, a staple of orientation for years. In late 2014, we learned that the "Gentlemen's Club" of Dalhousie University dentistry students had posted misogynist comments about female classmates on Facebook, voting on whom they wanted to have "hate" sex with and claiming the penis as a "tool used to wean and convert lesbians and virgins into useful, productive members of society" ("Dalhousie Delays," 2014, "Exams Postponed," para. 4). In the wake of Rehteah Parson's death, the government of Nova Scotia at the time struck a task force that highlighted the need for changes in the societal norms and beliefs that shape the nature, quality, and structure of relationships (Province of Nova Scotia, 2013).

In January 2014, the report *Student Safety in Nova Scotia: A Review of Student Union Policies and Practices to Prevent Sexual Violence* was released (Martell Consulting Services Ltd., 2014; henceforth referred to as the Students NS report or the report). Commissioned by Students Nova Scotia, the primary advocacy organization representing post-secondary students, in partnership with the Province of Nova Scotia, and prepared by Martell Consulting Services

Ltd., the main goal of the study was to "provide student unions with a set of strategies aimed at sexual assault prevention and the creation of safe and mindful cultures on campus" (p. 2). Three factors prompted this research: Students Nova Scotia's concern about sexual assault prevention, the tragedy of Rehteah Parsons' death, and the subsequent development of a provincial sexual violence strategy. A total of 73 interviews were conducted with student union and university representatives across six campuses, with an additional eight interviews with off-campus health experts.

The report represents "only a first step" to address sexual violence by student unions and other stakeholders "because students have the right to be safe and feel safe on our campuses" (p. 1). It states that a province-wide social media campaign would follow with funding available to help student unions implement report recommendations. As of April 2015, the funding allotted had been spent on initiatives across universities, including Bringing in the Bystander training and the More than Yes Campaign. The provincial sexual violence strategy, Breaking the Silence: A Coordinated Response to Sexual Violence in Nova Scotia, continues to unfold, engaging various communities, service providers, and government. The strategy launched a province-wide awareness campaign in October 2016; the strategy's training committee has developed an online training program for Nova Scotians on how to respond to sexual violence; and more than $3.7 million in grants has been dispersed to community groups for prevention, intervention, and coordination of community supports. The government has also expanded the Sexual Assault Nurse Examiner Program to provide services to victims across the province.

In my work in enhanced mental health and addiction services for women, I (Norma Jean) read the Students NS report and felt compelled to speak from my experience of over 30 years of feminist labour to stop "patriarchal violence" (Bannerji, 2000, p. 152). To honour women struggling to say the words, transgress the silence, organize, resist, and change their communities, I thought it would be instructive to critically analyze the report for inclusion in this timely volume. I (Nancy) am doing doctoral research that explores community responses to violence. From my reading and experience alongside victims of sexual assault, I know that the voices of victims are often silenced. I, too, have felt my own voice muted in my former role as clinical therapist in women's services in mental health and addictions. Privileged to occupy that space for ten years, I listened to hundreds of women's disclosures of abuse occurring throughout their life span, leading to a sense of outrage and oppression. During this time, I saw how a lack of provincial coordination and system champions for women presented formidable obstacles to connecting the lived experiences of women with community endeavours to address violence. At both personal and professional levels, I was inspired to discover pathways to community and political action for prevention of interpersonal violence. In this chapter, I wish to emphasize that sexual assault in a rape culture demands a political response, and that culture is something we can co-create, as communities and citizens, for a more respectful and humane society for women.

Our critical analysis of the Students NS report provides an opening for a broader discussion of campus sexual violence that employs a critique of the dominant and pervasive conceptions of sexualized violence in our society as a whole, and explores how these notions have permeated approaches to sexual violence prevention on campuses. We show why sexual assault must be understood as an issue of power and of structural inequalities, as such demanding a political response and commitment from governance structures, citizens, and communities to attain social change.

In this chapter we establish that the Students NS report fails to (1) adequately name the issue of power in social relations, particularly but not only in gender relations; (2) sufficiently highlight the structural and cultural elements at play in sexualized violence; and (3) fully examine discourses that assign undue responsibility to women. We argue that a comprehensive politicized framework and analysis would better mobilize congruent feminist and social justice strategies of cultural and structural change, as well as effective prevention and intervention programs in response to sexual assault on campus.

Before we turn our critical eye to the report, in order to sharpen our thinking about sexualized violence and our vision of changing rape culture we will explore the context for our analysis. Violence against women is the most pervasive yet unacknowledged human rights violation in the world (Heise, Ellsberg, & Gottemoeller, 1999; World Health Organization, 2013b). As many as one of every three women are victims of gender-based violence, making it one of the most widespread public health issues in the world today (United Nations Population Fund, n.d.). Such violence includes rape (predominantly a crime against women committed by men), sexual assault, sexual harassment, femicide, sexual slavery, intimate partner violence, physical and emotional torture, incest, child sexual abuse, female infanticide, and rape and sexual mutilation in war, among others.

Gender-based violence causes incalculable suffering for women. A major root of mental health issues, particularly depression (World Health Organization, 2013a), it often precedes women's mental health and substance use concerns (Canadian Women's Foundation, 2011). Women survivors of rape constitute the largest population with diagnosed post-traumatic stress disorder in the United States (Campbell & Wasco, 2005). Fear of men's violence, including rape, violates women's human rights of freedom of movement, association, and expression (Rozee & Koss, 2001) and impedes their full participation in society (Pickup, Williams, & Sweetman, 2001). In the context of women's education, violence against girls and women and its sequelae can greatly affect learning processes and social engagement in educational endeavours (American Association of University Professors, 2013; Horsman, 2000).

Given that many victims of adult sexual assault are women assaulted by men in the context of heterosexual relations, we focus on this particular reality here. At the same time, we recognize the need for more specificity in attending to sexual violence against populations that are structurally more vulnerable to violence overall (such as transgender persons), and against heterosexually identified men.

CRITICAL ANALYSIS OF *STUDENT SAFETY IN NOVA SCOTIA: A REVIEW OF STUDENT UNION POLICIES AND PRACTICES TO PREVENT SEXUAL VIOLENCE*

On the whole, Students Nova Scotia and participating student unions must be commended for breaking the silence and "formally acknowledging the existence of sexual assault on campus" (p. iii). The Students NS report calls on student leadership and other actors, such as senior university administration, to collaboratively build "a culture of prevention and intervention" (p. 1). It impressively advocates strategies for multiple actors at several levels to address the issue. These include the development of student union position papers on sexual violence; web presences providing information and resources; engagement of first- and second-year students in identifying core values and a vision of community; all-genders and gender-specific prevention programming; bystander programs; campus consultations on consent; changes in orientation to campus life; the formation of campus advisory committees on sexual violence; the establishment of peer education to focus on the link between alcohol consumption and sexual assault; and the implementation of a survey to determine the extent and nature of sexual assault on campuses.

The Students NS report should be applauded for naming sexual violence as a serious issue on campus and rape culture as the broader social context in which it occurs. Notably, it defines rape culture as one in which "rape is prevalent and pervasive and is sanctioned and maintained through fundamental attitudes and beliefs about gender, sexuality and violence" (p. 21). Moreover, the report recognizes that the aggressor is usually someone known to the victim—a friend, classmate, boyfriend, or ex-boyfriend. It identifies "a clear gender difference when it comes to who is most likely to sexually assault and who is most likely to be assaulted: 85% of victims ... are girls and women, and 98% of sexual offenders are men" (p. 7).

Despite these strengths, however, the report falls short of articulating a clear, coherent framework for an analysis of sexual violence that could inform recommendations for action. Although the report identifies rape culture, gender role socialization, and restrictive masculinity as elements at play in sexual violence, it does not explicitly name social power, privilege, and oppression as critical components in its framework, nor does it connect systemic gender inequity with sexual violence towards women. It neglects to locate sexual assault in the continuum of violence against women (Kelly, 1988), an act that is vital to understanding and addressing gender-based violence. Given the lack of connective tissue to make the links between the sometimes contradictory ideas presented in the report, it is difficult to get a sense of the nature of the desired change or the intentions of specific interventions. A comprehensive theoretical framework would clarify the contributing processes and factors involved in sexual assault and communicate their relevance for intervention, discursive or otherwise. We address these limitations in the following critique.

THE DISCOURSE OF RISK AND SEXUALIZED VIOLENCE

One evident shortcoming in the report resides in the framing of sexual violence in the discourse of risk. Although at first glance the concepts of "risk" and "risk factor" appear to allow us to tidily identify the circumstances in which sexual violence may occur, the notion undermines a deeper understanding of rape culture by shifting attention to the behaviour of individuals, most often women. Ultimately, the discourse of risk obscures the operation of heteropatriarchy and "the enduring social regulation of women" in our society (Scourfield & Welsh, 2002, p. 9)—in other words, the very conditions that place women "at risk." How does it do this?

Neo-liberalism and the discourse of risk

The discourse of risk as a central organizing principle in health and social services gained ground with the ascendancy of neo-liberal thought originating in the late 1970s (Gillingham, 2006; Lupton, 1993; Scourfield & Welsh, 2002; Swadener, 2010). "Responsibilisation," a key feature in this discourse (Liebenberg, Ungar, & Ikeda, 2013, p. 3), refers to the process through which individuals are made responsible for what should be the duty of another to perform, most often the state. In our current neo-liberal climate, social, cultural, political, and economic issues become reconstructed as individual responsibilities and choices, with the implication that amelioration can be achieved through the management of "risk" (Gillingham, 2006). By holding individual citizens primarily responsible for their plight, socio-political conditions such as precarious employment, stagnant wages, pay equity issues, weakening democratic participation, and growing social inequality are ignored, thereby transforming collective conditions into individual responsibility (Liebenberg et al., 2013). As the notion of a collective response through social policy and community action recedes, governments are able to justify reduced spending on social programs and the privatizing of public services, ultimately eliminating governmental and institutional accountability for public issues (Liebenberg et al., 2013; Swadener, 2010).

Liebenberg et al. (2013) give an example of how "responsibilisation" occurs in the discourse of risk. Scrutiny of the case notes of workers in child welfare, corrections, and mental health who provided services to youth revealed how front-line staff held youth responsible for practices of self-care and managing the risks they faced in their lives. Risks were conceived as conscious rational choices and outcomes determined by individual motivation and decision making to the exclusion of broader contextual factors at work. Consequently, youth were encouraged to see themselves as context-free individuals responsible for their own state of being regardless of whether the actions deemed appropriate for avoidance of "risk" were relevant or even feasible. As Swadener (2010) notes, actions in a world devoid of "nested contexts" are stripped of both meaning and context (p. 7).

Applying the discourse of risk to sexual assault

What can we expect if we apply the discourse of risk to sexual assault? The Students NS report states that risk factors are "either environmental (such as cultural norms or venues like off-campus house parties) or personal (such as decision-making around alcohol consumption) and can be related to victims and perpetrators, as well as bystanders" (p. vii). Alcohol is identified as "a high-risk factor for sexual assault" (p. iii), putting women at "higher risk" (p. 11). Using criminal justice language, the report also refers to "high-risk offender populations including student athletes and fraternity members" (p. iii) but misses an opportunity to explain what makes them "high risk" in campus rape culture. Another risk involves the targeting of victims by "sexual predators" (p. 8) in the first weeks of university attendance. Although a 1992 study cited in the report found that "60 percent [of male students] would commit sexual assault if they were certain they would not get caught" (p. 6), the report fails to explain the connection between the behaviours of "sexual predators" and this larger population of male students. This omission undercuts the reality that sexual assault against women is a pervasive social issue.

Applying the concept of risk to sexual assault on campus, we can predict that the gaze will fall on young women's deficits of self-care, for example, their heavy drinking or "provocative dress," to the exclusion of the aggressor's responsibility for his actions, or the cultural norms, ideology, language, and practices that sanction the abuse of power through sexual means. The discourse of risk works to reinforce the perception of sexual violence as something private and behavioural caused by poor decision making, judgment, and choices (Liebenberg et al., 2013). An interviewee's comment in the study illustrates this: "Alcohol removes inhibitions and allows women not to take responsibility for their actions. We see young women using alcohol as a means of losing control" (p. 17). When women are held responsible for controlling the factors that place them "at risk" in the first place, we can expect laments about why they "choose" to put themselves at risk—by drinking too much, walking alone at night, or going to a frat party.

Although young women do need to consider that others might sexually violate or exploit them if they drink too much or black out, telescoping social, cultural, and political arrangements into individual responsibilities and choices diverts attention from social relations of power, privilege, and oppression. When women are expected to manage risk in order to avoid rape, Burnett et al. (2009) clarify that "taking precautions to prevent date rape means the individual will also need to take on the responsibility if something were to happen. In other words, if an individual takes responsibility for the preparation to avoid date rape, then, by default, that individual must take the blame if rape occurs" (p. 476). This gendered victim-blaming dovetails with current health education lifestyle-risk discourse that apprises individuals of their responsibility for risky "lifestyle" behaviours when in actuality the control that individuals have over their living and working environments in late capitalist society has diminished (Lupton, 1993). Clearly, risk discourse about sexual violence serves a political function to obscure larger arrangements by blaming victims for their plight.

The discourse of risk conceives of women as objects vulnerable to risk at the same time that it holds them individually responsible for their victimization, erasing their resistance to power and their resiliency in the face of systemic oppression. Precisely for this reason, some rape prevention programs for women are called rape resistance programs, not "risk reduction." Resistance language points to the fact that women do resist—not some abstract, unnamed risk, but men's threatening behaviour, as well as sexism, racism, heterosexism, and so forth (Senn, 2011). The reality that women experience sexual violence in the context of the "insidious traumatization" of everyday racism, sexism, ableism, and heterosexism (Root, 1992) underscores the relationship between violence, trauma, and systemic oppressions (Burstow, 2003) and the need to understand violence as shaped by multiple dimensions of women's identity (Bannerji, 2000; Crenshaw, 1991; hooks, 1988; Razack, 1998). Finally, the discourse of risk tends to re-entrench sexist, heterosexist, and racist beliefs, for example, that women of colour are "promiscuous" and if they are raped, they must have been asking for it. Although we know that environmental conditions shape people's well-being more than the changes that individuals are able to make (McGibbon, 2012), the discourse of risk entices us to believe otherwise.

Rather than thinking of risk as disembodied from our cultural milieu, social institutions, social relations, forms of subjectivity, and everyday practices, as the Students NS report appears to do, how might we understand these "risks" if we took into account the connection between the individual and the social? In describing rape culture, the report states that "gender roles are strictly defined; men are hyper-masculine aggressors and women are their sexually provocative prey" (p. viii); yet, how heteronormativity and hypersexualization operate in campus culture, culminating in sexual violence, is inadequately explored. Heteronormativity is founded on the notion of binary and complementary sexes/genders that form conventional ideas of masculinity and femininity from which sexual desire is presumed to flow (Butler, 1999). Such ideas underlie deeply entrenched beliefs about gender, sex, and sexuality that shape female and male subjectivity and convey the inferiority of women, for instance, that men's drive to sexual intercourse co-exists with an inability to control it; that women must be gatekeepers of men's desire; and that women are temptresses and men are "natural" aggressors. Heteronormativity carries implications for everyone despite how people self-identify, given that non-conforming forms of sex, gender, gender expression, and sexuality are often devalued and targeted for violence. Consequently, universities as institutions must examine how they foster heteronormativity and the normalization of gender-based violence, including denial of the material conditions of women's lives. Rather than only identifying "risks" that get reduced to individual choice, we must also critique the social arrangements that shape our lives.

ALCOHOL, OBJECTIFICATION, AND SEXUAL ASSAULT

Summarizing the research on the link between alcohol and sexual assault, the Students NS report states that "while alcohol is not the cause of sexual assault, it appears to play a large role … half to over three-quarters of assaults involve alcohol consumption by the perpetrator or the survivor or both" (p. 8). It goes on to say that "alcohol consumption impairs higher order cognitive processes, thus enhancing the misperception of sexual intent to the point of forced sex" (p. 8). Notwithstanding that these "misperceptions" are portrayed as "acts without agents" (Lamb, 1991), the report fails to elucidate how the use of alcohol actually culminates in sexual assault, or in other words, how violence is connected to power and a sense of entitlement. Drinking can obviously bring about cognitive impairment, but does "misperception of sexual intent" necessarily or automatically result from cognitive impairment? In this vein, the report only addresses this issue once, in saying that "alcohol can also be used as a weapon, though it can also feed attitudes and judgements that may lead an individual to commit sexual assault" (p. 18).

Investigating the link between men's alcohol use and sexual violence perpetration, Gervais, DiLillo, and McChargue (2014) identify sexual objectification as a mediating factor between alcohol use and sexual aggression. Their study of undergraduate men found that the more college men drank, the more they evaluated women's bodies and made unwanted, explicit advances. Heteronormative discourses extolling men's drive to sexual intercourse and portraying women as sexually "provocative" objectify women as objects for men's use. Decades ago, radical feminists theorized that the objectification of women plays a vital role in the oppression of women as a class (Jaggar, 1988). Integral to sexism and misogyny, it reduces women to objects for the express purpose of the sexual gratification of another, without regard for their humanity and dignity.

Accordingly, any discussion of alcohol use and sexual violence today must attend to how the omnipresent processes of hypersexualization in our dominant culture produce such objectification. The gendered nature of hypersexualization not only teaches boys and men to sexually objectify girls and women, but conditions girls and women to turn the objectifying gaze inward. Girls may begin to self-objectify early in their lives, coming to view themselves from the perspective of the one who objectifies them as sex objects (Calogero, 2013). Devaluing their own feelings and appraisals, they experience conflicts between their own suppressed feelings and social expectations. These contradictions may, in turn, enable them to more readily justify their participation in the gendered status quo. A form of what feminist theories call "internalized oppression," the notion of self-objectification helps us to comprehend how young women subscribe to rape myths and engage in rape chants.

The Students NS report asserts that rape culture permeates all aspects of our society, fosters sexual violence on campus, and blames victims. It acknowledges that the alcohol industry, like others, sells "sexual provocation" to young women (p. 21) and that many young people are desensitized to the very environment in which they are immersed. The growth of substance use has been linked with disconnection and dislocation from self and self-identity; the alcohol industry exploits these feelings of inadequacy, particularly in young women (Alexander, 2008; Jernigan, 2011). Sensitive to the reality of victim blaming, the report recommends educational programming for women about the negative effects of heavy drinking framed around a "discussion of personal vulnerability, rather than responsibility" (p. 11). When we educate young women about heightened personal vulnerability, we need to facilitate making connections among sexualized violence, substance use, the psychosocial realities of objectification and self-objectification, and structural and individual power.

THE NORMALIZATION OF VIOLENCE IN DOMINANT AND CAMPUS CULTURES

The Students NS report states that discussions with student union leadership indicate that "there has been in general minimal concentrated effort to address the culture surrounding sexual violence" (p. 24). It describes an example of how campus culture "can normalize sexual assault and even something as explicit as a 'date rape night'" (citing rape culture manifest in an event called "rookie night; p. 20) and comments that the "implication ... [is] perhaps of still more far-reaching concern than the perceived or real risk from a single event or evening" (p. 20). Although this statement signals a glimpse of sexism and misogyny, the report does not make structural inequity and the normalization of violence against women explicit or visible, nor does it place them within a social justice framework.

Cultural violence refers to aspects of culture, including social media, advertising, music, pornography, clothing, and games, that suggest or justify violence (direct or structural) while obscuring its destructiveness (Galtung, 1990). Cultural violence is gendered violence, and nowhere is this more evident than in the highly gendered hypersexualization processes replete with violence that envelop boys and girls today from birth onward. Although these processes shape boys and girls differently and carry distinct consequences for each, the perpetuation of limiting gender roles for sexes in patriarchal societies constitutes a form of cultural violence. It is important to clarify here that socially organized material arrangements provide the frame for gender socialization and gender roles; women's subordination is not only a question of "gender socialization" but one of social power, structural dependency, and unequal gender relations (Andrew, Barnsley, Ellis, Lewis, & Wasserlein, 1986). For girls and women, structural features such as caregiving responsibilities, unequal pay for work of equal value, and occupational segregation interact with other inequities to perpetuate constructions of women as inferior. Although dominant culture constructs men as violence objects and women as sex objects (Gilligan, 2009), women and men do have agency to take up gender scripts in a myriad of ways and reject, partially or wholly, dominant constructions of heteronormative identities.

In making the connections between culture, the normalization of gendered violence, and individual behaviour explicit, the intersection of sexism, racism, and capitalism must not go unremarked. The globalized pornography and alcohol industries are two major forces shaping dominant culture and therefore the behaviour of young people. Both play a significant role in the early gendering that lays the foundation for children's emerging sense of self and identity and the forms of communication processes and behaviours expected of girls and boys (Katz, 2006; Kilbourne, 1999; Levin & Kilbourne, 2009). Given the mainstreaming of pornography, boys in Nova Scotia begin to watch it at an average age of 11 years. Writing about porn culture, Dines (2010) points out that

> it is affecting our girls and boys, as both are growing up with porn encoded into their gender and sexual identities. What is the impact? What we do know is that we are surrounded by images that degrade and debase women and that for this the entire culture pays a price. (p. 163)

The price paid by youth entails a constriction of horizons and potential to flourish, and for young women, poor body image, fragmented consciousness, and increased sexual violence and partner violence (Tobin, 2012).

In its attempt to acknowledge how campus culture can normalize sexual violence, the Students NS report falls short of situating this phenomenon within the context of feminist historical analyses of systemic sexism and misogyny. Much sexual violence exercised against women passes without visible outrage or overt comment. As Gavey notes, "everyday taken-for-granted normative forms of heterosexuality work as a cultural scaffolding for rape" (2005, p. 2) and make the sexual coercion of women by men normative (Senn, Gee, & Thake, 2011). Although some acts such as rape may be regarded as abhorrent, many forms of patriarchal violence, such as the sexual objectification of women, misogynist language, and sexual harassment, are normalized as part of everyday life and implicitly understood as part and parcel of gender relations (Kelly, 1988).

In a topical *Globe and Mail* article, Anderssen (2014) writes that a recent Massachusetts Institute of Technology student survey on sexual assault revealed that 72% of victims said that they did not regard their assault as serious enough to report, and 44% felt "at least partly responsible" for it. Furthermore, 25% of men and 15% of women thought that someone drunk would be "at least somewhat responsible." This is the milieu in which sexual assault is occurring on Canadian campuses, and we must ask probing questions about the elements in our society that converge to produce young men who harass women for sex and rape them when they are passed out, and young women who believe that assaults on their bodily integrity aren't serious and that the way they dress, drink, or flirt makes them at least somewhat responsible for inviting sexual attack. An historical context that traced feminist efforts to prevent sexual assault would have been helpful in this report to challenge the operation of power in social relations and individual subjectivities.

EDUCATION ABOUT CONSENT

The *Student Safety in Nova Scotia* report recommends campus-wide education about consent "since consent is not well understood by students, including women and men" (p. iii). In addition, the report defines rape culture as "a culture in which victim blaming is common (she was drinking, look what she was wearing) and in which consent is unclear (she was flirting, she didn't say no loudly enough or long enough)" (p. viii). The very idea that flirting or not saying no loudly enough can be construed as unclear consent indicates the need for a deeper analysis of rape culture. In other words, it is precisely because of inequitable power relations that consent is misunderstood.

Campuses across Canada have instituted campaigns about consent such as Yes Means Yes and Ask, Listen, Respect, to encourage clear communication and enthusiastic consent between sexual partners. The hope is that the line between consent and lack of consent will be less blurry. Although these campaigns may potentially help some students negotiate sexual encounters, do they imply that sexual violence is primarily the outcome of ambiguous communication while leaving questions of power and the sociopolitical context of violence unexamined? Since the prevalence of rape and sexual assault on university and college campuses has remained consistent for decades (Senn, 2011), even with No Means No campaigns, we raise the question at this juncture as to whether the emphasis on "miscommunication," "gray rape" (the blurred line between consensual and nonconsensual intercourse), and ignorance about the meaning of consent itself might add up to a reflection of misogynist culture.

According to "miscommunication theory," date rape often occurs when the man misinterprets the woman's verbal and non-verbal communication, erroneously believing that she wants sex. Since she presumably fails to say no clearly and firmly, the remedy lies in "assertive verbal communication" by the woman (Kitzinger & Frith, 1999, p. 294). Over a decade ago, Rozee and Koss (2001) questioned the validity of "miscommunication theory," citing studies showing that "the overwhelming majority of men and women who say 'no' actually mean no" and that men who self-report sexually aggressive behaviour are more likely to "misperceive" than other men or women (p. 302). Furthermore, most survivors of sexual assault actively communicate their nonconsent, with 70% saying no and physically fighting back (p. 300). On this point, we believe that women are the best judges of what they need to do in order to survive sexual violence and that physically fighting back may not be the optimal strategy in every situation.

To delve deeper into the lack of understanding about the meaning of consent, we must situate consent in the context of institutionalized power relations and ask what discourses young people have available to understand gendered relations. Through the use of conversation analysis, Kitzinger and Frith (1999) employed a feminist perspective on sexual refusal to challenge the assumption that young women find it difficult to refuse unwanted sexual activity. They found that culturally normative ways of doing refusals rarely involve saying no but are "elegantly crafted interactional activities" (p. 302).

> Both men and women have a sophisticated ability to convey and to comprehend refusals, including refusals which do not include the word no, and we suggest that male claims not to have understood refusals which conform to culturally normative patterns can only be heard as self-interested justifications for coercive behavior. (p. 295)

Beres (cited in Anderssen, 2014) concurs and asserts that sexual assault "is about someone making a decision to ignore the cues." Consequently, men's claim to be cultural dopes does not mean that women must then take up the task of "inventing new ways of doing refusals" to assuage men's allegations of ambiguity: "the problem of sexual coercion cannot be fixed by changing the way women talk" (p. 311). Accordingly, miscommunication theory mistakenly places the burden of responsibility for rape and sexual assault onto women, obscuring the larger context of socially organized patterns of gender relations (Kitzinger & Frith, 1999).

In her exploration of the heterorelational discourses that young women employ to understand sexual violence, Hlavka (2014) makes the point that we must pay attention to "how and why these violent acts are produced, maintained, and normalized in the first place," thus rendering them invisible (p. 2). She describes how, for interviewees in her study, relational dynamics were very much at play in naming their experiences. They understood boys and men as natural sexual aggressors and perceived their invasive behaviours as not serious. Through sexual scripts confounding romance and aggression, harassment was constructed as romance and flirting, entitling young men to violate the bodies of young women. Men's everyday violence was just what guys do and something that the young women "just dealt with" (p. 11). Constructed as gatekeepers of men's desire, the fear of being labelled a slut pitted young women against each other and served as a barrier to reporting rape. Young women appropriated heteronormative scripts to make sense of and normalize everyday harassment, coercion, and violence and to interpret and justify actions in ways that legitimated men's dominance.

According to Senn (2011), who designs rape resistance programs for Canadian female students, the miscommunication hypothesis must be thoroughly debunked (Senn et al., 2013), precisely because in situations of coercion, men persist even though most women report using direct refusals. Situating the sexual assault of women in the context of sexism and other forms of structural inequality, we know that societies with greater levels of sexism and gender inequity have higher rates of violence against women. Furthermore, attitudes of sexism and heterosexism are closely interrelated with negativity expressed towards individuals who are perceived as transgressing sex and gender norms (Martinez, Barsky, & Singleton, 2011). Despite these socially organized sex and gender norms, however, the Students NS report does not explicitly connect them to the issue of consent.

The Students NS report advocates ongoing education and discussion opportunities for students, in both separate and mixed spaces for males and females, on what constitutes and what does not constitute consent, with links to the Criminal Code and consequences of sexual assault. If, as some feminists have theorized, acquaintance rape is more difficult to recognize and resist because it is "built on a foundation of socially accepted norms and beliefs regarding female and male sexuality and relationships" (Senn et al., 2011, p. 74), then any superficial approach to education about consent that inadequately contextualizes the issue is unlikely to prevent sexual assault. Consent campaigns must go beyond the legal definition of consent to tackle our cultural and institutional beliefs and practices that foment and legitimize such violence. If consent campaigns are to have any purchase, they must address heterorelational discourses that normalize dominant cultural constructions of femininity and masculinity and sexual coercion. The fact that young women on campuses identify that they have been sexually violated signals that they do refuse scripts that justify violence against them.

Beres (2014) advocates rethinking the concept of consent for anti-violence education and activism. She argues that consent is of limited use in sexual violence prevention because the concept itself does not resonate with young people engaging in heterosex. In her research, she found that participants' descriptions of their practices of negotiating sex differ from how they understand consent. She suggests moving away from the use of the word "consent" to talk directly about a specific behaviour; for example, the campaign by Sexual Assault Voices of Edmonton uses phrases such as "Just because she isn't saying no … doesn't mean she is saying yes." Educators need to build on what young people already know about negotiating sex in order to see that negotiation is part of giving and receiving consent for sex. Drawing on Carmody's (2005) work, Beres proposes moving beyond talking about consent to talking about ethical sexual relations (Beres, 2014; Beres & Farvid, 2010). Such an approach may provide more freedom for "radical subversion of dominant forms of heterosexuality" (Beres & Farvid, 2010).

We advocate that any education about consent should be situated in a framework of social justice. One of the benefits of feminist and social justice education is that participants are encouraged to see both the structural implications of oppressive systems and norms and how they as individuals are implicated in them. Exploration of the meaning of consent must be located in a discussion of the social arrangements that shape women's and men's subjectivities and give rise to sexual violence. Topics for all sexes and genders should include social relations of power and privilege, compulsory heterosexuality (Rich, 1980), human rights and women's rights, and "gender equity education resistant to troubled, heteronormative binaries and cultural constraints that omit discourses of desire, gender, and sexuality" (Hlavaka, 2014, p. 19). Specific to sexual violence, subject matter must address power motivation and power–sex association (Rozee & Koss, 2001), rape myths and attitudes, rape resistance, and liberating discourses of desire (Senn, 2011).

THE ACCOUNTABILITY OF MEN AS AGGRESSORS

The Students NS report affirms that "social context helps frame sexual violence as everyone's concern" (p. 9). It goes on to say that the framing of sexual violence "as a woman's problem" has led to a "perceived polarization of the campus community—feminist versus misogynist—with many men (according to the interviews conducted for this study) reluctant to enter the conversation for fear of the misogyny label" (pp. 9–10). Although this statement is unclear, the language used appears to deflect attention from men's accountability in the perpetuation of patriarchal beliefs and practices (Rich, Utley, Janke, & Moldoveanu, 2010). It also hints at men's victimization by feminist demands for individual and social change. Gender-based violence clearly cannot be resolved solely as "a women's issue"; however, we must recall that women's movements across the globe have been responsible for making this a public issue. Canadian women's movements have long pushed for ideological and material gains towards gender equity. The fact that women have led this struggle ought not to serve as a justification for the disengagement of either men or communities.

In terms of framing sexual violence as everyone's issue, in the past decade or so men's violence against women has increasingly been recognized as a men's issue (Katz, 2006). The social construction of gender identities now includes critical analyses of masculinities and how they are constructed and performed (Katz, 2006; Minerson, Carolo, Dinner, & Jones, 2011). More recently, however, the development of inclusive masculinity theory in the context of a postfeminist sensibility in the academy has de-emphasized the issue of sexual politics and gendered power relations (O'Neill, 2015). Linking the social and the individual, Pease makes an important point that "men's violence is both socially constructed and individually willed" (cited in Carmody & Carrington, 2000, p. 14). Narrow scripts of masculinity foster a sense of isolation and separation that works to constrain engagement in the nurturing relationships central to moral and spiritual development. For example, for African Canadian men in Nova Scotia, the violence of racism shapes the construction of Black masculinity (James et al., 2010). Recognizing that the construction of masculinities occurs in a setting of systemic gender inequity, Rich et al. (2010) inquire into how men are gendered to concern themselves only with issues that they believe directly affect them, deny that sexual assault has anything to do with them, and refuse to see their role in the perpetuation of rape culture. These attitudes can arise when efforts are made to educate men about gender issues and sexual assault (Rich et al., 2010).

Rich et al. (2010) identify such attitudes as representative of "structural masculinity" or "hegemonic masculinity" (p. 270). They advocate that men understand the social and structural factors that inform hypermasculinity and rigid gender roles, as well as their own accountability in patriarchy as a social system. Since women have often been assigned the function of gatekeeping men's desire, heteronormative discourses have permitted men's limited accountability for aggressive, harassing, and criminal sexual conduct (Hlavka, 2014). Women and men can fail to hold men responsible for their actions through claims that men are just as much victims as women, for example, because men have been socialized to repress feelings. Although sexism does harm men, gender as a system of restraints tends to serve men's interests (power, domestic and sexual service, freedom from emotional responsibilities) more than women's and encourages power-over attitudes and behaviours; this is a fundamental difference in how restraints affect each social group (Sherwin, 1992). Although men are oppressed by racism and other systemic inequities, the discouragement in men of the development of skills and traits associated with what we call the "feminine" is a form of alienation, not oppression (Sherwin, 1992).

With respect to changing men's attitudes and behaviours regarding sexual assault, the Students NS report recommends male-only programming, facilitated by men, to help prevent sexual violence, including exploration of masculinity and clarification of the meaning of consent. What have rape prevention programs actually found in terms of their effectiveness in shifting men's attitudes and behaviours and holding them accountable for perpetrating sexual assault? In their review of the efficacy of education programs, Anderson and Whiston (2005) found that the majority lacked any evaluation of effectiveness. In programs that did produce short-term change in rape-supportive attitudes, such changes tended to last only briefly. Unfortunately, there was no change in behaviour, that is, in the reduction of sexual assault. Nevertheless,

Anderson and Whiston claim that interventions with content on gender-role socialization, information about rape, rape myths and facts, and risk-reduction strategies have more effect on participants' attitudes than rape empathy programs and interventions with vague contents.

Besides male-only education, the report advocates Bringing in the Bystander training for all student leadership and university staff, the athletic community, and students in general. Bystander training offers "a significant opportunity to provide education to the wider campus community and thereby impact the larger campus culture" (p. 12). Using a social norms approach, bystander programs "empower men to be stronger social justice allies of women by fostering interventions against the problematic behaviors of other men" (Fabiano, Perkins, Berkowitz, Linkenbach, & Stark, 2003, p. 109). Critical to changing social norms on campus, this approach builds on the healthy attitudes and behaviours of men who are willing to intervene to prevent violence; what other men think and do is the strongest influence on how men act (Fabiano et al., 2003).

In order for bystander programs to change social norms and foster social justice, McMahon and Banyard (2012) highlight the need to clearly define bystander intervention in the context of sexual violence prevention. For instance, does it mean intervention in situations where someone may be assaulted, as well as activism on campus to challenge rape culture, shift social norms, and build a respectful community that does not tolerate any form of violence (McMahon et al., 2013)? If bystander programs do advocate action in the broader sense of changing cultures of sexism, heterosexism, racism, and so forth, then the term "bystander" doesn't quite capture the essence of the change required in our communities because it suggests that one can somehow be outside and free of social relations of domination and oppression. Since this can't be so for anyone, a bystander would be better conceived as an engaged citizen contributing to building a healthy community based on respectful and equitable relations. In this regard, social justice education recognizes that men can act ethically and explores the opportunities for them to do so (Carmody & Carrington, 2000).

The Students NS report notes that sexual predators (male) exist on campus and target vulnerable first-year students (female) for rape by using "alcohol as a weapon to disable their victims" (p. 18). It also cites a Canadian survey which found that 20% of male students thought that forced sex was acceptable under circumstances such as if the couple had been dating or if the woman was drunk or stoned (p. 6). Use of the "predator" label constructs those who sexually assault as the "other," thus enabling men who consider aggression acceptable under any or certain circumstances to perceive themselves as "normal men." As long as discourses construct sexual aggressors as the "other," men can dissociate themselves from their role in maintaining sexism and rape culture (Rich et al., 2010). Narratives about "sexual predators," which tend towards one end of the continuum of sexual violence, encourage the disowning of this responsibility. The report's omission in naming sexism and misogyny as the common thread in sexual violence towards women undermines its recommendation of male-only programming to prevent violence.

EMPOWERING WOMEN THROUGH RAPE RESISTANCE EDUCATION PROGRAMS

The Students NS report recommends programming for "all genders on sexual assault statistics, gender role attitudes and socialization, and rape myths" and programming that "emphasizes that everyone has the right to refuse sex at any time, with anyone, regardless of their relationship or previous degree of sexual interaction" (p. iii). Women also need to know that "being inebriated makes them less effective in resisting unwanted sex and puts them at higher risk for sexual assault" (p. 11). Although the report recommends gender-specific programming with particular content for men, it does not explore in any detail programming for women.

Critiques of sexual assault prevention programs that focus primarily on women point out that these programs enable men to refuse responsibility for rape (Rich et al., 2010; Rozee & Koss, 2001; Stewart, 2013). Although many programs do focus on women to give them the tools and skills to prevent sexual assault, Senn et al. (2013) note that until there is widespread social change and effective programming for men, rape resistance education for women is their best hope for safety. Such programs offer women information on the behaviour of men who rape (male sexuality, scripts, and seduction tactics) and actual resistance strategies, including forceful physical defence and methods of overcoming emotional barriers to resistance (Senn, 2011). Rather than advance the unsupported claim that women who defend themselves suffer more harm (Senn et al., 2013), programs need to teach actual resistance strategies given the greater effectiveness of some strategies over others in avoiding rape (Rozee & Koss, 2001).

Nonetheless, rape resistance education alone, emerging out of feminist analyses of rape in the 1970s, is not enough to protect women from sexual assault, nor are co-educational and men's programs (Senn et al., 2011). Women need to know they cannot always prevent rape, including by altering their behaviour (Senn et al., 2013). In fact, the content and approach of the rape resistance programs promoted by Senn (2011) do not limit women's freedom nor remove responsibility from the aggressor. Given that "patriarchal notions of men and women's sexual needs, desires and perceptions of 'normal heterosexual practice'" put men's sexual needs ahead of women's, Senn (2011) argues that putting women's positive sexual desires at the centre of rape resistance education counteracts the "missing discourse of desire" for women, dominant masculinist biases, and the heterosexual intercourse imperative (pp. 127–128). She adds that "women's inability to resist sexual assaults by acquaintances may be due, at least in part, to the grey area created by patriarchal notions of 'normal heterosexual practice'" (p. 127).

In summary, rape education programs for women and men must be theoretically grounded, address the social roots of rape, and build a culture of community rights and responsibilities (Anderson & Whiston, 2005; Senn et al., 2013). Rape prevention means changing cultures and ideologies, social structures and policies, and everyday practices, not only preventing someone from being raped (Senn, 2011). Cultural messages and practices run deep, and it is unrealistic to expect a short training session on sexual assault to radically alter the beliefs and practices of students and undo years of envelopment in cultural and structural violence. This is particularly so when a typical response to unwanted, disconfirmatory information is minimization or dismissal as not personally relevant (Joseph, Gray, & Mayer, 2013). Social justice education that looks at systems of domination and oppression based on gender, sex, sexuality, race, class, ability, and so forth, would be a useful framework for contextualizing and educating about sexualized violence. The work already done in this field provides helpful approaches that encourage engagement and reflection in learning about social relations and the operation of power (Adams, Bell, & Griffin, 1997; Goodman, 2001).

The Students NS report mentions that the majority of college women survivors know their aggressors, and furthermore, many do not "label what happened to them as 'rape'" (p. 7). This statement is left unexplored. In her landmark book on sexual violence, Kelly (1988) explores how women come to name their experiences as sexual violence. Naming often involves questioning "common-sense" definitions, assumptions, and justifications about sexual violence and exploring the contradictions between dominant discourse and lived experience. Women need access to frameworks that help them describe and define their experiences as violence and challenge the limited range of men's behaviour deemed unacceptable in our society. Likewise, if young women do equally endorse rape myths on university and college campuses (Joseph et al., 2013), we need to encourage them to rethink these dominant cultural constructions.

The Student NS report underplays the role that safe spaces can play on campus for women, Indigenous people, and people of diverse sexualities and genders, to name some examples. In their study of disclosure and service use after sexual violence, Walsh, Banyard, Moynihan, Ward, and Cohn (2014) report that college students saw their experience of unwanted sexual contact as not serious (70% of victims) and a private matter (40%), and consequently did not use available services. Given the social messages that silence and blame victims, they were reluctant to define their experience as sexual assault. Studies of this kind point to the complexities involved in naming experiences of violence and to young women's need for support in this process. Safe spaces, whether on campus or community based, are critical for accessing alternative perspectives to the status quo.

Final Reflections

The Students NS report represents a positive beginning in tackling the issue of sexual violence on university and college campuses. The perennial question remains: How do we shift and change rape culture and structures rooted in capitalist colonialist racist patriarchy? Our critique of the report *Student Safety in Nova Scotia: A Review of Student Union Policies and Practices to Prevent Sexual Violence* demonstrates the imperative to foster social change grounded in social justice principles, equity, respect, and nonviolence in order to prevent sexualized violence. In our view, this change has to encompass shifts in ideology and discursive systems, institutional beliefs, policies and practices, and collective and individual actions.

In conceptualizing a map for change, Grosz (1990) helpfully outlines how women's oppression in patriarchal cultures operates at three intertwined levels, in (1) discursive systems, representations, and theories proliferating oppressive images of women and the feminine; (2) the underlying mode of social organization called patriarchy that places women and men in different positions in social, economic, and interpersonal relations and provides the meaning for sexist inequalities; and (3) unwarranted individual and collective acts of discrimination against women ranging from overt violence to the exclusion of women from certain social spheres and activities (pp. 149–150). A theoretical framework of social justice that recognizes all forms of social inequity must inform all change efforts, including violence prevention.

In Nova Scotia, the Antigonish Women's Resource Centre and Sexual Assault Services Association provides a theoretically grounded prevention project to end violence against women and gender-based violence at St. Francis Xavier University (Antigonish Women's Resource Centre and Sexual Assault Services Association, n.d.). The project uses an intersectional, gender-based community development approach to make gendered violence and its impact on the student body visible. Collaborating with students, faculty, staff, and administration, it works on three fronts: (1) to educate the university community about "how wider societal issues of gender impact institutional climate and individual constructions of gender and violence"; (2) to ensure that university policies and procedures (accountable to the campus community) are in place to address violence; and (3) to better serve the support needs of survivors and the safety needs of campus members. A key component of the prevention work involves community and campus collaboration.

The centre's prevention work recognizes that sexism, gender harassment, heterosexism, and partner violence create an unsafe campus environment and that particular populations are structurally more vulnerable to violence. Furthermore, different forms of oppression affect people's experience of, and vulnerability to, violence. Guy (2008) affirms that sexual violence cannot be eliminated by ending sexism alone; we must work to end all forms of oppression. Her visual conception of the sexual violence continuum situates violence in the context of multiple systems of interconnected oppressions. It is central to the development of a comprehensive vision of sexual violence prevention since "sexual violence is very rarely experienced as a discreet event and one's experience of sexual violence is impacted by one's experience of oppression" (p. 11).

In preventing sexual violence, Senn (2011) comments that "if we were to take rape prevention seriously, we would design theoretically grounded education programmes for men that would stop them from committing sexual coercion and sexual assaults, and educate men and women in ways that would substantially change our rape culture(s)" (p. 122). Although such education programs are crucial, including those that enhance the individual survival of young women, primary prevention must go beyond interventions directed at the personal and interpersonal. To illustrate this point, Hlavka (2014) asserts that "placing responsibility on women and girls to 'just say no' and excusing boys and men as they 'work a 'yes' out' works to erase institutional and structural responsibilities" (p. 18). On university and college campuses, attention must be paid to larger cultural discourses and practices of power, and institutional policies and practices must effectively protect people from assault and harassment (Hlavka, 2014). New policies that increase the reporting of sexual assaults or the numbers of campus police may be easier to institute (Hlavka, 2014); however, the kind of change required must go much deeper. Change efforts, including political action, must promote fundamental shifts in the complex ideological and attitudinal foundations of sexual violence (Hlavka, 2014; Rich et al., 2010). All prevention efforts should harness the expertise and experience of equity-seeking groups and organizations on and off campus.

Using lessons from feminism and other social movements, it is worth pointing out that "true primary prevention is population-based using environmental and system-level strategies, policies, and actions that prevent sexual violence from initially occurring" (American College Health Association, 2008, p. 5). These broader strategies aimed at changing communities (norms, traditions, local institutions, and workplaces) and society as a whole (broad social forces such as inequalities, oppressions, organized belief systems, public policies) tend to be more effective in changing individual attitudes and behaviours (American College Health Association, 2008). This is so because a comprehensive approach speaks both to how individual constructions of gender and so forth interface with the larger world and how norms, policies, and institutions shape the environment in which violence occurs (American College Health Association, 2008; Antigonish Women's Resource Centre and Sexual Assault Services Association, n.d.). Public health theory also advocates a systematic approach to promoting healthy behaviours such as egalitarian gender roles and healthy sexualities and suggests that sexual violence prevention efforts be specific to an intentional audience (American College Health Association, 2008). This specificity was evident in the Preventing Violence against Women at St. Francis Xavier University Project (Antigonish Women's Resource Centre and Sexual Assault Services Association, n.d.).

Clearly, the leadership of governments and institutions must be committed to creating safe and respectful teaching and learning environments on campuses. Through engaging in individual and collective political action, citizens must pressure leadership to respond to this significant social justice issue. In this regard, social movement theory offers significant insights into how social change occurs (Moyer, McAllister, Finley, & Soifer, 2001; Staggenborg, 2012). The university community advancing prevention efforts would benefit from a clear feminist and social justice theoretical framework to inform their efforts to change cultures, policies, and practices on campuses. Such a framework would have a consistent political message about what we understand to be the roots of sexualized violence, and clarity about how to manifest this understanding in all prevention and intervention work, discursive or otherwise. This would send a strong message that patriarchal violence and the politics of domination are public and community affairs. As feminists who have been part of the women's movement for decades, we know how hard it is to change a culture of misogyny; yet we still must work from the vision of a socially just and humane society for all.

REFERENCES

Adams, M., Bell, L. A., & Griffin, P. (Eds.). (1997). *Teaching for diversity and social justice: A sourcebook.* New York, NY: Routledge.

Alexander, B. (2008). *The globalization of addiction: A study in poverty of the spirit.* New York, NY: Oxford University Press.

American Association of University Professors. (2013). Campus sexual assault: Suggested policies and procedures. *Academe, 99*(4), 92–100.

American College Health Association. (2008). *Shifting the paradigm: Primary prevention of sexual violence.* Linthicum, MD: Author. Retrieved from http://www.acha.org/sexualviolence/docs/acha_psv_toolkit.pdf

Anderson, L. A., & Whiston, S. C. (2005). Sexual assault education programs: A meta-analytic examination of their effectiveness. *Psychology of Women Quarterly, 29*(4), 374–388.

Anderssen, E. (2014, November 15). Sex on campus: How no means no became yes means yes. *Globe and Mail*. Retrieved from http://www.theglobeandmail.com/life/relationships/sex-on-campus-how-no-means-no-became-yes-means-yes/article21598708/

Andrew, K., Barnsley, J., Ellis, M., Lewis, D., & Wasserlein, F. (1986). Feminist manifesto. *RFR/DRF, 15*(1), 46–47.

Antigonish Women's Resource Centre and Sexual Assault Services Association. (n.d.). Preventing violence at StFX. Retrieved from http://awrcsasa.ca/community-development-social-advocacy/preventing-violence-at-st-fx/

Bannerji, H. (2000). *The dark side of a nation: Essays on multiculturalism, nationalism and gender*. Toronto, ON: Canadian Scholars' Press.

Beres, M. A. (2014). Rethinking the concept of consent for anti-sexual violence activism and education. *Feminism & Psychology, 24*(3), 373–389.

Beres, M. A., & Farvid, P. (2010). Sexual ethics and young women's accounts of heterosexual casual sex. *Sexualities, 13*(3) 377–393.

Burnett, A., Mattern, J. L., Herakova, L. L., Kahl, D. H., Tobola, C., & Bornsen, S. E. (2009). Communicating/muting date rape: A co-cultural theoretical analysis of communication factors related to rape culture on a college campus. *Journal of Applied Communication Research, 37*(4), 465–485.

Burstow, B. (2003). Toward a radical understanding of trauma and trauma work. *Violence Against Women, 9*(11), 1293–1317.

Butler, J. (1999). *Gender trouble* (2nd ed.). New York, NY: Routledge.

Calogero, R. M. (2013). Objects don't object: Evidence that self-objectification disrupts women's social activism. *Psychological Science, 24*(3), 312–318.

Campbell, R., & Wasco, S. M. (2005). Understanding rape and sexual assault: 20 years of progress and future directions. *Journal of Interpersonal Violence, 20*(1), 127–131.

Canadian Women's Foundation. (2011). *Report on violence against women, mental health and substance use*. Toronto, ON: Canadian Women's Foundation and BC Society of Transition Houses.

Carmody, M. (2005). Ethical erotics: Reconceptualizing anti-rape eduction. *Sexualities, 8*(4), 465–480.

Carmody, M., & Carrington, K. (2000). Preventing sexual violence? *Australian and New Zealand Journal of Criminology, 33*(3), 341–361.

Crenshaw, K. (1991). Mapping the margins: Intersectionality, identity politics, and violence against women of color. *Stanford Law Review, 43*(6), 1241–1299.

Dalhousie delays dentistry exams amid misogyny case on Facebook. (2014, December 16). *CBC News*. Retrieved from http://www.cbc.ca/news/canada/nova-scotia/dalhousie-delays-dentistry-exams-amid-misogyny-case-on-facebook-1.2874489

Dines, G. (2010). *Pornland: How porn has hijacked our sexuality*. Boston, MA: Beacon Press.

Fabiano, P. M., Perkins, H. W., Berkowitz, A., Linkenbach, J., & Stark, C. (2003). Engaging men as social justice allies in ending violence against women: Evidence for a social norms approach. *Journal of American College Health, 52*(3), 105–112.

Galtung, J. (1990). Cultural violence. *Journal of Peace Research*, 27(3), 291–305.

Gavey, N. (2005). *Just sex? The cultural scaffolding of rape*. London, UK: Routledge.

Gervais, S., DiLillo, D., & McChargue, D. E. (2014). Understanding the link between men's alcohol use and sexual violence perpetration: The mediating role of sexual objectification. *Psychology of Violence*, 3(4), 1–14.

Gilligan, J. (2009). Sex, gender and violence: Estela Welldon's contribution to our understanding of the psychopathology of violence. *British Journal of Psychotherapy*, 25(2), 239–256.

Gillingham, P. (2006). Risk assessment in child protection: Problem rather than solution? *Australian Social Work*, 59(1), 86–98.

Goodman, D. J. (2001). *Promoting diversity and social justice: Educating people from privileged groups*. Thousand Oaks, CA: Sage.

Grosz, E. (1990). Philosophy. In S. Gunew (Ed.), *Feminist knowledge: Critique and construct* (pp. 147–174). London, UK: Routledge.

Guy, L. (2008). Re-visioning the sexual violence continuum. In American College Health Association, *Shifting the paradigm: Primary prevention of sexual violence* (pp. 10–11). Linthicum, MD: American College Health Association.

Heise, L., Ellsberg, M., & Gottemoeller, M. (1999). Ending violence against women. *Population Reports*, 27, 1–43.

Hlavka, H. R. (2014). Normalizing sexual violence: Young women account for harassment and abuse. *Gender & Society*, 20(10), 1–22.

hooks, b. (1988). *Talking back: Thinking feminist, thinking black*. Toronto, ON: Between the Lines.

Horsman, J. (2000). *Too scared to learn: Women, violence, and education*. Mahwah, NJ: Lawrence Erlbaum.

Jaggar, A. M. (1988). *Feminist politics and human nature*. Totowa, NJ: Rowman & Littlefield.

James, C., Este, D., Bernard, W., Benjamin, A., Lloyd, B., & Turner, T. (2010). *Race and well-being: The lives, hopes and activism of African Canadians*. Black Point, NS: Fernwood.

Jernigan, D. (2011). Framing a public health debate over alcohol advertising: The Center on Alcohol Marketing and Youth 2002–2008. *Journal of Public Health Policy*, 32(2), 165–179.

Joseph, J. S., Gray, M. J., & Mayer, J. (2013). Addressing sexual assault within social systems: System justification as a barrier to college prevention efforts. *Journal of Aggression, Maltreatment & Trauma*, 22(5), 493–509.

Katz, J. (2006). *The macho paradox: Why some men hurt women and how all men can help*. Naperville, IL: Sourcebooks.

Kelly, L. (1988). *Surviving sexual violence*. Minneapolis, MN: University of Minneapolis Press.

Kilbourne, J. (1999). *Can't buy my love: How advertising changes the way we think and feel*. New York, NY: Touchstone Press.

Kitzinger, C., & Frith, H. (1999). Just say no? The use of conversation analysis in developing a feminist perspective on sexual refusal. *Discourse & Society*, 10(3), 293–316.

Lamb, S. (1991). Acts without agents: An analysis of linguistic avoidance in journal articles on men who batter women. *American Journal of Orthopsychiatry*, 61(2), 250–257.

Levin, D., & Kilbourne, J. (2009) *So sexy so soon: The new sexualized childhood and what parents can do to protect their kids.* New York, NY: Ballantine Books.

Liebenberg, L., Ungar, M., & Ikeda, J. (2013). Neo-liberalism and responsibilisation in the discourse of social service workers. *British Journal of Social Work*, 1–16. doi:10.1093/bjsw/bct172

Lupton, D. (1993). Risk as moral danger: The social and political functions of risk discourse in public health. *International Journal of Health Services, 23*(3), 425–435.

Martell Consulting Services Ltd. (2014). *Student safety in Nova Scotia: A review of student union policies and practices to prevent sexual violence.* Halifax, NS: Students Nova Scotia.

Martinez, P., Barsky, A., & Singleton, S. (2011). Exploring queer consciousness among social workers. *Journal of Gay and Lesbian Social Services, 23*(2), 296–315.

McGibbon, E. A. (Ed.). (2012). *Oppression: A social determinant of health.* Black Point, NS: Fernwood.

McMahon, S., Allen, C. T., Postmus, J. L., McMahon, S. M., Peterson, N. A., & Hoffman, M. L. (2013). Measuring bystander attitudes and behavior to prevent sexual violence. *Journal of American College Health, 62*(1), 58–66.

McMahon, S., & Banyard, V. L. (2012). When can I help? A conceptual framework for the prevention of sexual violence through bystander intervention. *Trauma, Violence, & Abuse, 13*(1), 3–14.

Minerson, T., Carolo, H., Dinner, T., & Jones, C. (2011). *Issue brief: Engaging men and boys to reduce and prevent gender-based violence.* Ottawa, ON: Status of Women Canada.

Moyer, B., McAllister, J., Finley, M. L., & Soifer, S. (2001). *Doing democracy: The MAP model for organizing social movements.* Gabriola Island, BC: New Society.

O'Neill, R. (2015). Whither critical masculinity studies? Notes on inclusive masculinity theory, postfeminism, and sexual politics. *Men and Masculinities, 18*(1), 100–120.

Pickup, F., Williams, S., & Sweetman, C. (2001). *Ending violence against women: A challenge for development and humanitarian work.* Oxford, UK: Oxfam Great Britain.

Province of Nova Scotia. (2013). *Action Team on Sexual Violence and Bullying.* Halifax, NS: Author.

Razack, S. (1998). *Looking white people in the eye: Gender, race, and culture in courtrooms and classrooms.* Toronto, ON: University of Toronto Press.

Rich, A. (1980). Compulsory heterosexuality and lesbian existence. *Signs, 5*(4), 631–660.

Rich, M. D., Utley, E. A., Janke, K., & Moldoveanu, M. (2010). "I'd rather be doing something else": Male resistance to rape prevention programs. *Journal of Men's Studies, 18*(3), 268–288.

Root, M. (1992). Restructuring the impact of trauma on the personality. In L. Brown & M. Ballour (Eds.), *Personality and psychopathology* (pp. 229–265). New York, NY: Guilford Press.

Rozee, P. D., & Koss, M. P. (2001). Rape: A century of resistance. *Psychology of Women Quarterly, 25*, 295–311.

Scourfield, J., & Welsh, I. (2002). *New times or same old story? Risk, reflexivity and social control in child protection* (Working Paper Series, Paper 23). Cardiff, UK: School of Social Sciences, Cardiff University.

Senn, C. Y. (2011). An imperfect feminist journey: Reflections on the process to develop an effective sexual assault resistance programme for university women. *Feminism & Psychology, 21*(1), 121–137.

Senn, C. Y., Eliasziw, M., Barata, P. C., Thurston, W. E., Newby-Clark, I. R., Radtke, H. L., Hobden, K. L., & SARE Study Team. (2013). Sexual assault resistance education for university women: Study protocol for a randomized controlled trial (SARE trial). *BMC Women's Health, 13,* 25. Retrieved from http://.biomed central.com/1472-6874/13/25

Senn, C. Y., Gee, S. G., & Thake, J. (2011). Emancipatory sexuality education and sexual assault resistance: Does the former enhance the latter? *Psychology of Women Quarterly, 35,* 72–91.

Sherwin, S. (1992). *No longer patient: Feminist ethics and health care.* Philadelphia, PA: Temple University Press.

Staggenborg, S. (2012). *Social movements.* Don Mills, ON: Oxford University Press.

Stewart, A. L. (2013). The Men's Project: A sexual assault prevention program targeting college men. *Psychology of Men & Masculinity, 15*(4), 481–485.

Swadener, B. B. (2010). "At risk" or "at promise"? From deficit constructions of the "other childhood" to possibilities for authentic alliances with children and families. *International Critical Childhood Policy Studies, 3*(1), 7–29.

Tobin, L. (2012). *Sensing the impacts of hypersexualization and opportunities for change in Nova Scotia.* Presentation at the ACIP 2012 Injury Prevention Conference, Moncton, NB.

United Nations Population Fund. (n.d.). Gender-based violence. Retrieved from http://www.unfpa.org/gender-based-violence

Vladutiu, C. J., Martin, S. L., & Macy, R. J. (2011). College- or university-based sexual assault prevention programs: A review of program outcomes, characteristics, and recommendations. *Trauma, Violence, & Abuse, 12*(2), 67–86.

Walsh, W. A., Banyard, V. L., Moynihan, M. M., Ward, S., & Cohn, E. S. (2014) Disclosure and service use on a college campus after an unwanted sexual experience *Journal of Trauma & Dissociation, 11*(2), 134–151.

World Health Organization. (2013a). Violence against women: "A global health problem of epidemic proportions." Retrieved from http://www.who.int/mediacentre/news/releases/2013/violence_against_women_20130620/en/

World Health Organization. (2013b). Violence against women: Intimate partner violence and sexual violence against women. Retrieved from http://www.who.int/mediacentre/factsheets/fs239/en/

PART IV

FIGHTING BACK

Anti-Violence Activism on Campus

CHAPTER 11

THE COALITION AGAINST SEXUAL ASSAULT

Activism Then and Now at the University of Saskatchewan

Elizabeth Quinlan and Gail Lasiuk

On January 1, 2012, a woman was drugged and sexually assaulted in a student residence of the University of Saskatchewan (UofS). One of her two attackers was a student at the university. Not yet a university student herself, the victim/survivor (referred to anonymously as "Linda") was working on upgrading her high school credits so she could enroll in nursing. In the days and weeks following the assault, Linda's mother valiantly tried many different ways to approach the university for help, to no avail. She was ignored, indeed shunned, by all the security and administrative personnel she contacted. When she called the president's office, she was told that no action could be taken unless there was a criminal finding of guilt—information the family later discovered was incorrect. Why was there nobody to respond to the mother when eight years previously, a victim advocate had been established to provide support, information, referrals, and advocacy to victims/survivors and their friends and families?

Despite the alarmingly high rates of sexual violence on Canadian campuses, universities are often unprepared and unwilling to address this issue in a meaningful way. Among them is the UofS. This chapter charts the UofS's changing responses to high-profile sexual assault starting in 2003, when the university's flagrant intransigence regarding two sexual assaults became a flashpoint for the authors of this chapter to organize a meeting of a small group of concerned students, faculty, staff, and parents. That meeting gave birth to the Coalition Against Sexual Assault–University of Saskatchewan (CASA–UofS). Within a very short time from its inception, the group successfully petitioned the university for a campus security audit and a victim advocate position, and organized a variety of events on campus and in the larger community, including a student forum on campus security, several December 6 vigils, and a healing ceremony on the site of one of the assaults. A subsequent assault again threw the university into the spotlight with national media coverage and tested the group's ability to effect change within an institution that by then had become even more impersonal and, we would argue, corporatized.

The UofS is a typical medium-sized Canadian university with a balance of liberal arts programs and professional colleges, including medicine, engineering, nursing, and law. It shares many characteristics of other universities across the country, in particular its adoption of a corporatized managerialism (see Chapter 3). As a result, the UofS has departed from its history of providing accessible public education in service to the local population's needs. Attending to sexual violence on campus is in keeping with the UofS's historic characterization of itself as a "people's university" in a province with a populist history (Hayden, 1983). But as the university strays further and further away from this mandate, advocacy to adequately address sexual violence has fallen on deaf ears.

The events analyzed in this chapter are not for the purpose of showcasing one university, for what happened in the wake of the assaults at the UofS is not unique. Instead, the story is offered as a means of exploring the changes at contemporary Canadian universities, most notably the increased application of cost-benefit metrics to the functions of these institutions that is linked to abdication of their social responsibility to respond to and educate about sexual violence. The chronology illustrates that gains made as recently as a decade ago can be unceremoniously rolled back, particularly when the media's interest wanes.

We start the chapter with a description of events at the UofS in 2003. We then move to the next high-profile assault and contrast the university's response to the assault almost a decade prior. We recognize the inadequacies of both "victim" and "survivor" as terms to identify women who have experienced sexual assault and would prefer to use the women's own term. However, because this is not always possible, we choose to use victim/survivor or a pseudonym.

ASSAULTS AT THE UOFS

In July 2003 in broad daylight, a student at the UofS was sexually assaulted in a building on the university campus less than 100 feet from one of the main city streets. The victim/survivor (referred to anonymously as "Lee") was a university student employed on campus for the summer. She was performing her work duties alone when she was violently attacked by a stranger.

In conversation with Lee's family, the university's senior administration was dismissive of the fact that the perpetrator had an extensive file with campus security that detailed a history of openly declared misogynist and racist views (Lee, personal communication, 2015). For these activities, he had been expelled from university, and yet there were no steps taken by administration or security to prevent him from coming back onto campus. Instead, the conversations with the administrators focused on the distinctive legal status of the building where Lee worked, which was a university affiliate rather than part of the university proper. This bureaucratic technicality was used to justify why the university administration as her employer should not bear responsibility for her safety. This contravened the intent, if not the specific provisions, of the province's Occupational Health and Safety legislation that governed all workplaces, including the university. Yet, when it came time to complete the "Accidents, Incidents, and Spills Report Form," Lee was considered an employee and presented with such irrelevant questions as, "Was there any property/equipment damage?" and, "Was the correct equipment/tool/material used?" Harm to the employee was nowhere captured on this form.

The building where the assault took place was closed immediately after the assault, with promises of upgrades to the archaic walkie-talkie security system and limited staffing. In follow-up email correspondence, the coordinator of Discrimination and Harassment Prevention Services reiterated the promise to the family, "with no qualifications" (Lee, personal communication, 2015). Several months later, the building reopened, no better equipped and only minimally staffed.

Then, in November 2003, a female student studying on campus was attacked by an unknown assailant in a heavy-traffic washroom on the main floor of the College of Arts and Science. This was the second reported stranger assault in a matter of a few months. The brutal attack was met with shock and outrage by many in the campus community, feelings compounded by the high-profile assault committed only months earlier that year. Yet, very shortly after the second assault, rumours began to swirl on campus. As in so many cases, the report of the victim/survivor (referred to anonymously as "Rose") was met with suspicion by university officials: she had invented the story; she had lied about the assault to get out of writing exams. These rumours flew in the face of the facts. A communiqué about the "alleged" assault was issued shortly after, despite the DNA evidence that had been recovered via a rape kit, other physical evidence found at the crime scene, and the fact that it was one of the university's own security officers who was the first to find Rose after the assault. The use of the legal term "alleged" served the administration's concern with legal liability and did nothing to dispel the circulating rumours. When Rose's mother asked senior administration to explain the use of "alleged," the university administration peremptorily shifted the responsibility by stating, "At the time of the announcement we had not heard any details from the City Police" (T. Whitworth, vice-president finances and resources, personal communication, December 24, 2003). Such an oblique response skirted the university's role as the legitimate agent of notifications to its own community members, unbeholden to outside agencies for their content.

In the flurry of media reports that followed the second assault, the director of Campus Security Services offered the following explanation for why bulletins were issued only under certain circumstances: "Campus security alerts are based on information it gets from the police and the victim/survivor's privacy and peace of mind are issues when deciding whether to issue a bulletin" (Rempel, 2003). According to Rose's mother, it was only because her family and the UofS's student union women's centre strenuously advocated for a security bulletin that the communiqué was issued at all, and then it was several days after the assault had occurred (CASA–UofS, 2004).

While Rose was quoted as urging the university to better inform students about incidents that happen on campus—"By not being aggressive and assertive about this, the university is providing a false sense of security"—a university safety official was reported as saying in the same media story that "the campus is safe" (Rempel, 2004). The university's president reiterated the blanket assurance—"The university is very concerned about the safety of faculty, staff and students"—and at the same time, the director of Campus Security Services made the covert plea for additional resources for his unit by noting that "special constables can't be everywhere at once" (Rempel, 2003). Several weeks later, using the classic tactic of victim-blaming, the president issued the following directive to the campus community in an email message: "While the University must be responsible in its approach to campus safety, individuals must also use the same caution on campus as they do anywhere else" (P. MacKinnon, email, January 13, 2004).

CASA GOES TO WORK

In the weeks following the second assault in 2003, many individuals on campus expressed fear, shock, and outrage. Their coffee-time conversations were rife with questions but short on answers: "How could these acts have occurred in such heavily frequented places?" "If it happened to these two women, it could easily happen to me." "What was the meaning of the administration's declaration, 'Our university is a safe place'?" "Why were more resources dedicated to protecting university property rather than the people who studied and worked on campus?"

In response to these concerns, CASA circulated a petition to press the UofS for an external audit of its security procedures and in the following few weeks collected over 1000 handwritten signatures of support. To give further voice and recognition to the community's growing apprehension, CASA sponsored a public forum where all members of the university community could express their concerns and offer suggestions for improvements to security on campus. The forum was moderated by the student union president, with a panel consisting of the authors of this chapter, a university administrator, the second assault victim/survivor and her mother, and the province's occupational health and safety inspector responsible for enforcing the legislation at UofS. The panel's opening remarks were followed by an open mic. Instantly, long lines formed at both stand-up microphones. One of the first to speak was a CASA member presenting the petition with over 1000 signatures to the university administrator on the panel. Several themes emerged from the comments of speakers representing the ranks of university faculty, staff, and students. Most notable was the widespread dissatisfaction with the university's highly institutional, "robotic," and emotionless response to survivors and their families. Practical suggestions about safety reform were offered. The attendees also displayed a refreshing willingness to engage in open discussion of the larger issues that perpetuate sexual assault. Especially encouraging was the participation of a number of young men at the forum who spoke publicly about the steps they were taking to expand their awareness of their role in preventing sexual violence.

Immediately following the forum, the university agreed to conduct an external safety audit (the primary demand of CASA's petition), to be carried out by two security experts from a neighbouring university. During the audit, CASA representatives met with the auditors and presented 36 recommendations compiled from the forum for improving safety on campus. Key recommendations included the following:

1. Implementing a student-directed victim advocate position designed to provide public education on sexual violence and specialized services to survivors of gender-related violence;

2. Developing guidelines for the content and format of safety alerts (e.g., avoiding the use of words such as "alleged") in consultation with members of the university community, particularly women's advocacy groups;

3. Refocusing the duties of the security constables to reflect greater attention to community policing rather than the existing focus on parking enforcement;

4. Extending the Safe Walk program (a program providing accompaniment to students walking alone on campus) by making it available 24 hours a day, 7 days a week, and financially compensating Safe Walk volunteers for their work;

5. Installing security alert boards in strategic places throughout campus (e.g., residences, washrooms, elevators);

6. Ensuring that safety alerts are posted electronically, via email, within 24 hours of an incident being reported to security;

7. Creating an advisor to the president on the status of women, recruited from faculty on a part-time, two-year rotational basis, to coordinate and chair the President's Advisory Committee on the Status of Women and the President's Advisory Committee on Personal Safety;

8. Changing academic requirements such that all incoming students must include an introductory women's and gender studies course in their program of study; and

9. Demonstrating leadership in addressing gendered violence issues by having senior administrators be the first to take gender-sensitivity training.

Several of these recommendations were reiterated by the auditors in their final report, despite its predominant focus on the restructuring of the Department of Security Services and the installation of more security cameras on campus. Although the recommendation of a victim advocate was not included in the auditor's report, the security audit, together with the forum that preceded it, clearly galvanized the creation of the victim advocate position by the UofS student union. Funded in part by a Status of Women Canada grant, the advocate's mandate included support, information, referrals, and advocacy to survivors and their friends/families, as well as public education to the campus community through presentations, awareness events, and poster campaigns. Over the next few years, the victim advocate spearheaded and collaborated on many projects, including an educational play for first-year students with content on sexual violence and the implementation of a *USSU Sexual Assault Survivors' Bill of Rights* and the *USSU Sexual Assault Protocol*, documents that are now published annually in the USSU student rights handbook. Despite the resulting increase in awareness activities on sexualized/gender-related violence, the victim advocate position was eliminated in 2008 without notice or reallocation.

Institutional change: Mediated by the media

The two stranger-perpetrated sexual assaults in 2003 quickly caught the interest of the campus student newspaper and the local media, which proved to be a mixed blessing. While the media coverage served to keep pressure on the university administration and forced them to be accountable for addressing safety concerns on campus, the quality of the coverage was often poor and heavily laden with myths and implicit and explicit variations on the theme of victim-blaming. Stories that undermined the legitimacy of the victims/survivors' accounts not only bolstered the university administration's strategy of minimizing the prevalence and social costs of sexual assault on campus, but they also discouraged other victims/survivors from reporting.

When the survivor of the second assault requested a reprieve from the strenuous police questioning, which forced her to relive her assault many times over, a front-page story appeared in the local newspaper strongly insinuating that she had fabricated the details of her assault to further her own interests. The inference was based solely on speculation and rape mythology, with no factual evidence to support it, a devastating accusation for the survivor and her family, and one that no doubt served to dissuade other women from coming forward in the future. Indeed, when a white, middle-class woman attacked by a stranger in her place of learning, with obvious physical injuries substantiated by medical reports and DNA evidence to support her case, is labelled a liar by the public media, other survivors understandably lose confidence in the systems that are supposed to provide support. Yet in the face of all evidence to the contrary, the university continued to assert that the campus was a safe place.

On the upside, a critically minded journalist on the staff of a community-based newspaper who followed CASA's activities wrote a series of articles in 2004 criticizing the UofS's response to sexual assault. She prevailed in the face of being threatened with a lawsuit by the university president at the time. Although it is not possible to point to tangible evidence, we think it is reasonable to believe that these articles contributed to the university's eventual capitulation to CASA's demand for an external audit. Certainly there is no question that the media's appetite for provocative stories put pressure on the university on numerous occasions. With every CASA-led event, a press release was distributed to local media outlets, and while the coverage was not always helpful and sometimes downright damaging, without this media attention the university's actions would not have been held up for public scrutiny, and change could well have been much slower.

However, in the absence of high-profile sexual assaults, media interest tends to wane. As later events at the UofS revealed, university administration can take advantage of reduced public awareness by undoing the gains achieved in support services and resources devoted to these issues, relying on an absence of public complaints as spurious proof that sexual violence is no longer problematic.

FAST-FORWARD TO 2012

On January 1, 2012, another female student, Linda, was sexually assaulted at the UofS. This assault was by no means the only one at the university since 2003. But, unlike many assaults in the intervening years, it became a lightning rod for media attention and activism on campus, thereby exposing the ground lost in reforms promised at the time of the 2003 assaults.

In February 2012, CASA organized a meeting with Linda, her mother, and the university's vice-president of student affairs. In the meeting, CASA members reminded the vice-president of the victim advocate position created in 2004 via a joint effort by CASA and the UofS student union. Despite the demonstrated value of the advocate's work (as described above), the position was unceremoniously dismantled in 2009 without consultation with the student body. Had this position still been in place, Linda's mother would have received the necessary support; instead, she was shunted from one office to another and wrongly told that no action could be taken unless there was a criminal suit and a finding of guilt.

CASA applauded those changes emanating from the 2004 security audit that had remained in effect, for instance, the adjustment to job profiles of the security constables that resulted in more resources for community policing; installation of 24-hour lighting in most washrooms; and the significant increase of security cameras. But, on balance, there were many more recommendations that were either works-in-progress or had been simply forgotten. For instance, the security alert boards that were posted across campus as a result of the audit had gradually fallen out of use, and CASA noted that the university had yet to adopt any proactive requirements regarding mandatory education or sensitivity training for its students or staff, an item we had brought to the attention of administrators several years prior in CASA's report card (2005; see Appendix). CASA reminded the vice-president of the university's promise to institute a key recommendation of the 2004 external audit: a campus-wide alert to be issued within 24 hours of a reported assault. We remarked on the passage of time so that nine years later, here we were still without a communication procedure that was consistent, respectful, timely, and comprehensive. But it would be a full six weeks after the January 1, 2012, assault before the university alerted the campus community to the assault—and this was only because of CASA's insistence. Students were understandably outraged. In an opinion piece in the student newspaper, "Giving Victim/Survivors a Voice: University's Handling of New Year's Eve Assault Too Little, Too Late," the university administration was roundly chastised:

> The suggested treatment of the release seemed to be: read it, forget it, move on. Why notify the community at all, if only to mute the message? ... Were we provided with statistics, we would at least be armed with empirical knowledge. Were we to have the details, then the actual perpetrator, conditions and risks associated with this particular instance might be of some use. (Vic M., 2012, p. 8)

In another student newspaper article, the president of the undergraduate student union articulated the concerns of his many constituents by noting that the university buried the recommendations from the 2004 security audit, especially those recommendations concerning campus alerts. He wrote, "Now nine years later, the university has forgotten these [recommendations]. In neglecting to inform the students and employees of this recent assault in a timely manner, the administration put the campus community at risk" (Hofmann, 2012, p. 5).

Shortly after the delayed alert was finally issued, the perpetrator of the sexual assault was charged and brought before the courts. Coincidently, on the same day as his first court appearance, Jack Froese, a perpetrator found on the UofS campus in 2005 with duct tape, pornography, and the names and pictures of several university cheerleaders, was charged in another western city for aggravated sexual assault. Perhaps the timing is not so coincidental considering the serial nature of most sexual crimes. The minimal media reporting on Froese's presence on campus in 2005 served as the only alert to the campus community. A scant year after the external audit recommended 24-hour notifications, the university had failed to issue an alert. With no high-profile assault to attract media attention over the intervening years, it wasn't until the assault of 2012 that widespread attention to the pattern of sporadic, inconsistent university alerts came to light.

TASK FORCES AND POLICIES: UNIVERSITY RESPONSES

In contrast to the university's response to the 2003 assaults, within months of the January 2012 assault, the vice-president of student affairs established a task force to raise awareness about sexual assault and examine new approaches to its prevention and response. In recent times, task forces similar to the one at the UofS have become a staple of university responses to high-profile sexual assaults (Lakehead University, 2013; Saint Mary's University, 2014; University of Ottawa, 2015). As an aspect of the growing corporatization of universities, these administrative bodies reflect a departure from the more representative academic decision-making structures that have historically provided a necessary vehicle of influence to faculty and students (Newson, 2015). Task forces are often composed of an unwieldy number of members and are not recruited via an inclusive call for interested volunteers, but chosen by the university's senior administrators. The UofS's task force included several faculty, but mostly staff from various departments including human resources, student services communications, and security. Importantly, the task force had no representation from groups in the larger community with experience and training in survivor advocacy and preventative public education campaigns.

CASA declined to participate in the task force because members were skeptical that it would offer fruitful outcomes. Instead, CASA organized a consultation with local community-based organizations involved in gender-based violence prevention in order to develop recommendations for the task force to consider. Funded by the University President's Advisory Committee on the Status of Women, this consultation resulted in the three main recommendations that were conveyed to the chair of the task force in April 2013: (1) enhance post-assault care for sexual assault/abuse victims/survivors and increase awareness throughout the campus community concerning sexual violence via the creation of dedicated specialized professional services and cohorts of peer volunteers; (2) provide single-point access to information about sexual assault on the University of Saskatchewan website; and (3) develop and implement a campaign utilizing "male champions" (well-known male figures) and other allies to advance public education concerning sexual assault. As of the writing of this chapter, two and a half years since receiving the results of CASA's community consultation, none of these recommendations have been implemented.

Coverage of the 2012 assault in a national newspaper in November 2014 (Poisson, 2014) precipitated another flurry of interest on the part of the university administration to attend to sexual assault. With the recent declining student enrolments,[1] the university was now especially vulnerable to media stories that might discourage potential students from enrolling. The story focused on what was considered a dearth of sexual assault policies at Canadian campuses. Not to be outdone by the many other universities fixated on policy development, the UofS responded to the media pressure with a promise to produce a sexual assault policy within a matter of months, with no mention of funding and other resources to build the necessary infrastructure for coherent policy implementation.

When the newly installed vice-president of student affairs approached CASA shortly after the Poisson (2014) article, to consult on policy development, we stressed the need for an underlying commitment to accountability and concrete action. CASA argued that the problem was not so much a policy deficit as a need for implementing, resourcing, and monitoring for policy effectiveness. We held that there was already an unwieldy surplus of disparate and uncoordinated policies relevant to sexual assault that would be adequate with some modifications. Accordingly, we recommended that a better use of administrators' time would be to resolve the following issues related to existing policies:

1. The Violence Policy, created to comply with the 1993 provincial Occupational Health and Safety legislation, offers all members of the

university community protection from sexual assault but fails to outline relevant procedures;

2. The Sexual Harassment Policy, created in consultation with the President's Advisory Council on the Status of Women, five years earlier,
   is directed primarily to university staff; and

3. The Non-Academic Student Misconduct Policy has no procedures
   specific to sexual assault, and in so doing, treats plagiarism and other
   non-criminal offences on par with sexual assault.

There is no clear procedure regarding which policies should apply and under
what circumstances. Similar to policy development at most other Canadian
universities, these policies have been developed incrementally with little
consideration to how they are coordinated to eliminate redundancies and
gaps. Further, they place the onus to initiate a complaint solely on the victim/
survivor. This requirement places undue and onerous emotional effort on the
person who is already vulnerable after assault, and additionally carries consequential risk of ostracizing the victim/survivor from peers, faculty, and other
sources of potential support.

Another glaring omission in policy is the failure to include victims/survi-
vors in critical decisions in the wake of registering a complaint. For instance,
in the Non-Academic Student Misconduct Policy, the complainant has no
say in whether the complaint is handled via a formal hearing or an alternative
dispute resolution (ADR) as the default process. Nor is there provision for
decision-making power over the disclosure of communication. In the qua-
si-legal procedures of a formal hearing, procedural decisions such as in-person
versus written testimony are made by the tribunal panel, and the testimony
provided by the victim/survivor to the panel can be available to the courts if
the perpetrator is involved in a criminal case pertaining to the assault. For
the sexual assault victim/survivor, the possibility of coming face to face with
the perpetrator under such consequential circumstances can be devastating.
While the Non-Academic Student Misconduct Policy might work well for
theft or damage related to university property, it is spectacularly unsuited to
dealing with sexual assault.

Another difficulty with existing policies and procedures is the absence of
self-monitoring mechanisms to determine their success and failure in dealing
with sexual assaults. For instance, the Non-Academic Student Misconduct
Policy endows the university president with the authority to suspend a student
immediately when deemed necessary to protect the interests of other students, faculty members, or other university employees. However, suspensions
of sexual assault perpetrators are seldom made public, so it is impossible to
know how often this authority is invoked. It is CASA's opinion that the regular,

transparent dissemination of information on reported sexual assaults (including anonymous reports), as well as the university's response (noting sanctions applied against confirmed perpetrators), would go a long way towards encouraging victims/survivors to come forward with disclosure. Perhaps the most notable problem with sexual assault policies discussed here is the glaring lack of procedures and resources sufficient to realize the intent of the policies: in particular, CASA has advocated a centre dedicated to prevention and response to sexual violence, staffed by full-time professionals, non-professionals, and volunteer student advocates, and governed by representatives from student groups, faculty, and the community at large.[2]

CONCLUSION

Improvements to campus sexual assault response and prevention at the UofS were achieved at the expense of the women who were assaulted. We honour the survivors of these and all horrific acts of violence, as well as all whose shared sense of outrage and desire for social action has brought them together. Our collectivity has nourished the deeply felt hope that one day our post-secondary institutions will be safe and positive spaces for all who study, work, and otherwise contribute to campuses in Saskatchewan, as elsewhere.

The 2012 sexual assault exposed the slippage in improvements at the University of Saskatchewan advanced earlier by CASA's advocacy: the victim advocate position was abolished without notice; the 24-hour communication/alert protocol promised in 2004 was reneged on. And CASA's 2005 report card (see Appendix) is sadly still relevant in key respects, for instance, that several areas need improvement if the UofS is to recognize its important social responsibility. Another indicator that needs attention now, as then, is to gather and analyze the stats on incidence of rape on campus, and use data wisely in service of change. Among other things, campus-wide education and training programs are still needed to address the root causes of sexual violence and its intersecting determinants of gender, race, class, and other social markers. And now, a decade later, when the university is preoccupied with task forces and new policy development, what is needed is a coherent review of existing policies and accompanying infrastructure, budget, and procedures to give them force. This policy review must be conducted with a level of transparency and inclusiveness befitting of a public institution. Policies, however good, are necessary but not sufficient vehicles for addressing sexual assault, as evidenced by the 95 universities in the United States now under review by the federal government for inadequacies in their handling of sexual assault, despite the legislative requirements for all U.S. universities and colleges to have sexual assault policies (in addition to many other requirements) in order to receive federal funding.

Our university is not so different from other Canadian post-secondary institutions. It too is subject to corporatized practices and the hegemony of austerity that converts students into "revenue-generating units" while simultaneously slashing expenditures for services critical to their safety and well-being. Lusting after student enrolments makes universities vulnerable to media stories that expose the truth of campus sexual assault. The UofS's habitual response to such media stories is the iterative chant that "our university is a very safe place." Ironically, a more effective marketing strategy might well be a regular dissemination of statistics related to sexual assault accompanied by widely advertised services available to victims/survivors—all in the context of more transparent and robust policies that cover the gamut from prevention to oversight and, sadly, aftermath of sexual assaults on campus. Such a forthright technique has yet to be tried by Canadian universities intent on competitive branding.

APPENDIX   University of Saskatchewan's Report Card

**COALITION AGAINST SEXUAL ASSAULT
YEAR ONE**

Date: April 2005

PROGRESS REPORT

Name: *University of Saskatchewan*

HABITS AND ATTITUDES

Works well with others	✔	(is improving)
Plays well with others	☹	(needs improving)
Listens carefully	✔	(is improving)
Begins work promptly	✔	(is improving)
Finishes work	✔	(is improving) (e.g., shows lack of follow-through in bringing external consultants back for progress review)
Takes initiative	☹	(needs improving) (e.g., lead the way to establish measurement criteria for status of women ratings in *Maclean's* university report)

PROGRESS IN SUBJECT AREAS

SECURITY SERVICES   A
- separation of parking enforcement from policing
- increase in foot patrol
- shows evidence of community policing model
- increase in Rape Aggression Defence course offerings

COMMUNICATING   D
- has installed *Alert* boards to raise awareness of incidents on campus but effectiveness is compromised by content of posted messages (e.g., makes claims like 'there is no threat')

VIOLENCE POLICY   A
- as per required by Sask Occupational Health & Safety legislation

EDUCATING ON GENDER ISSUES & PERSONAL SAFETY   F
[No work submitted]
(e.g., work with parents, students towards offering campus wide gender sensitivity training)

NUMBER WORK   B−
- learns number facts
- still needs to demonstrate that (s)he knows the meaning of numbers (e.g., stats on incidence of rape on campuses)

GRADING KEY

HABITS AND ATTITUDES	PROGRESS IN SUBJECT AREAS
? = Satisfactory Growth	A = 90–100 D = 50–64
✔ = Is Improving	B = 80–89 F = below 50
☹ = Needs Improvement	C = 65–79

Reproduced with permission from CASA.

NOTES

1 Student enrolments have been decreasing since 2012/2013, when they reached a peak of 23,813, after gradually rising over the previous decade.
2 See https://drive.google.com/file/d/0B8KMMLIQ8YWMSlREbUtXQXhfakE/view?pli=1.

REFERENCES

Coalition Against Sexual Assault–UofS. (2004). Transcripts from Forum on Campus Safety, January 29, 2004 (Unpublished).

Hayden, M. (1983). *Seeking a balance: The University of Saskatchewan, 1907–1982.* Vancouver: University of British Columbia Press.

Hofmann, D. (2012, February 29). New Year's Eve assault triggers reform: Almost a decade after notorious assaults, UofS lacks clear response protocols. *The Sheaf,* p. 8.

Lakehead University. (2014). *Report of Task Force on Sexual Assault Education, Prevention and Support.* Retrieved from https://www.lakeheadu.ca/sites/default/files/uploads/249/Report,%20Sexual%20Assault%20Task%20Force.pdf

MacKinnon, P. (2004, January 13). Campus safety: A message from President Peter MacKinnon to the campus community [Email message].

Newson, J. (2015). Introduction. In J. Newson & C. Polster (Eds.), *A penny for your thoughts: How corporatization devalues teaching, research, and public service in Canada's universities* (pp. 1–26). Ottawa, ON: Canadian Centre for Policy Alternatives.

Poisson, J. (2014, November 21). Rape victim's ordeal with University of Saskatchewan. *Toronto Star.* Retrieved from http://www.thestar.com/news/gta/2014/11/21/rape_victims_ordeal_with_university_of_saskatchewan.html

Rempel, S. (2004, January 3). Petition demands U of S beef up security after sexual assault. *Saskatoon StarPhoenix.*

Rempel, S. (2003, December 18). Security cameras needed at U of S, students say. *Saskatoon StarPhoenix.*

Sabina, C., & Ho, L. (2014). Campus and college victim responses to sexual assault and dating violence: Disclosure, service utilization, and service provision. *Trauma, Violence, & Abuse, 15*(3), 201–226.

Saint Mary's University. (2013). *Promoting a culture of safety, respect and consent at Saint Mary's University and beyond.* Retrieved from http://www.smu.ca/webfiles/PresidentsCouncilReport-2013.pdf

University of Ottawa. (2015). *Report of the Task Force on Respect and Equality: Ending sexual violence at the University of Ottawa.* Retrieved from https://www.uottawa.ca/president/sites/www.uottawa.ca.president/files/report-of-the-task-force-on-respect-and-equality.pdf

Vic M. (2012, March 1). Giving victims a voice: University's handling of New Year's Eve assault too little, too late. *The Sheaf*, p. 5.

Young, S., & Maguire, K. (2002). Talking about sexual violence. *Women and Language*, *26*(2), 40–51.

CHAPTER 12

COLLECTIVE CONVERSATIONS,
COLLECTIVE ACTION

York University's Sexual Assault Survivors' Support Line
and Students Organizing for Campus Safety

Jenna M. MacKay, Ursula Wolfe, and Alexandra Rutherford

In the fall of 2006, two female York University students were sexually assaulted a week apart while they were on their way home to The Village, an adjacent townhouse development that primarily houses York students. The women were reportedly dragged between houses and sexually assaulted. One assault occurred at gunpoint. Reluctant to take action, York's administration responded by increasing foot and vehicle security patrols "slightly beyond the perimeter of campus" (Cherry, 2006, p. B6). Women were urged "to be aware of their surroundings at all times" (Freed, 2006, p. B1). Students organized a Take Back the Night march through The Village and established a neighbourhood watch program (Thompson, 2007), and the York Federation of Students (YFS) called for an open forum to discuss safety concerns and long-term solutions to violence (Olimpo, 2006).

At this time there was a palpable climate of fear at York. Female students took extra precautions and changed their behaviour (i.e., walking in groups, carrying cellphones, and locking their doors). Wen-Do Women's Self Defence instructor Denise Handlarski recalls that due to fear, "women wouldn't attend their classes because their parents had concerns about them attending a campus that was frequently in the news" (D. Handlarski, personal communication, January 18, 2015).

In September 2007, a series of sexual assaults were perpetrated during frosh week in York's Vanier Residence. Two men, posing as students, gained unauthorized access to the dormitories and trespassed into six rooms. Together, they sexually assaulted three female students. The York administration responded by spending $3.1 million on new closed-circuit television cameras and hiring additional security personnel to watch the cameras and monitor "suspicious behaviour." A York spokesperson assured the public that the dormitories were safe (Henry, 2007). The survivors were chastised for not locking their doors. While the perpetrators were originally presumed to be from the nearby marginalized Jane and Finch community, the subsequent investigation revealed that they were a recent York graduate and his friend from the affluent suburb of Thornhill (C. Juniper, personal communication, January 31, 2015).

While the 2006 assaults generated a climate of fear, the 2007 assaults led to a climate of student protest. Students called on the York administration to take action on campus safety. To the best of our knowledge, the ensuing demand for an external safety audit was one of the biggest collective anti-violence movements organized by York student groups and is thus an episode that deserves to be documented and analyzed. What can it tell us about the role of student activism in organizational and cultural change? In this chapter, we (Jenna and Ursula), as two former York undergraduates who were coordinators of the Sexual Assault Survivors' Support Line (SASSL) during this time, present and reflect upon this episode from our perspective as student-activist participants.[1]

In a recent *Toronto Life* article documenting sexual violence on campus, it was reported that "York's students are notoriously hard to please. They'll protest anything" (Laidlaw, 2013, p. 69). The implication of this outlandish statement was that it was pressure from student groups that led President Mamdouh Shoukri to commission an external safety audit, which was released to the public in 2010 (Laidlaw, 2013). We, among countless other students in our cohort and before our time, were some of the "notoriously hard to please" students who helped pressure the administration to address sexual violence, and the Sexual Assault Survivors' Support Line was one of the student groups that mobilized for action.

SASSL is one of the oldest and longest-running student-run post-secondary sexual violence organizations in Canada (I. Gianvito, personal communication, January 30, 2015). Given the increased attention to sexual violence on university campuses in Canada, it is important to recognize the history and role of student-run organizations such as SASSL. This history includes student anti-violence activism that has had a significant impact on how sexual violence is understood and addressed on campus. Students who have participated in SASSL and the sexual assault activism at York have gained an incredible amount of expertise in how to address the problem of sexual assault. They have learned how to navigate bureaucratic systems and create relationships among diverse stakeholders to advocate for a safer and healthier campus environment. Students have successfully bridged gaps between the university's academic mission and the lived experiences of students who continue to develop as leaders in addressing campus sexual violence.

The activism that took place in response to the 2006 and 2007 sexual assaults led to a campus-wide safety audit conducted by an external organization that was driven by anti-violence and anti-oppression values. The activism was a collective effort among multiple student groups and pushed SASSL to engage with the wider campus community to address structural violence. Here we intertwine the organizational history of SASSL with the history of this particularly important collective action. In the development of this chapter, we have had conversations with alumnae from SASSL's founding to the present, as well as student organizers who were involved in anti-violence campus activism during our time. In constructing this history, we have also consulted materials from our personal archives (e.g., newspaper clippings, training manual, organizational documents). We hope this history can inform the work of student groups facing similar campus issues.

THE SEXUAL ASSAULT SURVIVORS' SUPPORT LINE

SASSL is an undergraduate student organization at York that was established in 1996.[2] Primarily, SASSL exists to provide feminist anti-violence education, support, and resources to survivors of violence. Since its inception, SASSL's core values have been described as pro-survivor (i.e., SASSL believes, supports, and does not blame the survivor); pro-feminist (i.e., SASSL recognizes societal power imbalances that inform experiences of violence); and pro-diversity (i.e., SASSL works from an anti-oppression perspective and supports individuals regardless of social location and identity).

History

SASSL was founded by Siobhan McEwan. During her graduate studies in clinical psychology, Siobhan worked as a human rights advisor at York's Sexual Harassment Education and Complaint Centre (SHEACC). While interning at York's Counseling and Development Centre, Siobhan became concerned by the number of survivors she worked with, and came to believe that "there was a need for a student-run centre so that survivors could talk anonymously to their peers, receive support, information and counseling" (S. McEwan, personal communication, January 26, 2015). Many of her colleagues shared this perspective, and through Siobhan's leadership, SASSL began as a special pilot project of SHEACC.

Over the 1995/1996 academic year, SHEACC facilitated focus groups with members of the York community. The focus groups included representatives from across the university.[3] It became clear that in the aftermath of the Montreal Massacre of 1989, many members of the university community recognized the need to address violence against women in society in general, and on campuses more specifically (I. Gianvito, personal communication, January 30, 2015). A result of these focus groups was a Women's Campus Safety Grant application to develop and implement SASSL, which was awarded by the Ministry of Training, Colleges and Universities.

During its first year, SASSL was led by a committee of student volunteers. SHEACC brought together individuals[4] in the field of violence against women to provide anti-violence training to the student volunteers. SASSL consulted the Sexual Assault Centre of the McGill Students' Society (SACOMSS) and received a donation of materials that were adapted for SASSL's needs (e.g., volunteer training manual). SASSL also adapted its values and organizational structure from SACOMSS.

In the 1996/1997 academic year, Founders College donated a residence room to SASSL, which became the call centre.[5] At this time SASSL officially began to provide a 24-hour peer-support telephone line. The existence of SASSL and its need for volunteers was advertised on campus through hot-pink posters,[6] flyers, free ads in student papers, and a pamphlet displayed in all student services offices. As a result of this advertising, 40 undergraduate volunteers were trained—a momentum that has been maintained each year forward. Organizations from the campus and across Toronto provided guest speakers at SASSL's first volunteer training. Once the first cohort of volunteers was trained, SASSL officially registered as a student organization.

By the 1997/1998 academic year, SASSL created and filled eight coordinator positions; these roles were funded through bursaries and work-study positions. The roles were modelled after those at SACOMSS. To deepen their understanding of sexual violence, coordinators travelled to two sexual violence conferences. According to Ida Gianvito, a SASSL alumna member from the first cohort, the conferences "provided a good training opportunity and inspired coordinators with ideas for new initiatives" (I. Gianvito, personal communication, January 30, 2015). For instance, following these conferences coordinators developed a public education outreach program for campus residences and high schools in Toronto and York Region.[7] SASSL was the first Canadian student organization of its kind to provide anti-violence education on campus and to local high schools (S. McEwan, personal communication, January 26, 2015).

Over the 1998/1999 academic year, SASSL volunteers and staff focused on securing funding. As noted by Ida Gianvito (personal communication, January 30, 2015), "For the first time, SASSL hired a Coordinator who had not been a SASSL volunteer, but who had considerable experience working with university government—a much needed asset that Coordinators at the time did not possess." SASSL put forward a referendum question asking whether students would be in favour of a SASSL tuition levy. An overwhelming majority were in favour and a $2.10 tuition levy has guaranteed funding for SASSL since September 2000. Today this tuition levy provides SASSL with its annual operating budget of over $100,000. Along with the dedication and passion of SASSL coordinators and volunteers, this levy has been instrumental to SASSL's longevity.

During the 2000/2001 academic year, SASSL moved into an office in the student centre. Along with this physical move, new coordinator positions were developed and SASSL ceased to be a special project of SHEACC. Operational documents were put in place to reflect the organization at that point in time, and an advisory board was established. The board meets twice a year and helps ensure that SASSL is fiscally accountable and transparent, and that projects are aligned with the organizational mission and values. The board may provide advice or mediation as needed, but has no decision-making power.

SASSL's programming

The core programming of SASSL has included volunteer training, operating a telephone peer-support line, and outreach and public education.[8] Volunteer training is generally undertaken at the beginning of the fall and winter semesters. Each training accommodates approximately 40 undergraduate students over several days. The majority of volunteers are young undergraduate women, although in the 2008/2009 academic year SASSL trained its first male volunteer.[9]

Training is intended to educate volunteers on SASSL's values and covers a variety of topics.[10] Training modules are facilitated by SASSL coordinators, external presenters from the York community, and organizations from across the greater Toronto area. Training not only provides volunteers with skills to provide peer support, but it also provides them with anti-oppression, feminist knowledge and skills to act as leaders in their communities. While SASSL does not actively recruit survivors, over the years many survivors have been drawn to volunteering and working at SASSL. They have been able to use their lived experiences to inform their work.

During the academic year, SASSL operates a 24-hour peer-support line. This line provides non-directive support, resources, and referrals to campus or community-based services that meet callers' specific needs. Occasionally the line has been a mechanism for survivors to request advocacy or accompaniment to services either within or outside of the York community (e.g., hospital sexual assault centres). During our time, the peer-support line was answered from the call centre during work hours and a SASSL member was responsible for answering a cellphone during evenings and weekends. At this time the peer-support line was under-utilized, although there were increased calls following advertising initiatives (i.e., a bathroom stall poster campaign, information letters and pamphlets distributed to all university services and departments). In addition to supporting survivors via the telephone, SASSL coordinators provided face-to-face support in the student centre office as needed.

In addition to the responsibilities outlined in staff role descriptions,[11] each coordinator was responsible for one special event per year. Events and special initiatives changed annually as they were unique to the skill set and interests of the coordinators and responsive to the current context. A large proportion of special initiatives involved campus outreach and public education that raised awareness of sexual assault and deconstructed rape myths.

SASSL has used various methods to raise awareness about violence, healthy relationships, and social issues related to violence and sexism. Some examples of SASSL's outreach and public education initiatives include tabling in busy corridors, tabling at campus events, handing out condoms and information on consent, distributing information on date rape drugs at pub nights, classroom presentations, ads/articles in student papers, radio show interviews, making zines, organizing marches and rallies, organizing buses to Toronto's Take Back the Night march, special events for December 6 and International Women's Day, candygrams, campaigns, film screenings, art shows, fashion shows, comedy nights, lectures with high-profile speakers, distributing materials in frosh kits, providing workshops on campus and for local high school students, and training the student residence dons. SASSL also organizes and funds Wen-Do Women's Self Defence courses each year, which not only teach physical techniques, but also empower women and incorporate a feminist, anti-oppression analysis to deconstruct myths around violence against women, such as "stranger danger" and victim-blaming.

Many of the members of SASSL's executive committee from 2006 to 2008 were anti-oppression political activists. This inevitably shaped our work during this time and how the SASSL collective responded to campus issues. From 2006 to 2008, SASSL and the York community faced the need to respond to a series of violent incidents that galvanized a long-standing concern: students, especially women, were not safe. It was also unclear what the university was prepared to do about it. From our work experience at SASSL, we understood that violence wasn't just happening to the individual; instead, there were structures that were supporting this violence. To enhance safety, the administration needed to examine the physical environments, as well as the policies, procedures, values, attitudes, and practices that make up York's culture. The SASSL collective began to discuss anti-oppression values and what it meant to put those values into action.

SEXUAL ASSAULT IN THE CONTEXT OF YORK UNIVERSITY

Toronto's York University, established in 1959 on a large expanse of land north of the city, has a long history of violence in general and sexual violence in particular. Students have experienced this violence both on campus and in The Village. York's history of violence includes everything from a high-profile murder case that took place in The Village (see Morrow, 2011) to the more subtle and generally invisible forms of normalized violence that occur daily. These numerous incidents have contributed to York's reputation as a campus that is fundamentally unsafe (Laidlaw, 2013; Wong, 2010).

Despite the ubiquity of sexual violence on university campuses, there are a few contextual factors that inform our understanding of sexual violence at York. Predominantly a commuter school, York is geographically isolated and it can be difficult to feel a sense of community. The lack of a sense of community is compounded by York's large size. York hosts over 55,000 students, staff, and faculty on the Keele campus and has been likened to a small city, or an island. Given York's size it relies on private security as first responders rather than local police. This contributes to perceptions of the York campus as inherently dangerous because its crime statistics are collected and reported by campus security at the university level rather than included in the general City of Toronto statistics (as is the case at the University of Toronto). York's campus security must notify the Toronto police when they wish and/or need to report particular incidents.

York is located close to Jane and Finch, a racialized and highly stigmatized neighbourhood that is home to many poor and low-income families. Due to systemic racism and classism, the Jane and Finch area is heavily policed and has been beset by gang violence, high crime rates, and a lack of adequate social services. Despite the proximity between the two communities, they have been separated by an invisible fence. The Jane and Finch community has often been a scapegoat for violence and crime at York (e.g., Laidlaw, 2013). York has fostered an attitude that "problems on campus stem from area residents and not students" (Criger, 2012, para. 1). This view underscores the extent to which systemic racial discrimination is embedded in university communications and actions. Indeed, students have spoken out about racial profiling at York, which has included questioning Black male students who were presumed to be too young to be on campus (Mendleson, 2012). Due to York's size, location, and diverse community, it is important to understand and address sexual violence from a perspective that views violence as occurring not only at the individual level, but also through social, political, and institutional structures.

Historically, York has focused on isolated incidents of sexual violence presumed to be perpetrated by external individuals who target the campus. By drawing upon an individual-level analysis of violence, York has failed to take into account, and failed to be accountable for, the systemic ways in which violence and oppression are perpetrated and perpetuated. An individual lens does not invest in contextualized prevention efforts to adequately meet students' needs.

SASSL AND STUDENTS ORGANIZING FOR CHANGE

Collective action: Student groups organizing for an external safety audit

In September of 2007, the York Federation of Students (YFS) called for an external safety audit to be conducted by the Metropolitan Action Committee on Violence Against Women and Children (METRAC). Students felt that METRAC shared their community-based, anti-oppression values and could bring a structural analysis to the audit. It was believed that an external audit would hold the university administration accountable to making cultural changes to prevent future violence. The demand for an audit arose from community focus groups on student safety that YFS facilitated (C. Juniper, personal communication, January 31, 2015). Led by a newly elected and politicized YFS executive, student groups across York formed a coalition to advocate for the METRAC audit. These groups included the Centre for Women and Trans People (CWTP), Trans Bisexual Lesbian Gay Asexual at York (TBLGAY), the York University Black Student Association (YUBSA), the Graduate Student Association (GSA), Glendon's Women's Centre, and SASSL. The sexual violence that occurred in the Vanier Residence in 2007 was the catalyst for the coalition, but student leaders had been calling for an external safety audit since at least 2004 (Poei & Solomon, 2008). (For more on METRAC's safety audits, see Chapter 8.)

Many student leaders felt that York's response to the sexual violence had been inadequate and significantly delayed. The administration was focused on the physical and environmental aspects of security; their focus did not extend to the social and cultural factors that so desperately needed to be addressed.

In advocating for the audit, students organized quickly and efficiently. Unfortunately, many student leaders expressed concerns that they were not being heard and that the administration was unwilling to work collaboratively with students. Several student leaders from organizations such as SASSL, TBLGAY, and CWTP believed that the administration was more concerned with the bottom line and the York brand than with student's safety.

During the 2007/2008 academic year, greater attention was given to sensationalized cases than to the ever-increasing forms of everyday violence that students were experiencing. There was a general sense that the university was not acting fast enough, that the administration was unequipped to address the diverse range of students' needs, and that students' needs were not a priority. In a 2008 TBLGAY monthly report, Lynnette Dubois wrote about the delay in obtaining an external audit:

> The Security Advisory Council (SAC)[12] Meeting clearly showed the difficulty that York Students face in getting straight answers from administration. Since the spate of sexual assaults this year, student groups led ably by the YFS and GSA have called on York to enact a comprehensive safety audit by an outside agency. The agency preferred by YFS and the students is METRAC. Still as of Wednesday, January 23rd, York Security actively stonewalled the establishment of such a safety audit claiming that any such hiring would have to go through a complex procurement procedure. Even though the SAC voted in favour of such an action 3 months ago.

Many students saw the procurement process as an unnecessary delay, indicating that student safety was being approached merely as a financial decision. Given that the school had fast-tracked the procurement process for more lighting (K. German, personal communication, January 30, 2015), students felt that the audit, a more effective strategy, should be given the same attention and urgency. From the students' perspective, the procurement process was a way of asking, "What really is the cost of students' safety?"

Although the SAC allowed input from student groups, students' contributions were often not taken seriously. These experiences only increased the motivation and need for student activism.

Compounding the pressing need for an external safety audit was the ever-increasing campus violence. On January 16, 2008, the front cover of the York University student paper *The Excalibur* featured the question "Are we safe?": "In the past week, a custodian was assaulted in the Student Centre, a female was sexually assaulted in a stairwell and York Security released a report revealing that one man was repeatedly beaten and robbed" (Valz, 2008, p. 1). Days after this news report was released, threatening hate speech directed towards Black students was scrawled on the door of the YUBSA office and in a nearby washroom in the student centre. This was the second occurrence of racist graffiti that month. The administration did not respond to the racist hate crime for two days (Girard, 2008; Valz, 2008).

This violence left many student leaders feeling that an immense shift in thinking was required to force the administration to address safety in meaningful, holistic, and sustainable ways: as a first step, they needed to prioritize student safety above all other concerns. We pushed for an external audit because we believed that METRAC would be able to conduct a comprehensive assessment of the underlying causes of violence and the factors that perpetuate it. We believed that the METRAC audit would address *all* forms of violence (e.g., sexism, racism, classism, ableism, transphobia) experienced by York's diverse student body. As Gilary Massa, YFS's vice-president of equity at the time, stated, the audit will go beyond the physical environment and will look at "the institutional frameworks that allow for sexual assault to happen" (Godfrey, 2008, p. 2).

Collective voices speak louder: The postcard campaign

Upon hearing of the violent incidents in mid-January, SASSL members were angry and sick of feeling powerless, so we got organized. SASSL members Katie German, Ursula, and Jenna quickly called an informal meeting of SASSL members to discuss how to take action and get involved in the growing campus activism. We felt that SASSL was a latecomer to the student coalition and on the periphery of activism when we should have been in the centre of it. Not all SASSL members attended this meeting, and there were mixed feelings about how the collective should respond. There was a fear that taking a political stance against the university could jeopardize SASSL's funding. Callie Stanley, past finance coordinator, investigated whether such a fear was grounded in an actual risk, and thankfully it was not. The fear and threat of losing funding has shaped and restricted the activism of many feminist anti-violence organizations in Canada (Bonisteel & Green, 2005).

Although SASSL's funds were not affected, it was a reminder that we were not a completely autonomous entity. SASSL was resisting dominant narratives and pushing for an alternative perspective within the confines of the institution we were trying to change. Although working from within is potentially powerful, it does impose limits. This meant that we had to find ways to work with (or around) the very people/structures that were acting as barriers.

To the best of our knowledge, before this time SASSL had not taken a public stance on most political issues. In addition to funding concerns, some members worried that taking such a stance would alienate survivors who may require SASSL's services. There was internal debate about whether or not SASSL was an explicitly political organization and how overt activism would affect its ability to carry out its peer-support function. However, this anti-violence campus struggle was clearly one in which SASSL needed to act. We quickly landed on the idea of a petition that would draw attention to the YFS's call for the METRAC safety audit in the form of a postcard.

The postcard campaign was created to raise awareness and gain support from the student body, while putting pressure on the administration to take action. Through talking to students in classrooms and common spaces about the campaign, we connected with concerned students, as well as those who were generally apathetic to campus issues. We created a series of postcards that represented the multitude of intersecting forms of violence York students were experiencing. Ursula designed the postcards using a font and colour similar to York's branding to directly reference that this violence was occurring on campus and that the administration was accountable and needed to address it. The front had bold red text on a black background with a single equation,[13] and on the back was a letter that called for an external safety audit that was endorsed by all campus groups in the coalition. For example, the front of some postcards read: "York = Rape," "York = Unsafe," "York = Sexism," "York = Transphobic," "York = Racism," "York = Classism," and "York = Ableism." The postcards were intended to echo what many of us felt—that students' perspectives and needs were not part of the equation.

Distribution of the postcards was paramount in gaining support for the audit. Informing the larger student body of the call for the METRAC safety audit and collecting signatures was done mainly by students affiliated with SASSL and the coalition of student groups named above. To collect signatures, we set up tables in busy corridors and made classroom announcements. Katie German (personal communication, January 31, 2015) recalls visiting empty classrooms to write messages on the chalkboards to inform students about the METRAC audit and when the next security meeting would be.

The strength of the postcard campaign was its capacity to include everyone in the campus safety conversation. It built community and communicated that safety was everyone's issue. The campaign had a clear goal and a firm backing from students, faculty, and staff. People were able to personally identify their experience with the range of statements represented by the ten postcards. We experienced students personalizing their postcards and taking significant care in deciding which one to sign.

Over one thousand students, faculty members, and campus staff signed postcards advocating for the METRAC audit. The SASSL office was overflowing with garbage bags full of signed postcards, yet we had no clear idea of what to do with them. A member of YFS advised us to simply do what we wanted with the signed postcards. So, in the absence of a strong directive, we spontaneously, without consulting other coalition members, decided that we would have the biggest impact through a "postcard bomb," where we would shove all one thousand plus postcards under the office door of a key administrator. We decided to "bomb" Livy Visano, vice-president external of the York University Faculty Association, given his role as chair of the University Safety Audit Committee. At six o'clock one morning, along with a SASSL volunteer, we hauled all the postcards into the administrative tower and shoved most of them under Livy's door. When they wouldn't fit we began to randomly place them under the doors of other vice-presidents.

That morning angry emails were sent to student groups that had endorsed the petition and YFS received an angry call. Rightfully so, allied student groups were upset with SASSL for taking such action without consulting them. We felt guilty for acting so urgently and for not communicating our plan with other student groups. SASSL issued a statement to campus groups and the administration taking full accountability for the action. Livy (who turned out to be an ally) called YFS and conveyed that the administration was finally listening and that things were going to change (C. Juniper, personal communication, January 31, 2015). Despite the anger SASSL received from the administration and some student groups, C. Juniper, a prominent student leader, expressed that both she and Livy believed that the postcard bomb was the catalyst that forced the administration's hand to secure an external audit (C. Juniper, personal communication, January 31, 2015).

The postcard campaign was initiated by and for students. The campaign successfully shaped the administration's decision making by ensuring the meaningful inclusion of student voices. Students actively assessed their own needs and took action within the confines of bureaucracy for the betterment of the university culture. Students were demonstrating that violence prevention could be done collectively. Although the "bomb" was an impulsive, rogue move that was not endorsed by the collective, it may have been the catalyst for change. In all likelihood the "bomb" would not have happened if consensus of coalition members was needed. If we did not deliver the petition in such an agitating and confrontational way, the external safety audit may have been further delayed.

THE METRAC SAFETY AUDIT, THE POST-AUDIT CLIMATE, AND THE POWER OF THE STUDENT ACTIVIST

In the spring of 2008, the administration agreed to engage METRAC in a campus-wide safety audit. The audit took two years to complete. When the final report was released in June of 2010, Mamdouh Shoukri, the president of York University, was credited with the idea of evaluating campus safety, thereby erasing the community struggle that demanded such an evaluation. The final report included over 100 recommendations in three broad areas: social environment, physical environment, and security services.[14] In terms of social environment, the report noted that while York had several programs, policies, and procedures in place for campus safety, there were gaps in the areas of violence against women, hate incidents, and systemic oppression. Alarmingly, the audit identified that York had no specific policy or procedure to address sexual assault.

According to public documents, York has completed or "seriously advanced" over 85% of the recommendations (see http://safety.yorku.ca/prevention-response-sexual-violence/). As recommended by the audit, York University developed a sexual assault policy, which was approved by the board of governors on February 23, 2015,[15] and is piloting a bystander program, in which the community is mobilized to recognize and intervene in situations that may escalate into sexual assault.

Although the administration believes they have "seriously advanced" a large proportion of the recommendations, in the years immediately following the audit students continued to protest and voice concerns about campus safety (Khandaker, 2012). Amid concerns that the university was moving too slowly in implementing important METRAC recommendations (see Howlett, 2011; O'Toole, 2011), students expressed growing frustration around the inadequacy of the safety communications (Casey & Aulakh, 2011). In the wake of the murder of York student Qian Liu,[16] questions arose around the university's responsibility towards safety in The Village (O'Toole, 2011). Finally, at the 2011 Safety Forum at York's Osgoode Hall Law School, Toronto Police Constable Michael Sanguinetti commented that "women should avoid dressing like sluts in order not to be victimized" (Rush, 2011, p. A2). This was the catalyst for the SlutWalk movement, which quickly became a transnational phenomenon.[17] Current SASSL members identify wider education initiatives for all students, staff, and faculty on gender-based violence, as well as training on York's policies and procedures, as an important step forward to continually create a safer pro-survivor culture.

SASSL, along with other student representatives, has been involved in the implementation of the METRAC recommendations, participating in various groups and committees. Specifically, SASSL (1) collaborated on the development of York's Sexual Assault Awareness, Prevention, and Response Policy and Procedures; (2) helped develop a campus-based mobile safety app; (3) promoted the SaferTogether campaign, which highlights campus services; (4) partners in an annual consent event with York's Centre for Human Rights; (5) provides training for frosh leaders; (6) worked with security to remove victim-blaming "safety tips" from campus security bulletins; and (7) continues to offer free Wen-Do self-defence classes. We do not know the particulars of how or if SASSL has sustained a structural response to violence on campus, as the collective (and its understanding of violence) changes year to year.

It is important to note that the postcard campaign was only one of the many activist projects responding to the sexual violence and advocating for the METRAC safety audit. Students from across the university spent countless hours writing letters to the administration, distributing leaflets, organizing conferences, and speaking to the media. Students also participated in meetings, seminars, forums, and lectures. The list goes on. Without this large net of activist work, the audit may never have materialized.

SASSL's beginnings as a peer-support, student-run organization became a source of strength in the student-run initiatives leading up to the safety audit. The students addressing campus sexual violence understood the importance of strategic partnerships and community development. They also understood that effectively addressing sexual violence meant going beyond the mediocre response of changing some physical structures on campus to transforming the cultural beliefs and institutional norms that foster and maintain such violence. Mandating that the student perspective be considered would help to ensure that the community looked to students for knowledge, which would also help to ensure that students' needs were met.

Through our role as coordinators of SASSL, we learned that our voices can be powerful forces of change. We learned that we can make a difference and that we can contribute to the struggle against violence. With regard to the postcard "bomb," we recognize that it was not a collective move. Our decision was made in part because there was a breakdown of communication in the coalition and coalition members were feeling frustrated by institutional barriers. Our challenge as activist students was twofold: we were struggling to combat violence in our community, and we were struggling to be heard as students. In hindsight, with greater life experience and maturity, we are not sure we would make the same decision. Today we assume that we would be more likely to communicate effectively with coalition members, and consider the ramifications of such a move. We are lucky that the "bomb" had a positive impact, but this positive impact may not have been possible if our direct action wasn't taking place in tandem with less agitating advocacy, activism, and ongoing attempts to build collaborative relationships between student leaders and the administration. However, if we were in our early 20s today and feeling angry, tired, and like we were hitting a wall, as we did then, we might repeat such an action. We believe that acting against the grain is important and that agitation is necessary but perhaps is most effective when carried out with complementary activist strategies that all aim to achieve the same goal.

Although students are often looked down upon for being young, naive, and inexperienced, our analysis of the problems at York was more comprehensive and multifaceted than that of some of the administrators. Without the energy and decisive actions of students, we believe that it is unlikely that campus change would have occurred. Through this experience we have learned that community ways of knowing are valid, that communities know what they need, and that community-based action is required when demanding change that threatens the existing power structure.

On a more personal level, many SASSL alumnae, ourselves included, have learned more from our involvement in SASSL than could have been possible if our undergraduate education was restricted to the classroom. We have learned invaluable activist and community organizing skills, how to build relationships, and how to be more responsive allies. We have further developed the social justice lens from which we view the world. These leadership skills have stayed with us. As long as there has been violence on York's campus, there have been student responses to campus violence. Students have resisted, reacted, and spoken back. SASSL has played an important role in coordinating these reactions and moving them into effective action. Despite the many challenges to creating community at an institution as large and divided as York, it may be the willingness of students to come together and "protest anything" that actually binds the York community together.

ACKNOWLEDGEMENTS

We would like to sincerely thank the following individuals who have been instrumental both in addressing violence at York University and in developing this chapter. In alphabetical order we acknowledge the insights shared with us by Bergamont, Lynette Dubois, May Friedman, Sabrina Friedman, Katie German, Ida Gianvito, Stephanie Gordon, Denise Handlarski, Caroline Juniper, Sarah McCardell, Siobhan McEwan, Yaa Otchere, and Nina Vitopoulos.

NOTES

1   The third author, Alexandra, was a member of the SASSL advisory board during this same time and has been a faculty member at York for 15 years.

2   In 2011 SASSL changed its name to the Sexual Assault Survivors' Support Line and Leadership to highlight the public education programming (M. Friedman, personal communication, January 23, 2015). Given that our chapter focuses on the organization before this time, we will refer to SASSL by its original name.

3   Members of the focus groups included Karen Solomon, Counselling and Development Centre; Yvette Benayoun-Schmidt, Status of Women; Cora Dusk, associate vice-president Campus Relations and Student Affairs; Cecilia von Egmond, student; Pat Loughrin, Health and Safety; Heather Dryden, Centre for Race and Ethnic Relations; Sharon Thomas, SHEACC; Alana Rom, student; and Siobhan McEwan, SHEACC.

4   This included graduate student Larissa Silver (whose role was funded by the Women's Studies Department) and undergraduate student Michelle Chai.

5   The location of the call centre was kept confidential due to violence experienced by staff and volunteers at other sexual assault centres. SASSL's call centre has since moved.

6   Because Student Affairs had no use for hot-pink paper (and a lot of it), the paper was donated to SASSL, which pragmatically became the organization's signature colour.

7   This initiative was spearheaded by Brena Parnes and Kathryn Nastos (Serravalle).

8   These categories are reflective of our experience and may not accurately reflect SASSL's current programming.

9   There was extensive discussion among the collective about whether to train a male volunteer and how to support male survivors in general, as in the months previous, SASSL received its first call from a male survivor. Following an interview with the potential

volunteer and ensuring he was aligned with SASSL's values, SASSL agreed to work with him and was interested in the possibility of facilitating anti-violence initiatives by men for men. It was agreed that male volunteers would not answer the telephone line.

10 These included SASSL's values, anti-oppression, racism, disability, active listening and peer support, self-care, suicidality, sexual health and healthy relationships, domestic violence, sexual assault, sexual assault and men, LGBTQ relationships, child abuse/incest, reporting sexual assault, police and legal procedures, hospital procedures, and security on campus.

11 In 2001/2002 the roles of SASSL staff changed. The executive committee became a committee of five volunteer coordinators (also known as team leaders) who supervised and managed a team of volunteers; four coordinators who managed specific portfolios (i.e., volunteer training, publicity, internal relations, and external relations); and an administrator. In 2010/2011 the roles changed due to a SASSL restructuring initiative.

12 According to the York website, the Security Advisory Council (SAC) is the advisory body mandated to advise the vice-president, finance and administration, and the Department of Security Services on personal safety and security at York, including the nature and quality of the security services provided at the university. The SAC invites broad participation from the university community, which includes administration, staff, and students from various functional areas.

13 The concept of the equation was inspired by the AIDS activist group ACT UP, whose logo reads "Silence = Death." This slogan was created by six gay activists in response to the 1980s AIDS crisis.

14 The report can be accessed here: http://safety.yorku.ca/files/2013/01/METRAC-Audit -Report.pdf. A summary of the recommendations and their implementation as of June 2, 2015, is available at http://safety.yorku.ca/metracsafetyaudit/recommendationreport/.

15 The sexual assault policy can be found at http://safety.yorku.ca/prevention -response-sexual-violence/.

16 Qian Liu was a 23-year-old international student at York who was sexually assaulted and murdered while chatting via webcam with her ex-boyfriend in China. The assault and murder was committed by man who was a tenant in the building she lived in in The Village.

17 The SlutWalk movement protests victim-blaming by insisting that no aspect of women's appearance or embrace of sexuality should be used to justify acts of sexual violence against them. The founders sought to reclaim the word "slut," which has historically negative connotations, to highlight women's sexual agency.

REFERENCES

Bonisteel, M., & Green, L. (2005). *Implications of the shrinking space for feminist anti-violence advocacy.* Fredericton, NB: Canadian Social Welfare Policy Conference. Retrieved from http://www.rapereliefshelter.bc.ca/sites/default/files/imce/ShrinkingFeministSpace_AntiViolenceAdvocacy_OCT2005.pdf

Casey, L., & Aulakh, R. (2011, July 18). University not warning us of assaults, York students say. *Toronto Star.* Retrieved from http://www.thestar.com/news/ crime/2011/07/18/university_not_warning_us_of_assaults_york_students_say .html#

Cherry, T. (2006, December 1). Student, 19, assaulted near York. *Toronto Star,* p. B6.

Criger, E. (2012, September 19). Jane-Finch residents protest York U newspaper. *City News.* Retrieved from http://www.citynews.ca/2012/09/19/jane-finch -residents-protest-york-u-newspaper/

DeKeseredy, W. S. (2011). *Violence against women: Myths, facts, controversies.* Toronto, ON: University of Toronto Press.

Freed, D. A. (2006, December 2). Women afraid at York. *Toronto Star*, pp. B1–B2.

Girard, D. (2008, January 25). Defiant students rally at York. *Toronto Star*, p. A6.

Godfrey, L. (2008, January 23). Hillel@York responds to sexual assaults. *Excalibur*, p. 2.

Henry, M. (2007, September 9). Dorm room rapes stun York U. *Toronto Star*, pp. A1, A3.

Howlett, K. (2011, May 9). Latest York attack raises safety concerns. *Globe and Mail*, p. A11.

Khandaker, T. (2012, November 28). Students organize rally to take control of security on campus. *Excalibur*, pp. 1–2.

Laidlaw, K. (2013, October). Fortress York. *Toronto Life*, p. 66.

Mendleson, R. (2012, November, 30). York University students allege racial profiling. *Toronto Star*. Retrieved from http://www.thestar.com/news/gta/2012/11/30/york_university_students_allege_racial_profiling.html

Morrow, A. (2011, April 21). Murder charge laid in death of York student. *Globe and Mail*, p. A16.

Olimpo, F. (2006, November 22). Student sexually assaulted. *Excalibur*, pp. 1, 4.

O'Toole, M. (2011, May 10). York called on to address student safety issues. *National Post*. Retrieved from http://news.nationalpost.com/2011/05/10/ york-called-on-to-address-student-safety-issues/

Poei, A., & Solomon, R. (2008, January 31). Fear lurks on campus after dark. *24 hours*, p. 6.

Rush, C. (2011, February 18). Cop apologizes for "sluts" remark at law school. *Toronto Star*, p. A2.

Thompson, V. (2007, January 24). Stay alert. *Excalibur*, p. 4.

Valz, R. (2008, January 16). Excalibur exclusive: Are we safe? *Excalibur*, p. 1.

Valz, R. (2008, January 23). Hate crime targets black students. *Excalibur*, pp. 1, 7.

Wong, J. (2010, October). What evil lurks. *Toronto Life*, pp. 38–39.

PART V

STRATEGIES FOR CHANGE

CHAPTER 13

FROM REACTING TO PREVENTING

Addressing Sexual Violence on Campus by Engaging Community Partners

Julie S. Lalonde

SEXUAL VIOLENCE ON CAMPUSES ACROSS NORTH AMERICA

Sexual violence on campuses is by no means a new phenomenon. University-aged women remain one of the most vulnerable groups in Canada. What we have seen over the past year, however, is a sustained conversation about rape culture on campuses. In 2014, the United States Department of Education's Office for Civil Rights released the names of 76 post-secondary institutions that were being investigated under the federal Title IX mechanism "for possible violations of federal law over the handling of sexual violence and harassment complaints." This news thrust the issue of sexual violence on campus into the limelight and ignited a conversation across North America. With prestigious universities like Harvard, Johns Hopkins, Princeton, and others under investigation for alleged mishandling of sexual assault on their campuses, it became difficult to deny the systemic nature of the problem.

Here in Canada, the federal Minister of the Status of Women announced in 2011 that she was "concerned complacency is getting in the way of ending violence against women on college and university campuses." The conversation continued in Canada with high profile incidents at Saint Mary's University, the University of British Columbia, and the University of Ottawa that drew widespread outrage. Viewed in isolation, each incident could be chalked up to a campus-specific reality: inadequate lighting on walking paths; too few security officials; a lack of training for frontline workers on campus; poor management of "Frosh Week" activities; campus location in a "bad neighbourhood."

Sexual assault is not unique to one campus, one community, or one neighbourhood. What makes the issue of sexual violence unique is the approach of each campus to addressing it. The *Toronto Star* recently launched a series on campus sexual violence and found that only 9 out of 100 Canadian campuses have a specific sexual assault policy. Concerns about universities' failure to generate sexual assault policies and about inadequate sexual assault policies have also been raised by community groups such as METRAC, which recently published a discussion paper on the topic.

When viewed as a whole, it is clear that campuses are dealing with a systemic problem that requires a multi-pronged approach. As the experts in this chapter demonstrate, campuses have traditionally focused on reactive measures rather than actively working to *prevent* sexual assaults. Furthermore, they've often failed to utilize the expertise of the full campus community, which includes their community partners, such as sexual assault centres and community health resources.

This chapter aims to fill that gap by speaking with community groups to better understand how campus–community partnerships can reduce levels of sexual violence on campus and provide students with a more supportive and responsive campus community.

METHODOLOGY

Over the summer of 2014, I conducted 19 semi-structured telephone and Skype interviews with individuals who were currently or had recently been working with a Canadian campus on the issue of sexual violence. They worked for frontline agencies such as community sexual assault centres, community resource centres, and women's centres across Canada. In a handful of cases, the people I spoke with worked directly within the university as faculty or staff.

The movement to end sexual violence in Canada has been led by women; however, the experts I interviewed varied in gender, race, age, and years of experience in the field. I spoke with advocates who had been doing frontline work with women sexual assault survivors for 30 years and recent social work graduates who were just entering the field.

The organizations and individuals I interviewed have worked with campuses across the country. There is geographical representation from the Atlantic Provinces to British Columbia. No post-secondary institutions from the Territories have been included.

A starting point for my outreach was contacting 20 organizations that were awarded a Status of Women Canada grant as part of the 2011 call for proposals to examine the issue of sexual assault on campus. I contacted these groups over the summer of 2014, when many were winding down their projects. I received responses from 15 of the organizations I contacted.

Although the mandate was to examine the specific responses of *university* campuses, many of the community groups were working with all the post-secondary institutions in their community, including les Collèges d'Enseigne-ment Général et Professionnel (CEGEPs). The Status of Women Canada grant was not specific to universities but included all post-secondary institutions. Lastly, the inclusion of CEGEPs in this chapter was emphasized as important by experts in Quebec. It is for these reasons that this chapter includes univer-sities, colleges, and CEGEPs.

I also conducted an open call via social media and within my own network. I received responses from a few community organizations and individual activ-ists who had worked to address sexual violence on their campus as students. It is important to note that the *vast* majority of people I interviewed would speak to me only if they could remain anonymous. Some of the people I spoke to refused to disclose which campuses they were working on, for fear that their feedback would not be entirely confidential. The resistance to talking openly about one's work to address sexual violence on campus is in line with a recent *Maclean's* piece on campus sexual violence in which the author encountered academics who weren't willing to speak openly about their research because it was "impossible to anticipate what the consequences might be" (Browne, *Maclean's*, 2014).

My interview subjects are recognized experts in their field, active members of their community, and respected advocates. However, they felt that their standing in their community and especially in relation to the campus they were working with was incredibly precarious. I got a strong sense that people feared reprisals for talking about the existence of sexual violence on campus, let alone any critical comments regarding the campus response to it.

Much of the concern centred on how publicly identifying themselves or their work would damage their precarious relationship with the campus. For groups that were doing work on campuses via the Status of Women grant, there was also apprehension about how critical their work could be under the rubric of their funding agreements. Many of the funding recipients I spoke to felt the tension of wanting to use their project grants as a window of oppor-tunity to shake things up on campus while also wanting to ensure a sustained relationship with both their funders and the campuses they were targeting.

For all these reasons, the individuals, organizations, and campuses spoken about in this chapter are not identified, with the exception of Dr. Charlene Senn (and the University of Windsor), whose work has been publicly lauded as an example of a best practice in the area of sexual violence prevention.

The interviews ranged from 30 minutes to two hours, based on the amount of information the individual wanted to provide. I used a semi-structured interview style, where I asked each interviewee to provide me with a quick overview of their role with the campus, the goal of their project and/or job description, and any major successes or challenges they faced in trying to address sexual assault on campus. I asked them to share with me what they viewed as best practices in regards to preventing sexual assault, supporting sexual assault survivors, and addressing rape culture more broadly.

Although the experts I spoke with were working across campuses from different communities, key themes quickly began to emerge in the interviews. I've fleshed out these themes in the Findings section. Some participants went on to share chapters or documents prepared as a result of their work, which have been included in the References section.

This chapter looks at campus and community partnerships to address sexual violence in over 30 universities and colleges across Canada, ranging from large, urban-centred university campuses to rural colleges. This chapter covers English and French institutions, including CEGEPs. In this chapter, I refer to the community agency's interpretation of "best practice" in regards to addressing sexual violence on campus, whether it was based on their own measurements of successes or on the assessment of an external evaluator.

With so many projects happening across so many campuses, it was impossible to set a baseline measure of "best practice" with the time and resources at my disposal. I deferred to the expertise of the people I spoke with as to what they deemed most beneficial. This was proven to be an effective method, as common themes kept emerging. All of the findings in this chapter were validated by the experts I interviewed and the findings reflect their recommendations. There was a consensus that if campuses followed through on these recommendations significant progress would be made to address sexual violence on campus. Despite the lack of an academically evaluated baseline definition of "best practice," I think this chapter provides a significant starting point for examining the importance of universities engaging with community partners to address sexual violence on campus.

FINDINGS

Partnerships are vital for ending sexual violence on campus

The community partners and campus community members that I spoke to were strongly in favour of partnerships between campus and community. Even in cases where community groups encountered incredible resistance to their work, they felt it was imperative to continue working with campuses.

When community groups spoke with those who had been sexually assaulted on campus, the latter responded positively to the engagement of community groups, because they provided a "neutral" party that survivors could rely on. Community groups received encouraging feedback from survivors who appreciated that their presence provided an alternative to institutionalized campus services such as security, health services, or human rights officers. Confidentiality is a major concern for any sexual assault survivor, but particularly in a campus setting. Since the community agency was generally viewed as an "outsider" group, students felt that they would be less likely to side with the institution and more likely to provide them with a "neutral" perspective. The idea of "neutrality" from a community group was raised by several individuals and organizations I spoke with as positive response they often heard from survivors.

For those who work on campus, collaboration with community is seen as an excellent means of tapping into years of knowledge regarding community-based research and advocacy. In some cases, those working to address sexual violence from within campuses referred to the expertise of community groups to represent the voices of survivors. Some campuses were aware that community organizations were more likely to receive disclosures and reports from their students than administration-run services. By engaging with community organizations, those working on this issue from a campus perspective could begin to investigate why students were so reluctant to report to campus-based services and hopefully undertake to address those concerns.

"Before we joined the Sexual Assault Committee on campus, I think the administration was really naïve about what was actually going on at their school," said one woman working for a community agency that had recently partnered with their local campus. "At the same time, I don't think the school had any idea what we did, the services we offered, the years that we'd spent advocating for victims."

Partnerships between community groups and campuses created possibilities for knowledge exchanges. Community groups were able to gain access to academic research while campuses were able to learn about grassroots responses to violence. If these relationships are nurtured, they can be mutually beneficial in many ways.

It was interesting to note how many community agency workers had experience that predated that of their campus counterparts. Several of the individuals I spoke to had been leading anti-sexual violence work in the community for significantly longer than those who were doing this work at the campus. This sometimes created tension between the two groups. Community agencies might have had more years of experience than their campus-based counterparts, but their expertise was often seen as inherently less valuable because it was not academic.

In some cases, campus administrators and academic experts were shocked to learn from community groups how the campus had traditionally responded to sexual violence "incidents." Such moments could be tense, but community groups felt that if their campus counterparts approached the issue respectfully, this dialogue could be a great opportunity for building trust and mutual understanding of the complexity of addressing sexual violence. Furthermore, these interchanges could be important reminders of how past approaches to addressing sexual violence can taint future efforts. If community groups had historically been "burned" by the campus administration or vice versa, these awkward, albeit important, relationship breakdowns needed to be named in order for the groups to move forward together.

The most common way in which campus and community formally engaged was through a sexual assault advisory committee. These varied slightly depending on the campus and the community, but were generally committees formed on campus and made up of community, administration, and student groups who had the mandate to address sexual violence in their work. Some committees were very structured, with members having fixed-year terms, while others were more informal and had flexible membership.

Community groups had varying experiences with these committees. A number were described as productive, effective at moving the agenda forward, and ensuring that the work was not done in isolation. In these cases, the community groups felt like their membership in the committee was a positive use of their time and a great way of ensuring they were connected to what survivors needed on campus.

In other cases, community groups found membership in these types of committees to be very difficult. Many groups were dogged with internal conflict, often over political differences. Overworked advocates and frontline workers from community agencies felt like their presence were merely tokenistic or that their voices were actively silenced. They expressed frustrations about the level of knowledge that campus members brought to the table. One west coast community group addressed the knowledge gap within the advisory committee by developing and implementing training for the committee members to ensure everyone was grounded in survivor-centred, anti-oppression politics. Although it was an investment of their organization's time, they felt it was a long-term investment worth making because it allowed them to focus their meeting times on the practicalities of addressing sexual violence on campus.

Members of one community agency told me about their frustration in having to sit through meetings with members of the campus community, who often held incredibly problematic views on sexual violence. Members of the campus community who sat on these committees would downplay the prevalence of sexual violence on campus, resist critiques about campus services, and outright deny survivor stories. When this happened, it would create tension and division within committees. Community members on these committees refused to acquiesce to the resistance, but also found it frustrating to spend a large portion of their time educating the members of the committee rather than focusing on the work itself.

The importance of building strong relationships between campus and community groups cannot be downplayed. One community group I spoke to listed all the successes of their campus engagement project, including the creation of a campus-specific bystander campaign, partnerships with the athletic department, and a successful needs assessment process. But for them, the biggest success of all was building a new partnership with the campus administration that they felt was respectful and best of all, sustainable.

Another community interviewee perfectly summed up the importance of engaging community: "As frustrating as it is to navigate a system that is *so* politically different from our own, campus work is important work and we're going to stick it out as long as we can."

Government funding is an effective means of getting the ball rolling, but success requires a long-term funding commitment from campuses

Many agencies had never partnered with the campuses in their community prior to the Status of Women funding grant and felt it was an amazing opportunity to build a sustained relationship with those in their catchment area. The funding allowed them to hire someone specifically focused on campus work and gave them the capacity to build new relationships and strengthen alliances in the community. Once the funding ran out, however, and the projects were completed in the eyes of Status of Women Canada, the future of the partnerships on campuses were often uncertain.

A fear that community groups were to continue doing this work for free or risk losing ground was palpable for many. They often had not realized until their project-based funding ran out that the campus was relying on the community group to do most of the "heavy lifting." Administrations and academic experts were supportive of the work being done, but many community groups felt that at the end of the day the work fell on them to do. Furthermore, there were many concerns that if the community groups were to pull out, the campus would rely on the free labour of students to continue the work or abandon the issue completely.

Although every individual and organization I spoke with felt it was imperative that students and student groups have positions of leadership on campus regarding sexual violence, there was fear that a reliance on free student labour meant that projects would be short-lived. Students have notoriously over-burdened schedules; community groups felt that making students the sole organizers of this work on campus meant that the latter would burn out. Community groups were also aware that relying strictly on students to lead the movement meant that sustainability would be difficult, as students transition out of campus life every four years or so.

Community groups felt that their expertise should be valued through compensation by university/college/CEGEP administrations and that the same should apply to student organizers. Many of the experts I interviewed were opposed to the reliance on free student labour, for practical and political reasons, saying, "if campuses value this work so much, they should pay for it."

This was a common response to the issue of sustainability in their work. Community groups expressed frustration that in many cases, the campus response to sexual violence felt like lip service.

Administrations expressed a desire to address sexual assault on campus, but were not willing to "put their money where their mouth is." From the perspective of overworked and underpaid community agencies, the expectation that they would continue this work for free once the grant money expired was offensive. As one community-based frontline worker told me, "To expect us to lead the projects and basically do all the work but to not compensate us for it speaks to how little they value what we bring to the table."

Another agency's experience drives home the point about devaluing feminist, community-based work. The small pocket of funding that supported their work had run out, and so they were forced to rely on volunteer labour to keep up the momentum they had built on campus. They believed in the work so they kept at it. However, they soon realized that other community groups were doing similar work but being funded. "To see the campus funding *other* community agencies to do work around mental health and addictions, for example, while we're volunteering our time to ensure survivors are heard on campus is really, *really* insulting."

Through the Status of Women Canada funding to address sexual violence on campus and other project-specific initiatives, many community groups performed needs assessments with their local campuses. As part of those assessments, they produced a list of recommendations for addressing gaps in the existing services and responses on campus.

A common recommendation across different campuses was the need to establish a long-term committee and/or point person within the university to ensure lasting success. Groups felt this was imperative to ensure the work continued long past the media focus on a specific "incident," the timelines of a particular project, or the legacy reach of one key ally within the administration. Investing in such a committee or point person was a recommendation made to me by every person or organization I spoke to while preparing this chapter. Community groups were adamant that campuses needed to monetarily invest in this work in order to demonstrate a true commitment to ending sexual violence on campus.

Campuses need to focus on prevention rather than simply reacting to specific "incidents"

While I was conducting my interviews, it was very interesting to note the clear differences between campuses where there had been a recent "incident" versus those where there had been no recent public case of sexual violence or example of rape culture on campus. Early on in my conversations with community groups, they would indicate to me whether there had been some sort of precipitating factor in their relationship with the campus. "We were contacted by the school after X incident" was a common refrain from community groups.

A high-profile "incident" or "scandal" was a mixed blessing for community groups, who were outraged at the incidents in question but grateful that it meant a fire had been lit on campus. In the vast majority of cases where there were active partnerships going on between community groups and campuses, it was as a result of an incident that had brought the issue of sexual violence to light in a public way.

Although community organizations were unanimous in their frustration that it took a media frenzy for the university to come aboard, they were all grateful that at least the campus had chosen to respond by engaging with them. It is important to note that in many cases, community groups were the ones who made the initial contact with campuses and not the other way around. Community agencies would see that sexual violence was a concern and approach the campus to provide support. It could certainly be argued that community groups simply "got to them first," but in a few cases, community groups wanted it to be noted that they had worked to create that relationship. For them, it was a noteworthy distinction because it pointed to a campus that was not connected to its community partners. There was also a sense from many that their expertise was not recognized by the university/college/CEGEP.

Many of the community-based experts I spoke to talked about their sense of being devalued by academic institutions. There was nothing explicit that they could point to, other than a general sense of dismissal of their expertise and approach. They did not have specific proof as to why this was the case, but speculated that their use of a grassroots rather than a medical model and/or an explicit feminist, political stance might be why the campus administration was reticent to engage them. A few of the individuals I interviewed spoke of the irony of the situation where the institution that is clearly struggling to address sexual violence is acting like it is the expert on the issue. "Meanwhile, we've got decades of experience doing this work and doing it well, and we're being passed over because we don't have academic credentials backing us up." I mention the issue of respecting the expertise of community groups and acknowledging that community-based groups are often the catalyst for partnerships between campus and community because it speaks to the larger approach regarding prevention.

Evidently, if a campus's approach to sexual violence only addresses high profile cases, then it is not adequately focused on prevention. As for campuses that had not had a high-profile incident or "scandal," it was harder for community groups to engage the campus administration. Agencies trying to work with campuses that had not had a recent incident found it incredibly difficult to do so. There was a strong sense that campuses felt it was not an issue for them and that doing public anti-sexual violence work would only bring upon them the kind of attention they were grateful to have avoided thus far.

One campus that has successfully taken on prevention work is the University of Windsor, through the work of Dr. Charlene Y. Senn and Dr. Anne Forrest. They have worked to bring bystander intervention training to students as a means of preventing sexual violence. By embedding the workshops into classrooms, they've been incredibly successful at bringing their message to a large number of students, many of which are not traditionally reached by public education strategies. The success of their *Bringing in the Bystander*™ program is a great example of how campuses can prevent sexual violence while maintaining a positive image.

In fact, none of the individuals I spoke to who were working on a campus without an "incident" had any luck in moving the issue forward. It is important to recognize that this could simply have been reflective of the timing of when I contacted them. Nonetheless, without exception, every individual or organization that I spoke with who was working on a campus or in a community that was not affected by a "scandal" felt that their work up to that point had been a major struggle leading nowhere. One campus-based expert I spoke with expressed great frustration that their campus was missing a major opportunity to "get ahead" of the issue. "We don't have a 'scandal' yet, but it's only a matter of time before we do, so why not focus on prevention now?"

Regardless of how relationships were formed between campus and community groups, the community members I interviewed felt that campuses were talking very little about sexual violence and when they were, the focus was almost entirely on reacting. An emphasis on encouraging survivors to report is one example of how campuses focus on reacting to sexual violence rather than preventing it.

Many of the individuals I interviewed were frustrated with their administration's focus on getting victims to report. Campuses were quick to dismiss concerns about sexual violence on campus because their statistics did not show that it was an issue on campus. However, when presented with feedback from survivors, students, and community groups on how few assaults are reported, the administration would often respond with the assertion that the "issue" is a lack of reporting and that survivors should be encouraged to report.

Community organizations that are rooted in the experiences of survivors were resistant to making "reporting" the primary concern because they felt it ignored the larger issue of hostility and victim blaming that discourages survivors from speaking out. "It's like putting the cart before the horse," one woman told me. "You can't just say, 'We need more people to report,' you have to make the environment safer for survivors to come forward. That's a much bigger project than simply saying 'Reporting is important.'"

A focus on reporting is fundamentally at odds with prevention. Hoping that a survivor comes forward after they have been assaulted does not prevent that assault from happening. Although it could be argued that reporting can reduce the chances of a perpetrator victimizing others, it still does not eliminate sexual violence completely. Furthermore, making reporting the sole focus of a campus anti-sexual violence strategy can be read as victim blaming, for it places the onus entirely on those who have already been assaulted to take action.

There is, however, an encouraging trend towards innovative public education ca[illegible]ns, particularly in the realm of bystander intervention. *Bringing in the [illegible]er* is a program from the University of North Hampshire discusse[illegible]hat has been adapted by the University of Windsor. The campaign [illegible]n prevention by engaging bystanders of all genders to learn about their [illegible] preventing sexual violence, challenging myths about sexual assault, and supporting survivors.

Bringing in the Bystander has been evaluated and found to be an effective means of empowering students to make a difference. The university made the innovative program more accessible by integrating the bystander intervention training workshops into existing course content. In doing so, it was able to engage students in areas such as business and law who do not traditionally take these workshops.

Since the University of Windsor launched the campaign, it has trained about 60 facilitators and over 800 students have participated in workshops. The campaign is currently in its second phase and evaluating the long-term results of its training.

Green Dot Etcetera is another acclaimed, American-based, bystander intervention campaign with programming specific to campuses. The campaign's philosophy is that every incident of violence is a red dot on a map, whereas every incident of bystander intervention is a positive and therefore shown as a green dot. The goal is to create maps of campuses, communities, and entire cities covered in green dots rather than red ones. In this way, the campaign engages bystanders to choose who they want to be, a red dot or a green dot.

The campaign has been picked up and adapted by various organizations and campuses across North America, including York University and the University of Toronto. One Canada-specific bystander intervention campaign is draw-the-line.ca/traçons-les-limites.ca. Developed and managed by the Ontario Coalition of Rape Crisis Centres and Action ontarienne contre la violence faite aux femmes, the campaign uses a variety of scenarios to engage bystanders in thinking about their role in ending sexual violence. The campaign includes a user guide for workshop implementation, an interactive website, posters, postcard-style pamphlets, and resources such as YouTube clips and a radio PSA. Draw-the-line.ca/traçons-les-limites.ca employs a flexible copyright approach in which the campaign rollout can be tailored to each campus. For example, at Laurentian University, a short video was developed in which students spoke about how they would "draw the line." The guide and all campaign resources can be downloaded for free from the website, which allows for easy rollout of campaign workshops. The campaign is currently in its second phase of evaluation and has been picked up by a number of campuses across the province including Carleton and McMaster, in addition to Laurentian.

This trend towards bystander intervention campaigns is positive because it signals a desire for campuses to prevent, rather than simply react to, sexual violence. In my interviews, the experts I spoke to were encouraged to see bystander intervention approaches picking up steam. Bystander intervention campaigns are generally well evaluated academically, and the groups I spoke to felt they were better received by students. Focusing on everyone's positive role in ending sexual violence rather than painting men as perpetrators and women as victims was a welcome change by community and campus groups alike.

Community organizations also appreciated a focus on bystander intervention because it facilitates a continuous dialogue about sexual violence on campus. In talking about sexual violence as everyone's responsibility, community-based advocates felt that campuses can move away from reacting to specific incidents on campus and instead focus on creating a positive culture on campus where everyone looks out for each other.

Importance of engagement with senior administration
Bringing community, students, staff, faculty, and administrators together to address sexual violence is crucial. However, it is also important to bring together those who are in a position to make decisions. Often, community groups felt they were wasting their time sitting on committees that had no real power to create change. There was a sense of frustration felt by many that there were keen, well-intentioned people coming together on a regular basis whose work was often felt to be in vain.

The tone of the committees shifted drastically when there was strong engagement from senior administration and other powerful campus leaders. Community groups struggled with the recognition that advisory committee members were often made up of a mixture of folks who were keen but powerless and those who were perhaps less interested in the issue but held more decision-making power. In other cases, nobody sitting on the committee had any power within the academic institution itself. In the cases where the committees were only there as advisers, members felt their participation was less fruitful. Members did not maintain the same level of commitment, and advancing specific projects or initiatives was slow. In some cases, the committees fell apart and dissolved completely. In cases where there was strong buy-in from senior administration, however, decisions moved forward and real change happened. Lengthy committee meetings resulted in concrete plans, speedier decision-making, and an overall sense of effectiveness from committee members. This resulted in a stronger commitment from members as a whole.

Often, having an engaged senior administrator at the table was the sole deciding factor between success and failure. One organization told me that "once there was a change of upper admin and we got someone who was really invested in the issue, we were in business. The entire tone of the project changed and we felt like we could finally get our hands dirty."

Having a strong commitment from senior administrators was a key to ensuring concrete change was going to happen on campus. However, this was not easy to attain, seemingly due to personalities as much as campus structure. But the people I spoke to were unanimous in naming an engaged senior administrator as a deciding factor in whether a campus adequately addresses sexual violence or not.

The role of campus communications departments

When asked what their biggest challenge was, the parties I spoke to were unanimous in naming the campus communications/public relations/marketing department as a major impediment to addressing sexual violence on campus. Although these departments vary from campus to campus, everyone I spoke to was quite clear in naming them as the biggest barrier to moving forward.

Some community organizations felt they had to water down the work in order to get it approved by the university communications departments. One campus was censored from using the word "rape" in the project's Facebook group because it was "too alarming" and "not in line" with the "tone" the administration wanted to set on campus.

Other organizations felt that they were completely unable to name the issue of sexual violence and/or rape culture on campus because of resistance from the communications department. Many campus groups talked about the delicate maneuvering needed to get words like "sexual violence," "violence against women," or "rape culture" included in their projects and campaigns. Across many campuses, there was a desire from the administration to subsume the work under umbrella terms like "mental health," "bullying," or "harassment."

Although the mandate of many advisory committees was to address sexual violence, gender-based violence, or violence against women, the administrators often pushed for vague language such as "respect," "healthy communities," or "safety."

There was particular resistance to gendered language. Naming the problem of sexual violence was difficult enough but ensuring that a gender-based analysis was applied proved to be particularly difficult for many campuses. This was often a serious point of contention for community groups. Gender-neutral language was overwhelmingly preferred by campus communications departments. This was often taken as an insult by community groups. One organization in particular expressed clear outrage that at every turn, the communications department was pushing back against its gendered lens. "I work for an organization whose name and mandate is explicitly about violence against women and yet campus kept insisting that we act as though men and women are equally affected by rape culture."

I heard versions of stories like this from several different people I interviewed. From the perspective of community groups and their allies within the administration, naming the problem of sexual violence and clearly identifying its primary victims is imperative to addressing the problem. However, what they heard from campus communication teams was that the language is often too "controversial" or "political" for their liking.

The issue might appear on its surface as simply a matter of semantics, but it was evident from everyone I spoke to that it was indicative of political differences. For community-based advocates, calling the issue "sexual violence," "rape culture," or even "violence" was imperative to addressing sexual assault on campus. Yet they felt deep resistance from campus administrators who told them that the terms were alarmist. It was also quite clear to me that community groups and their campus allies felt it was just disingenuous for campuses to strike committees meant to tackle sexual violence on campus while removing the committee's ability to name the very issue it was trying to address.

From a logistical standpoint, this meant lengthy meetings and conference calls that many felt had stalled the progress of the projects, campaigns, or committees. In some cases, entire projects had to be rewritten due to fears from the communications departments that the language, tone, or approach would reflect badly on the campus. Projects meant to address sexual assault against women on campus were rewritten to meet the strict demands of communications teams. For example, words like "sexual violence," "rape," or "rape culture" were changed to "sexual harassment," "bullying," or "creating a culture of respect."

Several project managers I spoke with had their timelines shifted because getting approval from campus communications took much longer than anticipated and in many cases, these delays were a significant cause of stress. Press releases, recruitment posters, and communications to students about initiatives on campus were listed as examples of straightforward documents that many community agencies were shocked to discover took days and even weeks to approve because of careful maneuvering by the campus's communications department.

For many community agencies, this was a source of deep frustration because they felt campuses were being hypocritical. Campuses were relying on the expertise and knowledge of community groups while at the same time trying to depoliticize their work in order to preserve the campus's image.

For many community partners, this was difficult terrain for them to navigate. "How do I stay true to the work while ensuring I don't burn a bridge with campus?" In light of the findings mentioned above regarding the importance of partnerships and the need for that work to be continually funded, one can see how community organizations would struggle to strike the perfect balance.

CONCLUSION

Across the country, there are admirable individuals and organizations working to end sexual violence. By tapping into this vast network of experts, college, university, and CEGEP administrations can move towards making their campuses safer and more inclusive spaces.

The following recommendations emerged from this study:

- Campuses must meaningfully engage with their community partners. Grassroots community organizations have been fighting to end sexual violence for decades and have a wealth of expertise. Campuses would gain a great deal by creating advisory-type committees that include community partners and giving them a substantive role. Campuses must compensate community partners performing the work appropriately and be willing to engage them through a long-term commitment, not simply as a means of addressing a "scandal."

- Campuses must fund anti-sexual violence work on a sustained basis. Simply allocating this important issue a tiny pocket of money or project-based funding will not provide the needed momentum to address sexual violence on campus. A financial commitment to addressing sexual violence would include, for example, the funding of a permanent point-person on campus who is dedicated solely to addressing gender-based violence and the funding of continuous public education initiatives.

- Campuses must prevent sexual violence and not simply react to it. Administrations need to place an emphasis on addressing the campus culture that allows sexual violence to happen. They must invest in strong public education that focuses on engaging the campus community in ending sexual violence.

- Campus initiatives to address sexual violence must include senior administration. Any projects, committees, or initiatives must include members of the senior administration who have the power and authority to create change on campus. The inclusion of senior administration demonstrates the campus's prioritizing of the issue.

- Campuses must name the problem. Sexual violence on campus can only be eliminated if it is named. Communications departments, public relations offices, and/or marketing teams must make the brave choice to be transparent about sexual violence and the work being done on campus to address it.

APPENDIX A: SELECTION OF PREVENTION CAMPAIGNS

Bringing in the Bystander™
  http://cola.unh.edu/prevention-innovations/bringing-bystander%C2%AE

Draw-the-line.ca / traçons-les-limites.ca

"Green Dot Etcetera."
  https://www.livethegreendot.com/

"No Means No." Canadian Federation of Students.
  http://cfs-ns.ca/no-means-no/

"Start the Conversation." Carleton University.
  http://carleton.ca/equity/sexual-assault/sexual-assault-psas/

APPENDIX B: SELECTION OF GUIDES OR REFERENCES ON ADDRESSING SEXUAL VIOLENCE ON CAMPUS

"Campus Toolkit for Combatting Sexual Violence." Canadian Federation of Students.
  http://cfsontario.ca/en/section/210

"Developing a Response to Sexual Violence: A Resource Guide for Ontario's Colleges and Universities." Ontario Women's Directorate. January 2013.
  http://www.women.gov.on.ca/owd/docs/campus_guide.pdf

"Making the Grade? Findings from the Campus Accountability Project on Sexual Assault Policies." SAFER: Students Active for Ending Rape. October 2013.
  http://www.safercampus.org/blog/wp-content/uploads/2013/10/2013-Campus
  -Accountability-Project-Full- Chapter.pdf

"Making Noise @ Humber: Gender Based Violence Prevention Project." Urban Alliance on Race Relations, 2014.
  http://urbanalliance.files.wordpress.com/2012/08/officialgbvtoolkit.pdf

METRAC.
    http://www.metrac.org/what-we-do/safety/campus/

METRAC. "Sexual Assault Policies on Campus: A Discussion Paper." October 30,
    2014.
    http://www.metrac.org/resources/sexual-assault-policies-on-campus-a-discussion
    -paper-2014/

"Chaptering on Sexual Assault: A Toolkit for Canadian Media." Femifesto. 2013.
    http://femifesto.ca/wp-content/uploads/2013/12/FemifestoToolkitFinal.pdf

"Promoting a Culture of Safety, Respect and Consent at Saint Mary's University and
    Beyond." December 2013.
    http://www.smu.ca/webfiles/PresidentsCouncilChapter-2013.pdf20

APPENDIX C: METRAC HAS IDENTIFIED FIVE FACTORS THAT IMPROVE SAFETY FOR STUDENTS ON CAMPUS

1. Space layouts, building features, and security provisions that increase
   monitoring and reduce isolation and barriers to access/movement

2. Robust policies and practices that address dating abuse, sexual assault,
   and other gender-based violence with an understanding that violence
   most often happens between people who know each other

3. Training for staff, faculty, first responders, and students on violence and
   how to deal sensitively with survivors/victims

4. A holistic spectrum of programs and services that integrate prevention,
   intervention, risk assessment, and crisis response

5. Regular "temperature checks" that measure attitudes on violence,
   evaluate interventions, and monitor unchaptered incidents

NOTE

This chapter was commissioned by the University of Ottawa Task Force on Respect and Equality and is printed as part of the task force's report. It is reprinted here with permission.

REFERENCES

Browne, Rachel. "Why don't Canadian universities want to talk about sexual assault?"
    Maclean's. October 30, 2014. http://www.macleans.ca/education/unirankings/why
    -dontcanadian-universities-want-to-talk-about-sexual-assault/

Coker, Ann L., Patricia G. Cook-Craig, Corrine M. Williams, Bonnie S. Fisher, Emily R.
    Clear, Lisandra S. Garcia, and Lea M. Hegge. "Evaluation of Green Dot: An Active
    Bystander Intervention to Reduce Sexual Violence on College Campuses." *Violence Against Women*. June 2, 2011. http://www.livethegreendot.com/pdfs/
    VAWA_2011_article.pdf

Sexual Assault Centre Hamilton (SACHA). "It's Time: Key Recommendations." June
    2014. http://sacha.ca/our-centre/it-s-time-project

Tamburri, Rosanna. "Bystander intervention program changes attitudes about sexual assault." *University Affairs.* October 15, 2014. http://www.universityaffairs.ca/news/news-article/bystander-intervention-program-changes-attitudes-sexual-assault/

Unsilence the Violence StFX. Antigonish Women's Resource Centre and partners at St. Francis Xavier University. http://unsilencetheviolencestfx.wordpress.com/about-the-project/170-2/

CHAPTER 14

WHY THEORY MATTERS

Using Philosophical Resources to Develop University Practices and Policies Regarding Sexual Violence

Ann J. Cahill

Institutions of higher education in Canada and in the United States have recently become increasingly aware not only of the phenomenon of sexual violence on college campuses, but also of their own legal and ethical responsibilities in the face of that phenomenon. For institutions in the United States, one of the first steps in such awareness is an understanding of the many forms of federal legislation that are involved in university policies regarding sexual violence, including the *Violence Against Women Act* (VAWA), Title IX, and the *Clery Act*.

This volume, of course, focuses on Canadian universities and college campuses, for whom the situation is different, given the lack of federal legislation on the matter. However, at the time of publication of this volume, two provinces, British Columbia and Ontario, have passed legislation requiring colleges and universities to develop policies regarding sexual assault on campus (Chow & Macmillan, 2016; Dhillon & Hunter, 2016). Because this article focuses not on which practices and policies do or do not meet legal requirements, but rather on how universities should go about creating those practices and policies, the discussion is relevant for any Canadian college and university engaged in that process, whether it is legally mandated or not. I want to argue that universities should utilize faculty expertise, particularly from those faculty whose scholarship focuses on sexual violence, in order to develop more effective approaches to this all-too-common phenomenon. Even more specifically, I want to argue that faculty with expertise in feminist theory on sexual violence should have a seat at the table.

To make this argument, I will first defend the claim that universities should aspire to more than mere legal compliance (for which purposes legal experts, not theorists, would surely be sufficient). I will then present two specific ways in which theoretical work on sexual violence, particularly work grounded in feminist analysis, raises issues central to university policies that otherwise may be ignored or badly mishandled.

Throughout this discussion, it is helpful to keep in mind that institutions of higher education often constitute subcultures of their own, marked by their particular history, constituencies, practices, and norms. It is to be expected too that individual colleges and universities hold different positions vis-à-vis the culture(s) within which they are located (some, for example, are more integrated into the culture of their local city or region than others). With these cultural differences in play, there is no reason to assume that all university policies and procedures with regard to sexual assault should be identical. Yet it is also safe to assume that colleges and universities are embedded in larger cultures that experience high rates of gender-based violence, and that colleges and universities can be agents of change not only on their own campuses, but beyond. To transform cultural norms surrounding sexual assault on college campuses is but one facet, albeit a currently highly visible one, of the larger cultural change that is needed.

BEYOND COMPLIANCE

In the United States at least, the legislation surrounding the prevention of, response to, and reporting of sexual violence on campus is both complicated and dynamic; regulations, and guidelines for implementing those regulations, are frequently updated, sometimes in substantial ways (see, for example, the negotiated rulemaking on VAWA that was completed in 2014; "Violence Against Women Act," 2014). Given this complex set of legal requirements, it is understandable that some universities set their sights on compliance. While, as mentioned above, Canadian universities face the opposite problem—an acute absence of legislation specifically aimed towards institutions of higher education—they too have faced court cases. York University has been sued twice for allegedly failing to protect its students from sexual assault (Diamond, 2014; "Rape Victim Sues," 2010), and Carleton University faced similar allegations (Pinchin, 2009). If the university's goal is merely to meet the letter of the law, the only experts that should be involved in developing policies should be lawyers; philosophers and other scholars with expertise in sexual violence would have little to offer in such a task. Yet I would argue that mere legal compliance is a standard that universities, as institutions of higher education, should aspire to exceed.

Within the U.S. context, legislation dictates what universities must and should do, but by and large is silent with regard to the meanings of sexual violence and its place within larger structures of sexual injustice. Those kinds of questions are precisely the purview of feminist philosophers who study sexual violence. It matters, for example, that the harms that sexual violence imposes have been described differently in various historical periods and cultural contexts. Rape has been understood as a crime against male private property, such that restitution consisted of monetary compensation provided to the woman's father, or, at times, as a conceptual impossibility within marriage (because one cannot steal one what already possesses; see Bourke, 2009, for a more comprehensive discussion of the history of rape). To assume that there is a commonly held understanding of what sexual violence is, and what it means to individuals and communities, is to fail to recognize its historical and political nature. Delving into these admittedly very difficult questions will empower universities to craft policies that respond more effectively to the realities of sexual violence.

Perhaps even more importantly, the fact that universities should and must comply with all relevant legislation ought not to distract the institution from its primary mission, which is educational. If a primary goal of institutions of higher education in democratic societies is to prepare students to be critical, effective, educated citizens (lofty as that sounds, it is a goal that I believe such institutions should endorse), then their policies regarding sexual violence should forward that goal as well. In order to do so, the process that results in such policies must take up questions of community, citizenship, freedom, and justice, and must take up those questions in the specific cultural context of each university. Following the letter of the law will not be sufficient to meet that educational mission.

Finally, universities must comply with existing laws because they are legal entities that function within and benefit from legal recognition from a larger culture. Yet their cultural relevance extends far beyond their legal status. Universities are privileged sites within democratic societies, sites where new ideas are tested, and where new knowledge and insight is generated. In short, what universities do matters, and in developing practices and policies regarding sexual violence, universities have the opportunity to develop innovative, progressive, and potentially effective approaches to a systemic cultural problem.

These institutions should embrace that challenge, but in order to do so, they will need to muster more than legal expertise (although that expertise will also, of course, be crucial). Specifically, they should reach out to faculty who have scholarly knowledge regarding sexual assault, its cultural and political history, and its role in larger structures of gender injustice. Such scholars could come from a variety of disciplines (psychology, sociology, history, just to name a few). Yet I want to make a particular plea for seeking out and including scholars whose expertise includes the distinctly philosophical questions surrounding sexual violence. Although such scholars are perhaps most likely to be found within the discipline of philosophy, scholars who work in inter-disciplinary fields such as women's/gender studies, or whose disciplinary work emphasizes theoretical foundations, would also be excellent candidates.

In the next two sections, I will delineate two sets of theoretical concerns that are well developed (although, of course, still contested) within the feminist philosophical literature on sexual violence. These concerns are examples of ideas and challenges that exceed the legal questions surrounding sexual vio-lence, but that should be taken up within university conversations regarding policies. As I argue below, the absence of these questions within those conver-sations would risk the development of policies that would be less effective, and quite likely less progressive, than policies developed with these ideas in mind.

THE MEANING(S) OF SEXUAL VIOLENCE

Although it is painfully obvious that sexual assault is a harmful act, identi-fying the particular harms that sexual assault imposes on a person proves to be a challenging philosophical task. Some thinkers argue that sexual assault is harmful in the same way that any physical assault is harmful, and that to focus on the sexual aspect of the assault is distracting, or serves to intensify the degree of control that the neo-liberal state has over sexuality in general, or risks opening the door to blaming the victim (see Brownmiller, 1975, for an example of this approach). Other approaches to sexual assault might include a notion of theft, where one person's sexuality or sexual being was stolen by another (such an approach might view the rape of a virgin as more harmful than the rape of a sexually active person). Still others, lest we think that there is complete consensus around the belief that rape is deeply harmful, argue that our culture has overemphasized the harms of rape (Baber, 1987).

In contrast to all these approaches, several contemporary feminist theorists (myself included; see Cahill, 2001; but see also Du Toit, 2009, and Miller, 2009) have articulated an understanding of sexual violence as a violation of bodily autonomy, that is, an undermining of a person's ability to determine their own bodily experiences and interactions. It is important to note that this approach, which explicitly understands personhood as necessarily embodied (more on that below), goes well beyond the idea of consent, which will be addressed in more detail in the following section. Understanding sexual violence as an embodied act that undermines bodily autonomy moves the ethical conversa-tion from whether one person consented to a specific offer to a richer, more nuanced conversation about the connections among dignity, moral worth, and the ability to have significant say over one's embodied experience and being.

To grasp the ways in which this approach differs from other approaches, it helps to understand a common critique that many feminist theorists have made against western conceptualizations of the self and personhood, namely, that such models do not sufficiently recognize the ways in which the body is central to identity and personhood. That is, many predominant ways of understanding and conceptualizing the human person privilege (allegedly) disembodied aspects of personhood over embodied aspects of personhood (the U.S. constitution, for example, protects the rights to "life, liberty, and the pursuit of happiness," but does not guarantee food, housing, water, etc.). This marginalization of the body is then implicated in a variety of systems of injustice, as it tends to support the unequal treatment of categories of human beings who are viewed as more associated with the body, or whose work is more body centred.[1]

So here we have two powerful ideas emanating from the field of feminist philosophy: one, that sexual violence is a blow not against some abstract set of rights, but against bodily autonomy in particular, and two, that the body is central to personhood. Let's add one more in there: the importance of relations. Many feminist theorists have argued that common western theories of the self are overly individualistic, and tend to conceptualize the human person as either isolated from or prior to social relations. Mainstream social contract theory is a good example of this kind of model, insofar as it constructs social relations as primarily voluntary relations that rational, autonomous subjects enter into in order to satisfy particular needs. Feminist theorists, on the other hand (and particularly those working in the subfield of care ethics), argue that human persons develop from and within the context of relations, and that to view the human person as atomistic, as existing apart from relations, is to fundamentally misunderstand the human experience. Particularly interesting for the purposes of this article is the work on relational autonomy, that is, the idea that a human person's capacity for autonomy, for self-determination and agency, is a product of the particular relations that person has experienced. In other words, freedom isn't something that individual beings possess in some innate form; it's something that individual beings develop as they relate to each other, and it's something that relies on the actions and behaviours of others to be sustained (Meyers, 2010).

THE HARMS OF SEXUAL VIOLENCE, AND THE CHALLENGES OF RESPONSE

Putting these three ideas together (that sexual assault is embodied, that the body is central to personhood, and that relations are central to personhood) can help to develop an understanding of just how destabilizing sexual violence can be, and how some common responses to incidents of sexual violence can be retraumatizing to the survivor. The first two in particular can serve as preventive measures against a culture that often minimizes the harm of sexual violence. If sexual violence undermines a person's sense of bodily autonomy, and if matters pertaining to the body are central to a person's identity, moral dignity, and very being, then an act of sexual violence can be seen as deeply harmful. Two aspects of this harm are particularly important: first, these theories help us to understand the collective phenomenon of sexual violence as a systematic set of injustices that, insofar as they are disproportionately targeted towards one social group (women), constitute an attack on female personhood. Sexual violence as a cultural phenomenon does not merely consist of a series of bad actions; cumulatively, it adds up to a systematic denial of the possibility of full, equal personhood for women. Second, these theories can help us understand individual survivors of sexual violence as persons who have undergone a profoundly traumatic and destabilizing event.

Now it is important not to utilize such theories in an overly determinate way: different survivors understand and experience that trauma in radically different ways. Feminist theory can help here too, insofar as it generally rejects the notion that all women share some common set of traits or experiences. Given that the category of women is marked by significant differences (class, race, physical ability, age, just to name a few), and that there are many forms of sexual violence, each with its own cultural and political context, it would be foolhardy to expect all women to react to sexual violence in the same way, emotionally, psychologically, or physiologically. There are many ways of experiencing an undermining of one's bodily autonomy, but however it is experienced, such an undermining causes suffering—precisely because our bodily experiences are central to who we are.

What of relationality? How does the idea that who we are, and what we can do, is grounded in relation help us to understand sexual violence and the persons who have been subjected to it? For one, the emphasis on relationality reveals all incidents of sexual violence as exploitations of a fundamental, irrevocable vulnerability. The fact that we need others in order to be and become who we are necessarily means that what others do with and to us can, and must, affect us. This existential situation cannot be overcome or protected against—there is no way to wall oneself off from other human beings completely. To exist as a human is to be vulnerable to other humans, and in fact, to need other humans to act in certain ways such that one's own life can both continue and flourish (for more on this concept of vulnerability, see Fineman, 2000, 2008, and 2010). Thus, while some human beings, happily, are spared the actual experience of interpersonal violence, any human life entails the possibility of such violence.

Yet so often, particularly in cultural and political contexts where structures of violence are hidden by shame and taboo, that vulnerability is forgotten or repressed. To put it another way, human beings (particularly those who enjoy the privileges that go along with belonging to dominant groups based on gender, race, socio-economic status, sexual orientation, physical ability, etc.) can sometimes walk through the world relying upon while simultaneously failing to perceive their dependence on other human beings. From such a perspective, an experience of sexual assault can constitute a painful, embodied invocation of the central truth that human beings have the power to cause each other great suffering. While it is just as central, and just as important, that human beings have the power to cause each other great joy, and to enhance each other's lives, it is the vulnerability to harm that is most real to survivors of sexual violence in terms of their, for lack of a better term, healing process.

In addition to clarifying the role of vulnerability with regard to human existence, the emphasis on relationality helps us to see that how other individuals respond to a survivor's experience of sexual violence is absolutely crucial. After all, the importance of relationality does not stop with the incidence of sexual violence; if a human being's sense of self and capacity for action can be undermined by other persons, then it can also be enhanced by the actions and statements of others. Knowing that a survivor of sexual violence has had their bodily autonomy attacked, and has had their interpersonal vulnerability abused, can help university staff who interact with that survivor to focus their actions and speech on re-establishing the survivor's bodily autonomy. Indeed, understanding relationality can help such staff understand that part of the challenge of recovering from sexual assault is coming to grips with the vulnerability that has been revealed in its exploitation. Understood in this light, re-establishing autonomy is not a matter of returning the survivor to a previous state, where that vulnerability was not understood and perhaps not even perceived, but of integrating the existential fact of vulnerability into a necessarily transformed mode of being in the world, a process described in compelling detail in Susan Brison's *Aftermath: Violence and the Remaking of a Self* (2002).

The particular means by which a person's bodily autonomy is re-established are somewhat beyond the purview of the discipline of philosophy; empirical studies would need to establish what techniques are most effective. Yet philosophy can offer some general principles that can be helpful. For example, the concept of relationality would encourage those working with survivors to understand the process as necessarily intersubjective; that is, the process will take into account the particular experiences, interests, perspectives, and skills of all the persons involved. Not only is each survivor of sexual violence different, as noted above, but each person who interacts with survivors is different. Neither can be treated either as a blank slate or a predetermined, predictable member of a certain group. The emphasis on embodiment ought to remind the persons involved of the importance of bodily self-trust (MacLeod, 2002), and because the experiences of so many survivors of sexual violence are denied, doubted, and dismissed, responders should be highly attuned to the ways in which their behaviour and language (both verbal and nonverbal) express a trust in the survivor's own perceptions.

So far, I have highlighted contributions that feminist philosophy can make to our understandings of sexual violence, its harms, and the effects of certain forms of responses that survivors might encounter. In the next two sections, I turn my attention to more specific concerns that universities need to address in their policies, arguing that the feminist theories I have described above should play a central role as universities grapple with these concerns. The two specific matters I have chosen to address—the questions of and the decision to report (or not report) a sexual assault—do not exhaust the controversies relevant to university policies, but they are sufficient to demonstrate the importance of a distinctly feminist theoretical approach.

THE PROBLEM OF CONSENT

Earlier in this chapter, I mentioned that understanding sexual violence as related importantly to embodiment would have the effect of transforming the ethical concerns traditionally associated with sexual violence into a more complex, subtle line of ethical consideration. In this section, I will expand on that insight, arguing that mainstream understandings of the role of consent with regard to sexual interactions are deeply problematic, and that university policies cannot rely on those understandings if they seek to play a part in creating a sexually just campus culture. Although I would argue that the centrality of consent to sexual ethics ought to give way to a more complex set of ethical concerns, it is certainly the case that transforming our understanding of consent is an important step towards a cultural conversation about sexual assault that is simultaneously more robust and more subtle.

Contemporary understandings of sexual violence often focus on the category of nonconsensual sex. And at first glance, such a definition of appears to be helpfully clear: sexual assault occurs when one person sexually interacts with another person who has not given consent for that interaction. Yet feminist philosophers (myself included) have pointed out that focusing on consent presents a myriad of problems (Cahill, 2001; Pateman, 1988). For example, when consent is used as the hallmark of an ethical sexual interaction, there is almost always an underlying assumption that it is the female-identified partner who is giving or withholding consent; the male-identified partner is assumed to be offering that which can be consented to, or not. This framework assumes a heteronormative sexual narrative in which heterosexual men are the primary desirers of sex, and women do not so much desire sex as concede to it.

In addition, the focus on consent is marked by an underlying assumption that, by and large, women's sexual consent is viewed as meaningful, and is only ignored or overridden in the supposedly exceptional cases of sexual violence. This assumption is occasionally given voice in so-called rape prevention tips that (among other useful nuggets of advice) instruct women to communicate their sexual preferences and boundaries clearly and directly to their partners. Such advice obfuscates to the point of misrepresentation contemporary sexual politics, where hesitation on the part of a female-identified partner is frequently seen as a mere hurdle to be overcome, and where women often have justifiable fears about potential consequences of not conceding to their male partner's sexual requests or demands.

There is more to be said about the troubling ways in which focusing on consent hides rather than illuminates sexual inequality (for example, demanding that women clearly and consistently identify and then express their sexual desires while providing virtually no sexual education that would assist them in either difficult task seems particularly cruel). And indeed, there are several philosophical texts that offer detailed critiques of consent as an ethical yardstick. Yet the philosophical work on consent does not necessarily mean that university policies can or should avoid any and all mentions of it; the fact of the matter is that consent remains a coin of the realm, albeit one that is perplexing enough that even the U.S. federal government refrains from providing a definition of it, preferring instead to leave that task up to individual universities. However, understanding the ways in which consent can be utilized poorly should inspire universities to write policies and conduct educational programming that counters, rather than assumes, heteronormative, patriarchal models of sexual interactions. For example, policies should clearly state the need for affirmative consent (thus undermining the assumption that saying or doing nothing can be reasonably perceived as consent), and should understand consent as an ongoing aspect of sexual interactions (although one should also take the warning issued in the work of Lise Gotell [2008], who has criticized how the standard of affirmative consent has played out in Canadian courts of law). Although Antioch College was roundly mocked in the 1980s for its policy that required explicit, verbal consent for each individual action within the context of a sexual interaction, contemporary understandings of sexual ethics emphasize the fact that different acts have different meanings to different individuals, and thus consent must be continually expressed over the course of a sexual interaction. Colleges and universities also ought to follow the burgeoning discussion of enthusiastic consent, a riff on consent models that promises a more sex-positive model of sexual ethics ("On the Critical Hotness of Enthusiastic Consent," 2010).

AUTONOMY AND THE DECISION TO REPORT—OR NOT TO REPORT—AN ASSAULT

Too often, legislative or policy-centred approaches measure success in terms of the number of incidents of sexual violence that are officially reported. And there is no doubt that sexual violence is drastically under-reported, and that universities have come under fire for both under-reporting the number of incidents that occur on their campuses ("Washington Weighs In," 2014) and discouraging students from reporting, most likely with the intent to spare the university negative publicity. Under-reporting of incidents of sexual violence is seen as problematic not only because it results in an inability on the part of universities to grasp the real scope of the problem, but also because it reflects a cultural tendency to blame the victim. Accurate reporting of incidents of sexual violence, the logic goes, would help to reduce the shame associated with being a survivor of sexual violence, allow for more accurate data regarding sexual violence, and, not unimportantly, help to bring more perpetrators of sexual violence to justice, as implied in this language that was present on the RAINN website at least until February 2015:

> We hope you will decide to report your attack to the police. While there's no way to change what happened to you, you can seek justice and help stop it from happening to someone else. Reporting to the police is the key to preventing sexual assault: every time we lock up a rapist, we're preventing him or her from committing another attack. It's the most effective tool that exists to prevent future rapes. In the end, though, whether or not to report is your decision to make. ("Reporting the Crime to the Police," 2009, paras. 1–2)

Given these negative ramifications of under-reporting, it would be tempting for university staff working with survivors to actively encourage those survivors to report their experiences. Doing so would seem to be striking an important blow to rape culture. However, when keeping in mind the ethical responsibility to assist in re-establishing the survivor's bodily autonomy, it becomes less and less clear that such encouragement is ethically acceptable.

For one, such encouragement has the distinct potential to undermine the survivor's autonomy in the short term. Once a survivor embarks upon any kind of judicial process, the particular bureaucratic procedures that are involved—which are drastically different among universities, and often difficult to ascertain in detail prior to making an official report—do not, in general, have the survivor's autonomy as a primary goal. Thus, the survivor may be forced to relate aspects of their experience (both related to the incident of sexual violence itself, and in some cases, unrelated to that incident) that they would otherwise not choose to share. They may or may not be able to have an advisor with them during some proceedings, and if an advisor is allowed to be present, that advisor may or may not be allowed to provide counsel. At some universities, the accused is allowed to question the complainant, a situation that can cause significant harm to the survivor; at others, the accused is allowed to call character witnesses, but the complainant is not.[2]

Moreover, especially if such encouragement is framed by the possibility of achieving justice for the survivor, it risks not sufficiently preparing the survivor for the ways in which judicial processes, whether taking place within the university or within the public judicial system, themselves perpetuate damaging cultural assumptions about sexual violence and its survivors. Moving forward with judicial processes often involves the making public of various aspects of a survivor's private life; the repeated retelling, sometimes to an explicitly hostile or suspicious audience, of the survivor's experience; and the inevitable adjudication of the matter in the court of public opinion, which is hardly known for its friendliness to survivors.

The notion that justice for sexual violence is to be found in a courtroom, in fact, seems fairly farfetched. Not only are conviction rates for sexual violence and rape extremely low—one study showed that 13% of rape cases resulted in conviction, and that number goes down to 9% in cases where the accused was an intimate partner of the victim (Koss, 2000, pp. 1334–1335)—but many cases brought to the attention of prosecutors are rejected for charging (that is, the prosecutor opts not to bring any charges) (Koss, 2000, p. 1134). Not only should survivors skeptical that if they just "tell their story," justice will follow, but in fact they should be wary of the way in which their story will be told and heard within a judicial setting. Feminist scholarship has established in some detail the ways in which the space of the courtroom constructs survivors (Hengehold, 1993).

In short, there is little reason to believe that, by and large, judicial processes of any sort will serve the purpose of enhancing a survivor's sense of autonomy or need for justice. However, this state of affairs does not justify *discouraging* survivors from reporting. For some survivors, telling their story publicly and/or exercising their right to seek redress for the harms that were done to them in the cultural site that represents fairness and truth—the court of law—is a crucial part of working through the trauma of sexual violence. While survivors should be given clear information about what moving forward with a judicial process entails, they should also, if they choose to pursue that path, be provided with complete and consistent support for doing so.

In other words, when re-establishing the survivor's autonomy is the clear focus of interactions among the survivor and the university members who are in a responding role, then, when it comes to the choice of whether to pursue a judicial avenue, neither encouragement nor discouragement is appropriate. Instead, the goal should be to help the survivor determine which course of action is best for them, and then to work to ensure, as much as possible, that the choice is respected by the university.

Keeping the focus on the survivors and their own self-determined needs should help universities to avoid pressuring survivors to act in a way that the university would find advantageous. Although much of the negative publicity surrounding the ways in which particular universities have handled cases of sexual violence has focused on the tendency of university officials to discourage official reports (for fear, as mentioned above, of negative press), in today's current climate, it's all too easy to imagine that universities may have an interest in having students officially report sexual violence. An increase in reports may allow a university to claim, for example, that it has become proactive in tackling the issue of sexual violence, or that it has earned the trust of survivors, or that it is taking appropriate steps to punish perpetrators. University staff must have a consistent and shared commitment to the primacy of the survivor's experience in order to make sure that institutional interests, however inadvertently, do not end up imposing even more harm.

CONCLUSION

The careful reader will notice that nowhere in this discussion have I made specific recommendations regarding practices and policies that universities should develop. This is quite intentional; those practices and policies should arise out of the particular culture of each university, and should utilize the specific expertise to which each university has access. As I mentioned at the beginning of this chapter, universities are not only embedded in a larger culture, but constitute their own culture, and should develop ways of responding to and preventing sexual assault that are consistent with their cultural strengths (and, of course, that address their cultural flaws and challenges). This is yet another reason to include faculty with expertise regarding sexual assault in any discussions about policies. Not only will they bring crucial disciplinary expertise, but they have a perspective on the particular university culture that is irreplaceable.

Of course, while that perspective is irreplaceable, it is not sufficient. Other voices must be brought to bear here as well. While this chapter has focused on the participation of faculty, particularly those who approach the question of sexual assault from a feminist perspective, universities ought also to ensure that survivors of sexual violence (both those who have availed themselves of any university policies and procedures and, if possible, those who have chosen not to) participate in the creation or revising of those policies and procedures. This is the constituency, after all, who has the highest stake in developing policies that are fair and effective.

There are, of course, barriers to the inclusion of faculty with relevant expertise to the conversations devoted to developing or improving policies and practices regarding sexual violence on campus. The fact that such faculty self-identify as feminist may prove to be a significant stumbling block, as some members of the university community may perceive such faculty as biased rather than expert. There may be considerable political opposition to any explicitly feminist approach to sexual assault, as such an approach is, to more mainstream perspectives, uncomfortably critical of many beloved cultural practices. While it is difficult to imagine any university community member explicitly and openly defending either sexual assault or rape culture, a feminist perspective that connects sexual assault to other forms of gender inequality is often perceived as "going too far," precisely due to its more systematic and holistic analysis.

And then there are more general challenges as well. Some faculty may see such nitty-gritty work as not as worthy a use of their time as, say, teaching or producing new scholarship; some community members may perceive the need to develop compliant policies and practices as so urgent that it precludes the investment of time that these sorts of conversations demand. Even more basically, many universities and colleges may not have faculty with the relevant expertise on staff.

In situations where such barriers are either absent or surmountable, however, universities should take steps to integrate cutting-edge theoretical knowledge about sexual violence into the measures they develop to prevent and respond to such violence. Doing so honours the educational mission that is at the heart of institutions of higher knowledge, makes good use of the intellectual resources that such institutions contain, and could potentially develop approaches to sexual violence that go well beyond compliance with legal mandates. As this volume goes to press, institutions of higher education are the primary focus of mainstream reporting on sexual assault. While they are not the only cultural institution to grapple with the phenomenon of sexual violence, they are perhaps uniquely poised, precisely because of the expertise within their walls, to address these challenges in creative and effective ways.

NOTES

1 By now, the feminist literature on philosophy of the body is so extensive that a comprehensive list of works that develop this idea is impossible to provide. For a representative sample, however, see Ahmed (2000), Bartky (1990), Bordo (1993), Diprose (1994), Gatens (1996), Grosz (1994), Weiss (1999), and Young (2005).

2 In the United States, legislation such as the recent *Campus SaVE Act* has sought to create some clarity within and consistency among university policies on these and related matters, indicating clearly that all parties to any university process have the right to be accompanied by an advisor of their choice (including, if they wish and are able to provide one, an attorney). Moreover, there is increasing clarity that any processes must offer identical procedural possibilities to both the complainant and the accused. However, not all institutions have complied with these requirements as of yet, and some may eventually challenge these and other requirements in court.

REFERENCES

Ahmed, S. (2000). *Strange encounters: Embodied others in postcoloniality*. London, UK: Routledge.

Baber, H. E. (1987). How bad is rape? *Hypatia, 2*(2), 125–138. Retrieved from JSTOR database.

Bartky, S. L. (1990). *Femininity and domination: Studies in the phenomenology of oppression*. New York, NY: Routledge.

Bordo, S. (1993). *Unbearable weight: Feminism, western culture, and the body*. Berkeley: University of California Press.

Bourke, J. (2009). *Rape: Sex, violence, history* (Reprint ed.). Berkeley, CA: Counterpoint Press.

Brison, S. (2002). *Aftermath: Violence and the remaking of a self*. Princeton, NJ: Princeton University Press.

Brownmiller, S. (1975). *Against our will*. New York, NY: Fawcett.

Cahill, A. J. (2001). *Rethinking rape*. Ithaca, NY: Cornell University Press.

Chow, C., & Macmillan, S. (2016). New sexual violence and harassment legislation: New duties for colleges, universities and employers. *Canadian Labour and Employment Law*. Retrieved from http://www.labourandemploymentlaw.com/2016/03/new-sexual-violence-and-harassment-legislation-new-duties-for-colleges-universities-and-employers/

Dhillon, S., & Hunter, J. (2016, April 27). Sex-assault policy now mandatory for all B.C. postsecondary institutions. *Globe and Mail*. Retrieved from http://www.theglobeandmail.com/news/british-columbia/bc-introduces-law-mandating-sexual-misconduct-policies-for-universities/article29777655/

Diamond, J. (2014). Why we're suing York University for $20 million. Retrieved from http://jeremydiamondlaw.com/why-were-suing-york-university-for-20-million/

Diprose, R. (1994). *The bodies of women: Ethics, embodiment and sexual difference*. London, UK: Routledge.

du Toit, L. (2009). *Routledge Research in Gender and Society: Vol. 19. A philosophical investigation of rape: The making and unmaking of the feminine self*. London, UK: Routledge.

Fineman, M. A. (2000). Cracking the foundational myths: Independence, autonomy, and self-sufficiency. *The American University Journal of Gender, Social Policy & the Law, 8*(1), 13–29.

Fineman, M. A. (2008). The vulnerable subject: Anchoring equality in the human condition. *Yale Journal of Law & Feminism, 20*(1), 1–23.

Fineman, M. A. (2010). The vulnerable subject and the responsive state. *Emory Law Journal, 60*(2), 251–276.

Gatens, M. (1996). *Imaginary bodies: Ethics, power and corporeality.* London, UK: Routledge.

Gotell, L. (2008). Rethinking affirmative consent in Canadian sexual assault law: Neoliberal sexual subjects and risky women. *Akron Law Review, 41*(4), 865–898.

Grosz, E. A. (1994). *Volatile bodies: Toward a corporeal feminism.* London, UK: Routledge.

Hengehold, L. (1993). Rape and communicative agency. *Hypatia, 8*(4), 56–71. Retrieved from JSTOR database.

Koss, M. P. (2000, November). Blame, shame and community: Justice responses to violence against women. *American Psychologist,* 1332.

MacLeod, C. (2002). *Self-trust and reproductive autonomy.* Boston, MA: MIT Press.

Meyers, D. (2010, January). Feminist perspectives on the self (E. N. Zalta, Ed.). Retrieved from Stanford Encyclopedia of Philosophy website: http://plato.stanford.edu/entries/feminism-self/

Miller, S. C. (2009). Atrocity, harm and resistance: A situated understanding of genocidal rape. In A. Veltman & K. Norlock (Eds.), *Evil, political violence, and forgiveness* (pp. 53–76). Lanham, MD: Lexington Books.

On the critical hotness of enthusiastic consent. (2010, October 27). Retrieved from Feministing website: http://campus.feministing.com/2010/10/27/on-the-critical-hotness-of-enthusiastic-consent/

Pateman, C. (1988). *The sexual contract.* Oxford, UK: Polity Press.

Pinchin, K. (2009, August 10). Sex-assault victim sues Carleton for negligence. *Maclean's.* Retrieved from http://www.macleans.ca/education/uniandcollege/sex-assault-victim-sues-carleton-for-negligence/

Rape victim sues York U. for $3.5m. (2010, April 14). *National Post.* Retrieved from http://www.canada.com/story.html?id=4f156a59-01c0-407a-b870-d14b479bf42c

Reporting the crime to the police. (2009). Retrieved from RAINN website: https://www.rainn.org/get-information/legal-information

Violence Against Women Act: A Proposed Rule by the Education Department, 79 Fed. Reg. 35417 (proposed June 20, 2014). Retrieved from https://www.federalregister.gov/articles/2014/06/20/2014-14384/violence-against-women-act

Washington weighs in on campus assaults [Editorial]. (2014, May 3). *New York Times,* p. A18.

Weiss, G. (1999). *Body images: Embodiment as intercorporeality.* New York, NY: Routledge.

Young, I. M. (2005). *On female body experience: "Throwing like a girl" and other essays.* New York, NY: Oxford University Press.

CHAPTER 15

RESPONDING TO SEXUAL ASSAULT ON CAMPUS
What Can Canadian Universities Learn from U.S. Law and Policy?

Elizabeth Sheehy and Daphne Gilbert

Across Canada universities are being scrutinized and shamed for the actions of their students and staff, whether for "pro-rape" frosh chanting, sexual assaults occurring on and off campus, or the online activities of their students in debasing women. York University has been subject to intense and disproportionate media scrutiny (Dehas, 2013), starting in 2007 and continuing to the present, for men's perpetration of sexual assaults on or near campus, as well as to feminist critique for its handling of sexual assault prevention (Caron, Redford, & Teekah, 2010; Ikeda & Rosser, 2010). At the University of British Columbia, offending rape chants ("UBC Frosh Students," 2013) were followed by another frosh activity that denigrated Indigenous women (Justice, 2013), which was followed by a string of six sexual assaults by a serial perpetrator on its campus over several months (Bailey, 2013), all in the fall of 2013. During that same period, Saint Mary's also responded to a rape chant scandal (Taber, 2013), and Lakehead faced exposure after a former student wrote a letter to the editor of a local paper describing what it was like to have to attend classes with the student she alleged to have sexually assaulted her ("Lakehead Student's Rape Allegation," 2013).

Not long after, in March of 2014, the University of Ottawa was in the media when an allegation of sexual assault by several members of the men's hockey team was brought to the president's office around the same time that Facebook pages, wherein five male members of student leadership at the university discussed their female president in sexually derogatory and threatening terms, were made public ("Allan Rock," 2014; "Anne-Marie Roy," 2014). Meanwhile, Dalhousie's Faculty of Dentistry struggled with the negative publicity generated by the public airing of Facebook pages of male students discussing raping women using chloroform and denigrating their female colleagues, and Mount Saint Vincent fired a professor for "the non-disclosure of a sexual relationship with a student, which resulted in academic bias" (Zaccagna, 2015, para. 3).

The media interest in these events and the pressure on university administrators to respond quickly and decisively have no doubt been fuelled by high-profile developments occurring simultaneously in the United States. There campus student protests, a very effective national student lobby, litigation, and federal investigations have emerged, culminating in at least 85 U.S. universities (as of October 2014) being subject to potential loss of federal funding for failure to respond appropriately to individual complaints of sexual assault, as well as for inadequate prevention and reporting policies and practices (Kingkade, 2014).

Rightly, the question has been asked in Canada whether our universities are failing women students: do they or should they have similar legal responsibilities to deal with sexual violence (Rotstein, 2014)? Media reported that of 87 Canadian universities surveyed, only 9 have policies that specifically address sexual assault (Mathieu & Poisson, 2014a). Unevenness among university policies both within and across the provinces is the norm. Another investigation compared university data on sexual assaults reported to campus authorities, exposing a "patchwork approach" and concluding that only a "handful" of Canadian universities make this data public (Sawa & Ward, 2015b). Ironically, while universities might be loathe to "advertise" their sexual violence data, those campuses with the highest levels of reported violence may be doing the best job in terms of grappling with the issue and providing safe spaces for disclosure by women (Yung, 2015).

Canadian universities have undertaken self-study in response, producing reports, recommendations, and new policies and procedures. In each the deliberative body has responded to its specific incident(s) and has made recommendations that touch on all aspects of the university mission, understandably emphasizing education and prevention strategies (President's Council, 2013; UBC Point Grey Campus Safety Working Group, 2015; UBC's President's Task Force on Gender-Based Violence and Aboriginal Stereotypes, 2014; University of Ottawa, 2015). Saint Mary's, Lakehead, and the University of Ottawa have also recommended annual data gathering on students' experiences of sexual violence, the development of a sexual violence policy and response team, and mechanisms to investigate and discipline perpetrators. Lakehead goes somewhat further to recommend obligations on faculty and staff to respond appropriately to disclosures and a statement of the rights of complainants

(Lakehead University, 2014). Other Canadian universities are acting proactively by considering new policies before their students are in the news and social media (Mathieu & Poisson, 2014b).

The desirability of educational and sexual violence prevention obligations for universities seems incontrovertible, as does the need to develop specific sexual violence policies, consistent with the recommendations of the Ontario government (Ontario Women's Directorate, 2013) and METRAC (2014). Most Canadian universities already have student codes of conduct and/or sexual harassment policies that are at least theoretically available to respond to sexual violence on campus. Yet these policies are unclear in their application and sometimes contradictory; we also know that sexual assault is not like any other form of student misconduct, suggesting the need for focused inquiry into whether it is advisable to create new or enhanced disciplinary processes to be invoked by women who experience sexual violence connected with the university. These processes can be made available in addition to or in substitution for other forms of recourse found in the criminal justice system, in damages through civil litigation, or in compensation provided under criminal injuries compensation schemes.

On the one hand, university disciplinary processes arguably "decriminalize" and "privatize" men's sexual violence against women. As illustrated by U.S. cases, complainants may be discouraged from pursuing criminal or disciplinary processes by university personnel, and disciplinary consequences may be trivial and/or withheld from the public, the university community, and even the complainant. Most processes at Canadian universities include mediation as an alternative to investigation and adjudication; the penalty range is wide, from written reprimand through to expulsion; and the complaint and its resolution may be kept out of the public realm. These are undeniably serious concerns and worrisome implications of treating sexual assault as a non-academic disciplinary infraction. And, as we discuss further below, disciplinary models that are more adjudicative and punitive will attract more litigation and the involvement of lawyers, to the detriment of complainants.

On the other hand, practically speaking, sexual assault in Canada has already been decriminalized and privatized. Recovery of damages in tort law or compensation under criminal injuries schemes may be undercut by women's decision not to report to police or by the failure to secure convictions. Yet the rate at which women report sexual assault to police is extremely low: negative police, prosecutorial, defence lawyer, judicial, and jury responses to sexual assault allegations are so notorious that women must be what one Australian judge called "heroines of fortitude" to carry the burden of reporting and testifying for the prosecution (New South Wales Department for Women, 1996). The terrible personal, physical, psychological, relational, and economic costs of men's sexual violence are largely absorbed by women alone, whether or not they report to police.

In fact, there is some evidence that universities are doing an even worse job than the criminal justice system of creating processes that encourage reporting by women. For example, while UBC's data show that 16 sexual assaults were reported on campus for the period 2009–2013, the RCMP data show 70 sexual assaults for the same period (Sawa & Ward, 2015a). Women's experience of sexual violence undermines their academic success and puts at risk their ability to complete their programs (University of Ottawa, 2015), such that women also bear the educational costs of men's sexual violence and experience unequal access to post-secondary education.

While women students must be supported in their legitimate demand that police investigate and charge those men who engage in sexual violence, universities and colleges also have a role and a responsibility. Why wouldn't we insist that universities and colleges support women who seek police intervention and cooperate with police investigations? Shouldn't we also provide women with an alternative recourse to name the wrong that is less personally costly than the criminal law? And further, how could the criminal law possibly respond with the speed and the remedies needed to allow women to complete their education or continue their employment? Don't universities owe an obligation to their students and staff to provide interim and emergency measures to allow them to work, live, and study safely on campus?

Our starting point is that universities should provide avenues of redress for women who experience sexual violence and that these cannot simply be absorbed into pre-existing disciplinary codes and sexual harassment policies. Canadian governments have the power to impose uniform reporting and disciplinary procedures on universities, but in the absence of national or provincial standards, best practices should be identified for such policies. We first turn to a brief discussion of the legal context in which Canadian post-secondary institutions operate, particularly federalism, provincial human rights codes, the *Charter of Rights and Freedoms*, and tort law. Second, we describe the legal context in which U.S. universities and colleges sit: Title IX, the *Clery Act*, the Obama Task Force and its 2014 report, and the ongoing investigations and litigation arising from federal regulation. Third, we look at what Canadian institutions might learn from the U.S. experience specifically on the issues around reporting obligations, disciplinary measures, and protections for women who report sexual violence.

In our view, a comparative overview is useful given that the United States has more legislative experience in systemically addressing sexual violence on campus. Noting the ongoing challenges on U.S. campuses is helpful to identifying problems and concerns as we frame the early stages of a Canadian response. There are two important caveats with respect to the value of comparative legal analysis in this context. First, criminal law in the United States is a state power, unlike in Canada where it is a federal responsibility. This makes it more difficult for the White House and Congress to offer a coordinated plan to address sexual violence on campus where every state defines sexual assault and the rules of evidence differently, some in far from modern terms. Second, the sheer number of university and college campuses in the United States, operating in very different social and cultural settings than we experience in Canada, means that some of the lessons are not necessarily applicable here. For example, the powerful role that university sports plays—particularly college football—and fraternity culture in shaping and often limiting institutional responses to sexual violence in the United States is arguably[1] not as deeply embedded on Canadian campuses.[2]

LEGAL FRAMEWORK IN CANADA

In Canada responsibility for post-secondary education falls to provincial jurisdiction by virtue of the *British North America Act* (*BNA Act*) and because the federal government has abdicated any national leadership that could be exerted through federal funding. Under the division of powers between federal and provincial governments, the provinces have responsibility for the vast majority of social programs, including education, pursuant to section 93 of the *BNA Act*. However, in the period 1967–1976, the federal government shared the cost of funding for post-secondary education equally with provincial governments, giving the federal government the potential power to set national goals and standards.

Instead, the federal government began withdrawing from shouldering an equal burden and reduced federal transfers in the period 1977–1995. In 1995 it made a deep cut of $7 billion to social welfare, health care, education, and housing, further reducing federal funds for colleges and universities. Since that time, the federal government has at times provided new funding, but the funding has usually been targeted at specific federal goals in new projects (such as dedicated funds for research facilities or research chairs) as opposed to current operations. As of 2013 federal transfers were still $400 million short of 1992 levels. There is no indication that the federal government has any interest in using its funding powers to establish national educational standards, let alone standards for sexual violence aimed at women's equal access to post-secondary education.

Provincial governments could legislate on the issue or tie funding to post-secondary institutions to compliance with a provincial standard regarding a sexual violence policy. In Ontario, the government has taken a leadership role in putting the need for a sexual violence policy on the agenda, most recently signalling an intention to legislate in the area and impose data collection and reporting obligations upon post-secondary institutions. It has facilitated colleges in reaching agreement on some key elements and general contours, although the model policy leaves the details of disciplining defendants to the individual colleges (Benzie, Mathieu, & Poisson, 2015); universities are engaged together in the same process (Mathieu & Poisson, 2014c). In other provinces, human rights codes, the *Charter of Rights and Freedoms*, and even tort law might be invoked to force a university to address sexual violence.

All provinces have human rights codes that prohibit discrimination in employment and in the provision of services such as education. These codes also prohibit sexual harassment, which is broadly defined to extend to nonconsensual sexual contact. Human rights codes not only respond after the fact to acts of discrimination and harassment, but can also have a preventative effect by prompting universities to proactively develop policies and procedures to educate, deter, and sanction sexual harassment and violence. The liability of universities under human rights laws for sexual harassment can extend to failure to institute such proactive policies (*Ford v. Nipissing University*, 2011), which is also arguably a form of prohibited sex discrimination (*Janzen v. Platy Enterprises Ltd.*, 1989).

Universities may also be vulnerable in *Charter* litigation for failing to put in place adequate measures to deal with the known and therefore predictable problem of sexual violence on campus. Sexual assault, for example, has been recognized as an issue of sex equality for women under section 15 of the *Charter* (*R. v. Osolin*, 1993, p. 669). The issue of whether the university's acts or omissions are considered "government action" for the purposes of the application of the *Charter* is, however, complex. While universities are created by provincial statute and funded provincially, they are usually otherwise autonomous and thus free from *Charter* scrutiny, according to the Supreme Court (*McKinney v. University of Guelph*, 1990). However, in specific cases, greater degrees of government involvement may result in the opposite conclusion (*Douglas/Kwantlen Faculty Assn. v. Douglas College*, 1990; *Pridgen v. University of Calgary*, 2012),[3] pointing to the need to scrutinize the legislative context and degree of governmental control, and whether the university is carrying out a particular government policy.[4] Thus, if a government pursues legislation that imposes specific obligations on post-secondary institutions, the effect may be to open to *Charter* attack both the content and the application of sexual violence policies by complainants and defendants alike.

Were a university to be characterized as engaged in "government action" in a given circumstance, a student could conceivably bring suit for a remedy, whether a declaration that the university is in violation of the *Charter* or damages, both available under section 24(1) of the *Charter* (*Little Sisters Book and Art Emporium v. Canada,* 2000; *Vancouver (City) v. Ward,* 2010). It is also possible that liability in negligence law could be established if it could be shown that the university failed to take action with respect to a foreseeable risk of sexual violence, whether that failure is characterized as failing to warning women of a perpetrator (*Jane Doe v. Metropolitan Toronto Commissioners of Police,* 1998), failing to respond appropriately to disclosures of sexual violence, or failing to alleviate physical conditions that jeopardize women's safety or adopt policies and practices to deter and denounce sexual violence. In the United States, for example, Brett Solokov, CEO for the National Center for Higher Education Risk Management, tells university and college adminis-trators that they must deal promptly and assiduously with sexual violence complaints given the risk of serial perpetration:

> The first rape by a perpetrator is free. The second one is going to cost you seven figures. That's the way the law works; it is a horrible thing to say … the first one you didn't know was coming, it wasn't foreseeable, you didn't know he (perpetrator) could do that; the second time he does it, shame on you. And that's exactly how the law will process this. (as cited in Burke, 2013, p. 11)

Thus Canadian universities not only face mounting political pressure to respond to sexual violence, but may also fear complaints and lawsuits by stu-dents and employees if they fail to do so. For example, suits have been filed by women students who claim that lax security by the university in maintaining residences and facilities like labs facilitated men's sexual assaults against them (Pinchin, 2009; "Rape Victim Sues," 2010); lawsuits by students alleging that universities have responded inadequately after sexual violence has been per-petrated are in process (Hoffman, 2015a).

Of course, the legal question would be whether existing university policies regarding sexual harassment or student disciplinary codes that include sex-ual violence adequately address the university's obligation to respond to the unique harms and challenges posed by sexual assault. A recently filed human rights complaint against York University makes precisely this argument (Hoff-man, 2015b). In fact, there is precedent to suggest that university policies can fall short of their human rights obligations when they fail to account for forms of male violence such as anonymous stalking and the changed technological environment that facilitates it (*Ford v. Nipissing,* 2011, para. 72). Assuming that it is not appropriate simply to absorb sexual violence and sexual assault into pre-existing policies and that common standards are worth aiming for, what can we learn from the U.S. experience?

OVERVIEW OF THE SITUATION ON U.S. CAMPUSES

Brief overview of Title IX

Title IX of the *Education Amendments of 1972*[5] is a federal civil rights law that prohibits discrimination on the basis of sex in any education program or activity that receives federal funding.[5] Sex discrimination includes sexual harassment and all forms of sexual violence that are severe and pervasive enough to effectively bar a victim's access to an educational opportunity or benefit.[6] One incident of sexual violence can be severe enough to trigger a Title IX remedy. The legislation requires schools to be both proactive and appropriately reactive to sex discrimination. So, for example, schools that receive federal financial assistance must take necessary steps to prevent sexual assault on their campuses, and to respond promptly and effectively if an assault is reported. The Department of Education's Office for Civil Rights (OCR) is charged with enforcing Title IX in schools receiving financial assistance from the department. The OCR can initiate investigations or respond to complaints. Violators risk losing federal funds. The Department of Justice (DOJ) is also responsible for coordinating the enforcement of Title IX across all federal agencies and may initiate its own investigations or compliance review of schools receiving DOJ financial assistance.

A person who believes that her school has violated Title IX can file a complaint. Complainants can include students, faculty, or staff who have experienced an incident of sexual harassment or violence, or anyone who has faced retaliation for speaking out. Title IX investigations focus on the school's handling of the alleged misconduct, not on the complainant's experience of the misconduct. A person is protected under Title IX even if she does not directly experience harassment or violence. A school is required to take proactive steps to address potential misconduct and can be censored for creating a hostile environment if it knows of discriminatory behaviour and does nothing to address it. Schools must have an established procedure for handling complaints of sex discrimination and must have a Title IX coordinator to manage complaints.

Title IX guidance suggests that schools use a "preponderance of the evidence" standard to determine the outcome of a complaint (U.S. Department of Education, Office for Civil Rights, 2011). Schools must take immediate action to ensure that a complainant can continue her education free of ongoing sex discrimination by, for example, issuing a no-contact directive to the defendant and making reasonable changes to housing, class or sports schedules, campus jobs, or extracurricular activities. The 2011 Title IX guidance clearly prohibits schools from allowing mediation between a defendant student and a complainant in sexual violence cases. Such a diversion process is available only in cases of sexual harassment.

The Clery Act

The Jeanne Clery Disclosure of Campus Security Policy and Campus Crime Statistics Act (the *Clery Act*) requires colleges and universities that participate in federal financial aid programs to report annual statistics on crime, including sexual assault and rape, on or near their campuses, and to develop and use prevention policies. It is enforced by the Department of Education's Federal Student Aid (FSA) office. The FSA conducts on-site reviews to ensure compliance and can impose fines for violations.[7]

The Obama task force

On January 22, 2014, the White House announced the establishment of the White House Task Force to Protect Students from Sexual Assault ("Memorandum Establishing a White House Task Force," 2014). The memorandum announcing the task force asked the Office of the Vice President and the White House Council on Women and Girls to join in leading an interagency effort to address campus sexual violence, including the coordination of federal enforcement efforts. The task force was designed as advisory only, with a view to making recommendations on a wide variety of issues relating to campus sexual assault. The task force mission focused on education, consultation, and coordination. Its initial functions included establishing evidence-based best practices for preventing and responding to rape and providing guidelines to institutions; coordinating among agencies engaged in addressing sexual violence on campus and those charged with bringing institutions into compliance with the law; and broadening public awareness. Within 90 days (by mid-April) the task force had to produce a report to the president with proposals and recommendations for

1. Instructions, policies, and protocols for institutions on rape prevention and response, complaint and grievance procedures, investigations, adjudicatory procedures, disciplinary sanctions, and training;

2. Measurement tools for success of response efforts;

3. Greater transparency and accessibility for students in appreciating federal enforcement efforts; and

4. Promotion of increased coordination and consistency among agencies that enforce federal laws ("Memorandum Establishing a White House Task Force," 2014).

As promised, in April 2014, the task force released its first report. *Not Alone* presented a set of action steps and recommendations focusing on

1. The creation of a toolkit for a campus climate survey on sexual violence;

2. The creation of a set of public service announcements by the president, vice president, and various celebrities on the meaning of "consent";

3. The creation of a model reporting and confidentiality protocol with a specific aim of giving complainants more control over the process;

4. A checklist for schools in drafting or re-evaluating their sexual misconduct policies;

5. The promise of the development of trauma-informed training programs for school officials and campus and local law enforcement;

6. The promise of future assessment of different models for investigating and adjudicating campus sexual assault cases with a view to identifying best practices;

7. The provision of a sample agreement for partnering with local rape crisis centres and the future development of such an agreement for forging partnerships with local law enforcement;

8. The creation of a website (NotAlone.gov) that offers students a roadmap for filing a complaint against their school for failing to live up to obligations, and to find information on available services and applicable laws; and

9. The release of a guidance document with FAQs about Title IX and the *Clery Act* (White House Task Force to Protect Students from Sexual Assault, 2014).

In furtherance of the task force initiatives, on September 19, 2014, President Obama and Vice President Biden launched the It's On Us campaign, an awareness program to denounce sexual assault on university campuses. The campaign's "hook" is to ask everyone—men and women—to "step off the sidelines" and be part of the solution to campus sexual assault. The president announced, "It is on all of us to reject the quiet tolerance of sexual assault and to refuse to accept what's unacceptable" (Somanader, 2014, para. 5). In remarks at the event to launch the campaign, President Obama summarized White House efforts on this issue, including the creation of the task force; the establishment of guidelines for every school district, college, and university that receives federal funding on their legal obligations to prevent and respond to sexual violence; and a review of existing laws to make sure they adequately protect victims of sexual violence.

The Campus Sexual Violence Elimination Act (Campus SaVE Act)

The *Campus SaVE Act* went into effect in March 2014 as an added measure in the *Violence Against Women Reauthorization Act* of 2013. *Campus SaVE* specifically addresses the needs of women on university and college campuses. It has many positive features: most notably it broadens the focus in sexual violence from "stranger rape" cases to recognizing the danger of intimate sexual violence perpetrated by acquaintances and partners. It has a heavy educational component aimed at changing behaviours on campus (including bystander intervention training, for example). It also requires universities to have adjudicative processes for dealing with sexual violence complaints. The rule-making process under *Campus SaVE* is under way and there are kinks to iron out, most notably around the failure to specify the appropriate evidentiary burden.[8]

LESSONS FROM THE U.S. AND CANADIAN EXPERIENCES

The legislative experience in the United States is complex and varied, unsurprisingly given the number of colleges and universities governed by the statutes. Generally speaking, the following issues arise as important to complainants and experts in the field of sexual violence in both the United States and Canada. Before any kind of process responding to sexual violence kicks in, universities should consider two related efforts to avoid the problem: prevention and education. Once an incident occurs, universities must have policies to address the conflict. We have surveyed the U.S. experience in broad terms to identify issues and raise questions about continuing challenges.

Prevention policies

Campus prevention policies include practices around official events and alcohol availability, orientation week activities, and specific prevention/training/monitoring for sports programs and student athletes. Many universities have had long-standing practices they consider "preventative" of assault, like extra lighting, volunteer "don't walk alone" programs, and even self-defence training for female students. Critics argue these programs focus on the rare "stranger rape" scenarios and do nothing to address the more common sexual assault patterns on campuses (Ikeda & Rosser 2010). Moreover, by counselling women to curtail their lives and freedoms to avoid rape—essentially off-loading the responsibility to women to protect themselves, projecting myths about rape, and blaming women for their own rapes—universities echo the words of rapists[9] and engage in prohibited sex discrimination. A recent study sheds a more positive light on what is described as "resistance training." The study, led by a professor at the University of Windsor, concluded that incidents of sexual violence were reduced by half when women students participated in half-day resistance training programs. The training is particularly successful at teaching women to recognize the danger of sexual assault by acquaintances or friends as opposed to focusing on attacks by strangers (Marchione, 2015). U.S. colleges and universities have turned to bystander programs that teach others how to intervene to disrupt perpetration,[10] as well to education models in order to more effectively pursue prevention strategies.

Education and training

The need for campus education efforts to provide sexual assault training for faculty, staff, student residence leaders, teaching assistants, student leaders, and sports teams is acute. A recent poll by the Canadian Women's Foundation suggests that the majority of Canadians (67%), for example, does not understand the legal definitions of consent for sexual contact, and one in ten does not know or does not agree that consent is required within marriage and long-term relationships (Canadian Women's Foundation, 2015). Sexual assault prevention depends on widespread educational efforts—for potential perpetrators and bystanders—as does an effective response. Women who have experienced sexual assault may be slow to label it as such due to the disparity between legal definitions and social understandings, but also because a survivor's adaptation to trauma may be to repress the experience.

A key focus of the U.S. federal strategy is therefore trauma-informed sexual assault training for all employees who are first responders, investigators, and adjudicators for sexual assault complaints (Washington Coalition of Sexual Assault Programs, 2015). Trauma interferes with cognitive functioning, producing delayed recall and memory loss and fragmentation in sexual assault victims. Those without insight into these impacts may judge women's accounts unfairly. Unconscious biases and beliefs inconsistent with legal standards around sexual violence and consent must also be addressed through training, or investigators will simply fail in their legal duty (*Jane Doe v. Metropolitan Toronto Commissioners of Police*, 1998).

Trauma-informed training is therefore critical for a non-discriminatory campus response, but also to stop employees from causing further harm to women who report by retraumatizing them with appalling remarks. For example, one U.S. student who was part of a five-student federal lawsuit against her university was told by a campus police officer that "women need to stop spreading their legs like peanut butter or rape is going to keep happening until the cows come home" ("UConn to Pay $1.3M Settlement," 2014). In another multi-student lawsuit, one woman alleges that "she was raped anally and her testimony was questioned by a 'specially trained panelist' who didn't 'understand how it's possible to have anal sex without using lubrication first'" (Dockterman, 2014, para. 7).

These educational initiatives should therefore address

1. The role of the bystander and ways to safely intervene;[11]
2. The role that alcohol plays in campus sexual violence and how to intervene when suspected alcohol abuse within sports teams, residences, fraternities, and other sanctioned university activities is an issue;

3. The appropriate way to respond to complaints of sexual violence, including training on campus protocols for reporting, intervening, and calling police; and

4. Specific training for all those who implement sexual violence policies and protocols regarding the unique experiences and needs of those who have been sexually assaulted, including campus security, faculty and staff who administer student services, counselling services and accommodations policies, and those who are involved in investigating, carrying, or adjudicating allegations of sexual violence.

Providing urgent support and clear information following sexual violence

The Obama task force counsels universities and colleges to develop clear and accessible online information for those who experience sexual violence on campus as to how to request emergency services, counselling and support, interim measures, and any disciplinary response. The Ontario government has followed suit, urging colleges and universities to provide an easy-to-find link on the university's website (repeated throughout its pages and especially visible on any page frequented by students) that offers contact information for campus security and a sexual assault hotline or other 24/7 counselling service.[12] Campus police should be trained specifically to receive sexual violence complaints and to direct complainants to the appropriate emergency services (a hospital, walk-in clinic, sexual assault support centre, police, etc.). Campus security should also be trained to spot emergency cases that require immediate medical attention.

Given the prevalence of sexual assault on campuses, universities might be well advised to enter into partnership arrangements with autonomous sexual assault support services whereby clinics and/or counselling support services have space right on campus that is easily accessible to students. Autonomy for counselling services is key to preserving the privacy of complainants, for any records generated by university employees (including university counselling staff) belong to the university. Universities should not have access to this information given that they are in control of the disciplinary process.[13]

Once the initial "emergency" is handled, university websites should offer a clear indication of "next steps" for complainants. A protocol should be established that offers advice as to how a complainant can lodge a formal complaint against a defendant. If there are different routes for sexual violence and sexual harassment complaints, the guidelines should clearly indicate the consequences of making that choice (or delineate very clearly what conduct falls within each broad heading). Ideally, the complaint process would be streamlined to provide a single contact office for any complaint of sexual violence, whether against faculty, staff, or a fellow student.

The website should clearly outline what steps need to be taken by the complainant to file a complaint. (Is a written complaint necessary? Can the complainant book an appointment to see someone? Is there an advocate who can guide the complainant through the process?) The website should offer some guidance as to remedies that may be immediately available, such as a change of residence accommodation, change in course assignment, no-contact orders, and so on. These interim or emergency remedies will need to be tailored to specific incidents, but complainants should be able to access basic information about some options so they can discuss a potential plan with the designated office. Most importantly, neither the process of seeking information nor the form of interim measures should place burdens upon complainants, who may be in no position to vigorously assert their rights or bear the responsibility of avoiding the defendant.[14]

Finally, the steps of whatever disciplinary process a university adopts should be presented on a website in as detailed an overview as possible. Must the complainant be named or is there a process available for anonymous reporting? What will the process look like if she proceeds with a complaint? What are estimated timelines? What information will she need to present? What rights does a defendant have? What corresponding rights does a complainant have? What sanctions are available? All of this should be presented as clearly as possible so that complainants can formulate the questions to ask the designated office and can mull over their decisions on proceeding with some degree of knowledge as to what lies ahead if they go ahead with a formal complaint.

A staff person in the designated office should be equipped to counsel complainants as to the full range of options. If the complainant decides not to proceed with a formal complaint, can informal remedies persist around course/class assignment or residence accommodation? Can a no-contact order continue? If a complainant decides not to proceed, can the university proceed anyway if it has valid concerns about the safety of the university community? This scenario is not a remote possibility: one U.S. study of male college students' self-reported behaviour suggests that two-thirds of campus sexual violence is committed by serial predators, who averaged 5.8 rapes (Lisak & Miller, 2002).

To guide their creation of "first response" websites, a university might imagine a stereotypical first-year student in the fall of her first semester who is assaulted at a party in her residence. That student returns to her room and needs help. The university's website (and its trained campus security) should be easy for that student to access and navigate. She should be able to easily find 24/7 emergency assistance. She should be able to sit in the quiet of her own safe space and find the information she needs to make first-level decisions about reporting and next steps. If she does disclose to faculty or staff, they must provide information as to where she might go for medical/counselling/ complaint follow-up.

Interim measures pending investigation or a hearing

The immediate aftermath of a sexual violence incident is a crucial period for complainants. For those who live on campus, their living and work space becomes a dangerous place. Universities need clear guidelines on immediate remedial steps that can be taken upon a report of sexual violence, including temporary solutions to protect complainants. In a U.S. survey of 152 on- and off-campus crisis counsellors and service providers working with students who report rape, "these counselors cited institutional barriers on campus more often than any other factor as a discouragement to students pursuing complaints of sexual assault" (Jones, 2009, para. 12). One of the biggest barriers is deans who refuse to believe complainants or who encourage complainants to let the allegations go or "do nothing."[15]

It is evident that universities should not take the approach of "doing nothing" when a student alleges sexual assault. Even before an official complaint is lodged, there are interim/initial measures that can be taken. For example, universities can facilitate changes in residence room and course section assignment, and can prohibit contact between a complainant and defendant and/ or his supporters. In cases where criminal charges are in process, universities may be obligated to ban an accused from the campus (Caldwell, 2015). There might be immediate sanctions available if a complainant is harassed, bullied, or threatened because she came forward. Policies governing interim measures should clearly state that their imposition must not be construed as indicative of a breach of student discipline or "guilt."[16]

Some of these solutions may involve negotiation with the defendant and other faculty or staff. Complainant confidentiality should be respected insofar as is possible. There may not be a boilerplate solution to what is needed in the immediate aftermath, but universities should put in place guidelines and expectations that staff can turn to in their efforts to help a complainant feel safe within the university community. The issue of how interim measures intersect with the police response is discussed below.

A protocol for police involvement

A clear protocol is needed on facilitating police involvement if the complainant asks to speak to police. Complainants should be supported in their decision making without bias as to whether police should be called or not. There is a perverse incentive for universities to discourage reporting so as not to go "public" with sexual assault on campus, and so it is vital that women are told that sexual violence is a criminal matter and are offered support in contacting police should they so wish. Campus security should be trained to support complainants in either calling police or not, as the woman chooses. Consideration should be given to whether and how accompaniment can be provided (either by security or sexual assault counsellors on campus) when needed by complainants. The experience of reporting to police often involves secondary victimization whereby police "unfound" women's reports or even threaten charges against women who police believe are lying. The backing of campus security or counselling services may comfort the woman and motivate police. In particular, universities may have fiduciary obligations to their foreign students to help them navigate this difficult process.

Complainants should be given information about next steps if the police are involved and whether or how that will change any internal university process that goes forward. University processes are distinct from criminal proceedings, such that universities should not be held hostage waiting for a criminal matter to be resolved. A university must be able to act expeditiously to protect the safety of its community, and needs flexible policies to respond appropriately in individual circumstances. If complainants have reported to police and an investigation or prosecution proceeds, it may be necessary to delay internal proceedings in order to avoid tainting the criminal process from the standpoint of the complainant. The creation, accumulation, or exposure of complainants' personal records in the university context may also jeopardize the criminal trial. For their part, defendants who face criminal charges may be reluctant to participate in internal processes for fear that their actions could be construed as an admission of guilt or that they will unwittingly provide disclosure to the complainant of their criminal trial strategy.

If charges proceed in the criminal justice system and the university delays internal discipline, then interim measures to protect the complainant and community safety may be both necessary and justified on the basis of the criminal charges. Automatic imposition of some measures would alleviate the conundrum for an accused who does not want to appear "guilty" by agreeing to changes to class schedules, and so forth, and would relieve the complainant of the additional burden of having to persuade the university to adopt these measures. At the same time, an internal process should not be precluded by the complainant's decision not to report to police, police refusal to lay charges, or an acquittal in criminal court, because disciplinary proceedings serve different objectives, use less formal processes and lesser burdens of proof, and impose different sanctions. If, however, criminal proceedings culminate in conviction, the university should be able to act on that finding in its internal decisions because the standard of proof is so much higher in criminal law, and of course to avoid further traumatizing complainants.

Determining the obligations of faculty and staff

One issue that is the subject of some discussion within universities is whether faculty and staff who receive complaints from members of their community should be obligated to disclose those complaints to a designated office. Some U.S. institutions now make such reporting mandatory, in response to their federally imposed obligations to collect and disclose their data. At Ohio University, for example, there is a mandatory reporting requirement for all faculty and staff, unless they are counsellors or health care providers with specific privacy rules.[17] In Virginia a bill before the legislature would criminally punish employees who fail to convey these reports to police, regardless of the wishes of complainants (Anderson & Portnoy, 2015). Given that proposed Ontario law will mandate data collection and reporting, there may be pressure on institutions to require their employees to pass on all disclosures to a designated office. The policy drafted for all Ontario colleges includes such a clause, and some policies in place already seem to contemplate this obligation for employees.[18]

On the one hand, complainants may disclose an incident with an expectation of confidentiality that suggests the recipient of the disclosure should guard her privacy and respect her wish that nothing further be done. Some worry that this reporting obligation will discourage students and others from disclosing to trusted faculty and staff and put employees in an untenable position of having to interrupt or stave off a disclosure by warning the woman of their duty to report her disclosure (Flaherty, 2015; Jones, 2009). Those who disclose sexual assault should be able to make the decision for themselves about further disclosures and the inherent jeopardy to confidentiality this would entail.

On the other hand, a number of U.S. complaints involve complainants who have reported sexual violence to university employees, who have in turn discouraged further steps, failed to provide assistance, or neglected to pass the information on to anyone who could have helped. A related problem is that universities can resist knowledge regarding the true numbers of sexual violence reports on their campuses if their employees have no obligation to pass the information on to an office. Further, universities have responsibilities to protect their members, and in some cases safety concerns may outweigh the individual's wish to control the process or shield her confidential disclosure. Thus a reporting obligation may be necessary to ensure that someone in authority engages in the balancing of needs in particular situations, especially in the case of an alleged serial perpetrator.

If there is an obligation on employees to report disclosures, then universities must devise processes that guard confidentiality and leave the decision regarding next steps to the complainant if at all possible. Faculty and staff should be instructed as to how to respond to the complainant so that she feels supported, but is also made aware that her confidentiality may not be fully protected. In fact, some U.S. universities inform their members in unequivocal terms that their disclosures to employees must be passed to Title IX officials on campus.

Data collection

Universities must ensure a process for accurately recording incidents and resolutions of reported sexual violence, and compliance with laws, such as that forthcoming in Ontario, which require public reporting. Part of our current challenge is a lack of accurate and reliable data. Policies are being formulated now based on incomplete records. Refinement of those policies to best address the systemic nature of campus sexual violence will depend on more compelling and complete data from across the country. A related function of data gathering and analysis is the potential for identifying serial perpetrators and misogynistic cultures, as well as common risks or environmental factors that may play a role in facilitating sexual violence.

Universities need to train all personnel involved in receiving reports and collecting and disclosing data to attempt to offset the inherent biases against women who experience sexual violence and the gaps in many employees' understanding of applicable legal standards (Yung, 2015). These biases and gaps can short-circuit good policies. Further, it must be recognized that even if a province requires public reporting of data, U.S. experience tells us that universities are unlikely to collect and publicize fulsome sexual violence data in the absence of regular auditing by government (Yung, 2015, p. 5). This experience suggests that universities that are committed to this project need to set up mechanisms of external review to keep them on track.

The publication of results of reports by complainants, whether resolved through mediation processes or adjudicative hearings (including sanctions imposed), can contribute to a Canadian university-specific case law to be used by future hearing panels. Annual reports on incidents of reported sexual violence to police, campus security, a designated office, and faculty/staff would help us understand both the nature and extent of the problem.[19] Additionally, universities should consider creating a venue for complainants to report their experiences with its processes so that on an annual basis problem areas can be identified and modifications sought. Even if the outcomes of individual mediation processes must be kept strictly confidential, women must have a safe place to share their accounts of these processes and develop their political analysis, for the benefit of all.

Codes of conduct

Once a complainant decides to proceed with a complaint, the university disciplinary processes become key to both parties. This is an area of considerable scholarship and an equal amount of disagreement among experts. There are many contextual factors that shape the conversation. Three significant challenges surround the creation or modification of a disciplinary process.

First, universities must decide whether to separate sexual violence complaints from all other non-academic offences on campus. Should there be a distinct process for sexual violence incidents? Sexual violence is predicated upon inequality and reinforces women's subordination, making it a symbolic as well as a material act. Thus sexual violence is not easily absorbed into ordinary disciplinary processes because the complainant will experience acute forms of inequality in consequence. She will be vulnerable psychologically; physically (as trauma also manifests in the body); socially, in terms of isolation; and financially, given the economic costs of sexual assault that frequently include loss of employment, including teaching and research assistantships, and housing, and the high cost of counselling services and independent legal advice.

From the defendant's point of view, the accusation of sexual violence may be more stigmatizing than other disciplinary offences and may provide strong incentive to seek a lawyer's service and contest the allegation strenuously. We can predict that many of the same practices used by defence lawyers to intimidate, shame, and discredit women who allege sexual violence will be attempted in university processes as well. Such allegations also incite controversy on campuses and can become very politicized in ways other disciplinary infractions do not.

Second, universities must place their chosen process within either a negotiation/non-adversarial or adjudicative/adversarial model (or somewhere on that continuum). The first approach is often presented as "students' rights and responsibilities" and the latter as a "student code of conduct." The decision as to whether to prefer adversarial or non-adversarial models lays the key foundation for what follows. Some argue that universities should negotiate solutions between parties, further fulfilling their educational mission by focusing on restorative justice, rehabilitation, and reformation. Others argue that universities are ill-equipped to "rehabilitate" sexual offenders and that equality rights for women mandate adjudicative processes that respect the seriousness of the violation and the necessity of focusing on community safety (Schroeder, 2014, p. 1217).[20]

As noted above, in the U.S. Title IX guidance prohibits mediation for sexual violence complaints but permits it for sexual harassment. Complainants can feel considerable pressure to "mediate" or engage in "restorative justice" processes when their alleged assailant is a member of their own community. Prohibiting these more collaborative processes protects complainants from undue pressure and puts the onus on an impartial hearing panel to determine a reasonable and fair outcome. A more adjudicative model recognizes that systemic sexual violence on campuses makes universities hostile teaching and learning environments for women. However, the more closely a university's process resembles a criminal or civil process, the more the parties (and particularly defendants) argue for elevated protections in the investigation and hearing stages. The choice of model is a key determinant in the specifics of delivering it.

Universities will therefore have to decide whether to bar mediation and restorative justice options, whether for all forms of sexual violence or only the most extreme manifestations.[21] Those universities that require mediation as an aspect of either restorative justice or discipline must consider how such a process can be reconfigured to address systemic inequalities experienced by complainants, as well as the acute disempowerment sexual violence engenders. How can the reprivatization of sexual violence be avoided if mediation is used? How can the community be protected by private or individual, mediated solutions?

A third and related consideration is that students unhappy with university disciplinary processes are entitled to seek judicial review of those decisions and the processes that produced them. A body of jurisprudence elaborates "justification, transparency and intelligibility" (*AlGhaithy v. University of Ottawa*, 2012) as basic principles of fairness that universities need to pay attention to when crafting and implementing these processes. As mentioned earlier, tribunals situated within university disciplinary processes geared to producing remedial effects and contributing to student learning, which do not invoke adversarial norms, will have more leeway to set their own processes and deviate from strict evidentiary rules (*Kane v. Board of Governors of the University of British Columbia*, 1980).

Thus, courts have said that where no complex legal issues are involved, in the interests of expediency and cost-effectiveness, the university has the autonomy to design a simple and informal hearing that allows the defendant to use the assistance of a member of the university community but precludes legal counsel (*Ahvazi v. Concordia University*, 1992). In one case, for example, the court acknowledged that disclosure of documents might be limited to guard the confidentiality of the complainant's name when she cannot endure further distress (*Healey v. Memorial University of Newfoundland*, 1992), and in another case the court said cross-examination may be barred for the same reason if no serious issue of credibility arises (*Re B and W et al.*, 1985).

However, when these processes resemble judicial ones, where the language used echoes legalistic and particularly criminal law terminology, and when the potential penalty is not only serious but also realistically feasible, then courts have required higher degrees of compliance with traditional due process criteria. For example, where credibility is at issue and the stakes are high, such as loss of an academic year, an oral hearing may be required (*Khan v. University of Ottawa*, 1997), and the defendant may also be able to insist on the right to cross-examine the complainant or other witnesses (*Hajee v. York University*, 1985). Certainly when the conduct targeted is of a criminal nature and where disciplinary consequences will affect the student's reputation and prospects for employment, a right to counsel will likely be required (*Hajee v. York University*, 1985).

Students have the right to know the case against them, receive any document that will be relied upon in the decision, be judged by an unbiased decision maker, be given reasons for the decision, and have access to an appeal process. Although some informalities in process can be "corrected" by appeal avenues that allow for revisiting of fact finding (*AlGhaithy v. University of Ottawa*, 2012), there are limits. For example, even an early stage of disciplinary process, such as a meeting between the student and a vice-provost where an initial finding is made, may, if serious penalties are implicated, require that the student be permitted legal representation (*Telfer v. University of Western Ontario*, 2012).

Looking to the United States, we can see that the more informal processes recommended by Title IX guidelines, such as limits on the parties' ability to question or cross-examine each other, and other rules adopted by some universities that prevent lawyers from speaking during hearings or that make Title IX officers responsible for investigating, charging, and deciding both initial hearings and appeals, have sparked a tremendous backlash by defendants and their lawyers. In the past three years alone, dozens of lawsuits have been filed against universities alleging due process violations and sex discrimination against men in the disciplinary process (Yoffe, 2014). While most have been dismissed (Henrick, 2013, p. 78), there were some successful claims (Taylor, 2014). Emily Yoffe (2014) reports that "the higher education insurance group United Educators did a study of the 262 insurance claims it paid to students between 2006 and 2010 because of campus sexual assault, at a cost to the group of $36 million. The vast majority of the payouts, 72 percent, went to the accused—young men who protested their treatment by universities" (para. 19). It is reasonable to expect that Canadian lawyers will also initiate litigation wherever due process gaps appear in a sexual violence policy such that universities need to take this threat into account when designing their policies (Dube, 2015).[22]

Regardless of what model is chosen, the process should be clearly defined and the steps required easily accessible. Here are some issues that universities must consider.

Defining the scope of a sexual violence policy. One foundational issue is the definition of "sexual violence" for the purposes of any policy and process.

Does it include harassment? Intimate partner violence? Stalking? Cyber-harassment? The Ontario Women's Directorate (2013) has recommended a broad definition that includes but is not limited to all these forms of sexual violence.[23] This approach simplifies the policy by removing ambiguity and allowing for new forms of woman abuse to be captured by the policy.

It seems obvious that any sexual violence policy adopted by a university will apply to sexual misconduct between members of the university commu-nity, whether students, staff, or faculty. It may also be obvious that accommo-dation policies and support services should be provided for by the policy for students who experience sexual violence unrelated to the university, whether contemporaneous with the student's educational pursuits or historic, just as universities accommodate other physical and mental health needs of their members.

However, unlike most forms of non-academic misconduct, sexual vio-lence may frequently take place off campus. Codes that target only on-campus sexual violence can leave women without redress, even when that violence produces and reproduces inequalities on campus.[24] Universities should recon-sider restrictive definitions and examine the broader concepts used by some policies that include any conduct reasonably seen as having an adverse effect on the rights of members of the community to use and enjoy the learning and working environment (University of Western Ontario, 2010), and the specific inclusion of social media such as email, Twitter, and Facebook (York University, n.d.).

Role of the complainant. Universities must carefully sort out the role of a complainant in both restorative justice processes and disciplinary code models where the parties might have primary carriage of their case. A com-plainant may not be psychologically able to participate in questioning her alleged offender or in discussing any other physical evidence relevant to the case (Higgins, 2015). She may not be able to converse with or be in the pres-ence of the defendant. Universities will need specific supports for complainants who, while in the grip of trauma, cannot be expected to organize, present, or sustain their case. Universities may want to consider student advocates or ombudspersons to assist complainants because this is probably not a role that can be fulfilled by university legal counsel. We again stress that the unique power differential in sexual assault allegations, as opposed to other disciplinary charges, warrants specific redress and support for complainants who cannot be expected to carry the burden of the complaint alone.

While universities must have an objective process that respects the interests of both parties, they should consider the special needs of complainants and offer some support as well as maintain flexibility where needed. In particular, universities might consider allowing a complainant to choose which form of redress she wishes to pursue, a restorative justice process or a disciplinary one.

Timing issues. A rapid, simplified process that addresses the complaint before too much of a school year passes by should be the goal of any policy. While some investigative time may be needed, ordinarily these complaints should not require months of pre-hearing time. A rapid resolution is fair to all concerned, and universities should ensure that sufficient resources are allocated to move things along within predictable timelines. Again, however, flexibility may be required to respect the criminal process or respond to the needs of complainants who may not be able to cope with meeting the defendant face to face in the immediate aftermath of an alleged assault.

Representation. Specific provisions in supporting or prohibiting each party to be represented in either restorative justice processes or at a hearing (by their chosen representative, possibly including lawyers) must be included in the policy.[25] Lawyers can turn any process into an adversarial contest and may both lengthen and complicate any process. For this reason, some universities leave the discretion to determine whether counsel will be permitted in the hands of the chair of the disciplinary committee, emphasizing that they are conducting an inquiry, not a trial (University of British Columbia, 2012).

Of course, best practices suggest that if the defendant is represented, the complainant should have the option to be as well. Universities will have to decide whether representatives are an entitlement or an option to be negotiated depending on the seriousness of the alleged offence. Universities will also have to decide whether the representative can participate actively in the hearing or simply advise prior to it.

If lawyers are permitted, a further challenge will be determining who should pay. If a defendant engages counsel, does the complainant have to pay for her own lawyer?[26] Should student fees subsidize the availability of counsel for either party? Both parties? If one party is faculty or staff, union representation will likely be available. Universities should decide how to equalize the playing field so that both parties are fairly represented throughout the process. The complications added by lawyers may be one reason in favour of prohibiting representation if the matter is a simple one without many witnesses or other evidence.

Burden of proof. A clear standard of evidentiary proof is necessary. In the United States, the "Dear Colleague Letter" that offers guidance in Title IX complaints suggests that a "preponderance of evidence" or "balance of probabilities" is the appropriate standard (U.S. Department of Education, Office for Civil Rights, 2011). The failure to make that standard mandatory in *Campus SaVE* is one of the major critiques levelled at the legislation. Critics argue it leaves universities the option of a higher burden of proof (something like a "clear and convincing" evidence standard, which is closer to the criminal standard of "proof beyond a reasonable doubt"). Advocates for defendants' due process rights argue that the higher burden of proof is necessary to avoid highly stigmatizing findings of sexual misconduct and because those adjudicating lack judicial training and may feel pressure to enter a finding of misconduct in light of the potential loss of Title IX funding (Henrick, 2013, pp. 65–66).

Others point out that the lower standard is preferred in order to encourage complainants to come forward, to err on the side of protection of students and the university community, and to reflect the simplified processes of a disciplinary proceeding, which is more analogous to a civil proceeding as opposed to a criminal one using "proof beyond a reasonable doubt" (Weizel, 2012). In the United States, the standard of proof issue remains controversial, despite legislative guidance. For example, a group of influential Harvard law professors took a public stance against their own university's policy, denouncing it as too favourable to complainants.[27] Canadian universities need to be aware of these controversies when they specify the burden of proof and train those conducting the hearings on how to apply it to any evidence or testimony presented. Currently, most Canadian disciplinary codes use the lower balance of probabilities standard, with some exceptions such as the University of Toronto, which uses "clear and convincing evidence" as its standard for all offences (University of Toronto, 2002).

Rules governing the restorative justice process or hearing. There must be clear rules for how mediation and hearings will be conducted and training provided to those who implement these processes on sexual violence, for the needs and rights of complainants, and for the entitlements of defendants. Rules should be set out that protect the privacy of a defendant until the complaint is resolved; that address whether and how the parties can question each other and identify any inappropriate cross-examination subjects; that prohibit the use of a complainant's past sexual history; and that bar the introduction of any third-party records (therapeutic, medical, other). For example, St. Thomas University (2012) provides as follows: "In the course of an investigation, the dress or sexual history of the complainant will not be a factor in determining whether an event was consensual, nor will it be considered relevant" (s. viii).

It may be preferable to have each party offer written submissions that can be exchanged prior to a hearing so that there is some disclosure of the "case to be met." Witnesses should be called only if they can offer directly relevant evidence about the sexual violence incident. While evidentiary rules must be more relaxed than those used in a judicial hearing,[28] universities should take care to have clear guidelines on hearings (and train personnel appropriately) to avoid any badgering of complainants and to ensure rapid resolution of the complaint. Universities might consider prohibiting direct questioning of the parties by the parties and instead requiring all questions to be filtered through the chair (University of British Columbia, 2012), although one author warns that the chair may not be well equipped to detect unfair or malevolent questions (Burke, 2013, p. 36).[29]

Privacy protection. There must be rules protecting a complainant's privacy insofar as is possible. In the criminal law context, we know that women may be more likely to come forward with a complaint when they know there will be a publication ban on any identifying information. Such bans are routine. Similarly, our courts use initials for the name of an accused if releasing his name will also identify his complainant. Different considerations are at play within a university community, but universities should at a minimum ensure that the school newspaper and other media do not report on a complainant's name or identifying information.[30] Any publication of the results of a disciplinary process should use only initials for the complainant, and universities should endeavour to involve as few people in the process as possible. Complainants will most likely (and hopefully) remain members of the university community after the process concludes, and their privacy is key to their future comfort and safety, as well as to the university's ability to inspire the confidence in community members to report.

Sanctions. Disciplinary processes always need clear sanctions that are both publicized and regularly enforced. If a defendant is found responsible for a serious sexual violence incident, expulsion should be the default position. The protection of both the complainant and the wider university community requires the removal of predatory sexual violators. Some U.S. commentators argue complainants should be given a role in determining whether a defendant is expelled (Kitchener, 2012). On the other hand, complainants may be less likely to come forward, or be the object of considerable peer pressure, if expulsion of a defendant is a real possibility.

It will be a challenge to build a system of appropriate and graduated sanctions for offences that do not merit expulsion. In the criminal law context, we have an entire sentencing regime with detailed guidelines and hundreds of precedent cases. Universities should work together to share best practices regarding sanctions. A sort of university-style "case law" could assist those running hearings in determining the appropriate range of penalties. Sanctions ought to include the possibility of releasing the defendant's name to further campus safety and in the interests of transparency.

Possible "sanctions" arrived at through mediation or restorative justice processes present difficult issues. Mediation is often premised on confidential settlement between the parties. The development of a university-specific "case law" on sexual violence requires transparency in the process and, most importantly, the sanctions imposed. Privacy considerations must be kept distinct from the public disclosure of the nature of the incident, the process invoked, and the result.

CONCLUSION

It is clear that Canadian universities must tackle the issue of sexual violence directly and urgently. Scandals aside, there is a moral imperative to deal fairly with women employees and students who are victimized while at home and work on campus. It is axiomatic that the university community must be a safe space for women, although it has not been so for many.

Moreover, sexual violence sits on a continuum of violence against women, which extends to woman-killing or femicide. The U.S. experience of campus mass murders tells us that the shooters are always men; that the targets are often women; that many if not most are motivated by male rage at women; that sexual violence by the shooter can precede the rampage; and that these attacks seem to be correlated with institutional cultures that tolerate sexual violence, discrimination, and harassment (Cantalupo, 2009). Most recently, a campus feminist group has filed suit against their university for failing to prevent and respond to sexual harassment and threats against members of Feminists United after one of their outspoken members was murdered ("Student Sues Virginia University," 2015). While Canadian universities thankfully have far less experience with mass shootings, none of us will ever forget the Montreal Massacre and the fact that we too are vulnerable to the most extreme forms of misogyny. Now that a men's rights group has not only set up on many Canadian campuses but also received the legitimization of charitable status (McLaren, 2015), the stakes are even higher for our universities to address male resentment towards women and the forms of rape culture that manifest on campus.

We have raised many more questions here than we are able to answer, and we have not touched on other issues that universities must address. These include whether and what kinds of limitation periods should be used for initiation of complaints;[31] the potential for conflict of interest to affect the impartiality of an investigation or adjudication (Burke, 2013, pp. 20–28; Henrick, 2013, pp. 80–86); the need to encourage reporting by providing amnesty to complainants and witnesses who might otherwise be caught by other disciplinary offences for alcohol or drug use;[32] and the need for an appeals process that protects the interests of both defendants and complainants (METRAC, 2014, p. 12).

Ultimately, we recommend three positive steps that universities can take immediately to deal with sexual violence: first, they must acknowledge that sexual assault is not only a societal issue but specifically a university problem that requires direct action; second, they must develop clear and transparent processes to address sexual violence, involving students as agents of change (METRAC, 2014, p. 9), and with flexibility to evolve as our collective experience with the issue matures; and third, they must report honestly about the incidents of violence, the institutional response, and the ongoing challenge. Clarity, transparency, and responsiveness are crucial contributions to the conversation for university leadership. The U.S. experience teaches us that legislative solutions alone will not change the culture on campus. University leaders must make use of the tools at their disposal—legislation, policy, research, partnerships, and activism. But the administration must lead: sexual violence cannot be allowed to compromise women's ability to study, to work, and to thrive in the university.

ADDENDUM

This chapter relies on research that was up to date as of the fall of 2015. Since that time, much has changed ... yet the issues remain the same. The number of U.S. federal investigations of Title IX violations regarding sexual violence has risen to 304, implicating 223 colleges and universities (Anderson, 2017). In Canada, both Ontario and British Columbia have passed legislation that requires post-secondary institutions to develop stand-alone sexual violence policies and provide information, educational and prevention programs, resources, and accommodations for students who have experienced sexual assault (*Sexual Violence and Harassment Action Plan Act* [Ontario, 2016]; *Sexual Violence and Misconduct Policy Act* [British Columbia, 2016]). Manitoba has a similar bill (*The Post-Secondary Sexual Violence and Sexual Harassment Policies Act*, 2016) that has not yet moved beyond first reading. Ontario has also promulgated regulations to ensure that institutions make available information about how sexual violence allegations will be investigated and adjudicated, the due process measures that will be in place, and any avenues of appeal (*Sexual Violence at Colleges and Universities Regulations*, 2016). Given that post-secondary institutions across Canada are adopting different policies with variable protections for complainants and due process features, we expect turbulent times ahead, as the legitimacy of sexual violence policies is tested through litigation and in the court of public opinion.

NOTES

This chapter appeared originally on the SSRN website in August 2015. Available at: https://papers.ssrn.com/sol3/papers.cfm?abstract_id=2641844. It is reprinted with permission.

1   But see, for example, Montgomery (2013) and Chiose (2014a).
2   The unique position of powerful and rich fraternities on U.S. campuses is highlighted in a recent documentary on sexual violence on campus, *The Hunting Ground* (Ziering,

2015). The film also explores the role of college football in protecting male athletes from accountability for sexual assault, and features the story of football star Jameis Winston, accused of rape at Florida State University, who was drafted first overall in the 2015 NFL draft. See Howard (2015).

3   In *Pridgen*, one justice among the three also based her decision on *Charter* grounds, and a second judge, without deciding that the *Charter* applied, ruled that the disciplinary decision was "unreasonable" because the decision maker failed to even consider the two male students' countervailing right to freedom of expression.

4   *Lobo v. Carleton University* (2012) distinguished *Pridgen* because there the university was "delivering a specific government program in partnership with the government."

5   The *Civil Rights Act of 1964* also requires public schools to respond to sexual assaults committed against their students.

6   See Title IX (2015). See also Title IX: The Basics, retrieved from http://knowyourix. org/title-ix/title-ix-the-basics/. Sexual violence includes attempted or completed rape or sexual assault, sexual harassment, stalking, voyeurism, exhibitionism, verbal or physical sexuality-based threats or abuse, and intimate partner violence.

7   See, for example, a report on 2011 violations by Yale University, https://studentaid.ed.gov/ sa/about/data-center/school/clery-act-reports#. The database is searchable by school and by year.

8   For an excellent overview of the complete U.S. legislative position, including a description of *SaVE*, see Duncan (2014), p. 4443, and Schroeder (2014), p. 1195.

9   Daniel Katsnelson, who predated upon women in a York University residence dorm by looking for unlocked doors, said to his parole officer prior to entering a guilty plea to sexual assault, "Now maybe she will know to keep her doors locked" ("York U Rapist," 2010, para. 15).

10   See, for example, the Step Up! program (http://stepupprogram.org/topics/sexual -assault/); "Jackson Katz Speaks" (2017); Choise (2014b).

11   A new advertising campaign by the Ontario provincial government launched in March 2015 features a graphic television spot where men engaging in assaultive behaviours look at the camera and thank the viewer for "not telling anyone." See Uechi (2015).

12   In March 2015 the Ontario provincial government released its plan to address sexual violence, including on university campuses. It promised that the government would "introduce legislation to require colleges and universities to adopt a sexual assault policy, developed with significant input from students, and renewed—with student involvement—every four years." See Ontario (2015).

13   For example, in January 2015 a complainant sued the University of Oregon for mishandling her rape case. In defending itself against a claim of emotional distress, the university gave its counsel her therapy records from its on-campus counselling centre. See Pryal (2015).

14   A dilemma that arises in the imposition of no-contact orders or other measures to prevent the parties from engaging with each other is that of who should bear the burden of avoidance. Thus, complainants may be told to avoid coming to campus at times when a defendant will be on site. However, to restrict a defendant's access to campus would involve telling him of the complainant's schedule, and she may prefer to avoid that sort of disclosure to her alleged perpetrator. Furthermore, although it is beyond the scope of this paper, complications as to scheduling are more acute when the defendant is a staff person or faculty member who is not suspended from employment duties.

15   For example, Jones (2009) reports:

> In December 2007, Elizabeth Ryan, who was finishing up her first semester on the New Paltz campus of the State University of New York, was summoned to speak to the Dean of Students in the austere Haggerty Administration Building.

The dean's office had just learned she filed a police report alleging that she was raped by another freshman at an off-campus fraternity house. (Elizabeth Ryan is not her real name; she has asked to use a pseudonym to protect her privacy.) Ryan says she immediately knew that what had happened to her was rape. The nurse who administered the rape kit, and others who heard her story, seemed shocked, Ryan recalls, by the trauma that she conveyed, and by the bruises on her breasts. But when she told the story to the dean, a veteran student affairs administrator named Linda Eaton, it was Ryan's turn to be shocked. One of her options was to "do nothing," she says the dean told her. Even now, Ryan, 20, has a hard time rationalizing that response. "If I wanted to do nothing, I would have kept my mouth shut," she says. "I wouldn't have gone to my RA, or to the campus police, or to the New Paltz police, or to the hospital. I wouldn't have said a word to anybody right from the start," she says. "It was insulting. This guy had just raped me ... and that's her answer?" ("Troubling Tale at SUNY New Paltz," paras. 1–3)

16 See, for example, University of Toronto (2002).

17 But see Jones (2009):

> Char Kopchick, assistant dean of students at Ohio University, says that her university's efforts at increasing sexual assault reporting rates several years ago achieved just the opposite effect. The university put in place a mandatory reporting requirement—meaning that all faculty and staff were obligated to report a sexual assault to police, unless they were counselors or health care providers specifically bound by privacy rules. As a result, Kopchick says, students stopped showing up. ("Overcoming Perceptions, para. 5)

18 The Brock University *Sexual Assault and Harassment Policy* (Brock University, 2015) provides that "where an employee of the University becomes aware of an allegation that a sexual assault has been perpetrated by another University employee, there is a requirement to immediately report the incident to the Associate Vice-President, Human Resources (or designate) who will coordinate the investigation and University response." The St. Thomas University (2012) policy on sexual assault complaints by students provides that "as soon as he or she is able to do so, the first person to come into contact with the person who has been sexually assaulted should report the incident. The incident should be reported to a Complaint Officer, or a member of the Residence Life staff, as applicable, who in turn should contact the Director of Student Services and Residence Life for further guidance" (p. 26).

19 See Ontario (2015). The Ontario government pledged to introduce legislation to "require universities and colleges to report publicly on incidence of sexual violence, as well as initiatives underway to address sexual violence and harassment, and their effectiveness" (p. 27).

20 See also the controversy surrounding the use of a restorative justice process at Dalhousie University's dentistry school to address complaints of sexual harassment in Facebook postings (Thomson, 2015).

21 See Hampson (2015). The article explains the fallout from an incident of Facebook harassment at the Dalhousie dentistry school in the fall of 2014. Some of the women targeted by male colleagues agreed to a restorative justice process, as did 12 of the 13 men involved in the harassment. Those who opted out of the university's chosen method for resolving the issue were left without any remedial process.

22 See, for example, the class-action lawsuit launched by members of the men's varsity hockey team at the University of Ottawa when the president suspended the team after an allegation of sexual assault by two team members was received ("University of Ottawa Men's Hockey Players," 2015).

23 *Developing a Response to Sexual Violence* (Ontario Women's Directorate, 2013) proposes the following: "No person shall commit an act of sexual violence against any other person or threaten another person with sexual violence. This includes, but is not limited to, sexual assault, sexual harassment, stalking, indecent exposure, voyeurism, degrading sexual imagery, distribution of sexual images or video without consent, cyber harassment and cyber stalking" ("Student Code of Conduct," para. 2).

24 See the case of Charles Barrons, discussed in Hampson (2015).

25 For example, the University of Alberta's *Code of Student Behaviour* allows either party to be accompanied by an "advisor," defined as follows: "A person who will assist the Appellant or the Respondent during the disciplinary process. Assistance may be provided by the Student OmbudService, Student Legal Services, legal counsel or another Advisor as the Appellant or Respondent choose" (s. 30.2.4). The University of Saskatchewan's *Standard of Student Conduct in Non-Academic Matters* provides, "The complainant and the respondent have a right to bring an advocate (which may be a friend, advisor, or legal counsel) to a hearing, and to call witnesses, subject to the provisions below with respect to the rights of the hearing board" (p. 11).

26 It is beyond our scope to address sexual violence when faculty and staff are involved, but universities should consider the imbalance in unionized environments when collective agreements entitle members to legal representation. For a detailed discussion of the unfairness generated by additional due process and representational rights accorded to faculty in the context of Amherst's policies, see Burke (2013, pp. 39–47).

27 See for example, Robbins (2012); Jacobs (2015); and "Rethink Harvard's Sexual Harassment Policy" (2014). For one student's account of what it is like to be accused of sexual misconduct, see Witt (2014).

28 See our discussion in "A Protocol for Police Involvement" of the problems presented when a criminal case is proceeding. More relaxed rules in a disciplinary process may present particular challenges to parties in a criminal case, and universities may have to stall an internal process pending resolution of the criminal prosecution.

29 Burke (2013, p. 50) argues instead for a civil rights–based investigatory process over an adversarial one.

30 This is particularly urgent if a criminal complaint is under way and there is a legal publication ban on identifying information in that process.

31 Flanagan and Tso (2014) describe a reform achieved by student activism at Tufts University, removing a previous limitation period of 12 months for filing a claim and instead permitting such claims as long as the alleged perpetrator remains enrolled at the university.

32 See Burke (2013, pp. 33–34) and METRAC (2014, p. 8), which revealed that of 15 Canadian universities and colleges studied, none had such a policy.

REFERENCES

Ahvazi v. Concordia University, 1992 49 Q.A.C. 108.

AlGhaithy v. University of Ottawa, 2012 O.N.S.C. 3172.

Allan Rock calls University of Ottawa incident "repugnant." (2014, March 5). *CBC News.* Retrieved from http://www.cbc.ca/news/canada/ottawa/allan-rock-calls-university-of-ottawa-incidents-repugnant-1.2561604

Anderson, N. (2017, January 18). At first, 55 schools faced sexual violence investigations. Now, the list has quadrupled. *Washington Post.* Retrieved from https://www.washingtonpost.com/news/grade-point/wp/2017/01/18/at-first-55-schools-faced-sexual-violence-investigations-now-the-list-has-quadrupled/?utm_term=.a6ad4f0463ca

Anderson, R., & Portnoy, J. (2015, January 26). Va Senate panel advances mandatory reporting bill for campus sexual assault. *Washington Post*. Retrieved from http://www.washingtonpost.com/local/virginia-politics/va-senate-panel-advances-mandatory-reporting-bill-for-campus-sexual-assault/2015/01/26/6154700c-a56a-11e4-a2b2-776095f393b2_story.html

Anne-Marie Roy, uOttawa student leader, subject of explicit online chat. (2014, March 2). *CBC News*. Retrieved from http://www.cbc.ca/news/canada/ottawa/anne-marie-roy-uottawa-student-leader-subject-of-explicit-online-chat-1.2556948

Bailey, I. (2013, October 29). RCMP hunting serial predator in UBC sexual assaults. *Globe and Mail*. Retrieved from http://www.theglobeandmail.com/news/british-columbia/one-suspect-now-believed-responsible-for-six-ubc-campus-sex-assaults/article15141220/

Benzie, R., Mathieu, E., & Poisson, J. (2015, February 1). Ontario colleges create sex assault policy. *Toronto Star*. Retrieved from http://www.thestar.com/news/canada/2015/02/01/ontario-colleges-create-sex-assault-policy.html

Brock University. (2015, May). *Sexual Assault and Harassment Policy*. Retrieved from https://brocku.ca/human-rights/wp-content/uploads/sites/55/Brock-Sexual-Assault-and-Harassment-Policy.pdf

Burke, T. (2013). *Your first rape is free ... your second rape will cost you seven figures* (Doctorate in Education, American International College). Retrieved from http://papers.ssrn.com/sol3/papers.cfm?abstract_id=2363295

Caldwell, B. (2015, June 1). Judge blasts WLU for its handling of residence rape. *The Record*. Retrieved from http://www.therecord.com/news-story/5655782-judge-blasts-wlu-for-its-handling-of-residence-rape/

Canadian Women's Foundation. (2015). *Only 1 in 3 Canadians know what sexual consent means*. Retrieved from http://canadianwomen.org/press-consent

Cantalupo, N. C. (2009). Campus violence: Understanding the extraordinary through the ordinary. *Journal of College and University Law, 35*(3), 613–690.

Caron, B., Redford, M., & Teekah, A. (2010). Post scripts from YorkU. *Canadian Woman Studies, 28*(1), 43–44.

Chiose, S. (2014a, October 5). McGill staff knew charged football player's past. *Globe and Mail*. Retrieved from http://www.theglobeandmail.com/news/national/mcgill-staff-knew-charged-football-players-past/article20939357/

Choise, S. (2014b, October 31). Male bystander intervention can help end sexual assaults, expert says. *Globe and Mail*. Retrieved from http://www.theglobeandmail.com/news/national/male-bystander-intervention-is-key-to-ending-sexual-assault/article21418259/

Civil Rights Act of 1964, IV U.S.C. § 42.

Dehas, J. (2013, April 19). Is the media fair to York University? *Maclean's*. Retrieved from http://www.macleans.ca/education/uniandcollege/is-the-media-fair-to-york-university/

Dockterman, E. (2014, April 24). Students file Title IX sexual assault complaint against Columbia University. *Time*. Retrieved from http://time.com/76762/students-file-title-ix-sexual-assault-complaint-against-columbia-university/

Douglas/Kwantlen Faculty Assn. v. Douglas College, [1990] 3 S.C.R. 570.

Dube, D. E. (2015, January 13). University of Ottawa Gee-Gees hockey players file $6M lawsuit. *Ottawa Sun*. Retrieved from http://www.ottawasun.com/2015/01/13/live-gee-gees-hockey-players-sue-school

Duncan, S. H. (2014, November 3). The devil is in the details: Will the campus SaVE Act provide more or less protection to victims of campus assaults? *Journal of College and University Law, 40,* 4443.

Education Amendments of 1972, 20 U.S.C. § 1681.

Flaherty, C. (2015, February 4). Endangering a trust. *Inside Higher Ed.* Retrieved from https://www.insidehighered.com/news/2015/02/04/faculty-members-object -new-policies-making-all-professors-mandatory-reporters-sexual

Flanagan, A., & Tso, P. (2014, February 19). Inside the student activist movement: Tufts and sexual violence. *Jezebel.* Retrieved from http://jezebel.com/ inside-the-student-activist-movement-tufts-university-1526094401

Florizone, R. (2015, January 9). *Terms of reference for the Task Force on Sexism, Misogyny and Homophobia in the Faculty of Dentistry.* Retrieved from http://www.dal .ca/content/dam/dalhousie/pdf/cultureofrespect/Task%20Force%20Terms%20 of%20Reference.pdf

Ford v. Nipissing University, 2011 H.R.T.O. 204.

Hajee v. York University (1985), 11 O.A.C. 72.

Hampson, S. (2015, March 6). How the dentistry-school scandal has let loose a torrent of anger at Dalhousie. *Globe and Mail.* Retrieved from http:// www.theglobeandmail.com/news/national/education/how-the-dentistry -school-scandal-has-let-loose-a-torrent-of-anger-at-dalhousie/article23344495/

Healey v. Memorial University of Newfoundland (1992), 106 Nfld. & P.E.I.R. 304 (Nfld. S.C.T.D.).

Henrick, S. (2013). A hostile environment for student defendants: Title IX and sexual assault on college campuses. *Northern Kentucky Law Review, 40*(1), 49–92.

Higgins, L. (2015, February 23). A Montrose woman says Stony Brook University required her to prosecute her own sex attacker at a disciplinary hearing. *Journal News.* Retrieved from http://www.lohud.com/story/news/local/westchester/2015/02/22/ stony-brook-student-prosecute-alleged-sex-attacker-lawsuit-says/23743857/

Hoffman, K. (2015a, March 3). York University fails to support sex assault victims, woman says. *CBC News.* Retrieved from http://www.cbc.ca/news/canada/manitoba/ york-university-fails-to-support-sex-assault-victims-woman-says-1.2979396

Hoffman, K. (2015b, June 30). York University's sexual assault policy sparks human-rights complaint. *Globe and Mail.* Retrieved from http://www.the globeandmail.com/news/national/education/york-universitys-sexual -assault-policy-sparks-human-rights-complaint/article25194134/

Howard, A. (2015, March 3). Why "The Hunting Ground" could cast a shadow over Jameis Winston. Retrieved from http://www.msnbc.com/msnbc/jameis -winston-unwitting-star-campus-rape-film-the-hunting-ground

Ikeda, N., & Rosser, E. (2010). *You* be vigilant! Don't rape! *Canadian Woman Studies, 28*(1), 37–43.

Jackson Katz speaks at the University of Cape Town. (2017). Retrieved from Mentors in Violence Prevention website: http://www.mvpnational.org/

Jacobs, P. (2015, February 18). Harvard professor explains the biggest problem with school's new sexual assault policy. *Business Insider.* Retrieved from http://www.business insider.com/janet-halley-harvard-law-professor-sexual-assault-policy-2015-2

Jane Doe v. Metropolitan Toronto Commissioners of Police (1998), 39 O.R. (3d) 487 (S. Ct).

Janzen v. Platy Enterprises Ltd., [1989] 1 S.C.R. 1252.

The Jeanne Clery Disclosure of Campus Security Policy and Campus Crime Statistics Act (Clery Act), 20 U.S.C. § 1092(f)(1)-(15) (2012).

Jones, K., (2009, December 2). Barriers curb reporting on campus sexual assault. Retrieved from the Center for Public Integrity website: http://www.publicintegrity .org/2009/12/02/9046/barriers-curb-reporting-campus-sexual-assault

Justice, H. (2013, September 20). What's wrong with the CUS FROSH Pocahontas chant? *Artswire* UBC. Retrieved from http://wire.arts.ubc.ca/featured/whats -wrong-with-the-cus-frosh-pocahontas-chant/

Kane v. Board of Governors of the University of British Columbia, [1980] 1 S.C.R. 1105.

Khan v. University of Ottawa (1997) 34 O.R. (3d) 535 (C.A.).

Kingkade, T. (2014, October 15). 85 Colleges are now under federal investigation for sexual assault cases. *Huffington Post*. Retrieved from http://www.huffingtonpost .com/2015/04/06/colleges-federal-investigation-title-ix-106_n_7011422.html

Kitchener, C. (2012, August 23). How to encourage more college sexual assault victims to speak up. *The Atlantic*. Retrieved from http://m.the atlantic.com/national/archive/2013/08/how-to-encourage-more-college-sexual -assault-victims-to-speak-up/278972/

Lakehead student's rape allegation prompts task force. (2013, October 22). *CBC News*. Retrieved from http://www.cbc.ca/m/news/canada/thunder-bay/lakehead -student-s-rape-allegation-prompts-task-force-1.2159004

Lakehead University. (2014, June). *Sexual Misconduct Policy and Protocol*. Retrieved from https://www.lakeheadu.ca/faculty-and-staff/policies/general/ sexual-misconduct-policy-and-protocol

Lisak, D., & Miller, M. P. (2002). Repeat rape and multiple offending among undetected rapists. *Violence and Victims, 17*(1), 73–84.

Little Sisters Book and Art Emporium v. Canada, 2000 S.C.C. 69.

Lobo v. Carleton University, 2012 O.N.S.C. 254.

Marchione, M. (2015 June 10). Rape prevention training greatly lowers risk of sex assault: Study. *Global News*. Retrieved from http://globalnews.ca/news/2047791/ canadian-universities-study-shows-rape-prevention-training-greatly-lowers -risk-of-sex-assault/

Mathieu, E., & Poisson, J. (2014a, November 20). Canadian post-secondary institutions failing sex assault victims. *Toronto Star*. Retrieved from http://www.thestar.com/ news/canada/2014/11/20/canadian_postsecondary_schools_failing_sex_assault _victims.html

Mathieu, E., & Poisson, J. (2014b, November 21). Queen's, University of Saskatchewan pledge to implement sexual assault policies. *Toronto Star*. Retrieved from http:// www.thestar.com/news/canada/2014/11/21/queens_university_to_fast_track _policies_on_sexual_assault.html

Mathieu, E., & Poisson, J. (2014c, December 23). Ontario universities commit to multi-prong sexual violence plan. *Toronto Star*. Retrieved from http://www.thestar.com/ news/canada/2014/12/23/ontario_universities_commit_to_multiprong_sexual _violence_plan.html

McKinney v. University of Guelph, [1990] 3 S.C.R. 229.

McLaren, L. (2015, March 12). How's men's rights groups are distorting the debate about equality. *Globe and Mail*. Retrieved from http://www.theglobeandmail.com/life/relationships/leah-mclaren-are-men-really-the-victims/article23426535/

Memorandum establishing a White House Task Force to Protect Students from Sexual Assault. (2014, January 22). Retrieved from https://www.whitehouse.gov/the-press-office/2014/01/22/memorandum-establishing-white-house-task-force-protect-students-sexual-a

METRAC. (2014). *Sexual assault policies on campus: A discussion paper*. Retrieved from https://www.metrac.org/resources/sexual-assault-policies-on-campus-a-discussion-paper-2014/

Montgomery, S. (2013, November 1). Former Richmond high school football star facing sex assault charges. *Richmond News*. Retrieved from http://www.richmond-news.com/former-richmond-high-school-football-star-facing-sex-assault-charges-1.681299

New South Wales Department for Women. (1996). *Heroines of fortitude: The experiences of women in court as victims of sexual assault* [Report]. Woolloomooloo, NSW: Author.

Ontario. (2015, March). *It's never okay: An action plan to stop sexual violence and harassment*. Retrieved from https://dr6j45jk9xcmk.cloudfront.net/documents/4170/actionplan-itsneverokay.pdf

Ontario Women's Directorate. (2013). *Developing a response to sexual violence: A resource guide for Ontario's colleges and universities*. Ottawa, ON: Queen's Printer for Ontario. Retrieved from http://www.women.gov.on.ca/owd/docs/campus_guide.pdf

Pinchin, K. (2009, August 10). Sex-assault victim sues Carleton for negligence. *Maclean's*. Retrieved from http://www.macleans.ca/education/uniandcollege/sex-assault-victim-sues-carleton-for-negligence/

President's Council. (2013). *Promoting a culture of safety, respect and consent at Saint Mary's University and beyond: Report from the President's Council*. Retrieved from http://www.smu.ca/webfiles/PresidentsCouncilReport-2013.pdf

Pridgen v. University of Calgary, 2012 A.B.C.A. 139.

Rape victim sues York U for $3.5m. (2010, April 14). *National Post*. Retrieved from http://www.canada.com/story.html?id=4f156a59-01c0-407a-b870-d14b479bf42c

Re B and W et al. (1985), 52 O.R. (2d) 738 (H.C.J.).

Pryal, K. R. G. (2015, March 2). Raped on campus? Don't trust your college to do the right thing [Commentary]. *The Chronicle of Higher Education*. Retrieved from http://chronicle.com/article/Raped-on-Campus-Don-t-Trust/228093/?cid=at&utm_source=at&utm_medium=en

Rethink Harvard's sexual harassment policy [Opinion]. (2014, October 15). *Boston Globe*. Retrieved from http://www.bostonglobe.com/opinion/2014/10/14/rethink-harvard-sexual-harassment-policy/HFDDiZN7nU2UwuUuWMnqbM/story.html

Robbins, R. (2012, May 11). Harvard's sexual assault policy under pressure. *Harvard Crimson*. Retrieved from http://www.thecrimson.com/article/2012/5/11/harvard-sexual-assault-policy/

Rotstein, S. (2014, August 29). Are Canadian universities doing enough to prevent sexual assault on campus? *Huffington Post*. Retrieved from http://www.huffingtonpost.ca/samara-rotstein/sexual-assault-on-campus_b_5737596.html

R. v. Osolin, [1993] 4 S.C.R. 595.

Sawa, T., & Ward, L. (2015a, February 9). UBC sex assault reports out of sync with police statistics. *CBC News*. Retrieved from http://www.cbc.ca/news/canada/ubc-sex-assault-reports-out-of-sync-with-police-statistics-1.2950264

Sawa, T., & Ward, L. (2015b, February 11). Canadian campuses lack US-style transparency on sex assault reports. *CBC News*. Retrieved from http://www.cbc.ca/news/canada/canadian-campuses-lack-u-s-style-transparency-on-sex-assault-reports-1.2953078

Schroeder, L. P. (2014). Cracks in the ivory tower: How the Campus Sexual Violence Elimination Act can protect students from sexual assault. *Loyola University Chicago Law Journal, 45*(4), 1195–1243.

Sexual Violence and Harassment Action Plan Act (Supporting Survivors and Challenging Sexual Violence and Harassment) (2016). Statutes of Ontario, c-2.

Sexual Violence and Misconduct Policy Act (2016). Statutes of British Columbia, c-23.

Sexual Violence at Colleges and Universities Regulations (2016). Ontario Regulation 131/16.

Somanader, T. (2014, September 19). President Obama launches the It's On Us campaign to end sexual assault on campus [Blog post]. Retrieved from https://www.whitehouse.gov/blog/2014/09/19/president-obama-launches-its-us-campaign-end-sexual-assault-campus

St. Thomas University. (2012, December). *Disciplinary Processes for Cases of Social Misconduct. Appendix B: Procedures with Respect to Sexual Assault Complaints by Students.* Retrieved from http://w3.stu.ca/stu/currentstudents/documents/CodeofConductDecember2012.pdf

Student sues Virginia University after campus feminist group member killed. (2015, May 7). *The Guardian*. Retrieved from http://www.theguardian.com/us-news/2015/may/07/university-of-mary-washington-feminist-group-lawsuit-death

Taber, J. (2013, September 5). Saint Mary's student president says rape chant was "biggest mistake ... probably in my life." *Globe and Mail*. Retrieved from http://theglobeandmail.com/news/national/saint-marys-student-president-says-rape-chant-was-biggest-mistake-of-my-life/article14142351

Taylor, J. (2014, November 10). Database: Lawsuits against colleges and universities alleging due process and other violations in adjudicating sexual assault. Retrieved from http://www.avoiceformalestudents.com/list-of-lawsuits-against-colleges-and-universities-alleging-due-process-violations-in-adjudicating-sexual-assault/

Telfer v. University of Western Ontario, 2012 O.N.S.C. 1287.

The Post-Secondary Sexual Violence and Sexual Harassment Policies Act (2016). Bill 204, 1st Session, 41st Legislature Manitoba.

Thomson, A. (2015, March 11). Restorative justice for dental students at Dalhousie University brings scrutiny. *CTV News*. Retrieved from http://www.ctvnews.ca/canada/restorative-justice-for-dental-students-at-dalhousie-university-brings-scrutiny-1.2275033

Title IX. (2015). Retrieved from Know Your IX website: http://endrapeoncampus.org/title-ix/

UBC frosh students sing pro-rape chant. (2013, September 7). *CBC News*. Retrieved from http://www.cbc.ca/news/canada/british-columbia/ubc-investigates-frosh-students-pro-rape-chant-1. 1699589

UBC Point Grey Campus Safety Working Group. (2015, February). *Interim report of the UBC Point Grey Campus Safety Working Group.* Retrieved from http://vpstudents .ubc.ca/files/2014/02/Interim-Report-from-the-UBC-Point-Grey-Campus-Safety -Working-Group.pdf

UBC's President's Task Force on Gender-Based Violence and Aboriginal Stereotypes. (2014, February 18). *Transforming UBC and developing a culture of equality and accountability: Confronting rape culture and colonialist violence.* Retrieved from http:// vpstudents.ubc.ca/files/2014/03/IGBVAS-Recommendations-for-Community -Consultation2.pdf

UConn to pay $1.3M settlement in sexual assault lawsuit. (2014, July 18). *Al Jazeera.* Retrieved from http://america.aljazeera.com/articles/2014/7/18/uconn-sexual -assaultsettlement.html

Uechi, J. (2015, May 6). Ontario gets enlightened about sexual harassment. *Vancouver Observer.* Retrieved from http://www.vancouverobserver.com/news/ powerful-tv-ad-hammers-sexual-assault-and-harassment-bystanders-video

University of Alberta. (2016). *Code of Student Behaviour.* University Governance. Retrieved from http://www.governance.ualberta.ca/en/CodesofConductandResi- denceCommunityStandards/~/media/Governance/Documents/Codes%20of%20 Conduct%20and%20Residence%20Community%20Standards/Code%20of%20 Student%20Behaviour/COSB-Updated-May-30-2016.pdf

University of British Columbia. (2012). *Rules for the President's UBC Vancouver and UBC Okanagan Non-Academic Misconduct Committees.* Retrieved from http:// universitycounsel.ubc.ca/files/2012/02/Rules-for-the-Presidents-Non-Acad -Misconduct-Committees.pdf

University of Ottawa. (2015). *Report of the Task Force on Respect and Equality: Ending sexual violence at the University of Ottawa.* Retrieved from https://www.uottawa .ca/president/sites/www.uottawa.ca.president/files/report-of-the-task-force-on -respect-and-equality.pdf

University of Ottawa men's hockey players to file class-action law suit. (2015, January 13). *CBC News.* Retrieved from http://www.cbc.ca/news/canada/ottawa/university -of-ottawa-men-s-hockey-players-to-file-class-action-lawsuit-1.2899006

University of Saskatchewan. (2012). *Standard of Student Conduct in Non-Academic Matters and Regulations and Procedures for Resolution of Complaints and Appeals.* Retrieved from https://www.usask.ca/secretariat/student-conduct-appeals/ StudentNon-AcademicMisconduct2016.pdf

University of Toronto. (2002). *Code of Student Conduct.* Retrieved from http://www .governingcouncil.utoronto.ca/Assets/Governing+Council+Digital+Assets/ Policies/PDF/ppjul012002.pdf

University of Western Ontario. (2010). *Code of Student Conduct.* Retrieved from http:// www.usc.uwo.ca/government/documents/Western_Code_of_Student_Conduct .pdf

U.S. Department of Education, Office for Civil Rights. (2011, April 4). *Dear Colleague letter.* Retrieved from http://www2.ed.gov/about/offices/list/ocr/letters/ colleague-201104.pdf

Vancouver (City) v. Ward, 2010 S.C.C .27.

Violence Against Women Reauthorization Act of 2013, Pub. L. No. 113-4, S.304, 127 Stat. 54, 89-92 (2013).

Washington Coalition of Sexual Assault Programs. (2015). *Creating trauma-informed services: A guide for sexual assault programs and their system partners.* Retrieved from http://www.wcsap.org/sites/default/files/uploads/resources_publications/special_editions/Trauma-Informed-Advocacy.pdf

Weizel, M. L. (2012). The process that is due: Preponderance of the evidence as the standard of proof for university adjudications of student-on-student sexual assault complaints. *Boston College Law Review, 53*(4), 1613–1655.

White House Task Force to Protect Students from Sexual Assault. (2014). *Not alone.* Retrieved from https://www.justice.gov/ovw/page/file/905942/download

Witt, P. (2014, November 3). A sexual harassment policy that nearly ruined my life. *Boston Globe.* Retrieved from http://www.bostonglobe.com/opinion/2014/11/03/sexual-harassment-policy-that-nearly-ruined-life/hY3XrZrOdXjvX2SSvuciPN/story.html#

Yoffe, E. (2014, December 8). The university sexual assault overcorrection: How efforts to protect women have infringed on men's civil rights. *National Post.* Retrieved from http://news.nationalpost.com/news/the-university-sexual-assault-overcorrection-how-efforts-to-protect-women-have-infringed-on-mens-civil-rights

York University. (n.d.). *Code of Student Rights and Responsibilities.* Retrieved from http://www.yorku.ca/oscr/pdfs/CodeofRightsandResponsibilities.pdf

York U rapist gets 8 year sentence. (2010, April 14). *CityNews.* Retrieved from http://www.citynews.ca/2010/04/14/york-u-rapist-gets-8-year-sentence/

Yung, C. R. (2015). Concealing campus sexual assault: An empirical examination of Clery Act data. *Psychology, Public Policy & Law, 21*(1),1–9.

Zaccagna, R. (2015, January16). MSVU dismisses instructor who had sexual relationship with student. *The Chronicle Herald.* Retrieved from http://thechronicleherald.ca/metro/1263504-msvu-dismisses-instructor-who-had-sexual-relationship-with-student

Ziering, A. (Producer) & Dick, K. (Director). (2015) *The hunting ground* [Motion picture]. United States: Weinstein Company. Available at http://www.thehuntinggroundfilm.com/ .

ABOUT THE AUTHORS

SHEENA BANCE is a doctoral candidate in the Department of Applied Psychology and Human Development at the University of Toronto. Her research interests focus on post-traumatic mental health in women and in the workplace, and the role of cultural background in women's mental health.

MELISSA BENDIG is a Saskatchewan-based researcher, educator, and policy analyst. She holds a master's degree in public health from the University of Saskatchewan and has worked for several years in a variety of health-policy-related fields, including community programming, research, and post-secondary instruction.

JENNIFER L. BILLAN is actively involved in community projects and is passionate about working with communities promoting health and healing. She recently earned her master's degree in kinesiology and health studies at University of Regina, where she explored the identity and health of Indigenous grandmothers who are caring for grandchildren.

CARRIE BOURASSA is Chair of Indigenous and Northern Health at Health Sciences North Research Institute and Scientific Director of the Institute of Aboriginal Peoples' Health at the Canadian Institutes of Health Research based in Sudbury. She is a member of the College of New Scholars, Artists and Scientists of the Royal Society of Canada. She publishes in the areas of Indigenous end-of-life care, Métis health, and violence against Indigenous women. Carrie is Métis, belonging to the Regina Riel Métis Council #34.

ANN J. CAHILL is professor of philosophy at Elon University, and is the author of *Overcoming Objectification: A Carnal Ethics* (2010, Routledge) and *Rethinking Rape* (2001, Cornell University Press). She recently co-edited a special issue of the *Journal of Social Philosophy* on the theme of "Miscarriage, Subfertility, and Death."

CURTIS FOGEL is an associate professor in the Department of Sport Management at Brock University. In 2016, he was appointed as a research fellow in Canadian Studies at the University of California, Berkeley. He is the author of *Game-Day Gangsters: Crime and Deviance in Canadian Football* (2013, AU Press). His research interests include sports law, ethics, doping, and violence.

ANNE FORREST is Director of Women's and Gender Studies at the University of Windsor. Her field of research is labour relations. Her participation in the Bystander Initiative arises from her scholarly and personal interest in organizational change.

DAPHNE GILBERT teaches law at the University of Ottawa. Her research interests lie primarily in the *Charter of Rights and Freedoms*, with a particular emphasis on equality rights, reproductive rights, and animals and the law.

ANDREA GUNRAJ is an author, communicator, and community development professional. Currently in the youth homelessness sector, she has worked with diverse communities on issues of safety, gender-based violence, social justice, and equity. Andrea worked with METRAC on Violence for several years in a variety of roles to build safer and inclusive communities and spaces and has a background in criminology.

JUDY HAIVEN is a professor in the Management Department in the Sobey School of Business at Saint Mary's University, Halifax, Nova Scotia. She teaches industrial relations. Her areas of research include women and work, women in trade unions, and equity issues and human rights in the workplace. Prior to becoming an academic, she worked as a factory worker, a filmmaker, and a journalist.

SARAH HOROWITZ recently completed her Ph.D. in the Department of Applied Psychology and Human Development at the University of Toronto. Her research and clinical interests focus on violence against women, post-traumatic mental health, and non-suicidal self-injury in young adults.

JULIE S. LALONDE is an Ottawa-based social justice advocate, support worker, and public educator. She has been working in the field of sexual violence for over a decade. Julie has won wide recognition for her work, including the 2013 Governor General's Award in Commemoration of the Persons Case and Volunteer Ottawa's Best Volunteer in a Leading Role award. She has been a support worker to survivors at the Sexual Assault Support Centre of Ottawa since 2006.

GAIL LASIUK is a founding member of the Coalition Against Sexual Assault–University of Saskatchewan. She is the technicians' representative on the Canadian Union of Public Employees Local 1975 Executive and is a long-time activist in numerous social justice projects.

JENNA MACKAY is an artist, community organizer, and qualitative researcher and program evaluation consultant in Toronto. She worked at the Sexual Assault Survivors Support Line from 2006 to 2009.

ERIC J. OLESON is the Indigenous health research supervisor at the First Nations University of Canada. His background is in social policy, economics, and intimate partner violence. Eric has worked in Indigenous health for the past five years, focusing on HIV/AIDS community-based research and interventions.

NATALIE OWL is a member of Sagamok Anishnawbek. She recently completed her master's degree with the thesis *The Effects of the Intergenerational Residential School Experience and Negative Racial Stereotyping on Ojibwe Speech Patterns in Mid-Northern Ontario Anishnawbek.*

CASSANDRA A. OZOG is a sessional instructor and course developer at both the University of Regina and the First Nations University of Canada. She is also a Ph.D. student at the University of Regina in the field of disaster recovery and community health.

NORMA JEAN PROFITT has a long history of activism in feminist movements in Nova Scotia and Costa Rica, with a focus on violence against women. During her tenure as associate professor in the School of Social Work, St. Thomas University, she developed the first course on Lesbian, Gay, Bisexual, and Two-Spirit Peoples and Social Work. She also pioneered a course called International Perspectives on Violence against Women in the UNB Certificate in Family Violence Issues offered by the Muriel McQueen Fergusson Centre for Family Violence Research. Her current interests include spirituality and social justice, and the intersection of institutional oppression and relational trauma. In 2016 she was recipient of a Governor General's Award in Commemoration of the Persons Case.

ANDREA QUINLAN is an assistant professor in the Department of Sociology and Legal Studies at the University of Waterloo. Her research focuses on intersections of law, science, technology, and medicine in legal responses to sexual violence, and the influence of anti-violence movements on sexual assault policy, law, and institutional practice. She is the author of *The Technoscientific Witness of Rape: Contentious Histories of Law, Feminism, and Forensic Science* (U of T Press, 2017).

ELIZABETH QUINLAN is a faculty member in the Department of Sociology at the University of Saskatchewan. She is a founding member of the Coalition Against Sexual Assault. Her research on sexual violence, workplace health, and caring labour employs arts-based strategies to engage participants from the outset through to innovative knowledge translation.

NANCY ROSS currently works at the School of Social Work, Dalhousie University, and is near completion of a Ph.D. in peace studies at the University of Bradford, England. Her prior work as a clinical social worker contributed to her passion in working to reduce and end all forms of interpersonal violence, as expressed in her research interests and involvement with the Be the Peace Institute. She embraces a combined critical clinical perspective that aims to link individual experiences of violence with community measures to end cultural, structural, and direct forms of violence.

KATE ROSS-HOPLEY is a recent graduate from the Master in Public Health program at Columbia University and is currently pursuing her medical degree at the University of Saskatchewan.

ALEXANDRA RUTHERFORD is a professor of psychology at York University in Toronto. She directs the Psychology's Feminist Voices oral history and digital archive project and served as an advisory board member of the Sexual Assault Survivors' Support Line.

CHARLENE Y. SENN is a faculty member in the Department of Psychology and cross-appointed to Women's and Gender Studies. She is a national expert in the study of male violence against women, with a particular focus on sexual assault interventions developing women's capacity to resist sexual assault.

ELIZABETH SHEEHY is a full professor at the University of Ottawa Faculty of Law, where she teaches and researches in the area of criminal law and legal responses to male violence against women. She is a Fellow of the Royal Society of Canada. In 2015 her book *Defending Battered Women on Trial: Lessons from the Transcripts* (2014) received the David Walter Mundell award, from the Attorney General of Ontario, for fine legal writing.

LANA STERMAC is a professor in the Department of Applied Psychology and Human Development at the University of Toronto. Her research interests focus on sexual violence against women and women's education. She has served on several advisory and education committees addressing sexual violence on campus.

GAIL TAYLOR holds an M.A. in liberal studies and an M.Ed. in adult education. She has worked in a variety of roles in adult education and community development, which informs her current work in the field of mental health peer support and outreach. A published writer, she also works as a writing specialist and editor for academic and community projects, as well as community health research collaborations. She has particular interest and experience in feminist issues such as violence against girls and women, pay equity, and poverty.

MADISON TRUSOLINO is a Ph.D. student in the Faculty of Information Studies at the University of Toronto. Her interests are in political economy, intersectional feminism, and gender and labour in the cultural industries.

URSULA WOLFE is a yoga and movement instructor and a Student Affairs professional at Wilfrid Laurier University in Waterloo. She specializes in the graduate student experience and student health and wellness. Ursula was a coordinator of the Sexual Assault Survivors' Support Line at York University.

INDEX